# FTCE GENERAL KNOWLEDGE

FLORIDA TEACHER CERTIFICATION EXAMINATIONS

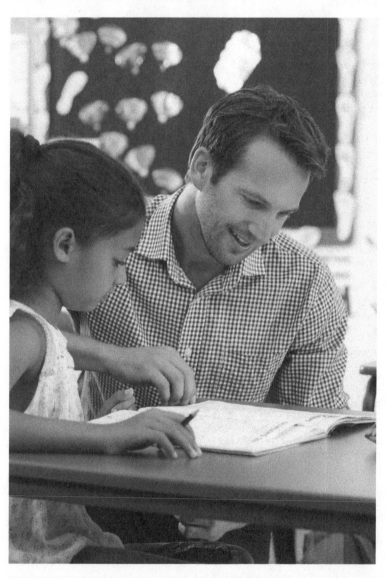

**Erin Mander, Ed.D.**
University of Central Florida
Orlando, Florida

**Tammy Powell, M.Ed.**
University of Central Florida
Orlando, Florida

*Research & Education Association*
www.rea.com

***Research & Education Association***
258 Prospect Plains Road
Cranbury, New Jersey 08512
Email: info@rea.com

**Florida FTCE General Knowledge Test
with Online Practice Tests, 4th Edition**

**Published 2021**
Copyright © 2019 by Research & Education Association, Inc.
Prior editions copyright © 2015, 2011, 2006 by Research &
Education Association, Inc. All rights reserved. No part of this
book may be reproduced in any form without permission of the
publisher.

Printed in the United States of America

Library of Congress Control Number 2018963086

ISBN-13: 978-0-7386-1251-5
ISBN-10: 0-7386-1251-0

The competencies presented in this book were created and implemented by the Florida
Department of Education. For further information visit *www.fl.nesinc.com*.

Cover image: © iStockphoto.com/monkeybusinessimages

All trademarks cited in this publication are the property of their respective owners.

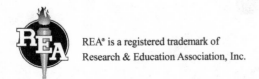

REA® is a registered trademark of
Research & Education Association, Inc.

J20

# Contents

## About Our Authors

**Dr. Erin Mander** is president of a curriculum consulting firm in Orange County, Florida, and teaches both the FTCE General Knowledge and Professional Education classes through the University of Central Florida Continuing Education Program. Dr. Mander studied curriculum and instruction at Wheaton College (B.A.), Walden University (M.A.), and the University of Central Florida (Ed.D.). She is a certified teacher who has been working in education for 15 years. Her goal in education is to preserve the dignity of each individual learner through an approach that is both inspirational and engaging.

**Tammy Powell** leads the FTCE General Knowledge Mathematics and FTCE Elementary Education K–6 test prep programs at the University of Central Florida. A UCF graduate and a certified teacher specializing in math and science, Mrs. Powell has been working in education in Florida's Orange County for more than a decade and a half. She has taught at the elementary, middle school, and high school levels. She is certified by the State of Florida in K–6 Elementary Education, 5–9 Mathematics, and 6–12 Journalism. Mrs. Powell holds a master's degree in Mathematics Curriculum and Instruction from Concordia University. Her goal in the classroom is to make even the most difficult concepts easy to understand while using thorough preparation to overcome the test anxiety that many adults experience.

## About REA

Founded in 1959, Research & Education Association (REA) is dedicated to publishing the finest and most effective educational materials—including study guides and test preps—for students of all ages.

Today, REA's wide-ranging catalog is a leading resource for students, teachers, and other professionals. Visit *www.rea.com* to see a complete listing of all our titles.

## Acknowledgments

We would like to thank Larry Kling, Editorial Director, for supervising development; Pam Weston, Publisher, for setting the quality standards for production integrity and managing the publication to completion; John Cording, Technology Director, for coordinating the design and development of the REA Study Center; Alice Leonard, Senior Editor, for project management; and Diane Goldschmidt, Managing Editor, for editorial review.

We also gratefully acknowledge Transcend Creative Services for typesetting this edition.

# Passing the FTCE General Knowledge Test

Congratulations! By taking the FTCE General Knowledge Test, you are on your way to a rewarding teaching career. Our book and the online tools that come with it give you what you need to succeed on this important exam, bringing you one step closer to being certified to teach in Florida.

Our FTCE General Knowledge Test Book + Online Prep package includes:

- Complete overview of the exam

- Comprehensive review of all competencies

- Online diagnostic test to pinpoint your strengths and weaknesses and focus your study

- Three full-length practice tests, two in the book and one online, with powerful diagnostic tools to help you personalize your prep

- Detailed answer explanations

There are many different ways to prepare for the FTCE General Knowledge Test. What's best for you depends on how much time you have to study and how comfortable you are with the subject matter. Our book and practice tests give you the tools you need to customize your prep so you can make the most of your study time.

##  How to Use This Book + Online Prep

### About Our Review

The review chapters in this book are designed to help you sharpen your command of all the skills you'll need to pass the FTCE General Knowledge Test. Each of the skills required under each competency is discussed at length to optimize your understanding of what the test covers. Keep in mind that your schooling has taught you most of what you need to know to answer the questions on the test. Our content review is designed to reinforce what you have learned and show you how to relate the information you have acquired to the specific competencies on the test. Studying your class notes and textbooks together with our review will give you an excellent foundation for passing the test.

### About Our Practice Tests

REA's FTCE-GK test prep is a complete, flexible study system that allows you to make the most of your study time. At the online REA Study Center (*www.rea.com/studycenter*), you'll get feedback right from the start on what you know and what you don't.

Before you review with the book, go to the REA Study Center to take our online **diagnostic test**. Your detailed score report will pinpoint topics for which you need the most review to help you focus your study.

Our **3 full-length practice tests** (2 in the book + 1 online) cover all the topics you can expect to see on the actual exam. As you take each practice test, use your score reports to identify areas where you need extra study, until you're confident that you've mastered the topics that challenge you the most.

Our full-length online exam simulates the computer-based format of the actual FTCE-GK, building your confidence as you practice under test-like conditions. Features of our online exam include:

- **Automatic Scoring**—Find out how you did on your test, instantly.

- **Diagnostic Score Reports**—Get a specific score tied to each competency, so you can focus on the areas where you need the most help.

- **Detailed Answer Explanations**—Learn not just why a response option is correct, but also why the other answer choices are incorrect.

- **Timed Testing**—Manage your time as you practice, so you'll feel confident on test day.

To achieve the best results, we recommend you take both our printed and online exams. The more you practice, the more comfortable you will be with the format of the FTCE General Knowledge Test—helping you to score higher!

## Getting Started

Before you work through this book, we strongly recommend that you visit the Florida Teacher Certification Examinations website at *www.fl.nesinc.com*. There you'll find the most current information on the exam, including registration information, testing sites, testing format, test-day advice, registration cost, and FTCE-developed test preparation materials.

## An Overview of the Test

### Who Takes the Test and What Is It Used for?

The FTCE-GKT is used by the State of Florida to assess knowledge of teacher certification candidates. If you do not achieve a passing score on the FTCE-GKT, don't panic. You can take the test again, so you can work on improving your score in preparation for the next time you take it.

### About Computer-Based Testing

The FTCE-GKT is offered only on computer at flexible times and locations throughout the year. Minimal computer and typing skills are required to complete computer-based tests. You will need to select answers on-screen to multiple-choice questions, and type a response to the essay assignment.

### When Should the FTCE-GKT Be Taken?

The FTCE-GKT is usually taken immediately before completing a teacher certification program at a college or university. This gives you enough time to retake the test if necessary. Our practice tests will familiarize you with the format of the exam so that you do not have to go through the anxiety of learning about the FTCE-GKT during the actual exam.

## When and Where Is the Test Given?

The FTCE-GKT is administered at various times and locations in Florida and in select cities nationwide. To find a testing center near you, visit the official website: *www.fl.nesinc.com*.

The registration bulletin for the FTCE-GKT contains test dates and administration sites. You may obtain a registration bulletin by contacting:

> FTCE/FELE Program
> Evaluation Systems Group of Pearson
> PO Box 226
> Phone: (413) 256-2893
> Amherst, MA 01004
> Website: *www.fl.nesinc.com*

The Test Information Guide became available in a new, interactive format beginning in August 2018. This new format replaced the previous PDF documents.

This new, interactive design includes:

- embedded links for faster movement on the server, enabling you to focus on specific areas of interest;

- a single test item and response options on each screen (The related competency is included.);

- the ability to answer the question on the screen and then see if you are right or wrong before you move on;

- the ability to enlarge text; and

- a revised introduction containing new preparation strategies and study methods.

## Is There a Registration Fee?

Yes, you must pay a fee to take the FTCE-GKT. Fee waivers are available for candidates who cannot afford the registration fee. You must be enrolled in a college undergraduate program and must prove that you are required by a registered score recipient to take the exam. Details regarding income eligibility levels are contained in the registration bulletin.

## What is Assessed on the Test?

The FTCE General Knowledge Test ensures that you have the essential knowledge and skills to teach the state-required curriculum in Florida.

Whether you are a student, a graduate from a Florida state-approved teacher preparation program, or an educator who has received certification in another state, you should familiarize yourself with the requirements for teaching in Florida at the FTCE website. The FTCE General Knowledge Test is a required component of full certification in teacher preparation programs in Florida.

The following chart shows the approximate percentages devoted to each subject covered on the exam's four subtests:

| Subtest | Percentage of Subtest |
|---|---|
| **English Language Skills (40 minutes/Approx. 40 questions)** | |
| Knowledge of language structure | 25% |
| Knowledge of vocabulary application | 25% |
| Knowledge of standard English conventions | 50% |
| **Reading (55 minutes/Approx. 40 questions)** | |
| Knowledge of key ideas and details based on text selections | 40% |
| Knowledge of craft and structure based on text selections | 25% |
| Knowledge of the integration of information and ideas based on text selections | 35% |
| **Mathematics (100 minutes/Approx. 45 questions)** | |
| Knowledge of number sense, concepts, and operations | 17% |
| Knowledge of geometry and measurement | 21% |
| Knowledge of algebraic thinking and the coordinate plane | 29% |
| Knowledge of probability, statistics, and data interpretation | 33% |
| **Essay (1 essay/50 minutes)** | |

## Scoring

The FTCE General Knowledge Test is a pass/fail test. The subtests are administered, scored, and reported independently.

### Scoring the English Language Skills, Mathematics, and Reading Subtests

Upon completion of your General Knowledge exam, you will receive an unofficial score report for the multiple-choice subtests: English Language Skills, Mathematics, and Reading. Official score reports for the above three subtests will be available approximately 3 to 6 weeks after your test date.

The minimum percentages needed to earn a passing score on these subtests are as follows:

- English Language Skills: 70 percent of items correct.

- Reading: 75 percent of items correct.

- Mathematics: 72 percent of items correct.

### Scoring the Essay Subtest

Your Essay Subtest score will be released approximately six weeks after your test date. The passing score for the General Knowledge Essay Subtest is at least 8 out of 12 points. Your essay will be read and scored by two independent and qualified raters. The two independent scores are combined to create the total score for the Essay subtest.

### What if I don't pass each subtest?

If you fail any of the subtests, you are required to retake only the subtest(s) failed. For example, if you fail the Mathematics subtest and pass all the other subtests, you only have to retake the Mathematics subtest.

## Preparing for the Test

It is never too early to start studying for the FTCE-GKT. The earlier you begin, the more time you will have to sharpen your skills. Do not procrastinate. Cramming is not an effective way to study. Work out a schedule and stick to it. Be sure to set aside enough time—at least two hours each day—to study. The more time you spend studying, the more prepared and relaxed you will feel on the day of the exam.

When you take the practice tests, be sure to simulate the conditions of the test as closely as possible. Turn off all electronic devices and sit down at a table free from distraction. Read each question carefully, consider all answer choices, and pace yourself.

As you complete each test, score your exam and review the detailed explanations for the questions you answered incorrectly. Concentrate on one problem area at a time by reading the question and explanation, and by studying our review until you are confident that you have mastered the material. Give extra attention to the review chapters that cover your areas of difficulty, as this will build your skills in those areas.

### Study Schedule

| Week | Activity |
|------|----------|
| 1 | Take the online Diagnostic Test at the REA Study Center (*www.rea.com/studycenter*). Your detailed score report will identify the topics where you need the most review. |
| 2–3 | Study the review chapters, using your score report from the diagnostic test to focus your study. Some useful study techniques include highlighting key terms and special information. You might want to write in the margins or take notes as you read the review. |
| 4 | Take Practice Test 1 in the book. Identify topics where you need more review. Pay special attention to the detailed explanations for the questions you missed. |
| 5 | Take Practice Test 2 in the book. Restudy the appropriate review sections until you are confident you understand the material. Because the Essay test is difficult to self-assess, you might want to ask a friend or two to help you to grade your practice essays (chapter 5). |
| 6 | Take Practice Test 3 online at *www.rea.com/studycenter*. Use your remaining time before the actual test to restudy any topics you missed. |

## Test-Taking Tips to Boost Your Score

Even though you have probably taken standardized tests like the FTCE-GKT before, you may still experience some anxiety about the exam. This is perfectly normal, and there are several ways to help alleviate test-day nervousness. Here are some tips to help you raise your score.

### 1. Guess Away

One of the most frequently asked questions about the FTCE General Knowledge Test is: Can I guess? The answer: absolutely! There is no penalty for guessing on the test. That means that if you guess incorrectly, you will not lose any points, but if you guess correctly, you will gain points. Thus, while it's fine to guess, it's important to guess smartly, or as the strategy is called: use process of elimination (see Strategy No. 2). Your score is based strictly on the number of correct answers. So answer all questions and take your best guess when you don't know the answer.

### 2. Process of Elimination

Process of elimination is one of the most important test-taking strategies at your disposal. Process of elimination means looking at the choices and eliminating the ones you know are wrong, including answers that are partially wrong. Your odds of getting the right answer increase from the moment you're able to get rid of a wrong choice.

### 3. All in

Review all the response options. Just because you believe you've found the correct answer, don't neglect to look at each choice so you don't mistakenly jump to any conclusions. You are asked to choose the *best* answer; be sure your answer is really the best one.

### 4. Letter Choice of the Day

What if you are truly stumped and can't use the process of elimination? It's time to pick a fallback answer. On the day of the test, choose the letter choice (i.e., A, B, C, or D) that you will pick for any question you cannot smartly guess. According to the laws of probability, you have a higher chance of getting an answer right if you stick to one chosen position for the answer choice when you have to guess an answer instead of randomly picking one.

### 5. Use Choices to Confirm Your Answer

The great thing about multiple-choice questions is that the answer has to be staring back at you. Have an answer in mind and use the choices to *confirm* it. For the Math subtest, you can work out the problem and find the match among the choices, or you may want to try the opposite: *backsolving*—that is, working backwards—from the choices given.

### 6. Watch the Clock

Among the most vital point-saving skills is active time management. The breakdown and time limits of each section are provided as you begin each test. Keep an eye on the timer on your computer screen. Make sure you stay on top of how much time you have left for each section and never spend too much time on any one question. Remember: Most multiple-choice questions are worth one raw point. Treat each one as if it's the one that will put you over the top. You never know, it just might. For the essay subtest, make sure you have enough time to write a well-organized essay. The last thing you want on test day is to lose easy points because you ran out of time and focused too much on difficult questions.

### 7. Read, Read, Read

It's important to read through all the multiple-choice options. Even if you believe answer choice A is correct, you can misread a question or response option if you're rushing to get through the test. While it is important not to linger on a question, it is also crucial to avoid giving a question short shrift. Slow down, calm down, read all the choices. Verify that your choice is the best one, and click on it.

### 8. Take Notes

Use the erasable notepad and pen provided to you to make notes to work toward the answer(s).

### 9. Isolate Limiters

Pay attention to any limiters in a multiple-choice question stem. These are words such as *initial, best, most* (as in *most appropriate* or *most likely*), *not, least, except, required,* or *necessary*. Especially watch for negative words, such as "Choose the answer that is *not* true." When you select your answer, double-check yourself by asking how the response fits the limitations established by the stem. Think of the stem as a puzzle piece that perfectly fits only the response option(s) that contain the correct answer. Let it guide you.

### 10. It's Not a Race

Ignore other test-takers. Don't compare yourself to anyone else in the room. Focus on the items in front of you and the time you have left. If someone finishes the test 30 minutes early, it does not necessarily mean that person answered more questions correctly than you did. Stay calm and focus on *your* test. It's the only one that matters.

### 11. Confirm Your Click

In the digital age, many of us are used to rapid-clicking, be it in the course of emailing or gaming. Look at the screen to be sure to see that your mouse-click is acknowledged. If your answer doesn't register, you won't get credit. However, if you want to mark it for review so you can return later, you can do so—but only within a subtest. Before you click "SUBMIT," use the test's review screen to see whether you inadvertently skipped any questions.

### 12. Creature of Habit? No Worries.

We are all creatures of habit. It's therefore best to follow a familiar pattern of study. Do what's comfortable for you. Set a time and place each day to study for this test. Whether it is 30 minutes at the library or an hour in a secluded corner of your local coffee shop, commit yourself as best you can to this schedule every day. Find quiet places where it is less crowded, as constant background noise can distract you. Don't study one subject for too long, either. Take an occasional breather and treat yourself to a healthy snack or some quick exercise. After your short break—5 or 10 minutes can do the trick—return to what you were studying or start a new section.

### 13. Knowledge is Power

Purchasing this book gave you an edge on passing the FTCE General Knowledge Test. Make the most of this edge. Review the sections on how the test is structured, what the directions look like, what types of questions will be asked, and so on. Take our practice tests to familiarize yourself with what the test looks and feels like. Most test anxiety occurs because people feel unprepared when they are taking the test, and they psych themselves out. You can whittle away at anxiety by learning the format of the test and by knowing what to expect. Fully simulating the test even once will boost your chances of getting the score you need. Meanwhile, the knowledge you've gained will also save you the valuable time that would have been eaten up puzzling through what the directions are asking As an added benefit, previewing the test will free up your brain's resources so you can focus on racking up as many points as you can.

### 14. B-r-e-a-t-h-e

What's the worst that can happen when you take a test? You may have an off day, and despite your best efforts, you may not pass. Well, the good news is that a test can be retaken. In fact, you may already be doing this—this book is every bit for you as it is for first-timers. Fortunately, the FTCE General Knowledge Test is something you can study and prepare for, and in some ways to a greater extent than other tests you've taken throughout your academic career. Yes, there will be questions you won't know, but neither your teacher education program nor state licensing board expects you to know everything. When unfamiliar vocabulary appears or difficult math problems loom, don't despair: Use context clues, process of elimination, or your letter of the day to make your choice, and then press ahead. If you have time left, you can always come back to the question later. If not, relax. It is only one question on a test filled with many. Take a deep breath and then exhale. You know this information. Now you're going to show it.

## The Day of the Test

### Before the Test

On the day of the test, you should wake up early after a good night's rest. You should have a good breakfast and dress in layers that can be removed or added as the conditions in the testing center require. Arrive at the testing center early. This will allow you to relax and collect your thoughts before the test, and will also spare you the anguish that comes with being late. Keep in mind that *no one will be admitted into the testing center after the test has begun.*

Before you leave for the testing site, make sure that you have your admission ticket and two unexpired forms of identification. The first form of identification must be government issued and must contain a recent photograph, your name, and a legible signature. This can be a driver's license, state-issued identification card, passport, or U.S. military identification. The second identification form must have either a clear photograph or a signature. Examples of these could be a student ID or a Social Security card. If you do not have proper identification, you will not be admitted to the testing site. Be sure to check the FTCE website close to the date of your test just in case there are any changes to these requirements.

There are also very strict rules about what you may not bring to the testing site. You may not bring watches of any kind, cell phones or any other electronic communication devices. Scrap paper, written notes, books, and any printed material is prohibited. Smoking, eating, or drinking are not allowed, so do not bring any food or drinks, including water, to the site. Finally, weapons of any kind are banned, as are any visitors, including relatives.

### During the Test

Once you enter the test center, follow all the rules and instructions given by your test supervisor. Failure to do so may result in your dismissal from the testing center. You may also have your scores canceled.

### Are there any breaks during the test?

If you take all four subtests of the General Knowledge exam in a single session, you will **be given a 15-minute break** between subtests. Instructions will appear on the computer screen at the appropriate time and will indicate how long the break is. While taking a scheduled break **you may access personal items** that you stored before the exam, including but not limited to cell phones, exam notes, and study guides. **You may leave** the test center during this scheduled break. Following your break, the proctor will check your ID and may capture your palm vein image before taking you back to your seat so you can resume your test.

You may also take an unscheduled break on your own, but the **exam clock will not stop**. The test proctor will set your workstation to break mode. You **may not access** your personal items except for food, drink, or medications. You **may not leave** the test center. The test proctor will check your identity before you are escorted back to your station.

## After the Test

Keep in mind that several versions of the FTCE-GKT are administered during each testing period. The test-takers around you were very likely working on tests with completely different questions and answers from yours. Do not be alarmed when talking to friends and acquaintances about their FTCE-GKT test-taking experiences to discover that you do not "remember" the questions they are discussing. And be sure to keep such discussions private: You'll be signing a non-disclosure agreement when you sit for the test.

Good luck on the exam! You are well on your way to certification.

# FTCE GENERAL KNOWLEDGE TEST

## Content Review

# Reading

This chapter will prepare you for the Reading section of the FTCE-GKT. You will be guided through a step-by-step approach to focus on the reading passages and questions. Also included are tips to help you quickly and accurately answer the questions that will appear in this section of the exam. You will have 55 minutes to complete the 40-question section, which covers the following key competencies:

- Knowledge of key ideas and details based on text selections. (40%)

- Knowledge of craft and structure based on text selections. (25%)

- Knowledge of the integration of information and ideas based on text selections. (35%)

## The Passages

The selections in the Reading section are specially designed to be on the level of the types of material in your college textbooks. They will present you with very diverse subjects. The passages will be both expository and narrative. Although you will not be expected to have prior knowledge of the information presented in the passages, you will be expected to know the fundamental reading comprehension techniques presented in this chapter. Only your ability to read and comprehend material will be tested.

## The Questions

Each passage will be followed by a number of questions, with 40 questions spanning approximately five passages. The questions will ask you to make determinations based on what you have read. You will encounter different questions that target the skills below. The questions will ask you to:

- Identify textual evidence to support conclusions.

- Identify explicit meaning and details.

- Determine inferences and conclusions.

- Discriminate between inferences, conclusions, and assumptions.

- Determine and analyze the development of central ideas or themes.

- Summarize one or more texts.

- Determine how and why specific individuals, events, and ideas develop.

- Determine the cause-and-effect relationship(s) among individuals, events, and ideas.

- Interpret the meaning of words and phrases.

- Analyze how specific word choices shape meaning or tone.

- Analyze how the author uses organization and text structure to convey meaning.

- Contrast the point of view of two or more authors.

- Analyze how point of view and purpose shape the content and style of text.

- Evaluate and relate content presented in diverse formats.

- Evaluate specific claims in text based on relevancy, sufficiency, and validity or reasoning.

- Synthesize information from a range of texts to develop a coherent explanation of a process, phenomenon, concept, or theme.

- Analyze multiple texts to differentiate approaches authors take to develop similar themes.

# General Strategies

Eight key strategies should guide you in this section:

- Attack each passage immediately by determining the author's purpose and tone.

- Identify the main ideas of each paragraph.

- When a question asks you to draw inferences, your answer should reflect what is implied in the passage, rather than what is directly stated.

- Use the context of the sentence to find the meaning of an unfamiliar word.

- Determine whether the writer is using facts or opinions.

- Recognize key transitions and identify dominant patterns of organization.

- Commit to a response and move on. Don't get frustrated by the more troublesome passages. If you haven't gotten answers after two attempts, answer as best you can and go to the next question.

- If you have time at the end, go back to the passages that were difficult and review them.

# General Strategies for Reading Passages

*When reading each passage*, this is your general plan:

Step 1: Read quickly while keeping in mind that questions will follow.

Step 2: Uncover the main idea or theme of *the passage*. It is typically contained within the first few lines.

Step 3: Uncover the main idea of *each paragraph*. Usually it is contained in either the first or last sentence.

Step 4: Skim over the detailed points of the passage; you can always go back and look for details if a question calls for that.

When you take the Reading Section of the FTCE-GKT, you will have two tasks:

1. Read the selection.

2. Answer the questions.

Of the two, carefully reading the passage is more important; answering the questions is based on an understanding of the passage. Here is a three-step approach to reading:

Step 1: Preview.

Step 2: Read actively.

Step 3: Answer the questions.

## Step 1: Preview

A preview of the reading passage will reveal its purpose and rationale. Before beginning to read the passage, you should take about 30 seconds to look over the passage. An effective way to preview the passage is to read the first sentence of each paragraph and the concluding sentence of the passage.

It is critical as a test-taker that you analyze the stem of each question in order to determine the reading strategy needed to successfully answer the question. Don't spend time reading the answer choices for each question. The stem alone should guide you as you read.

The stems will be similar to the following:

1. The main idea of the passage is best stated in which of the following?

2. The main purpose of the writer in this passage is to . . .

3. Of the following, which fact best supports the writer's claims?

4. Among the following statements, which states an opinion expressed by the writer rather than a fact?

5. The list of topics below that best reflects the organization of the topics of the passage is . . .

6. Which paragraph below is the best summary of the passage?

7. Based on the passage, the rationale for fact-pattern analyses arises out of what theoretical groundwork?

8. Based on data in the passage, what would most likely be the major cause for the climax of the selection?

9. In the context of the passage, _____ might be most nearly defined as which of the following?

## Step 2: Read Actively

After your preview, you are now ready to read actively. This means that as you read, you will be engaged in such things as recognizing important words, topic sentences, main ideas, and words denoting the tone of the passage. Carefully read the first sentence of each paragraph since this often contains the topic of the paragraph. During this stage, you should also determine the writer's purpose in writing the passage, as this will help you focus on the main points and how the writer structures the passage. You can determine the author's purpose by asking yourself:

- What is the writer's overall goal or objective?

- Is the writer trying primarily to persuade you by proving or using facts to make a case for an idea?

- Is the writer trying primarily to inform and enlighten you about an idea, object, or event?

- Is the writer attempting primarily to amuse you? To keep you fascinated? To persuade you?

Read these examples and see if you can decide what the primary purpose of each numbered statement is.

(1) Jogging too late in life can cause more health problems than it solves. I will allow that the benefits of jogging are many: lowered blood pressure, increased vitality, better cardiovascular health, and better muscle tone. However, an older person may have a history of injury or chronic ailments that makes jogging counterproductive. For example, the elderly jogger may have hardening of the arteries, emphysema, or undiscovered aneurysms just waiting to burst and cause stroke or death. Chronic arthritis in the joints will only be aggravated by persistent irritation and use. Moreover, for those of us with injuries sustained in our youth—such as torn Achilles' tendons or torn knee cartilage—jogging might just make a painful life more painful, canceling out the benefits the exercise is intended to produce.

(2) Jogging is a sporting activity that exercises all the main muscle groups of the body. That the arms, legs, buttocks, and torso voluntary muscles are engaged goes without question. Running down a path makes you move your upper body as well as your lower body muscles. People do not often take into account, however, how the involuntary muscle system is also put through its paces. The heart, diaphragm, even the eye and face muscles, take part as we hurl our bodies through space at speeds up to five miles per hour over distances as long as 26 miles, which is marathon distance.

(3) It seems to me that jogging styles are as identifying as fingerprints! People seem to be as individual in the way they run as they are in personality. Here comes the Duck, waddling down the track, little wings going twice as fast as the feet in an effort to stay upright. At about the quarter-mile mark, I see the Penguin, quite natty in the latest jogging suit, body stiff as a board from neck to ankles and the ankles flexing a mile a minute to cover the yards. And down there at the half-mile post—there comes the Giraffe—a tall fellow in a spotted electric yellow outfit, whose long strides cover about a dozen yards each, and whose neck waves around under some old army camouflage hat that probably served its time in a surplus store in the Bronx rather than in Desert Storm. Once you see the animals in the jogger woods, you can identify them from miles away just by seeing their gait. And by the way, be careful whose hoof you're stepping on, it may be mine!

In (1) the writer makes a statement that a number of people would debate and which isn't clearly demonstrated in science or common knowledge. In fact, common wisdom usually maintains the opposite thesis. Many would say that jogging improves the health of the aging—even slows down the aging process. As soon as you see a writer point to or identify *an issue open to debate* and standing in need of proof, she or he is setting out to persuade you to one side or the other. You'll notice, too, that the writer in this case takes a stand. It's almost as if the writer is saying, "I have concluded that . . ." But a thesis or arguable idea is only a *hypothesis* until evidence is summoned by the writer to prove it. Effective arguments are based on factual or demonstrable evidence, not opinion.

In (2) the writer is simply stating a fact. This is not a matter for debate. Instead, the writer's evidence is used to *explain* and *describe* what is meant by the fact. She or he proceeds to *analyze* (break down into its elements) the way the different muscle groups come into play or do work when jogging, thus explaining the fact stated as a main point in the opening sentence. That jogging exercises all the muscle groups is not in question or a matter of debate. Besides taking the form of explaining how something works, or what parts it is made of (for example, the basic parts of a bicycle are . . .), writers may show how the idea, object, or event functions. A writer may use this information to prove something. But if the writer doesn't argue to prove a debatable point, then the purpose must be either to inform (as here) or to entertain.

In (3) the writer is taking a stand, but she or he is not attempting to prove anything, but instead merely pointing to a lighthearted observation. Moreover, all of the examples the writer uses to support the statement are either fanciful, funny, odd, or peculiar to the writer's particular vision. Joggers aren't really animals, after all.

Make sure to examine all of the facts that the author uses to support the main idea. This will allow you to decide whether or not the writer has made a case, and what sort of purpose the writer supports. Look for supporting details—facts, examples, illustrations, expert testimony or research—that pertain to the topic in question and *show* what the writer *says* is so. In fact, paragraphs and theses consist of *show* and *tell*. The writer *tells* you something is so or not so and then *shows* you facts, illustrations, expert testimony, or experience to support it.

The FTCE-GK Test requires you to distinguish between fact and opinion. Let's look at the following examples. In each case, ask yourself if you are reading a fact or an opinion.

1. Some roses are red.

2. Roses are the most beautiful flowers in the world.

3. After humans smell roses, they fall in love.

4. Roses are the worst plants to grow in your backyard.

No. 1 is a fact. All you have to do is go look at the evidence. Go to a florist. You will see that No. 1 is true. A fact is anything that can be demonstrated to be true in reality or that has been demonstrated to be true in reality and is documented by others. For example, the moon is in orbit an average of about 239,000 miles from Earth.

No. 2 is an opinion. The writer claims this as truth, but since beauty is an abstract quality, it remains to be seen. Others will hold different opinions. This is a matter of taste, not fact.

No. 3 is an opinion. There is probably some related coincidence between these two, but there is no verifiable or repeatable and observable evidence that this is always true—at least not the way it is true that if you throw a ball into the air, it will always come back down to Earth on its own. Opinions have a way of sounding absolute, and may be held by the writer with supreme confidence, but are not backed up by factual evidence.

No. 4, though perhaps sometimes true, is a matter of opinion. Many variables contribute to the health of a plant in a garden—factors such as soil, temperature range, and amount of moisture. This is a debatable point that the writer would have to prove.

As you read, note the structure of the passage. The most common paragraph structures are explained below.

## Main Types of Paragraph Structures

1. Main idea plus supporting arguments

2. Main idea plus examples

3. Comparison and contrast

4. Advantages and disadvantages

5. Chronological order

6. Cause and effect

7.   Problem and solution

8.   Order of importance

9.   Summary

The structure contains several different aspects of one idea. For example, a passage on education in the United States in the 1600s and 1700s might first define education, then describe colonial education, then give information about the separation of church and state, and then outline the pros and cons of taxation to support public education. Being able to recognize these structures will help you recognize how the author has organized the passage. Examining the structure of the passage will help you answer questions that ask you to organize the information in the passage, or to summarize the information presented in that passage.

For example, if you see a writer using a transitional pattern that reflects a sequence moving forward in time, such as "In 1982 . . . Then, in the next five years . . . A decade later, in 1997, the _____ will . . .," chances are the writer is telling a story, reciting history, or the like. Writers often use transitions of classification to analyze an idea, object, or event. They may say something like, "The first part . . . Second . . . Third . . . Finally."

You may then ask yourself what the analysis is meant to accomplish. To explain or to persuade me of something? These transitional patterns may also help reveal the relationship of one part of a passage to another. For example, a writer may be writing "on the one hand . . . on the other hand . . ." This should alert you to the fact that the writer is comparing or contrasting two things. To what end? Is one better or worse than the other?

By understanding the *relationship* among the main point, transitions, and supporting information, you may more readily determine the pattern of organization as well as the writer's purpose in a given piece of writing.

As with the earlier paragraph examples showing various possible purposes, you examine the relationship between the facts or pieces of information presented (that's the "show" part) and what the writer is trying to point out to you (that's the "tell" part) with that data. For example, the discussion presented about education in the 1600s might be used:

- to prove that it was a failure (a form of argument),

- to show that it consisted of these elements (an analysis of the status of education during that time), or

- to show that education during that time was silly.

In the two sections below, consider the different relationship between the previous data and the thesis, and how that thesis changes the discussion from explanation to argument:

(1) Colonial education differed from today's schooling in several ways. Education in those days meant primarily studying the three "R's" (reading, writing, and arithmetic) and the Bible. Church and state were more closely aligned with one another—education was, after all, for the purpose of serving God better, not to earn more money.

(2) Colonial "education" was really just a way to create a captive audience for the Church. Education in those days meant studying the three "R's" in order to learn God's word—the Bible—not commerce. The Church and state were closely aligned with one another, and what was good for the Church was good for the state—or else you were excommunicated, which kept you out of Heaven for sure.

The same information is cited in both cases, but in (1) the writer treats it analytically (". . . differed . . . in several ways . . ."), not taking any real debatable stand on the issue. What is, is. However, the controlling statement in (2) puts forth a volatile hypothesis, and then uses the same assertion to support that hypothesis.

## Step 3: Answer the Questions

In Step 2 (Read actively) you gathered enough information from the passage to answer questions dealing with establishing the main idea, how the thesis is supported, its purpose and organization, differentiating fact from opinion as well as analyzing bias, tone, the relationships between sentences, validity, and logic. Let's look again at these questions.

*When answering the questions,* this is your plan:

1. Answer each question one at a time. Read it carefully.

2. If the question is asking for a general answer, such as the central idea or the purpose of the passage, answer it immediately.

3. If the question is asking for an answer that can be found only in a specific place in the passage, save it for last since this type of question requires you to go back to the passage, which takes more of your time.

4. For the detail-oriented questions, try to eliminate or narrow down your choices before looking for the answer in the passage.

5. Go back to the passage, utilizing key words and context to find the answer.

6. When you cannot find the correct answer, use the process of elimination to the greatest extent and then guess.

Now that you have a general framework for addressing the Reading section, it is critical for you to understand the skills that support each of the three competencies.

## Competency 1: Knowledge of Key Ideas and Details Based on Text Selections

### Skill 1.1: Identify textual evidence to support conclusions drawn from text.

While you are reading, it is critical that you distinguish between key ideas, author bias, and the evidence for those ideas. *Evidence* is anything used to prove that an idea is true, real, correct, or probable. *Bias* is the author's personal feelings on the topic and what she or he believes, which may not be based in fact.

### Types of Evidence

Only a few forms of evidence are available to the writer of each selection. The kinds of evidence that a writer can summon to support his or her position or assertion are as follows: (1) facts and statistics, (2) the testimony of an authority, (3) personal anecdote, (4) hypothetical illustrations, and (5) analogy. Strictly speaking, the last two in this list are not true evidence, but only offer common-sense probability to the support of an argument.

*Documented facts and statistics* are the most powerful evidence a writer can bring to bear on proving an idea or supporting the main thesis. Documented facts and statistics must be used fairly and come from reliable sources. For example, *Funk and Wagnall's Encyclopedia* is a reliable source but Joe the Plumber's *Guide to Waterfowl in the Everglades* is not. This is true because, first of all, Joe is a plumber, not an ornithologist (a bird scientist), and second, no one has ever heard of Joe the plumber as an expert in a field other than plumbing. Reliable sources for facts and statistics are the best information that can be offered.

*Expert testimony* is the reported positions, theses, or studies of people who are recognized experts in the field under discussion in the literature. A writer may use books, articles, essays, interviews, and so on by trained scientists and other professionals to support a thesis or position. Most often, this testimony takes the form of quotations from the expert or a paraphrasing of his or her important ideas or findings.

*Personal experience and anecdote* is the evidence of a writer's own personal experience, or a "little story" about an event, person, or idea that exemplifies the point he or she is trying to make. It holds weight if the reader trusts the writer and the story is relevant; it is not as powerful or as conclusive as documented facts or the testimony of experts (unless the writer is a recognized authority in the field about which he or she has written).

*Hypothetical illustrations* are examples that suggest probable circumstances in which something would be true. Strictly speaking, a hypothetical illustration is not "hard" evidence, but rather evidence of probability. For example, to demonstrate that "people will do whatever they can get away with," a writer might bring up the hypothetical illustration of someone at a ticket counter who gets back more change than the price of the ticket.

The chances are, the writer might point out, that the person would pocket the extra money rather than be honest and return it. In this case, the writer is not naming anybody in particular or citing statistics to make the point, but rather is pointing to *a situation that is likely but is not an actual documented case.* For the reader, this situation has either the weight of common sense or none at all.

*Analogies* are the last and weakest form of evidence. In fact, they are not evidence at all. An analogy is simply a comparison between items that are different but that also have some striking similarities. Analogies often use the term "like" to show the relationship of ideas. For example, the writer might say, "Life is like a tree: we start out struggling in the dirt, grow into the full bloom of youth, and become deeply rooted in our ways, until, in the autumn of our years, we lose our hair like leaves, and succumb ultimately to the bare winter of death."

While reading, determine what sort of evidence the writer is using and how effective it is in proving the writer's case. As you analyze evidence, it is critical to determine why the author chose the piece of evidence found within the passage. Then, determine the overall effect on the passage(s).

## Reasons for Evidence

To prove any thesis that the writer maintains is true, he or she may employ any one of the following seven strategies:

1. *Show* that a process or a procedure does or should work step-by-step in time;

2. *Compare or contrast* two or more things or ideas to show important differences or similarities;

3. *Identify* a problem and then explain how to solve it;

4. *Analyze* its components, or *classify* by its types or categories, an idea or thing to show how it is put together, how it works, or how it is designed;

5. *Explain* why something happens to produce a particular result or set of results;

6. *Describe* the particular individual characteristics of a place, person, time, or idea;

7. *Define* what a thing is or what an idea means.

*Bias* can be identified in passages in which the author is comparing and contrasting two arguments. To analyze the relationship between ideas in opposition (pro and con), first identify the claim each side is making. (Of course, in many situations there are more than two sides.) Pay attention to the intricacies of the position; many arguments are not simply for or against something, but instead are qualified positions with exceptions. For example, the claim that Medicare should pay for standard prescriptions is different from the claim that Medicare should pay for prescriptions. The word "standard" qualifies the argument; perhaps experimental drugs or preventative treatments are excluded from the proposal.

In analyzing an argument, be sure to find the edges of the argument, where the arguer would not want to press the argument further and where there may be bias. After analyzing the argument, locate and evaluate the reasons that the author uses to support the claim. Ask yourself, "Why is the author's claim important?" Then examine the reasons the author gives: Are they good reasons and are they connected to the claim? Finally, examine the evidence the author uses to support the reasons. The evidence should come from reliable sources and be pertinent to the reasons and claim. In examining two or more opposing arguments, you will judge which best supports its claim.

## Skill 1.2: Identify explicit meaning and details within text.

Comprehension strategies are conscious plans—sets of steps that good readers use to make sense of text. The utilization of strategies helps you become a purposeful, active reader who is in control of your reading comprehension. Review the comprehension strategies discussed below in order to find the explicit meaning and details within a single selection or between two selections.

### Strategy 1—Making Connections

I know . . . about this topic.

- A good reader interacts with the text and brings his/her experiences to what he/she reads.

- Competent readers make three types of connections:
    1. relating text to self (personal experiences)
    2. relating text to another text (one piece of information to another)
    3. relating text to the world around them

### Strategy 2—Predicting/Inferring

Predicting while reading requires some intuition, but predicting is also based on using one's experiences, solid clues from the text, and the ability to anticipate what could logically happen next.

- Ask, "What do you think will happen next?" Read on to see if that actually happens.

- Inferring involves complex thinking.

- As you read, act as a detective gathering logical clues to piece together the solution to some mystery.

- Inferring is often called "reading between the lines."

- You must use clues to infer what the author means when he or she doesn't explicitly tell you in the text.

## Strategy 3—Questioning

- Self-questioning during reading provides clarity and predictions to keep you engaged.

- Good questions to consider are known as the five W's and the H: who, what, when, where, why, and how.

## Strategy 4—Monitoring and Clarifying

- As a good reader, you must correct mistakes in understanding by rereading and looking for answers to what is confusing.

- Good readers make sure they understand the meaning, and stop to figure it out when they don't understand.

- Rereading is a good idea!

## Strategy 5—Summarizing

- Involves remembering what you have read and selecting only the most important points in a logical manner.

- Summarize as you read to boost your comprehension.

- Be intentional about remembering the order of the details within the selection.

## Strategy 6—Evaluating

- As you read, judge the selection by ranking important ideas and critiquing the author's writing.

- As you are ranking and critiquing, consider the arguments utilized by the author in the selection.

## Skill 1.3: Determine inferences and conclusions based on textual evidence.

Drawing conclusions requires ferreting out information that is implied or inferred. This means that the information is not clearly or explicitly stated. Writers often *tell* you more than they say directly. They give you hints or clues that help you "read between the lines." Using these clues to gain a deeper understanding of the text is called *inferring*. When you infer, you go beyond the surface details to see other meanings that the details suggest or imply. When the meanings of words are not stated clearly in the context of the text, they may be *implied*—that is, suggested or hinted at. When meanings are implied, you may infer them.

*Inference* is just a big word that means a conclusion or judgment. If you infer that something has happened, you do not see, hear, feel, smell, or taste the actual event. But from what you know, after you put the pieces of the puzzle together, it makes sense to believe that it has happened. You make inferences every day. Most of the time you do so without thinking about it.

Suppose you are sitting in your car stopped at a red traffic light. You hear screeching tires, then a loud crash and breaking glass. You see nothing, but you infer that there has been a car accident. We all know the sounds of screeching tires and a crash. We know that these sounds *almost always* mean a car accident has taken place. But there could be some other reason, and therefore another explanation, for the sounds. Perhaps it was not an accident involving two moving vehicles. Maybe an angry driver rammed a parked car. Or maybe someone played the sound of a car crash from a recording. Making inferences means choosing the most likely explanation from the facts at hand.

There are several ways to help you draw conclusions and inferences based on what the author says. Next we'll look at the various strategies to aid you in reaching a critical inference or conclusion.

### General Sense

The meaning of a word may be implied by the general sense of its context, as the meaning of the word *incarcerated* is implied in the following sentence:

Murderers are usually *incarcerated* for longer periods of time than robbers.

You may infer the meaning of *incarcerated* by answering the question, "What usually happens to those found guilty of murder or robbery?" If you answered that they are locked up in jail, prison, or a penitentiary, you correctly inferred the meaning of *incarcerated*.

## Examples

When the meaning of the word is not implied by the general sense of its context, it may be implied by examples. For instance,

> Those who enjoy belonging to clubs, going to parties, and inviting friends to their homes for dinner are *gregarious*.

You may infer the meaning of *gregarious* by answering the question, "What word or words describe people who belong to clubs, go to parties a lot, and invite friends over to their homes for dinner?" If you answered social or something like "people who enjoy the company of others," you correctly inferred the meaning of *gregarious*.

## Antonyms

When the meaning of a word is not implied by the general sense of its context or by examples, it may be implied by an antonym or by a contrasting thought in a given context. *Antonyms* are words that have opposite meanings, such as *happy* and *sad*.

> Ben is fearless, but his brother is *timorous*.

You may infer the meaning of *timorous* by answering the question, "If Ben is fearless and Jim is very different from Ben with regard to fear, then what word describes Jim?" If you answered with a word such as *timid*, or *afraid*, or *fearful*, you inferred the meaning of *timorous*.

## Contrasts

A contrast in the following sentence implies the meaning of *credence*:

> Dad gave *credence* to my story, but Mom's reaction was one of total disbelief.

You may infer the meaning of *credence* by answering the question, "If Mom's reaction was disbelief and Dad's reaction was very different from Mom's, what was Dad's reaction?" If you answered that Dad believed the story, you correctly inferred the meaning of *credence*; it means *belief*.

## Be Cautious

When a sentence contains an unfamiliar word, it is sometimes possible to infer the general meaning of the sentence without inferring the exact meaning of the unknown word.

> Whenever we invite the Paulsons for dinner, they never invite us to their home for a meal; however, when we have the Browns to dinner, they always *reciprocate*.

In reading this sentence, some students infer that the Browns are more desirable dinner guests than the Paulsons without inferring the exact meaning of *reciprocate*. Other students conclude that the Browns differ from the Paulsons in that they do something in return when they are invited for dinner; these students conclude correctly that *reciprocate* means "to do something in return."

In drawing conclusions (making inferences), you are really getting at the ultimate meaning of things—what is important, why it is important, how one event influences another, how one event leads to another. Simply getting the facts in reading is not enough—you must determine what those facts mean to you, especially within the framework of answering FTCE Reading questions.

## Skill 1.4: Discriminate among inferences, conclusions, and assumptions based on textual evidence.

As a test-taker, it is important not only to recognize inferences and conclusions as discussed previously, but also to differentiate between inferences, conclusions, and assumptions as you look at a selection. To be skilled within this area, you must think systematically as you read: Analyze each part of the selection and assess its quality, especially when looking at more than one vantage point on a given topic. As you are reading, you need to make logical inferences based on sound assumptions. This is an important skill that is often confusing for test-takers. Review the basic meanings below.

**Inference:** a piece of information which can be logically *deduced* from the given set of statements. An inference could be a logical deduction from a single statement or from a combination of two or more statements.

**Assumption:** a hidden or unstated premise. The two key words are "hidden" and "premise."

- A *premise* means that the assumption must be true for the conclusion to hold true.

- *Hidden* means it cannot be logically derived from existing information. New information must be presented. This is because there is no need to assume a thing that can be logically derived from existing information.

Now that you can clearly differentiate the two definitions, it is helpful to review how you will see these elements in the context of a question stem on the FTCE examination.

| Inference | Assumption |
|---|---|
| **Question Stem Structure**—If the statements above are true, which of the following must be true? | **Question Stem Structure**—Which of the following is an assumption on which the argument depends? |
| Inference is a statement that must be true, *if the given information is true.* | Assumption is a statement that must be true, *for the given information to be true; in other words, for the conclusion to hold true.* |
| An inference *can always be logically deduced* from the given information. | An assumption *can never be logically deduced* from the given information— it contains some new information. |
| It's very rare for an inference question to have a conclusion in the passage or the question stem. | An assumption question needs to have a conclusion in the passage or the question stem. |

## Skill 1.5: Determine and analyze the development of central ideas or themes from one or more texts.

Determining the central idea or theme requires you to identify the topic of the selection, all major events, and the central focus of the selection. Therefore, it is important that you have a strategy to address each one of these aspects.

### Identify the Topic of the Selection

To find clues to the topic:

— Look at the title (if available).

— Look at the first and last paragraph—the topic is usually named.

— Ask yourself: What is discussed throughout the whole selection? What subject spreads across the whole text? Look for clues to the topic in captions, pictures, boldface words, headings, and so forth. What do all of these have in common?

— Remind yourself: The topic must include all the major details and events from the selection.

   *Caution*: Not every detail has to do with the topic. The topic is the common element or connection between major details.

— What do all major details share?

**Check Yourself: It's Not the Central Idea if . . .**

— It's too general or too big. (Topic statement suggests or could include many ideas not stated in the text.)

— It's off the mark, totally missing the point.

— It captures only one detail, rather than all of the key details.

— It captures only some of the details—for example, maybe you didn't think about the ending.

**Questions to Check Yourself:**

— Does the topic I've identified give an accurate picture of what the whole selection is about?

— Was I as specific as possible?

— After naming the topic, can I now specifically picture in my mind what happened or was communicated in the text? Or might I picture something different that also fits my topic statement? If so, how can I change my topic statement to correct the problem?

## Identify all Major Events

Authors often plant important ideas in these elements:

(a) Details that reflect or refer to the title.

(b) Details at the beginning of a text.

(c) Details at the end.

(d) Surprises, revelations, whenever your expectations are not met.

(e) Repetition.

(f) Lots of attention given to a detail—for instance, a long explanation or description.

(g) Subheads and italicized text.

(h) Changes in character, tone, mood, setting, plot twists.

(i) A question near the beginning or the end.

**Check Yourself: It's Not a Key Detail if . . .**

— It's interesting but doesn't develop the topic or lead to the central focus.

— It reminds us of something and is even personally important, but if you were to remove it from the piece, the piece wouldn't lose any significant meaning or impact.

**Questions to Check Yourself:**

— Are all the details related to the topic?

— How do the key details relate to each other?

— What pattern do they make?

— What point do they repeat or add up to?

## Identify the Central Focus (the main idea or point the author makes about the topic)

— The statement of central focus must make a point about the topic and cover the whole selection.

— Ask yourself: Is the central focus directly stated? If not, it must be inferred.

— Which details help me decide on the central focus? Why are these details important?

— The central focus considers how the details relate to one another or lead to one another (what caused or led to what).

— The central focus must consider the ending and how the details or events lead to this final conclusion.

### Check Yourself: It's Not the Central Idea if . . .

— It is so literal and specific it doesn't allow the reader to apply the main idea to his/her life.

— It is too general—more like a topic statement than a main idea.

— It is true but misses the point of the text. It wasn't what the author was talking about.

— It misses the point.

— It fits only an isolated detail or event, not the whole text.

— It does not incorporate all details.

— It doesn't fit the ending or the final situation.

### Questions to Check Yourself:

— What point do the key details repeat and add up to?

— Is the central focus a statement about the topic?

— Is the central focus something useful that can help you to think or act in the world?

— Also consider: Do you agree with the statement as applied to life? Why or why not?

## ■ Skill 1.6: Summarize one or more texts using key supporting ideas and details.

A *summary* is a brief account of the main ideas and supporting details. As is the case with other skills within this domain, you will need an effective strategy. Try the Summarize Strategy. It involves pausing to review the text and create a summary of what you have read. The FTCE test is timed; therefore, it is critical that you have an efficient way to capture what is most important. The primary reason you should consider this strategy is because it helps you identify and keep track of a text's main ideas. When you summarize, you're more likely to remember what is important—and remembering important ideas makes for a satisfying reading experience. Summarizing also gives you a great starting point for discussing what you've read.

When you read, stop periodically and summarize what has happened so far in the text. If you're reading one selection, focus on the important characters and events. If you're reading a nonfiction text, look for the main points the author makes. If you have two selections, it is helpful to stop after each and summarize to consolidate what you've read.

When considering a question that asks for a summary of a particular section of the selection or the whole selection, always remember that a good summary focuses on the following aspects:

- Captures the main ideas and key information in the text

- Has the right amount of detail (not too much and not too little)

- Combines several ideas or facts into one statement

- Paraphrases (uses your own words) to convey that you understand the author's ideas.

## ■ Skill 1.7: Determine how and why specific individuals, events, and ideas develop based on textual evidence.

*Textual evidence* is supporting evidence from a text (fiction or nonfiction) that the author uses to flesh out his or her ideas. All textual evidence should:

- Support a specific point

- Be followed by a connection that explains the relationship of the evidence to the central idea being communicated by the author of the selection

There are four types of textual evidence that you will see as you read through the FTCE test's selections: referencing, summarizing, paraphrasing, and quoting. The types are listed, in sequence, from those that use general evidence (referencing) to those that use specific evidence (quoting). The most common type of textual evidence for literary analysis responses is quoting. Understanding each type of evidence across the spectrum will aid you in analyzing the strength of the evidence found within a given selection.

### Referencing

*Referencing* is mentioning a particular event or action in the text. This is helpful when the author wants to point out something in order to strengthen the author's voice on the topic. This is the most basic type of evidence given by an author.

### Summarizing

*Summarizing* is putting someone else's words into your own words. This is used by authors when they want to point to a larger section of text without using details of the original text.

### Paraphrasing

*Paraphrasing* means putting someone else's words into the author's words. A selection will utilize this when it needs more detail than a summary can provide, but less than a direct quote. A paraphrase focuses concisely on a single central idea.

### Quoting

*Quotations* illuminate a selection in the strongest way possible. It is the most convincing evidence of the four types because it adds credibility to the author's ideas. As with all textual evidence, it is when the author connects the quote to the main point that validation occurs.

## Skill 1.8: Determine the cause-and-effect relationship(s) among individuals, events, and ideas based on textual evidence.

Determining cause and effect is a strategy to find a causal relationship between or among events, conditions, or behaviors. When you are trying to determine the cause-and-effect relationship within one or between two selections, you will need to use a strategic form of analysis while reading. Cause and effect are subtle and often hard to distinguish. Be sure not to confuse cause with effect. To determine the cause of something, ask yourself *why* it happened. To determine the effect of a cause, ask *what* happened. Three general causal relations can exist when a cause-and-effect relationship exists:

- Necessary cause—one that must be present for the effect to occur.

- Sufficient cause—one that can produce an effect unaided, though there may be more than one sufficient cause of a given effect.

- Contributory cause—one that helps to produce an effect but cannot do so by itself.

Questions that can be raised to identify cause-and-effect relationships:

- Have I assumed a cause-and-effect relationship where none exists?

- Have I assumed only one cause when many causes may be appropriate?

- Have I incorrectly assumed a causal relationship between two events where one immediately follows another?

- Are there single or multiple causes?

- Are there single or multiple effects?

- Is a chain reaction involved?

Once a cause-and-effect relationship has been identified, then the task becomes to determine the nature of the relationship. Several kinds of causes exist.

- The primary cause (also know as the main cause, the necessary cause, or first cause) is the basis for a causal chain of events.

- The secondary cause or effect is usually an ancillary cause that contributes to an effect or an ancillary effect of a cause.

- The short-term cause or effect (also called the immediate cause or effect) is a single, immediately identifiable event.

- The long-term cause or effect (often referred to as the underlying cause) is an important contributing cause or effect that may be difficult to identify, but in the long run is more important than the immediate causes or effects.

Questions to be raised once a cause-and-effect relationship has been identified:

- To determine causes, ask, "Why did this happen?" or "What are the causes?" or "What are the factors that cause ___?"

- To determine effects, ask, "What happened because of this?" or "What is the effect or result?" or "What are the factors that resulted from this cause?"

- If a causal chain has been identified, ask, "What causal chain of events led to this effect?"

Often, many causes contribute to a single effect, or many effects may result from a single cause. What is most important for you as a reader is that you must be actively asking yourself the questions listed above as you read the selections. If you focus on this strategy, then you will be equipped to address a causal-relationship question stem. Finally, review the list of key words below in order to successfully recognize word clues.

**Word Clues for Causes**

- Because
- This leads to
- For one thing
- Due to
- Hence
- One cause is
- Another is
- For this reason

- For one thing
- Since
- So
- For
- First
- Second
- Another reason is
- If . . . then

**Word Clues for Effects**

- Consequently
- As a result
- For this reason
- This leads to
- On account of
- One result is
- Hence
- Later

- A result of this is
- Another result is
- Resulted in
- Therefore
- Thus
- So
- Then
- If . . . then

## Competency 2: Knowledge of Craft and Structure Based on Text Selections

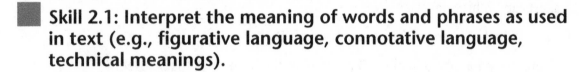

**Skill 2.1: Interpret the meaning of words and phrases as used in text (e.g., figurative language, connotative language, technical meanings).**

### Connotative Language

*Connotation* refers to a meaning that is implied by a word apart from the thing that it describes explicitly. Words carry cultural and emotional associations or meanings in

**FTCE GENERAL KNOWLEDGE**

addition to their literal meanings or denotations. For instance, "Wall Street" literally means a street situated in Lower Manhattan in New York City but connotatively it refers to "wealth" and "power."

## Positive and Negative Connotations

Words may have positive or negative connotations that depend upon the social, cultural, and personal experiences of individuals. For example, the words *childish*, *childlike* and *youthful* have the same denotative but different connotative meanings. *Childish* and *childlike* have a negative connotation as they refer to immature behavior. Whereas, *youthful* implies that a person is lively and energetic.

## Examples of Connotative Language

Below are a few examples of connotative language. The suggested meanings are shaped by cultural and emotional associations:

- *Dove* implies peace or gentility.

- *Home* suggests family, comfort, and security.

- *Politician* has a negative connotation of wickedness or insincerity while *statesperson* connotes sincerity.

- *Pushy* refers to someone loud-mouthed and irritating.

- *Mom* and *Dad,* when used in place of *mother* and *father*, connote loving parents.

## Examples of Connotation in Reading

In literature, it is a common practice among writers to deviate from the literal meanings of words in order to create novel ideas. Figures of speech are examples of such deviations.

### Example #1:

*Metaphors* are words that connote meanings that go beyond their literal meanings. Shakespeare in his Sonnet 18 says:

"Shall I Compare Thee to a Summer's Day"

Here, the phrase "a Summer's Day" implies the fairness of his beloved.

Similarly, John Donne says in his poem "The Sun Rising":

"She is all states, and all princes, I."

This line suggests the speaker's belief that he and his beloved are wealthier than all the states, kingdoms, and rulers in the whole world because of their love.

### Example #2

*Irony* and *satire* exhibit connotative meanings, as the intended meanings of words are opposite to their literal meanings. For example, we see a sarcastic remark passed by Antonio on Shylock, the Jew, in William Shakespeare's play "The Merchant of Venice":

> "Hie thee, gentle Jew.
>
> The Hebrew will turn Christian: he grows kind."

The word "Jew" has a negative connotation of wickedness, while "Christian" demonstrates positive connotations of kindness.

### Example #3

George Orwell's allegorical novel *Animal Farm* is packed with examples of connotation. The actions of the animals on the farm illustrate the greed and corruption that arose after the Communist Revolution of Russia. The pigs in the novel connote wicked and powerful people who can change the ideology of a society. In addition, Mr. Jones (the owner of the farm), represents the overthrown Tsar Nicholas II; and Boxer, the horse, represents the laborer class, etc.

### Function of Connotation

In literature, connotation paves the way for creativity by using figures of speech like metaphor, simile, symbolism, personification, etc. Had writers contented themselves with only the literal meanings, there would have been no way to compare abstract ideas to concrete concepts in order to give readers a better understanding. Therefore, connotative meanings allow writers to add to their works dimensions that are broader, more vivid, and fresher. As you are reading, look for these elements to create a greater picture of what is occurring within the given selection or set of selections.

## Figurative Language

While you are reading, it is important to recognize that the author will use many of the devices previously mentioned to describe things. Any time that the author describes something by comparing it with something else, he or she is using figurative language.

### Simile

A simile uses the words "like" or "as" to compare one object or idea with another to suggest they are alike.

**Example:** as busy as a bee

## Metaphor

Metaphor states a fact or draws a verbal picture by the use of comparison. A simile would say you are *like* something; a metaphor is more positive—it says you *are* something.

**Example:** You are what you eat.

## Personification

A figure of speech in which human characteristics are given to an animal or an object.

**Example:** My teddy bear gave me a hug.

## Alliteration

The repetition of the same initial letter, sound, or group of sounds in a series of words. Alliteration includes tongue twisters.

**Example:** She sells seashells by the seashore.

## Onomatopoeia

The use of a word to describe or imitate a natural sound or the sound made by an object or an action.

**Example:** snap crackle pop

## Hyperbole

An exaggeration that is so dramatic that no one would believe the statement is true. Tall tales are hyperboles.

**Example:** He was so hungry, he ate that whole cornfield for lunch, stalks and all.

## Idioms

An idiom is an expression that is peculiar to itself either grammatically (as in, "No, it wasn't me.") or in having a meaning that cannot be derived from the conjoined meanings of its elements.

**Example:** Fred is feeling *under the weather*.

## Clichés

A cliché is an expression that has been used so often that it has become trite.

**Example:** Many hands make light work.

**Skill 2.2: Analyze how specific word choices shape meaning or tone.**

## Word Choice and Tone

In any selection found on the FTCE examination, the writer chooses each word carefully. Some choices are made for the purpose of clarifying meaning, and other choices are made for style or effect. Writers can't use spoken language's intonation to convey their attitude toward a subject, so they must rely on their choice of words and details to communicate their tone. A writer's tone might be described as *admiring, stern, cynical, condescending, impatient,* or *hopeful,* for example.

Using the following strategies will help you examine word choice and tone:

- **Analyze the details.** One clue to a writer's tone is his or her choice of details. For example, does the writer of a biographical essay include only details that reveal the subject's flaws?

- **Examine word choice.** Look closely at the writer's choice of words or phrases. Do the words selected have positive or negative connotations, or associations?

For example, a writer might describe the following event in a variety of ways: *The politician explained his behavior.*

>   **Example 1:** The politician squirmed to excuse his indiscretions.

>   **Example 2:** The politician calmly and rationally justified his actions.

By looking closely at the choice of the words *squirmed, excuse,* and *indiscretions* in the first example, you can glean that the writer has a negative opinion of the politician. In the second example, however, the use of words with a positive connotation (*calmly, rationally,* and *justified*) reflects the writer's respect for the politician.

- **Analyze the effects.** Consider the cumulative impact of the writer's choices on the meaning and tone of the text. What do the details and language suggest about the writer's viewpoint on his or her subject? What impression of the topic do you get from reading?

## Word Choice and Meaning

Questions about word choice are very common within this examination. Often an FTCE test question will ask you to deal specifically with word choice. Other questions might ask you to consider word choice among other techniques. Words used in different contexts can have different connotations. When you answer a question about word choice, you are not only being asked what that word means but to consider how that meaning is affected by the context of the passage. You will be able to infer a great deal about writers' opinions from the words they use. Word-choice questions ask you to focus on the *connotation* rather than the *denotation* of a word.

Considering word choice is all about thinking beyond the obvious meaning of a word in order to explore what it suggests. Often words meaning almost the same thing imply quite different things. You need to be alert to recognize these when they occur.

### Example

One question asks,

> Should parents be allowed to smack their children?

and another asks,

> Should parents be allowed to strike their children?

The questions are almost the same, but the first seems to be less against smacking than the second, because the word *strike* suggests something more violent and aggressive than *smack*, which has connotations of a more gentle action, a slap rather than a blow.

### Example

Would you rather have a *crowd* outside your house, or a *mob*? Probably a crowd, since *mob* has connotations of an unruly, rather threatening group.

### Example

When a group of workers is looking for a raise, newspapers who support them will usually write something like:

> Sheet metal workers are *asking* for a 20% increase

while newspapers who are opposed to them will probably say they are *demanding* a 20% increase.

Why? Because, although the figures are the same, *demanding* suggests a more aggressive, unreasonable approach.

### Example

> She looked at Sharon's new hairstyle and snickered.

What does the choice of the word *snickered* here suggest about the observer's attitude about Sharon? Friendly? Sympathetic? Respectful? Surely not. If the writer had wanted to suggest that, she'd have chosen a word like *chuckle* or *giggle*, which would suggest a more friendly, warm kind of laughter. *Snickered* suggests a bit of contempt, a bit of a sneer.

**Skill 2.3: Analyze how the author uses organization and text structure(s) to convey meaning.**

Text structure is how information is organized in writing. Text structures, or patterns of organization, not only vary from one piece of writing to the next, but text structures may also change frequently from paragraph to paragraph within a single piece of writing. Though not all text can fit snugly into one of the patterns of organization listed below, it is critical to recognize how each selection is organized. Below are the most common ways to organize a selection:

### Chronological

When information in a passage is organized by the time during which a series of events occurred, it is organized chronologically. Nonfiction passages organized chronologically often contain dates. Fiction passages or narratives are more subtle and are organized chronologically, but usually have no dates. A narrative or story is a journey through time, and all of the events are arranged in order of time; therefore, every story has a beginning, a middle, and an end. Even if an author uses flashbacks, flash-forwards, or otherwise manipulates the time in his or her text, the events still occur along a timeline. Stories require the passage of time; therefore, all stories are organized chronologically.

### Compare-and-Contrast

Compare-and-contrast is a text structure or pattern of organization where the similarities and differences of two or more things are explored. It is important to remember that with the compare-and-contrast text structure, the text should be discussing similarities and differences. If the text only discusses similarities, it is only comparing. Likewise, if it only discusses differences, it is only contrasting. The text must do both to be considered compare-and-contrast.

> **Example:** Apples and oranges are both fruits, which means that they have seeds inside of them. Each has a skin, but orange skins are thick and easy to peel. Apple skins are thinner and do not peel easily. Oranges also contain more acid than apples, but both fruits are delicious.

### Order of Importance

In an order-of-importance structure, ideas or steps are prioritized by the writer or speaker according to a hierarchy of value. When using the order-of-importance pattern of organization, information can be structured from most to least important or least to most important. Both structures would be considered as the order-of-importance text structure.

> **Example:** The company has a clearly defined hierarchy. All major decisions go through the president, who controls the entire operation, but most daily decisions go to the board. Beneath the board members are the regional managers, who oversee the branch managers, who run each local branch.

## Sequence

Sequential order, or process writing, as it is sometimes called, is when information in a passage is organized by the order in which it occurs. This method of organizing text is generally used for instructions or directions, but it can also be used to explain processes in nature or society, such as how a president is elected.

Sequential organization is frequently confused with chronological order. To further confound the issue, sometimes people refer to chronological order as chronological sequence. But there is a key difference that distinguishes the two patterns: Texts organized chronologically occur at a specific time and setting, whereas texts describing processes or sequences do not occur at any specific time and place. To elaborate, if I tell the story of how I came home and made cookies, that information is organized chronologically. The story took place in my kitchen sometime in the past.

Alternatively, consider instructions on how to make cookies. When did that occur? That could happen anytime or at no particular time at all. This is because a recipe describes a process or sequence, one which is not attached to any specific chronology. Unlike chronologically ordered texts, information organized sequentially does not occur at any specific time but, rather, anytime.

Signal words: First, next, before, lastly, then

> **Example:** How to Make Cookies. First, get your materials. Then, make your dough. Lastly, cook your dough at 400 degrees for 10 minutes.

## Spatial

Spatial organization is when information in a passage is organized in order of space or location. If you were to describe the room in which you are sitting right now, you would be using spatial organization. Spatial organization may also be called descriptive writing; it is most frequently used when the narrator describes how something looks. Spatial organization is generally pretty easy to identify, but be aware that spatial organization is used in both fiction and nonfiction texts. Most fictional passages are organized chronologically, but in paragraphs where the narrator is describing a setting or the appearance of a character, the information may be organized spatially.

Some signal words that might indicate that the writer or speaker is following the spatial pattern of organization include: *next to, behind, across from, below that, above that, to the right of*, etc.

> **Example:** Volcanoes are a feared and destructive force for good reason. A volcano is like a pressure valve for the inner Earth, but they can also be very beautiful. One part of the volcano that people rarely see is the magma chamber. The magma chamber is way beneath the Earth's bedrock. It is tremendously hot. Running from the magma chamber to the crater of the volcano is the conduit. The conduit connects the magma chamber to the outer world. At the top of the volcano is the crater. This is where the magma exits. Volcanoes are a beautiful yet dangerous natural phenomenon.

## Cause and Effect

Paragraphs structured as cause and effect explain reasons why something happened or the effects of something. These paragraphs can be ordered as causes and effects or as effects and then causes. The cause-and-effect text structure is generally used in expository and persuasive writing modes.

To put it another way, when an author gives reasons why something happened, he or she is explaining what caused an effect (reasons are causes and the thing that happens is the effect). Also, when a writer explains the results of an action, he or she is explaining the effects of a cause (results are effects and the initial occurrence is the cause). The cause-and-effect text structure is used so commonly that you have probably written a paragraph using it and not noticed.

> **Example:** Many people think that they can get sick by going out in cold weather improperly dressed; however, illnesses are not caused by temperature—they are caused by germs. So while shivering outside in the cold probably won't strengthen your immune system, you're more likely to contract an illness indoors because you will have a greater exposure to germs.

In the above example, the paragraph explains how germs cause illnesses. The germs are the cause in the paragraph and the illness is the effect.

Here is another example of a paragraph that is written using the cause-and-effect text structure:

> **Example:** Students are not allowed to chew gum in my class. While some students think I am just being mean, there are many good reasons for this rule. First, some irresponsible students make messes with their gum. They may leave it on the bottoms of desks, drop it on the floor, or put it on other people's property. Another reason why I don't allow students to chew gum is because it is a distraction. When students are allowed to chew gum, they are more worried about having it, popping it, chewing it, and snapping it than they are in listening, writing, reading, and learning. This is why I don't allow students to chew gum in my class.

Identifying a text written using the cause-and-effect pattern of organization can be tricky. In most stories, events in the plot occur for various reasons. This can be mistaken for the cause-and-effect text structure; however, stories are organized chronologically, and the information in each passage is more likely to be organized by the time span during which each event occurred. Contrarily, cause-and-effect passages usually focus on explaining the reason why something occurs or occurred, and time will usually not pass in these paragraphs.

Here are some signal words that may indicate that information in a paragraph is organized as cause and effect: *because, as a result, resulted, caused, affected, since, due to, effect.*

### Problem and Solution

Problem-and-solution is a pattern of organization where information in a passage is expressed as a dilemma or concerning issue (a problem) for which a remedy (solution or attempted solution) was, can be, or should be sought. The problem-and-solution text structure may seem easy to recognize, but it is frequently confused with the cause-and-effect pattern of organization. However, if you read the passage and look specifically for both a problem and a solution to the problem, you should find it pretty easy to distinguish between cause and effect. Cause-and-effect passages do not propose solutions to any negative occurrences within the passage, but rather just explain why or how they happen.

> **Example:** It seems like there has been a surge in teen pregnancies these days. Teen pregnancies make it very difficult for young mothers to pursue their dreams and meet the demands of an infant. Fortunately, most teen pregnancies can be easily prevented by using birth control; however, even birth control is not 100% effective. The most effective way to prevent teen pregnancies is abstinence, which is 100% effective.

Here are some signal words that may indicate that a passage has a problem-and-solution organization: *propose, solution, answer, issue, problem, problematic, remedy, prevention,* and *fix.*

## Skill 2.4: Contrast the point of view of two or more authors on the same topic by analyzing their claims, reasoning, and evidence.

This skill focuses on the idea of differentiating and analyzing when examining two selections that generally cover the same topic. As a test-taker, you will find that there will be multiple accounts given from different perspectives.

A firsthand account of an event or topic is based on an author's personal experience. Diaries, autobiographies, and letters are firsthand accounts. The author's perspective on an event or topic may be influenced by his or her feelings about it.

A secondhand account of an event or topic is based on research rather than personal experience. Encyclopedia entries, biographies, and textbooks are considered to be secondhand accounts. The author's perspective on the event or topic is usually neutral. The author simply states the facts.

As you are reading the selection(s), you must analyze and take note of specific claims, reasoning, and evidence provided by the author.

Let's look at a passage and examine the claim, the reasoning, and the evidence.

### Indentured Servants

Early settlers in the American colonies had a lot of land but not enough people to work on it. So, beginning in the decade after the settlement of Jamestown, Virginia, in 1607, many men and women came to the colonies to live as indentured servants. In exchange for their
5 passage overseas and room and board, these men and women agreed to work for a period of between four and seven years. Then they would be considered free. Until then, they had to fulfill their contracts by working very hard. Their lives were harsh and restricted. People who tried to run away could be punished by having their contracts extended. If they
10 survived the hard labor, however, indentured servants received freedom packages that sometimes included at least 25 acres of land.

### Analysis

This passage is a secondhand account.

- The author of this passage was not an indentured servant and has no personal experience with indentured servitude.

- Instead, the author uses researched information to tell about indentured servants.

- The author's purpose for writing is to inform readers.

- The author's perspective with regard to indentured servitude is neutral. The author states facts about both the drawbacks and the potential positive outcomes of being an indentured servant.

**Claim:** What do you know? In other words, *what is the author's claim(s) or theory about the topic?*

**Evidence:** How do you know? In other words, *what is the evidence from the text that supports the author's claim(s) about the topic?*

### Types of Evidence

The types of evidence that a writer can summon to support his or her position or point are as follows: (1) facts and statistics, (2) the testimony of an authority, (3) personal anecdote, (4) hypothetical illustrations, and (5) analogy. Strictly speaking, the last two items in this list are not true evidence, but only offer common-sense probability to support an argument.

## Skill 2.5: Analyze how point of view and purpose shape the content and style of text.

Each selection is either written in first-person point of view or third-person point of view. It is important that you are able to identify the point of view and recognize how it shapes the content and style of the text.

**First-person point of view**—A character in the story is the narrator. This character is telling the story. The narrator uses the pronouns *I*, *me*, and *we*. In first-person point of view, readers learn about events as the narrator learns about them.

**Third-person point of view**—The story is being told by an outside observer (someone who is not in the story). The author uses the pronouns *he*, *she*, and *they*. In third-person point of view, the author can tell about the thoughts, actions, and feelings of the other characters.

### Author's Purpose:

As a general rule, the purpose of the selections are to inform/describe, persuade, or entertain.

### Point of View:

Position from which a writer addresses a topic to include beliefs, assumptions, and biases.

### Tone:

The attitude toward a subject, a character, or the reader. Choice of words and details convey the tone.

Every time an author writes, he or she has a **purpose** in mind. Understanding an author's purpose will help readers interpret the information. The author's **point of view** is often expressed through the purpose for writing. Review the following chart to be able to successfully recognize the purpose and point of view of the writer.

**Recognizing Purpose and Point of View**

| Type of Writing | Author's Purpose | Point of View and Tone |
|---|---|---|
| **Non-fiction**<br>• News articles<br>• Textbooks<br>• Biographies<br>• Documentaries<br>• Technical manuals<br>• Charts, graphs, tables | To inform, explain, give directions, illustrate, or present information. | The author's point of view and tone is primarily neutral. |
| **Persuasive Pieces**<br>• Editorials<br>• Advertisements<br>• Campaign speeches<br>• Bumper stickers<br>• Billboards<br>• Commercials<br>• Some charts and graphs | To persuade by expressing an opinion to convince readers to think/feel/act a certain way. | The point of view reflects the author's attitude about a subject. Sometimes the opinion is directly stated and other times it is implied. The author may try to convince readers by using tone to appeal to their feelings and/or values. |
| **Fiction**<br>• Short story<br>• Poetry<br>• Novels<br>• Plays | To illustrate a theme, event, or story that conveys a mood. Usually written to entertain. | The author may use characters or narrators to express attitudes in the story. The tone might be light and humorous, serious, or sad. |

# Competency 3: Knowledge of the Integration of Information and Ideas Based on Text Selections

## Skill 3.1: Evaluate and relate content presented in diverse formats.

This skill focuses on the aspects of gathering, assessing, and applying information from two selections. It is the process of analyzing selections in a strategic way in order to successfully answer the questions. The selections will come alive when you recognize how the ideas in the text connect to your experiences and beliefs, events happening in the larger world, understanding of history, and your knowledge of other texts.

"Text-to-Text, Text-to-Self, Text-to-World" is a strategy that helps you develop the habit of making these connections. This strategy helps you comprehend and make meaning of the ideas in the text. This strategy can be used when reading any text—historical or literary—and it can also be used with other media as well, including films. It can be used at the beginning, middle, or end of the reading process—to get you engaged with the texts and to understand the texts more deeply.

## Text-to-Text, Text-to-Self, Text-to-World

As you are actively reading the selections, ask yourself the following questions.

1.  **Text-to-Text**—How do the ideas in this text remind you of another text (story, book, movie, song, etc.)? Complete one of the following statements:

    - What I just read reminds me of _____ (story/book/ movie/song) because . . .

    - The ideas in this text are similar to the ideas in _____ because . . .

    - The ideas in this text are different from the ideas in _____ because . . .

**Are there similarities/differences in . . .**

| | |
|---|---|
| Genre | Plot |
| Text structure | Character |
| Author | Fact |
| Topic | Opinion |
| Theme | Information |
| Message | Vocabulary |

2.  **Text-to-Self**—How do the ideas in this text relate to your own life, ideas, and experiences? Complete one of the following statements:

    - What I just read reminds me of the time when I . . .

    - I agree with/understand what I just read because in my own life . . .

    - I don't agree with what I just read because in my own life . . .

**Are there similarities/differences in . . .**

| | |
|---|---|
| My family | Feelings I have had |
| My friends | Experiences |
| Trips I have been on | A place I have been |
| Things I have seen | |

3.  **Text-to-World**—How do the ideas in this text reading relate to the larger world—past, present, and future? Complete one of the following statements:

- What I just read makes me think about _____ (event from the past) because . . .

- What I just read makes me think about _____ (event from today related to my own community, nation, or world) because . . .

- What I just read makes me wonder about the future because . . .

**Are there similarities/differences in . . .**

| | |
|---|---|
| Something I have seen on TV | Current events |
| Radio news | Something I have studied before |
| A newspaper story | Real-world happenings—local and global |
| Historical events | A conversation |

 ## Skill 3.2: Evaluate specific claims in text based on relevancy, sufficiency, and validity or reasoning.

### Evaluating Evidence

For an argument to be logically convincing, your assertions (claims) must be backed up (supported) by evidence. Just as you learned in Competency 1, there are many types of evidence, but most fall into four major categories:

(1) Facts

(2) Statistics

(3) Examples/Anecdotes

(4) Expert Opinions

Remember, you cannot simply take evidence at face value. It may be that the writer has deliberately or unintentionally used evidence that is suspect. You, as the reader, recipient, or target of the persuasive argument must be prepared to evaluate the evidence, assess whether or not it is to be believed, and judge whether or not it really makes the case. Here are some typical questions that you need to ask:

*Is the evidence adequate and representative?*

- There should be a number of examples, so we can see a real trend.

- If it's a survey, there should be a large enough sample.

- The example, while credible, may in fact be a rare exception. Should we try to change a whole system in order to deal with an isolated problem?

*Is it accurate?*

- As you look closely at the evidence, do you see any flaws in it?

- While discovering a variety of minor errors does not in itself negate an argument, it does cast doubt on the overall credibility of the argument.

- If the facts in one source contradict evidence in other sources, then you must judge the accuracy.

*Is it relevant?*

- Does it really fit the situation that is being argued?

- Has it been taken out of context?

*Is the source of the evidence credible?*

- Is the source of the statistics or facts named?

- What kinds of credentials does the expert have (degrees, professional affiliations, employment, experience)?

- Is the source a professional, peer-reviewed journal?

- If a website, who is the owner/author of the website?

- If a scientific study, who commissioned or funded it?

- Does the source of the quotes or statistics have an interest in the matter?

- Generally, if an individual is speaking against his or her interests, the testimony will be more credible.

- The most credible sources will be written by individuals working for academic institutions (though they too may be paid industry consultants on the side), appearing in a peer-reviewed professional journal, or published by a university press.

- Do other credible sources refer to this source? That's usually a good sign of credibility (though it's also true that it may not apply to a source that is truly fresh and innovative).

- The more one gets to know about a subject, the more one works with sources related to this subject, the more one will be able to judge credibility.

Evidence is not the only means of supporting an argument, though it is the essential component. The writer can also make good use of analogy (comparing something abstract and unfamiliar with something concrete and familiar) and appeals (ethical/moral and emotional) to move the reader to agreement. Without supporting evidence, though, the argument will fall apart under scrutiny.

## Skill 3.3: Synthesize information from a range of texts to develop a coherent explanation of a process, phenomenon, concept, or theme.

Synthesizing involves merging new information with existing knowledge to create an original idea, see a new perspective, or form a new line of thinking to achieve insight. Synthesizing is the most complex of comprehension strategies. A true synthesis is an "Aha!" of sorts. As we take in information, we enhance our understanding.

Synthesizing lies on a continuum of evolving thinking. Synthesis allows you to process meaning and achieve new insight. Introducing the strategy of synthesizing in reading, then, primarily involves teaching the reader to stop every so often and think about what he or she has read. Each piece of additional information enhances the reader's understanding and allows him or her to better construct meaning by integrating the text with the reader's own thinking.

True synthesis is achieved when a new perspective or thought emerges from the reading. How does this type of insight come about? Nonfiction text, for example, often conveys information that helps the reader form a particular viewpoint. A reader's thinking changes as he or she ingests new information gleaned from the text. An article on rainforest deforestation might point a finger at governmental forestry policies. A synthesis could involve forming an opinion about the shortsightedness of government policies. This constitutes an evolution of thought: The new information combined with the reader's thinking leads to new insight.

To accurately synthesize when reading, readers need to get at the essence of the text. As you read a selection, it is your thinking about the text and the schema that you bring to the reading that creates an understanding of the selection. Here are some guiding questions to consider while synthesizing:

- What does the author believe? What shows me what the author is thinking?

- What else have I read that is like this text?

- Has this reading changed my opinion on this topic?

- Does this text make me think differently about things that I know or have experienced in my own life?

Synthesis is really the culmination of a reader's comprehension strategies. Synthesis is sifting through all of the information that a reader has available and creating new insight as thinking evolves.

## Skill 3.4: Analyze multiple texts to differentiate approaches authors take to develop similar themes (e.g., mode, author's craft, genre, point of view).

*Modes* are the purposes for writing. *Narrative, expository*, and *persuasive* are the three most commonly used terms to describe modes. All writing should allow room for mixing modes.

**Narrative**—Writing in which the author tells a story. The story could be fact or fiction.

**Expository**—Writing in which the author's purpose is to inform or explain the subject to the reader.

**Persuasive**—Writing that states the opinion of the writer and attempts to influence the reader.

Good writing never loses sight of its main purpose.

There are mini-modes, too. *Descriptive* is a good example. You can write with the sole purpose of describing something: a beautiful sunset over the ocean, a favorite childhood memory, your new truck, and so on. But we rarely do that; we more often use descriptive writing to make narrative, expository, and persuasive writing more effective.

*Genres* are categories of writing. In fiction, the genres are historical, realistic, mystery, humor, folk tales, science fiction, and so on. For nonfiction, visualize the Dewey Decimal System and how it is organized by category: biographies, science and nature essays, physical science, etc. You wouldn't go to the bookstore and ask for an expository book to plan your next trip to Italy. You'd ask for the travel section to find the category of books and resources about traveling to Italy.

*Formats* are structures of writing. If you write in the narrative mode, you'd likely write chronologically. If you work in the expository mode you might organize by comparison and contrast, point-by-point analysis, cause and effect, or any number of ways we construct nonfiction writing. Structures have to be modeled and taught so students know which to use to shape the writing. We use a variety of structures depending on the purpose for writing.

As a general rule of thumb, the terms *modes* and *formats* live in the writer's world. The term *genre* is more reader-centered. On the FTCE-GK test, it is critical that you are able to identify and analyze each.

## Paired Passages

Paired passages are a set of passages that are connected in some way. On the examination, you will have questions about each individual passage. You will also have questions that require you to analyze the passages simultaneously. Make sure you understand which passage the question is referring to within the evaluation. Also, you must note evidence provided by the author as you are reading in order to determine the best answer choice. The questions will be a combination of reading skills from central idea to structure to organization pattern. Having a strategy is critical:

### 4-Step Strategy

- **Read** both passages.

- **Explain** or understand the connection(s) between the two passages.

- **Analyze** similarities and differences of the passages.

- **Determine** the answers to the questions based on evidence from each passage.

## English as a Second Language: KEY READING STRATEGIES

If you are an English learner, it is critical that you be a strategic test-taker in order to be successful on the Reading portion of the examination. Below, you will find a set of strategies that can be applied:

1. **Be an Active Reader.** Ask yourself critical questions as you go:

   - What is the main message the author wanted to convey through the reading?

   - Who is the main audience of this text?

   - What is the author's main intention to write this text?

   - What do I already know about the topic?

2. **Be Sensitive to Context.** English is a very context-sensitive language. One word has multiple meanings, and the meaning changes depending on the context in which the word is used. Trying to learn the meaning of a new word by guessing from contextual clues is a useful skill to develop. Contextual clues may appear in the same sentence where the word is used or in the preceding or following sentences. This strategy is especially helpful when examining vocabulary questions.

3. **Write as You Read.** As key ideas and evidence jump out at you, make a note of them.

4. **Skim Text.** Skimming and scanning are usually considered speed-reading skills because they are not used for intensive reading, but for the GK Reading Section it is

an essential skill. Skimming a text involves running your eyes over it quickly to get the main idea or gist of the passage. This skill allows you to identify which parts of a long text you might need to read more closely to identify a correct answer.

5. **Scan for Key Words/Phrases.** Scanning, on the other hand, allows you to quickly search a text for a particular piece of information. Scanning is ideal when you are looking for a key idea from a test question or answer. Perhaps a subject needs to find a phone number in a directory, the date of a historical event, or the time their train is leaving.

6. **Summarize.** This skill requires you to take what you have read and put it into a concise word or phrase. Whether you have read a paragraph or a complete passage, it is critical that you can synthesize the ideas communicated by the author into one clear idea. Doing this while you read will help you find answers more easily.

7. **Visualize.** As you read through each passage, see what is happening through your "mind's eye." Using this strategy will aid you in focusing on key ideas within the text.

## Drill 1: Context Clues

**Directions:** Determine a working meaning for the underlined word in each of the following sentences by evaluating context clues.

1. Romeyn de Hooghe, the first <u>limner</u> to limit his work to narrative strips, used his talent to create pictorial criticism of the persecution of the Huguenots under Louis XIV.

2. The somber clouds and the dreary rain caused the child to <u>mope</u> about the house.

3. The <u>veracity</u> of the witness's testimony, revealed through his eye-to-eye contact with the jury and lack of stumbling over words, was not doubted.

4. Why isn't the evening sun described as <u>moribund</u>, not setting; after all, it is coming to the day's end?

5. As president, state warden, and security chief, the leader described in Gilbert and Sullivan's "The Mikado" is a <u>poohbah</u>.

6. Robin Hood's <u>audacious</u> actions included conducting dangerous rescues of Maid Marian and visiting enemy territory disguised as a local.

7. Among common household health products are <u>St. John's Wort</u> and <u>Echinacea</u>, herbs from the garden.

8. My father is a <u>numismatist</u>; he spends several hours each week studying his coins from other countries and time periods.

## Drill 2: Purpose/Point of View

**Directions:** Read the passages and answer the questions that follow.

### Passage 1

The Matsushita Electric Industrial Company of Japan has developed a computer program that can use photographs of faces to predict the aging process and, also, how an unborn child may look. The system can show how a couple may look after 40 years of marriage and how newlyweds' future children may look. The computer analyzes facial characteristics from a photograph, based on shading and coloring differences, and then creates a three-dimensional model in its memory. The system consists of a personal computer with a program and circuit board. It will be marketed soon by Matsushita.

1.    This passage is written in the point of view called

    (A)  first person.

    (B)  second person.

    (C)  third person.

    (D)  a combination of first and third person.

2.    The intended purpose of this passage is to

    (A)  persuade a couple to send in their photographs to use to predict their children's appearance.

    (B)  explain how the aging process of adults and the appearance of their children can be predicted by a computer.

    (C)  express an opinion about the technology of the future in Japan.

    (D)  describe one way a computer uses photographs.

### Passage 2

As a farmer from Conrad, Montana, I might be the last person expected to invent and patent a motorcycle helmet. (No, I don't wear a helmet while I am driving my tractor.) The law in the United States requires that all cars sold must carry a third, high-mounted brake light on the rear of the vehicle. If cars need this light, I thought, how much safer life would be for motorcyclists if they, too, had such a light. The problem, however, was to install it "high-mounted." I have designed a helmet with a brake light in the rear. Thus, motorcyclists wearing a helmet like mine are much safer on the road.

3.    The intended purpose of the passage is to

(A) tell about a farmer in Montana.

(B) explain a safety requirement for cars in the United States.

(C) describe a man's motorcycle helmet invention that makes riding motorcycles safer.

(D) show the versatility of some people.

4. The point of view of this passage is

(A) first person.

(B) second person.

(C) third person.

(D) first and third person.

## Drill 3: Structure/Key Details/Vocabulary

**Directions:** Read the passage and answer the questions that follow.

### Water

1      The most important source of sediment is earth and rock material carried to the sea by rivers and streams; the same materials may also have been transported by glaciers and winds. Other sources are volcanic ash and lava, shells and skel-

5      etons of organisms, chemical precipitates formed in seawater, and particles from outer space.

Water is a most unusual substance because it exists on the surface of the earth in its three physical states: ice, water, and water vapor. There are other substances that might exist in

10     a solid and liquid or gaseous state at temperatures normally found at the earth's surface, but there are fewer substances which occur in all three states.

Water is odorless, tasteless, and colorless. It is the only substance known to exist in a natural state as a solid, liquid, or gas

15     on the surface of the earth. It is a universal solvent. Water does not corrode, rust, burn, or separate into its components easily. It is chemically indestructible. It can corrode almost any metal and erode the most solid rock. A unique property of water is that it expands and floats on water when frozen or in the solid

20     state. Water has a freezing point of 0°C and a boiling point of 100°C. Water has the capacity for absorbing great quantities of heat with relatively little increase in temperature. When ***distilled***, water is a poor conductor of electricity but when salt is added, it is a good conductor of electricity.

25     Sunlight is the source of energy for temperature change, evaporation, and currents for water movement through the atmosphere. Sunlight controls the rate of photosynthesis for all marine plants, which are directly or indirectly the source of food for all marine animals. Migration, breeding, and other

30     behaviors of marine animals are affected by light.

Water, as the ocean or sea, is blue because of the molecular scattering of the sunlight. Blue light, being of short wavelength, is scattered more effectively than light of longer wavelengths. Variations in color may be caused by particles

35     suspended in the water, water depth, cloud cover, temperature, and other variable factors. Heavy concentrations of dissolved materials cause a yellowish hue, while algae will cause the water to look green. Heavy populations of plant and animal

40     materials will cause the water to look brown.

1.  Which of the following lists of topics best organizes the information in the selection?

    (A) I.    Water as vapor

        II.   Water as ice

        III.  Water as solid

    (B) I.    Properties of seawater

        II.   Freezing and boiling points of water

        III.  Photosynthesis

        IV.   Oceans and seas

    (C) I.    Water as substance

        II.   Water's corrosion

        III.  Water and plants

        IV.   Water and algae coloration

    (D) I.    Water's physical states

        II.   Properties of water

        III.  Effects of the sun on water

        IV.   Reasons for color variation in water

2.  According to the passage, what is the most unusual property of water?

    (A) Water is odorless, tasteless, and colorless.

    (B) Water exists on the surface of the earth in three physical states.

    (C) Water is chemically indestructible.

    (D) Water is a poor conductor of electricity.

3.  Which of the following best defines the word *distilled* as it is used in the last sentence of the third paragraph?

    (A) Free of salt content

    (B) Free of electrical energy

    (C) Dehydrated

    (D) Containing wine

4.   The writer of this selection would most likely agree with which of the following statements?

   (A)  The properties of water are found in most other liquids on this planet.

   (B)  Water should not be consumed in its most natural state.

   (C)  Water might be used to serve many different functions.

   (D)  Water is too unpredictable for most scientists.

## Drill 4: Inference

**Directions:** Read the passage and answer the questions that follow.

### The Beginnings of the Submarine

1      A submarine was first used as an offensive weapon during the American Revolutionary War. The Turtle, a one-man submersible designed by an American inventor named David Bushnell and hand-operated by a screw propeller, attempted
5    to sink a British man-of-war in New York Harbor. The plan was to attach a charge of gunpowder to the ship's bottom with screws and explode it with a time fuse. After repeated failures to force the screws through the copper sheathing of the hull of HMS *Eagle*, the submarine gave up and withdrew, exploding
10    its powder a short distance from the *Eagle*. Although the attack was unsuccessful, it caused the British to move their blockading ships from the harbor to the outer bay.

      On 17 February 1864, a Confederate craft, a hand-propelled submersible, carrying a crew of eight men, sank a Federal cor-
15    vette that was blockading Charleston Harbor. The hit was accomplished by a torpedo suspended ahead of the Confederate *Hunley* as she rammed the Union frigate *Housatonic*, and is the first recorded instance of a submarine sinking a warship.

20    The submarine first became a major component in naval warfare during World War I, when Germany demonstrated its full potential. Wholesale sinking of Allied shipping by the German U-boats almost swung the war in favor of the Central Powers. Then, as now, the submarine's greatest advantage was that it
25    could operate beneath the ocean surface where detection was difficult. Sinking a submarine was comparatively easy, once it was found—but finding it before it could attack was another matter.

During the closing months of World War I, the Allied Sub-
30  marine Devices Investigation Committee was formed to obtain
from science and technology more effective underwater detection equipment. The committee developed a reasonably accurate device for locating a submerged submarine. This device
was a trainable hydrophone, which was attached to the bottom
35  of the ASW ship, and used to detect screw noises and other
sounds that came from a submarine. Although the committee
disbanded after World War I, the British made improvements
on the locating device during the interval between then and
World War II, and named it ASDIC after the committee.

40  American scientists further improved on the device, calling
it SONAR, a name derived from the underlined initials of the
words sound navigation and ranging.

At the end of World War II, the United States improved
the snorkel (a device for bringing air to the crew and engines
45  when operating submerged on diesels) and developed the
Guppy (short for greater underwater propulsion power),
a conversion of the fleet-type submarine of World War II
fame. The superstructure was changed by reducing the surface
area, streamlining every protruding object, and enclosing the
50  periscope shears in a streamlined metal fairing. Performance
increased greatly with improved electronic equipment, additional battery capacity, and the addition of the snorkel.

1.  The passage implies that one of the most pressing modifications needed for the submarine was to

(A) streamline its shape.

(B) enlarge the submarine for accommodating more torpedoes and men.

(C) reduce the noise caused by the submarine.

(D) add a snorkel.

2.  It is inferred that

(A) ASDIC was formed to obtain technology for underwater detection.

(B) ASDIC developed an accurate device for locating submarines.

(C) the hydrophone was attached to the bottom of the ship.

(D) ASDIC was formed to develop technology to defend U.S. shipping.

3.  SONAR not only picked up the sound of submarines moving through the water but also

    (A) indicated the speed at which the sub was moving.

    (B) gave the location of the submarine.

    (C) indicated the speed of the torpedo.

    (D) placed the submarine within a specified range.

4.  According to the passage, the submarine's success was due in part to its ability to

    (A) strike and escape undetected.

    (B) move more swiftly than other vessels.

    (C) submerge to great depths while being hunted.

    (D) run silently.

5.  From the passage, one can infer

    (A) David Bushnell was indirectly responsible for the sinking of the federal corvette in Charleston Harbor.

    (B) David Bushnell invented the Turtle.

    (C) the Turtle was a one-man submarine.

    (D) the Turtle sank the *Eagle* on February 17, 1864.

## Answer Key

### Drill 1: Context Clues

1.  artist; line drawer
2.  unhappily move about
3.  truthfulness
4.  dying or dead
5.  leader who holds several offices
6.  daring
7.  herbs used for good health
8.  coin collector

## Drill 2: Purpose/Point of View

1. **(C)**

Choice (C) is the correct answer because the passage employs the point of view of an outsider through the use of pronouns such as *he, she,* and *it.*

2. **(B)**

The intended purpose is to explain. Although couples might be interested in sending in their photographs to see what their children may look like, choice (A), the passage is not encouraging this reaction from those who read it. Choice (C) is much too broad a response; also, the passage is not expressing an opinion. Choice (D) is too vague, although what it says is incomplete truth.

3. **(C)**

The focus of the passage is the motorcycle helmet, and the intended purpose is to explain why and how the helmet was invented. Choice (A) is a fact about the inventor—he is a farmer. Choice (B) is a true statement as well, but it is what prompted the writer's idea for a helmet. (D) is a general statement that is unrelated to this passage.

4. **(A)**

The personality of the speaker is revealed along with his ideas and actions. Notice also the use of the pronoun *I.* Choice (D) will attract some test-takers, but the first person point of view often uses third person pronouns along with first person pronouns.

## Drill 3: Passage Structure/Key Details/Vocabulary

1. **(D)**

The correct response is (D) because its precepts are summations of each of the composition's main paragraphs. (A) only mentions points made in the second paragraph. (B) and (C) only mention scattered points made throughout the passage, each of which does not represent a larger body of information within the passage.

2. **(B)**

The second paragraph states that this is the reason that water is a most unusual sub-stance. (A) and (C) list unusual properties of water, but are not developed in the same manner as the property stated in (B). (D) is not supported in the passage not only because electrical conduction is not water's "most unusual property," but also because water's electrical conduction properties vary depending on whether salt is present.

3. **(A)**

The sentence contrasts distilled water to that which contains salt, so (A) is correct. (B), (C), and (D) are not implied by the passage.

4. **(C)**

The correct choice is (C) because of the many properties of water ascribed to it in the passage, each of which might serve one practical purpose or another. (A) and (D) are contradicted within the passage, while (B) is not implied at all by the passage.

## Drill 4: Inference

1. **(A)**

Answer (A) is correct because of the importance of streamlining mentioned in the final paragraph. (B) and (C) are not suggested in the paragraph, and (D) is secondary in importance to (A).

2. **(D)**

Since it may be inferred from the general purpose of underwater detection equip-ment, (D) is correct. While (A) and (B) are true statements, they are not inferences. (C) is not implied in the passage.

3. **(D)**

Answer (D) is correct because the "R" in SONAR stands for "Ranging." (A), (B), and (C) are neither mentioned nor implied by the passage.

4.  **(A)**

As was mentioned in the third sentence of the third paragraph, (A) is correct. (B), (C), and (D) are not mentioned in the passage.

5.  **(A)**

It may be inferred that Bushnell's invention led to the success of the later version of the submarine. (B) and (C) are true, but are not inferences because they are directly stated in the first paragraph. (D) is not a true statement; the Turtle had no direct link to the 1864 incident.

# Mathematics

Are you ready to tackle the Math section of the FTCE General Knowledge Test? Well, you will be after you review some of the basic concepts contained in this chapter. The more familiar you are with these fundamental concepts, the better you will do on the math section. Our math review represents the various mathematical topics that appear on the exam. Once you have mastered these concepts, you will be prepared to apply them when solving the word problems that make up the majority of the mathematics subtest.

## Competency 1: Knowledge of Number Sense, Concepts, and Operations

### Skill 1.1. Compare real numbers and identify their location on a number line.

The numbers used in basic mathematics courses are called the **real numbers**. Real numbers are comprised of rational and irrational numbers. **Rational numbers** are numbers that can be written as a ratio of two integers. Rational numbers include integers, fractions, and decimals. **Integers** are the set of whole numbers and their opposites: $\{\ldots -3, -2, -1, 0, 1, 2, 3\ldots\}$. Whole numbers and natural (counting) numbers are subsets of integers. **Whole numbers** are all the positive integers and 0: $\{0, 1, 2, 3 \ldots\}$. **Natural or counting numbers** are the positive integers beginning with 1: $\{1, 2, 3, 4 \ldots\}$. You can remember that natural numbers start with 1 because it is *natural* to start with one when you are counting items. A **decimal number** is a number represented by the digits 0 to 9 and may include a decimal point. Examples of decimal numbers are 4.5, 0.003, and 367.0 (all whole numbers can be written with a decimal point to the right of the ones place). When reading a decimal number, you use the word *and* for the decimal place. For instance, the decimal 4.5 is read *four and five tenths* since it ends in the tenths place. The number 0.003 is read *three thousandths* since it ends in the thousandths place. **Fractions** are numbers that can be used to express parts of a whole. A fraction has a numerator and a denominator. The denominator is the number on the bottom, and it shows how many pieces the fraction is broken up into. The numerator shows how many parts of the fraction you have.

An **irrational number** is a number that cannot be expressed as the ratio of two integers. Decimals that never end (called non-terminating) and do not have a repeating pattern are irrational. Square roots of numbers that are not perfect squares are irrational numbers. The most well-known irrational number is the ratio of a circle's circumference to its diameter; it is represented with the symbol $\pi$ (pi). The decimal value of $\pi$ is non-repeating and non-terminating, even after a million places beyond the decimal point. During the FTCE exam, use 3.14 to substitute for $\pi$, which equals approximately 3.141592.

It is important to know that each number has a specific value and may be written in a number of different forms, such as a fraction, decimal, percent, or integer. All real numbers can be placed on a number line to show how they compare to each other. A number line is actually infinite, continuing infinitely in both directions forever. In order to make a physical representation of a number line, however, we are only able to draw a finite portion of it. Below is an example of a number line that shows the integers from −10 to +10. Although only the integers are marked, there are an infinite number of numbers that can be represented on the number line. The bottom number line shows you that between 0 and 1 you could place 0.3, $\frac{9}{20}$, 0.8, and $\frac{9}{11}$ because they are numbers greater than 0 and less than 1.

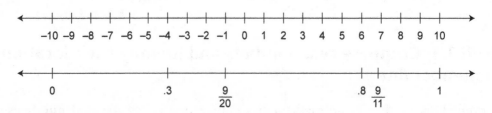

As you move to the right on a number line, numbers get larger. As you move to the left on a number line, numbers get smaller. This means that 10 is greater than 8, but −10 is less than −8. You can choose to show as many or as few numbers as you wish on a number line. In addition, you can divide the number line into whatever divisions suit the situation. When we want to compare numbers between 0 and 1, we only show the portion of a number line between 0 and 1, as seen above.

## Fractions

On the FTCE-GKT, you will need to compare fractions to identify which fraction is larger and which is smaller. If fractions are shown on a number line, the fraction to the right is the larger one. Comparing fractions is simple when the fractions have the same denominator, because you can directly compare the value of the numerators. For example, $\frac{9}{10}$ is greater than $\frac{7}{10}$ because 9 is larger than 7.

If the fractions do not have a common denominator, the easiest way to compare them is to use your four-function calculator to convert both fractions to decimals. This is done by dividing the numerator (the number on the top) by the denominator. For instance, if you were comparing $\frac{4}{5}$ and $\frac{9}{10}$, you would convert the fractions into two division problems: $4 \div 5 = 0.8$ and $9 \div 10 = 0.9$. Comparing the decimals, you would see that 0.9 is greater than 0.8, so $\frac{9}{10}$ is greater than $\frac{4}{5}$.

Another way to compare fractions is to find a common denominator for the fractions and then compare the numerators. In order to find a common denominator, you have to identify the **least common multiple (LCM)** of the denominators. Again, let's compare $\frac{4}{5}$ and $\frac{9}{10}$. The first few multiples of 5 are 5, 10, 15, and 20. Since 10 (the denominator we need) is a multiple of 5, we can use that as our common denominator. Since 10 is two times five, convert the fraction as shown below:

$$\frac{4 \times 2}{5 \times 2} = \frac{8}{10}$$

Now we have $\frac{8}{10}$ and $\frac{9}{10}$ and can easily see that 9 is greater than 8.

One last trick for comparing fractions is using the cross product method as shown below.

$$5 \cdot 13 = 65 \quad 12 \cdot 6 = 72$$

$$\frac{5}{12} \diagdown \frac{6}{13}$$

Since 72 is greater than 65, $\frac{6}{13}$ is greater than $\frac{5}{12}$. Don't forget to multiply from the denominator across to the numerator and place your answers at the top, otherwise your solutions will be on the wrong side to directly compare fractions.

It is also very important to remember that things look very different when comparing negative fractions! $-\frac{1}{4}$ is actually greater than $-\frac{1}{2}$, so we do not recommend this method when comparing negative fractions.

## PROBLEM

Which fraction is greater, $\frac{3}{4}$ or $\frac{2}{5}$?

## SOLUTION

Using a calculator, $\frac{3}{4} = 0.75$ and $\frac{2}{5} = 0.4$. Since 0.75 is greater than 0.4, $\frac{3}{4}$ is greater than $\frac{2}{5}$. ***Warning:*** *ALWAYS enter the numerator into the calculator first or your answer will be incorrect.*

If you choose to find the common denominator to compare the fractions, follow these steps:

**Step 1:** Find the least common multiple of the denominators.

**4:** 4, 8, 12, 16, **20**

**5:** 5, 10, 15, **20**

**Step 2:** Rename the fractions by identifying the relationship between the old denominator and the new denominator.

$$\frac{3 \times 5 = 15}{4 \times 5 = 20} \qquad \frac{2 \times 4 = 8}{5 \times 4 = 20}$$

**Step 3:** Compare the numerators of the renamed fractions, $\frac{15}{20}$ and $\frac{8}{20}$.

Since 15 is greater than 8, $\frac{3}{4}$ is greater than $\frac{2}{5}$.

It is recommended that you use the calculator method for comparing fractions, and reserve the time-consuming process of finding a common denominator for when you have to add or subtract fractions.

## PROBLEM

List the fractions shown from least to greatest: $\frac{3}{7}, \frac{8}{21}, \frac{7}{14}$.

(A) $\frac{3}{7}, \frac{8}{21}, \frac{7}{14}$      (B) $\frac{8}{21}, \frac{7}{14}, \frac{3}{7}$

(C) $\frac{7}{14}, \frac{3}{7}, \frac{8}{21}$      (D) $\frac{8}{21}, \frac{3}{7}, \frac{7}{14}$

## SOLUTION

Sometimes using common sense can reduce the amount of work needed to solve this type of problem. Notice that if you simplify $\frac{7}{14}$ you see that it is equal to $\frac{1}{2}$ because 7 is half of 14. If you think about it, it is obvious that $\frac{8}{21}$ and $\frac{3}{7}$ are less than $\frac{1}{2}$ because their numerators are **less than half of their denominators**. That lets us know that the largest fraction is $\frac{7}{14}$. Now all we have to do is compare $\frac{8}{21}$ and $\frac{3}{7}$. Using your calculator, $8 \div 21$ is approximately 0.38 and $3 \div 7$ is approximately 0.43, so $\frac{3}{7}$ is greater than $\frac{8}{21}$. The correct answer is (D).

Let's look at another example.

### PROBLEM

Place the following fractions in order from least to greatest: $\frac{2}{5}, \frac{7}{8}, \frac{3}{4}, \frac{6}{17}$, and $\frac{13}{14}$.

## SOLUTION

At first glance, this looks like a very time-consuming problem because all of the fractions have different denominators. However, when you look closely, you should notice that you can use your estimation skills to put the fractions in order. Ask yourself if any of the fractions are less than $\frac{1}{2}$? Notice that $\frac{2}{5}$ and $\frac{6}{17}$ are the only fractions that are less than $\frac{1}{2}$. You can tell because their numerators are less than half of their denominators. Therefore, you know that either $\frac{2}{5}$ or $\frac{6}{17}$ will be the smallest fraction. Can you use your estimating skills again to figure out which of the two fractions is smallest? Notice that $\frac{2}{5}$ is very close to $\frac{1}{2}$. $\frac{2.5}{5}$ would be exactly $\frac{1}{2}$. What about $\frac{6}{17}$? Notice that $\frac{6}{18}$ would be exactly $\frac{1}{3}$ and $\frac{6}{17}$ is very close to that. $\frac{1}{3}$ is smaller than $\frac{1}{2}$. Therefore, $\frac{6}{17}$ is smaller than $\frac{2}{5}$. Now, you have two of the five fractions in order, $\frac{6}{17}$ and $\frac{2}{5}$. Now examine the other three fractions: $\frac{7}{8}, \frac{3}{4}$, and $\frac{13}{14}$. Notice that $\frac{3}{4}$ can be easily rewritten as $\frac{6}{8}$.

Which is smaller, $\frac{6}{8}$ or $\frac{7}{8}$? $\frac{6}{8}$ is smaller, so you know that $\frac{3}{4}$ comes before $\frac{7}{8}$. The final fraction, $\frac{13}{14}$, is very close to one whole, which would be $\frac{14}{14}$. Therefore, you can put all five fractions in order from least to greatest as follows: $\frac{6}{17}$, $\frac{2}{5}$, $\frac{3}{4}$, $\frac{7}{8}$, and $\frac{13}{14}$.

**PROBLEM:**

Choose the signs that make the inequality correct.

$$-1\frac{1}{2} \; \bigcirc \; -\frac{7}{8} \; \bigcirc \; -\frac{1}{10}$$

**SOLUTION:**

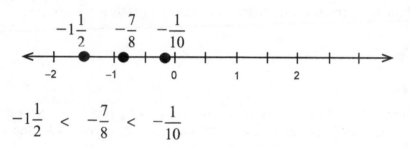

$$-1\frac{1}{2} \; < \; -\frac{7}{8} \; < \; -\frac{1}{10}$$

By placing the numbers on a number line, it is easy to see that $-1\frac{1}{2}$ is the smallest fraction since it is farthest to the left, and $-\frac{1}{10}$ is the largest because it is farthest to the right.

When working with problems that require comparing fractions, be sure to check to see if you can use estimation rather than exact computation. If you can, it will often take less time than performing tedious calculations.

## Conversions

Quantities can be presented in a variety of ways: as a decimal, a percent, or a fraction. Depending on the situation, it may be appropriate to use one form over another. Therefore, it is beneficial to know how to convert among the three forms.

Writing a fraction as a decimal is simple if the denominator of the fraction is a power of 10, such as 10, 100, or 1000. For example, $\frac{2}{10} = 0.2$ (two tenths), $\frac{17}{100} = 0.17$ (seventeen hundredths), and $\frac{45}{1000} = 0.045$ (forty-five thousandths). All you have to do is to make sure that you put the last digit of the numerator so that it ends in the place designated by the denominator. If the denominator is not a power of 10, then divide the numerator by the denominator as we did in the preceding section.

To write a decimal as a fraction, write the numbers of the decimal in the numerator of a fraction without the decimal point. Locate the digit that is farthest to the right in the number and write its place value as the denominator. If the fraction needs to be simplified, then rewrite it in lowest terms. To write 0.55 (fifty-five hundredths) as a fraction, write 55 in the numerator and 100 in the denominator: $\frac{55}{100}$. Next simplify the fraction by identifying the **greatest common factor (GCF)** that the two numbers share. The factors of 55 are $1 \times 55$ and $5 \times 11$, so 1, 5, 11, and 55 are the greatest common factors. The factors of 100 are $1 \times 100$, $2 \times 50$, $4 \times 25$, $5 \times 20$, and $10 \times 10$, so 1, 2, 4, 5, 10, 20, 25, 50, and 100 are the greatest common factors. The GCF of these two numbers is 5. Divide both the numerator and the denominator by 5 to reduce the fraction to simplest terms:

$$\frac{55 \div 5 = 11}{100 \div 5 = 20}$$

You should also be able to convert a percent to a decimal. The percent sign means "per hundred," so we calculate percent by dividing the original number by one hundred. This is easily accomplished by moving the decimal point in the number two places to the left. **If there is no decimal point, it means that the number in front of the percent sign is a whole number.** It is understood that every whole number has a decimal point at the end of the number. So the number 2 is actually **2.** and the number 10 is actually **10.** In the number 19, for example, the decimal point (not written) would be at the end of the number: 19. The value is the same as 19 without the decimal point. After moving the decimal point two places to the left, simply take away the percent sign. The process is shown below:

**Step 1:** Add a decimal if needed 19% =19.%

**Step 2:** Move the decimal two places to the left and drop the percent sign. Now we have 0.19.

On the FTCE General Knowledge Test, you will have a calculator at hand to solve percent word problems. When using the four-function calculator on this test, your answers will be in decimal form, and you will have to convert them to percent by reversing the process used in the preceding example. In this situation you will instead move the decimal two places to the right and add a percent sign.

## PROBLEM

Write 0.02 as a percent.

## SOLUTION

To write 0.02 as a percent, move the decimal place two positions to the right, then add a percent sign: 002.%. Now remove the zeros in the front of the number and the decimal at the end since your answer is a whole number: 2%.

Look at the relationships between some decimals and percents shown below. In each case, the decimal moves two places to the left and the % sign is dropped to change a percent to a decimal. To change a decimal to a percent, the decimal moves two places to the right and the % sign is added.

$$100\% = 1.00 \quad 75\% = 0.75 \quad 50\% = 0.50 \quad 25\% = 0.25 \quad 0.5\% = 0.005$$

## PROBLEM

Find the decimal equivalent of 14%.

(A) 14      (B) .14      (C) .014      (D) $\dfrac{1}{4}$

## SOLUTION

When converting a percent to a decimal, remove the percent sign and divide the number by 100 (which is the same as moving the decimal point two places to the left). 14% as a decimal would be 0.14. Choice (B) is the correct answer.

If you are required to write a percent as a fraction, write the number in front of the percent sign in the numerator of the fraction, then use 100 as the denominator. Remember to simplify the fractions when necessary. So $14\% = \dfrac{14}{100} = \dfrac{7}{50}$.

PROBLEM

How would you write 91% and 8% as fractions in *lowest terms*?

(A)  $\dfrac{91}{100}$  and  $\dfrac{2}{25}$      (B)  $\dfrac{91}{100}$  and  $\dfrac{8}{100}$

(C)  $\dfrac{91}{10}$  and  $\dfrac{2}{25}$      (D)  $\dfrac{.91}{10}$  and  $\dfrac{.08}{100}$

SOLUTION

To write a percent as a fraction, remove the percent sign. Put the number given as the numerator and 100 as the denominator. Simplify if necessary. 91% is equal to $\dfrac{91}{100}$. It is in lowest terms. 8% is equal to $\dfrac{8}{100}$. The greatest common factor of 8 and 100 is 4. Divide the numerator and the denominator by 4 to get $\dfrac{2}{25}$. Choice (A) is the correct answer.

If you need to write a fraction as a percent, follow the steps for writing a fraction as a decimal. Then follow the steps for writing a decimal as a percent.

**Example:** Write $\dfrac{1}{8}$ as a percent.

First, $1 \div 8 = 0.125$, then $0.125 = 12.5\%$.

If you are asked to compare numbers to each other and they are presented in a variety of forms, it is helpful to put them all in the same form—whichever is easiest for you or whichever form makes most sense in the problem. If you have to put the following numbers in order from least to greatest, 0.18, $\dfrac{1}{8}$, 15%, and 10%, you could rewrite $\dfrac{1}{8}$, 15%, and 10% as decimals. Then it would be easy to see how to order them. $\dfrac{1}{8} = 0.125$; 15% = 0.15; and 10% = 0.10. So, the numbers in order are 10%, $\dfrac{1}{8}$, 15%, and 0.18.

It is also helpful to know how to convert between mixed numbers and improper fractions. To explain how to rewrite a mixed number as an improper fraction, let's look at an example.

**Example:** Write $5\frac{3}{8}$ as an improper fraction.

**Step 1:** Multiply the denominator of the fraction by the whole number: $8 \times 5 = 40$.

**Step 2:** Add that answer to the numerator of the fraction: $40 + 3 = 43$.

**Step 3:** Write your answer as your new numerator over your original denominator: $\frac{43}{8}$.

To write an improper fraction as a mixed number, reverse the process.

**Example:** Let's write $\frac{27}{4}$ as a mixed number.

**Step 1:** Without your calculator, divide the denominator into the numerator: $27 \div 4 = 6$ remainder $3$

**Step 2:** Write your answer as the whole number: 6

**Step 3:** Make your remainder as the new numerator and KEEP your old denominator: $6\frac{3}{4}$

Therefore, $\frac{27}{4} = 6\frac{3}{4}$.

Most of the answer choices on the FTCE General Knowledge Test will be in simplest terms, but occasionally you'll see an improper fraction. Be prepared to simplify any answers. It is a good test-taking strategy to look at all of the answer choices before you begin solving the problem. This will help you decide the most efficient way to solve the problem and may save you valuable test-taking time. Since it is most common to write all fractions in lowest terms, always simplify your fractions so that the numerator and the denominator only share a common factor of 1. For example, $\frac{8}{15}$, $\frac{14}{19}$, and $\frac{25}{54}$ are all in simplest terms because the only factor that the numerator and the denominator of each fraction share is 1.

As mentioned earlier, to write a fraction in lowest terms, find the greatest factor that the numerator and the denominator have in common, then divide both the numerator and the denominator by that number. **Equivalent fractions** are two fractions that are equal to each other, but have different denominators; equivalent fractions simplify to the same fraction written in lowest terms. Some examples of equivalent fractions are:

$$\frac{2}{5} = \frac{4}{10} \qquad \frac{1}{4} = \frac{25}{100} \qquad \frac{2}{3} = \frac{6}{9}$$

It is also helpful if you watch for fractions that are equivalent to $\frac{1}{2}$, such as $\frac{2}{4}$, $\frac{5}{10}$, $\frac{25}{50}$, and $\frac{50}{100}$. Anytime the numerator is exactly half of the denominator, the fraction is equal to $\frac{1}{2}$.

**PROBLEM**

Simplify: $\frac{1}{10} + \frac{3}{5}$.

**SOLUTION**

Start by choosing a common denominator. Since 10 is a multiple of 5, we will use 10 as the denominator. Next rename the fraction by finding a fraction that is equivalent to $\frac{3}{5}$, but has 10 in the denominator.

$$\frac{3 \times ? = ?}{5 \times ? = 10}$$

Since $5 \times 2 = 10$, rewrite the problem as follows, then solve:

$$\frac{3 \times 2 = ?}{5 \times 2 = 10} \qquad \frac{3 \times 2 = 6}{5 \times 2 = 10}$$

Now that you have an equivalent fraction to $\frac{3}{5}$ you can solve the problem:

$$\frac{1}{10} + \frac{6}{10} = \frac{7}{10}.$$

**PROBLEM**

Simplify: $\dfrac{11}{12} - \dfrac{3}{8}$

(A) $\dfrac{8}{4}$      (B) $\dfrac{11}{12}$      (C) $\dfrac{13}{24}$      (D) $\dfrac{1}{2}$

**SOLUTION**

To complete this problem, you need to find a common denominator for 12 and 8. The first four multiples of 12 are 12, 24, 36, 48. The first four multiples of 8 are 8, 16, 24, 32. The least common multiple of 12 and 8 is 24, because 24 is the smallest multiple that 12 and 8 share. Now rename the fractions and solve. The correct answer is (C), $\dfrac{13}{24}$.

$$\frac{11}{12} = \frac{22}{24} \text{ and } \frac{3}{8} = \frac{9}{24} \qquad \frac{22}{24} - \frac{9}{24} = \frac{13}{24}$$

## Exponents and Exponential Notation

When a number is multiplied by itself a specific number of times, it is said to be **raised to a power**. This is written as $a^n = b$ where $a$ is the number or **base**, $n$ is the **exponent** or **power** that indicates the number of times the base is to be multiplied by itself, and $b$ is the product of this multiplication. For example, in the expression $3^2$, 3 is the base, and 2 is the exponent. This means that 3 is used as a factor two times ($3 \times 3$); the product is 9.

An exponent can be either positive or negative. A negative exponent implies a fraction such that if $n$ is a negative integer, then $b$ will be a fraction. For example, $3^{-2}$ is equal to $\dfrac{1}{3^2} - \dfrac{1}{(3 \times 3)} = \dfrac{1}{9}$. When you see a negative exponent, move it to the denominator and change the sign of the exponent to positive. For example, $2^{-4} = \dfrac{1}{2^4} - \dfrac{1}{(2 \times 2 \times 2 \times 2)} = \dfrac{1}{16}$.

If a number has an exponent of 1, which we don't write, the number stays the same. So $13^1 = 13$. Any number (except 0) with an exponent of 0 always equals 1, so $11^0 = 1$ and $1{,}234^0 = 1$. When computing the value of an expression in exponential form, it is often a good idea to write the expression out in expanded form to make sure you arrive at the correct answer. If you have $2^5$, a common error is to multiply 2 by 5 and get 10. $2^5$ is the same as $2 \times 2 \times 2 \times 2 \times 2$, which is 32. Writing the expression out in expanded form ensures that you do not make a mistake when simplifying.

### PROBLEM

Which of the statements below is true?

(A)  $2^3 = 3^2$        (B)  $4^0 \times 10^2 > 3^4$

(C)  $5^3 + 5^2 = 5^5$       (D)  $4^2 + 2^4 = 2^6$

### SOLUTION

**Choice (A):** $2^3 = 2 \times 2 \times 2 = 8$ and $3^2 = 3 \times 3$, which is 9.

These two expressions are not equal.

**Choice (B):** First solve the left side of the inequality.

$4^0 = 1$, because anything (except 0) to the 0 power is 1.

$10^2 = 10 \times 10 = 100$. The product of these values, $1 \times 100$, is 100.

Now solve the right side: $3^4 = 3 \times 3 \times 3 \times 3$, which is 81.

This would make the statement read 100 is greater than (>) 81, which is true.

**Choice (C):** $5^3 + 5^2$ is *not* the same as $5^3 \times 5^2$, which would be $5^5$.

The expression $5^3 + 5^2$ is $(5 \times 5 \times 5) + (5 \times 5)$.

This simplifies to $125 + 25$, which equals 150.

The right side of the equality is $5^5$.

This equals $5 \times 5 \times 5 \times 5 \times 5 = 3{,}125$. These are not equal.

**Choice (D):** $4^2 + 2^4$ equals $(4 \times 4) + (2 \times 2 \times 2 \times 2) = 16 + 16 = 32$.

When 32 is written as a power of 2, it is $2^5$ (not $2^6$ which equals 64).

Thus, the correct answer is (B).

If you are asked to multiply or divide exponents on the General Knowledge Test, the best strategy is to solve each individual term, then use order of operations to solve. There are rules, however, that can make this process easier if you take the time to learn them. To use these rules, the bases must be the same.

| Rule | Example |
|---|---|
| $A^b \times A^c = A^{b+c}$ | $3^2 \times 3^4 = 3^{2+4} = 3^6$ |
| $\dfrac{A^b}{A^c} = A^{b-c}$ | $\dfrac{3^6}{3^2} = 3^{6-2} = 3^4$ |
| $(A^2)^4 = A^{2\times4}$ | $(4^2)^3 = 4^{2\times3} = 4^6$ |
| $\dfrac{1}{A^{-b}} = A^b$ | $\dfrac{1}{7^{-2}} = 7^2$ |

## PROBLEM

Which of the statements below is *false*?

(A) $2^6 + 2^3 = 2^9$  (B) $5^3 \times 5^5 = 5^8$

(C) $\dfrac{10^9}{10^3} = 10^6$  (D) $\dfrac{8^5}{8^0} = 8^5$

## SOLUTION

When multiplying exponents whose bases are the same, add the exponents and keep the base the same. When dividing exponents whose bases are the same, subtract the exponents and keep the base the same. If you know these two rules, you can see that answer choices (B), (C), and (D) are true. (A) is false because you do not add the exponents when *adding* exponential expressions. Each expression must be simplified separately, and then combined. That is, $2^6 + 2^3$ would be $64 + 8$, which equals 72. This is not the same as $2^9$, which equals 512. The correct answer is (A) because it is the only false statement.

## PROBLEM

Simplify the expression: $\dfrac{x^3 \times x^9}{x^2}$

(A) $x^6$  (B) $x^8$  (C) $x^{10}$  (D) $x^{14}$

## SOLUTION

To solve this problem, you must know the rules of multiplying and dividing exponents with the same bases. First, simplify the numerator: $x^3 \times x^9 = x^{3+9} = x^{12}$. Now divide your numerator by your denominator: $x^{12} \div x^2 = x^{12-2} = x^{10}$. Choice (C) is correct.

**PROBLEM:**

Simplify $a^3b^3(ab)^2$

**SOLUTION**

According to the order of operations, we first have to take care of the $(ab)^2$, which is equivalent to $a^2b^2$. Now our expression reads $a^3b^3a^2b^2$. Next, since we are multiplying like bases, we add their exponents. This gives us $a^{3+2}b^{3+2}$, which is equal to $a^5b^5$.

## Square Numbers

**Perfect square numbers** are numbers that result from multiplying an integer by itself. The first 10 square numbers are 1, 4, 9, 16, 25, 36, 49, 64, 81, and 100.

There are an infinite number of square numbers; it is helpful to be able to recognize them. The reason they are called square numbers is because if you start with a positive integer, you can imagine that it is the side length of a square. When you multiply that number by itself, the answer you get can be represented by the area of a square. The diagrams below show the first six square numbers.

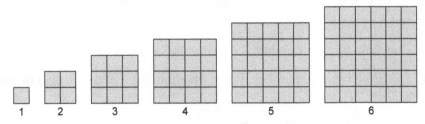

In each of the preceding figures, if you multiply the base times the height, you get a perfect square. For example, the last figure has a base and a height of 6. Multiply 6 times 6 and you have 36, a perfect square number.

## Square Roots

Just as you square a number, you can also find the **square root** of a number. To find the square root of a number, you must find a number that when squared, equals your original number. Each number has two square roots, a positive one and a negative one. Thus, the square root of 81 is 9 since $9 \times 9 = 81$. However, −9 is also a root of 81 since $(-9)(-9) = 81$. On the General Knowledge Test, your four-function calculator will not have a square root symbol, so you will only be asked to solve for the square roots of perfect squares. You may have to estimate the square roots of other numbers. For instance, if you know that $\sqrt{36} = 6$ and you know that $\sqrt{49} = 7$, you should be able to estimate that

$\sqrt{40}$ lies somewhere between 6 and 7. You will rarely be asked to use the negative roots on the test.

## Divisibility Rules and Prime and Composite Numbers

There are times you will want to know what numbers are factors of other numbers. In this case, you are looking for numbers that divide evenly into another number. Familiarity with divisibility rules will help you recognize factors quickly. How can you tell if a number is evenly divisible by another? You can simply try it out on your four-function calculator or learn to recognize the divisibility rules that follow:

- Divisible by 1: All whole numbers are divisible by 1.

- Divisible by 2 (also called even): If a number ends in 0, 2, 4, 6, or 8, it is an even number, so it is divisible by 2.

- Divisible by 3: Add up the digits of the number; if that sum is divisible by 3, then the number is divisible by 3. *Example: 81, 8 + 1 = 9, 9 is divisible by 3, so 81 is divisible by 3.*

- Divisible by 4: If the last two digits of a number are divisible by four, the number is divisible by 4.

- Divisible by 5: A number is divisible by 5 if it ends in 5 or 0.

- Divisible by 6: A number that is divisible by 2 and 3 is also divisible by 6.

- Divisible by 8: If the last three digits of a number are divisible by 8, the number is divisible by eight.

- Divisible by 9: A number is divisible by 9 if the sum of its digits is divisible by 9.

- Divisible by 10: If a number ends in 0, it is divisible by 10.

Every whole number is divisible by 1 and itself. If a number is only divisible by 1 and itself and has no other factors (therefore having only 2 factors), it is a **prime number**. The prime numbers less than 20 are 2, 3, 5, 7, 11, 13, 17, and 19. There are an infinite number of prime numbers. If a number has more than two factors, it is a **composite number**. The number 1 has only one factor; therefore, it is neither prime nor composite.

**PROBLEM**

Identify the following numbers as prime or composite, and list their factors.

(A) 36      (B) 91      (C) 13      (D) 384

**SOLUTION**

**Choice (A):** This number is composite. It is divisible by 2 since it is an even number. The sum of its digits is 3 + 6 = 9. 9 is divisible by both 3 and 9. Since it is divisible by both 2 and 3, it is also divisible by 6. So far we have identified 2, 3, 6, and 9 as factors. By dividing 36 by these numbers, we generate a complete list of 36's factors: 1, 2, 3, 4, 6, 9, 12, 18, and 36. Note: Even though 6 × 6 is equal to 36, we only list 6 one time on our list.

**Choice (B):** 91 passes our divisibility tests. It is divisible by 1, 7, 13, and 91, so it is not a prime number.

**Choice (C):** Thirteen is a prime number. It has two factors, 1 and 13.

**Choice (D):** 384 is a composite number. Use the divisibility rules to find the factors.

- **2:** It is an even number because it ends with a 4; therefore, 2 is a factor.

- **3:** The sum of the digits of 384 is 15. If the sum of the digits is divisible by 3, then 3 is a factor. 15 is divisible by 3, so 384 is divisible by 3.

- **4:** Since the last two digits are divisible by 4 (84 ÷ 4 = 21), 384 is also divisible by 4.

- **5 and 10:** It ends in a 4, so 5 and 10 are not factors.

- **6:** It is divisible by 2 and 3, so 6 is a factor.

- **7 and 8:** Try these in your calculator. 8 is a factor, 7 is not.

- **9:** If the sum of the digits is divisible by 9, then 9 is a factor. Since 15 is not evenly divisible by 9, 9 is not a factor.

The factors of 384 are 1, 2, 3, 4, 6, 8, 12, 16, 24, 32, 48, 64, 96, 128, 192, and 384. Notice that once you pass 8, you need your calculator to try other possible factors. These can also be generated by multiplying together other numbers from the list you have generated with your divisibility rules: 3 × 4 =12, 4 × 6 = 24, and 2 × 8 = 16. With larger numbers, this technique will narrow down which numbers you should check.

## Prime Factorization

Each number has a unique, distinct prime factorization. This is calculated by breaking down a number into only prime factors. A prime number such as 13 will have a simple prime factorization: $13 = 1 \times 13$. To express a composite number with prime factorization, you can break it down into its prime factors with a factor tree:

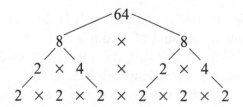

The prime factorization of 64 is $2 \times 2 \times 2 \times 2 \times 2 \times 2 = 2^6$. Another example is 50, which divides into $2 \times 25$, then $2 \times 5 \times 5$. Since both 2 and 5 are prime, the prime factorization of $50 = 2 \times 5^2$.

### PROBLEM

Which is the correct prime factorization of 150?

(A) $(10)(5)95)$　　　　(B) $(2)(3)(5^2)$

(C) $(2^2)(5)(3)$　　　　(D) $(2)(5)(5)(5)(5)$

### SOLUTION

The prime factorization of a number must only contain prime numbers. The order of the factors is not important. Answer choice (A) cannot be correct because 10 is not a prime number. An efficient way to find the prime factors of a number is to start with any two factors of the number and then break those factors down into primes (this may remind you of "factor trees"). $150 = 15 \times 10$. Then you can break 15 into $5 \times 3$, and you can break 10 into $2 \times 5$. Put all the factors together, and you see there are two factors of 5, one factor of 3, and one factor of 2. These factors are shown in answer choice (B), so this is the correct answer.

## Skill 1.2. Solve real-world problems involving the four operations with rational numbers.

When you are trying to solve a problem, you must read the details in the problem carefully to figure out what information you need and what information you can ignore. It is recommended that you read word problems at least twice before attempting to solve them. Do not assume that you must use every number that is given in a problem. Sometimes there is information included that is used to help clarify the situation, but the numbers are not needed to answer the question. This extra information is intended to distract you, so watch for it. Real-world problems do not come with the directions needed to solve them. You have to figure out what to do based on the context of the problem, and drawing a model can be very helpful when you are planning your solution. For example, the words "all together" and "the total" indicate that you will use addition. The words "how much more" or "how much taller" indicate subtraction. The chart that follows shows some vocabulary you may see that indicates each of the four operations.

| Addition | Subtraction | Multiplication | Division |
|----------|-------------|----------------|----------|
| Add | Subtract | Multiply | Divide |
| And | Minus | Times | Quotient |
| Plus | Difference | Product | |
| More than | Less than | | |
| Increased by | Decreased by | | |
| Sum | Take away | | |
| Total | Fewer | | |

You will be able to use a four-function calculator on this exam, which will help you with your computations, but BEWARE! You can only perform one mathematic function at a time. So if you have $5 \times 4 \div 2$, you have to first multiply 5 by 4 and record the answer, 20, then enter $20 \div 2$.

The other important point to remember is that you can not enter a negative sign as your first figure. So if you have $-2 + 3$, the negative sign will not record in the calculator. For this reason, it is better to do simple calculations by hand.

Mrs. Stanton is writing her will. She wishes to leave each of her five children an equal amount of her $800,000 estate. Which problem below will result in each child receiving the correct amount?

(A) $800,000 \div 5$  (B) $5 \times 800,000$

(C) $5 \div 800,000$  (D) $800,000 - 5$

### SOLUTION

To break up an amount into even groups, you must use division. To find how much money each child will receive, divide the total amount of money, $800,000 by the number of children, 5. $800,000 \div 5$ is the correct expression. This is answer choice (A).

Darnell put $2\frac{1}{4}$ cups of flour in a bowl along with $\frac{1}{2}$ cup of butter and $\frac{2}{3}$ cup of sugar. How many cups of ingredients does Darnell have?

(A) $2\frac{4}{9}$  (B) $3\frac{5}{6}$  (C) $3\frac{5}{12}$  (D) $2\frac{7}{24}$

### SOLUTION

To add these three fractions, find the common denominator for 2, 3, and 4. The least common multiple of 2, 3, and 4 is 12, so 12 is a common denominator you can use.

**Step 1:** Find the common denominator and rename the fractions:

$$2\frac{1}{4} = 2\frac{3}{12} \qquad \frac{1}{2} = \frac{6}{12} \qquad \frac{2}{3} = \frac{8}{12}$$

**Step 2:** Write the whole number 2, then add the numerators. Keep 12 as the denominator:

$$2\frac{3}{12} + \frac{6}{12} + \frac{8}{12} = 2\frac{17}{12}$$

**Step 3:** Rewrite $\frac{17}{12}$ as a mixed number. It is $1\frac{5}{12}$.

**Step 4:** Rewrite the problem $2 + 1\frac{5}{12} = 3\frac{5}{12}$. The correct answer is (C).

## Real-World Problems with Percent

There are several different types of problems you may encounter involving percent. If you want to find the percent of a number, the easiest way is to rewrite the percent as its decimal equivalent and multiply. If you need to know what percent one number is of another as in the problem, you should set up a "part over whole" proportion. You write the proportion with the numerator as the part you are given and the denominator as the whole, the largest number. For example, if your rent is $1,000 and you make $1,850 a month, the $1,000 is the part you are looking for and the $1,850 is your whole income. The percent of your income that you spend on rent is $\frac{1,000}{1,850} = .55555$. Move the decimal point two places right and add the percent sign and you have 55.55%.

### PROBLEM

What percent of 80 is 5?

(A) 16%     (B) 6.25%     (C) .0625%     (D) 40%

### SOLUTION

Using the part over the whole technique, you can divide 5 by 80. $5 \div 80 = 0.0625 = 6.25\%$. Notice that choice (C) is a distractor. This is the decimal representation of the solution before you convert it to percent. Choice (A) is also a distractor since this would be a possible solution if you incorrectly reversed your operation and entered the number 80 into the calculator before the 5. The correct answer is choice (B).

### PROBLEM

15% of what number is 30?

(A) 4.5     (B) 20     (C) 15     (D) 200

### SOLUTION

For this problem, it is better to use a proportion. If 30 is 15% of some number, $n$, then $\frac{15}{100} = \frac{30}{n}$. Once this problem is set up, you can use cross product ($15n = 30 \times 100$) to solve algebraically or merely notice that if 30 is twice 15, then $n$ must be $100 \times 2 = 200$, as shown:

$$\frac{15}{100} = \frac{30}{n} \qquad \frac{15 \times 2 = 30}{100 \times 2 = n} \qquad n = 200$$

### PROBLEM

Tom bought a piece of land selling for $65,000. If he had to pay 12% of the price as a down payment, how much was his down payment?

(A) $5,416    (B) $7,800    (C) $6,500    (D) $5,000

### SOLUTION

The most efficient way to find 12% of $65,000 is to multiply the decimal equivalent of 12% by 65,000. $0.12 \times 65,000 = 7,800$. Therefore, $7,800 is the down payment Tom must pay. Choice (B) is the correct answer.

### PROBLEM

A diamond necklace sells for $7,300. If you purchase it on a one-day sale, the price is reduced by 18%. What is the sale price of the necklace?

(A) $1,314    (B) $405    (C) $2,908    (D) $5,986

### SOLUTION

The price of the necklace is being reduced 18%. That means the price you pay for the necklace will be 100% − 18%, which is 82% of the original price. To find the sale price of the necklace, you can find 82% of $7,300 or find 18% of $7,300 and subtract it from $7,300. The first way is more efficient because it requires only one step. To find 82% of $7,300, rewrite 82% as a decimal (0.82) and multiply it by 7,300. $0.82 \times 7300 = 5,986$. The correct answer is (D). *Note: Answer choice (A) is the amount of discount, not the sale price.*

## Skill 1.3. Evaluate expressions involving order of operations.

Mathematics follows rules and procedures. If you encounter a problem with different operations, or one that also has parentheses and exponents in it, you must know in what order to simplify the problem. Without being given any instruction on this topic, you might think that you would simplify from left to right; however, this is not always correct. To make sure that everyone who completes the same problem gets the same answer, there is an order of operations to follow. The order of operations is as follows:

(1) Simplify everything inside grouping symbols, starting from the center symbols and working outward.

(2) Simplify exponents.

(3) Do multiplication and division from left to right. This means that if division appears first, you divide before you multiply.

(4) Do addition and subtraction from left to right.

People often use the mnemonic **PEMDAS** — "Please Excuse My Dear Aunt Sally" — to remember the order of operations. Let's start by looking at problems that contain only the four operations of addition, subtraction, multiplication, and division. By following the rules of the order of operations, do multiplication and division from left to right before addition and subtraction, always working from left to right. Therefore, in the following problem: $4 + 7 \times 2$, multiply 7 by 2 first, then add that answer to 4. The answer is 18. If you have the problem $6 \div 3 + 3 \times 2$, you would first complete the division ($6 \div 3 = 2$) and then the multiplication ($3 \times 2$) = 6. Your new problem would be $2 + 6 = 8$. If you merely worked from left to right, your solution would be 10, which would be incorrect.

Let's look at this problem: $12 \div 3 \times 5$.

This problem has both multiplication and division. Remember, neither multiplication nor division comes *before* the other; they are to be done as they occur from left to right. In this problem, divide 12 by 3 and then multiply that answer by 5. You get $4 \times 5$, which is 20.

If, in addition to any of the four operations, a problem has parentheses or exponents, you must solve what is inside the parentheses before addressing the exponents.

Let's look at a problem that has parentheses, exponents, and several operations.

$6 \times (8 + 2) \div 5 - 3^2$.

Follow the order of operations to complete the problem in the following order:

| | |
|---|---|
| $6 \times (8 + 2) \div 5 - 3^2$ | The original problem |
| $6 \times 10 \div 5 - 3^2$ | Simplify inside parentheses. |
| $6 \times 10 \div 5 - 9$ | Simplify exponents. |
| $60 \div 5 - 9$ | Do multiplication and division from left to right. |
| $12 - 9$ | Do multiplication and division from left to right. |
| $3$ | Do addition and subtraction from left to right. |

### PROBLEM

Simplify by following the order of operations: $18 - 12 \div (3 - 1)^2 \times 5 + 8$.

    (A) 15.5      (B) 8.3      (C) 4      (D) 11

### SOLUTION

Following the order of operations, the problem is simplified as follows:

| | |
|---|---|
| $18 - 12 \div (3 - 1)^2 \times 5 + 8$ | The original problem |
| $18 - 12 \div (2)^2 \times 5 + 8$ | Simplify inside parentheses. |
| $18 - 12 \div 4 \times 5 + 8$ | Simplify exponents. |
| $18 - 3 \times 5 + 8$ | Do multiplication and division from left to right. |
| $18 - 15 + 8$ | Do multiplication and division from left to right. |
| $3 + 8$ | Do addition and subtraction from left to right. |
| $11$ | Do addition and subtraction from left to right. |

The correct answer is choice (D).

## Parentheses, Brackets, and Braces

When solving order of operations problems on the General Knowledge Test, it is common to have problems with multiple sets of embedded parentheses ( ), brackets [ ], and braces { }. When these appear in a problem, always work from the inside out as seen in the following example:

| | |
|---|---|
| $7 + 2\{[3 + (2x - 2) + x] - 3\}$ | The problem |
| $7 + 2\{[3 + 2x - 2 + x] - 3\}$ | Look at the parentheses in the middle. You can't add a number ($-2$) to a variable with a coefficient ($2x$), so remove the parentheses. |
| $7 + 2\{[3 - 2 + 2x + x] - 3\}$ | Look inside of the brackets and regroup like terms. |
| $7 + 2\{[1 + 3x] - 3\}$ | Simplify the terms in the bracket. |
| $7 + 2\{1 + 3x - 3\}$ | Remove the brackets. |
| $7 + 2\{1 - 3 + 3x\}$ | Regroup like terms in the braces. |
| $7 + 2\{3x - 2\}$ | Simplify the terms in the braces. |
| $7 + 6x - 4$ | When a number is directly outside of the parentheses, you must multiply every term inside the parentheses by that term so multiply both $3x$ and $-2$ by $+2$. |
| $7 - 4 + 6x$ | Regroup like terms. |
| $3 + 6x$ | Simplify. |

## Absolute Value

The absolute value of a number is its distance from 0 on the number line and is written as $|a|$. The absolute value of a number is always positive because distance is always positive. For example, $|+4| = 4$, and $|-4| = 4$ because both numbers are four units from 0 on the number line. When simplifying expressions involving absolute value, pay attention to positive and negative signs and be sure to follow the correct order of operations. For example, the expression $-3|-5| - 1 = -3 \times 5 - 1 = -15 - 1 = -16$.

### PROBLEM

Simplify the following: $|3 - 12| + 6 \div 2 \times 3^2 - 5$

(A) 13      (B) 62.5      (C) 8.5      (D) 31

### SOLUTION

In addition to following the order of operations, for this problem you have to know how to simplify expressions that have absolute value bars. The expression in the bars, $|3 - 12|$, simplifies to $|-9|$. Then take the absolute value of $-9$ to get 9. The steps below show how to get the simplified answer to this expression.

| | |
|---|---|
| $|3 - 12| + 6 \div 2 \times 3^2 - 5$ | The original problem |
| $|-9| + 6 \div 2 \times 3^2 - 5$ | Solve inside the absolute-value bars. |
| $9 + 6 \div 2 \times 3^2 - 5$ | Simplify absolute value expression. |
| $9 + 6 \div 2 \times 9 - 5$ | Simplify exponents. |
| $9 + 3 \times 9 - 5$ | Do multiplication and division from left to right. |
| $9 + 27 - 5$ | Do multiplication and division from left to right. |
| $36 - 5$ | Do addition and subtraction from left to right. |
| $31$ | Do addition and subtraction from left to right. |

The correct answer is (D).

Now take a look at the following problem: $|3 - x| = 12$. When you encounter this type of problem on the test, it is important that you recognize that this equation has two solutions, the one where $|3 - x| = -12$ and the one where $|3 - x| = +12$, as shown:

$$|3 - x| = +12$$

$$
\begin{array}{ll}
3 - x = +12 & 3 - x = -12 \\
\underline{-3 \qquad -3} & \underline{-3 \qquad -3} \\
-x = \quad 9 & -x = -15 \\
\underline{\div -1 \quad \div -1} & \underline{\div -1 \quad \div -1} \\
x = \quad -9 & x = \quad 15
\end{array}
$$

As you can see, the solutions to $|3 - x| = 12$ are $-9$ and $+15$.

## PROBLEM

$$\frac{3}{4}(x - 2) = |5^2 - 9 \times 8| - 5$$

## SOLUTION

You may be tempted to distribute $\frac{3}{4}$ though $(x - 2)$, but that will only create more work. Notice that in the solution below, we wait until we have simplified the equation as much as possible, then eliminate the $\frac{3}{4}$ by multiplying both sides by its inverse, $\frac{4}{3}$.

| | |
|---|---|
| $\frac{3}{4}(x - 2) = |5^2 - 9 \times 8| - 5$ | The original problem |
| $\frac{3}{4}(x - 2) = |25 - 9 \times 8| - 5$ | Solve the exponent. |
| $\frac{3}{4}(x - 2) = |25 - 72| - 5$ | Multiply $-9$ times $+8$. |
| $\frac{3}{4}(x - 2) = |-47| - 5$ | Subtract 72 from 25. |
| $\frac{3}{4}(x - 2) = 47 - 5$ | Bring the $-47$ out of the absolute value bars. |
| $\frac{3}{4}(x - 2) = 42$ | Subtract 5 from 47. |
| $\left(\frac{4}{3}\right)\left(\frac{3}{4}\right)(x - 2) = \left(\frac{4}{3}\right)42$ | Multiply both sides by the inverse of $\left(\frac{3}{4}\right)$. |
| $x - 2 = 56$ | Cancel out $\left(\frac{4}{3}\right)$ and $\left(\frac{3}{4}\right)$, then multiply $\left(\frac{4}{3}\right)$ by 42. |
| $x - 2 + 2 = 56 + 2$ | Add 2 to both sides. |
| $x = 58$ | The solution |

## Competency 2: Knowledge of Geometry and Measurement

■ **Skill 2.1. Identify and classify simple two- and three-dimensional figures according to their mathematical properties.**

### Intersecting Lines and Angles

An **angle** is a collection of points that is the union of two rays having the same endpoint. An angle such as the one illustrated below can be referred to in any of the following ways:

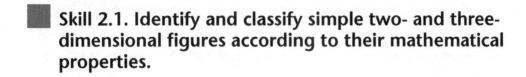

A) by a capital letter which names its **vertex** (common endpoint), i.e., $\angle A$;

B) by a lowercase letter or number placed inside the angle, i.e., $\angle x$;

C) by three capital letters, where the middle letter is the vertex and the other two letters are not on the same ray, i.e., $\angle CAB$ or $\angle BAC$, both of which represent the angle illustrated in the figure.

### Types of Angles

(A) **Vertical angles** are formed when two lines intersect. These angles are equal.

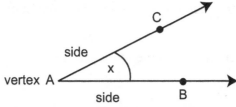

(B) **Adjacent angles** are two angles with a common vertex and a common side, but no common interior points. In the following figure, $\angle DAC$ and $\angle BAC$ are adjacent angles. $\angle DAB$ and $\angle BAC$ are not.

(C) A **right angle** is an angle whose measure is 90°.

(D) An **acute angle** is an angle whose measure is larger than 0° but less than 90°.

(E) An **obtuse angle** is an angle whose measure is larger than 90° but less than 180°.

(F) A **straight angle** is an angle whose measure is 180°. Such an angle is, in fact, a straight line.

(G) A **reflex angle** is an angle whose measure is greater than 180° but less than 360°.

(H) **Complementary angles** are two angles, the sum of the measures of which equals 90°.

(I) **Supplementary angles** are two angles, the sum of the measures of which equals 180°.

(J) **Congruent angles** are angles of equal measure.

PROBLEM

In the diagram below, ∠2 is equal to 128°. What is the measure of ∠3?

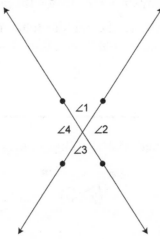

(A) 52 degrees

(B) 48 degrees

(C) It cannot be determined from the diagram.

(D) 128 degrees

## SOLUTION

Two intersecting lines create two pairs of **vertical angles**. Vertical angles are congruent (they have the same measure). The angles that are not congruent are supplementary (they add up to 180 degrees). Therefore, if you know the measure of one of the four angles, you can find the other three. In this problem, you are told that $\angle 2$ is 128 degrees and asked to find $\angle 3$. You can see that $\angle 3$ is supplementary to $\angle 2$. Therefore, 180 degrees − 128 degrees will give you the measure of $\angle 3$, which is 52 degrees.

## PROBLEM

Find the measure of $\angle B$ in right triangle $ABC$.

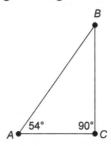

(A) It cannot be determined from the diagram.

(B) 36°

(C) 90°

(D) 44°

## SOLUTION

In a right triangle, the two angles that are not the right angle are complementary (they add up to 90 degrees). The sum of the three angles in any triangle is 180 degrees. Therefore, if one of the angles is 90 degrees, then the other two must also add up to 90 degrees (to have a total of 180 degrees in all three angles).

Solve the equation: $90 - 54 = x$ to find the measure of $\angle B$. $\angle B = 36°$. Choice (B) is correct.

## Two-Dimensional Shapes

### Polygons

Working with two-dimensional geometric shapes involves measures of one-dimension (length, width, height, perimeter, circumference, radius, and diameter) and two-dimension (area) measurements. Be prepared to recognize and name two-dimensional shapes.

| Number of sides in polygon | Name of polygon |
| --- | --- |
| 3 | Triangle |
| 4 | Quadrilateral |
| 5 | Pentagon |
| 6 | Hexagon |
| 7 | Septagon |
| 8 | Octagon |
| 9 | Nonagon |
| 10 | Decagon |

### Triangles

A closed three-sided geometric figure is called a **triangle**. The points of the intersection of the sides of a triangle are called the **vertices** of the triangle. The **perimeter** of a triangle is the sum of the measures of the sides of the triangle. A side of a triangle is a line segment whose endpoints are the vertices of two angles of the triangle. An interior angle of a triangle is an angle formed by two sides and includes the third side within its collection of points.

The first way to categorize a triangle is by the length of its sides. An **equilateral** triangle is a triangle having three equal sides, $AB = AC = BC$ and three equal angles, $\angle A$, $\angle B$, and $\angle C$.

A triangle having at least two equal sides is called an **isosceles** triangle. The third side is called the **base** of the triangle. A triangle with no equal sides is called a **scalene** triangle.

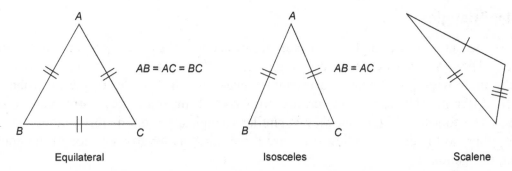

Equilateral                    Isosceles                    Scalene

The second way to categorize a triangle is by the size of its angles. A triangle with one obtuse angle (greater than 90°) is called an **obtuse triangle**. A triangle can only have one obtuse angle because the total interior measurements of a triangle have to equal exactly 180 degrees. An **acute triangle** is a triangle with three acute angles, which means they all measure less than 90°. A triangle with a right angle is called a **right triangle**. The side opposite the right angle in a right triangle is called the **hypotenuse** of the right triangle. The other two sides are called arms or legs of the right triangle.

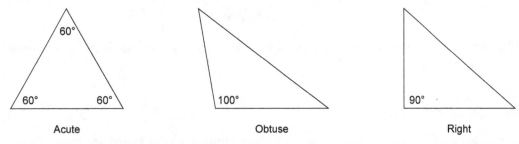

Acute                    Obtuse                    Right

When naming a triangle, you should choose one name from each list above. For example, if a triangle has sides of different lengths and an angle greater than 90 degrees, it is an obtuse scalene triangle. If the triangle has two sides the same length and one 90-degree angle, it is a right isosceles triangle.

## Area of Triangles

The area of a triangle is given by the formula $A = \frac{1}{2}bh$, where $b$ is the length of a base, which can be any side of the triangle, and $h$ is the corresponding height of the triangle, which is the perpendicular line segment from the vertex opposite the base to the base itself.

$$A = \frac{1}{2}bh$$
$$A = \frac{1}{2}(12)(5)$$
$$A = 30$$

## Similar Triangles

The measures of the angles of a pair of similar triangles are equal in a one-to-one fashion. Therefore, a triangle whose angles are 30°, 60°, and 90° is similar to every other triangle with those angle measurements, even though the sides of the two triangles may be different. The sides, however, are proportional, meaning they correspond to one another. The following figure shows two similar triangles, but one is three times the size of the other, so the corresponding sides are three times as long (even though the angles remain the same).

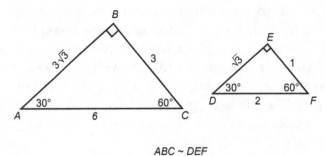

ABC ~ DEF

The sign for similar is ~ and the corresponding angles are listed in the same order: $\angle A = \angle D$, $\angle B = \angle E$, and $\angle C = \angle F$.

## Special Quadrilaterals

A quadrilateral is a polygon made up of four straight lines. There are many "special" quadrilaterals. Knowing their specific properties helps define them accurately, and will help you correctly identify them on the FTCE General Knowledge Test.

| Special Quadrilateral | Properties |
|---|---|
| Trapezoid | • Exactly one pair of parallel sides |
| Parallelogram | • Two pairs of parallel sides<br>• Opposite sides congruent |
| Rhombus | • All four sides congruent |
| Rectangle | • Two pairs of parallel sides<br>• Opposite sides congruent<br>• Four right angles |
| Square | • Two pairs of parallel sides<br>• All four sides congruent<br>• Four right angles |

## Area of Quadrilaterals

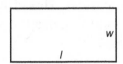  **Rectangle**  $A = lw$

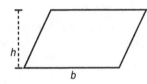  **Parallelogram**  $A = bh$

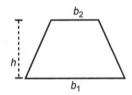  **Trapezoid**  $A = \dfrac{1}{2}h(b_1 + b_2)$

**PROBLEM**

Find the area of the trapezoid in the diagram in square units.

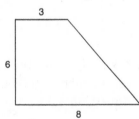

(A)  66          (B)  33          (C)  48          (D)  57

**SOLUTION**

Use the formula for the area of a trapezoid:

$$A = \frac{1}{2}h(b_1 + b_2)$$

The height of this trapezoid is 6. The two bases are 3 and 8. Substitute the numbers into the formula to find the area of the trapezoid.

$$A = \frac{1}{2}(6)(3 + 8)$$
$$A = (3)(11)$$
$$A = 33$$

The area is 33 square units. The correct answer is (B).

**Note:** Notice that the trapezoid only has one pair of parallel sides. This distinction separates it from the parallelograms, which include the following shapes: square, rectangle, and rhombus.

### PROBLEM:

Five tables were put together for a party. Two were 5 ft. 4 in. long and three were 2 ft. 4 in. long. How long was the total length of all the tables once they were put together?

(A)  7 ft. 8 in.

(B)  15 ft.

(C)  15 ft. 4 in.

(D)  17 ft. 8 in.

### SOLUTION:

Calculate the length of the tables by multiplying 5 ft. 4 in. by 2 and 2 ft. 4 in. by 3:

   2(5 ft. + 4 in.) + 3(2ft. + 4 in.) =

   10 ft. + 8 in. + 6 ft. + 12 in. =

   16 ft. + 20 in. =

   16 ft. + 12 in. + 8 in. =

   17 ft. 8 in.

The correct answer is (D). Notice how we broke apart the 20 inches into 12 + 8. This makes it easier to convert the inches to feet. You can also divide the 20 inches by 12 (inches per foot) if a question asked you to leave your answer in fraction form, which would make your solution $17\frac{8}{12}$ feet (simplified to $17\frac{2}{3}$ feet).

## Circles

A circle is a special two-dimensional geometric figure whose circumference is found by multiplying its diameter by the irrational number $\pi$. A circle's diameter is twice its radius. The area of a circle is found by the formula $A = \pi r^2$, and the circumference can be found by the formula $C = 2\pi r$ or $C = \pi d$. The diagram that follows shows the parts of a circle. The circumference of a circle is the distance around the circle. The radius is a segment from the center of a circle to a point on its circumference. The diameter is a segment from one point on the circumference to another point on the circumference passing through the center of the circle.

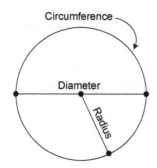

## PROBLEM

How many millimeters larger is the circumference of Circle *A* than Circle *B*?

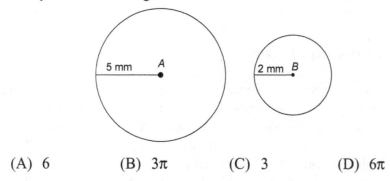

(A) 6          (B) 3π          (C) 3          (D) 6π

## SOLUTION

The formula for the circumference of a circle is $C = 2\pi r$. The question asks you to compare the circumferences of Circles *A* and *B*. Find the circumference of each circle.

| **Circle *A*** | **Circle *B*** |
|---|---|
| $C = 2\pi r$ | $C = 2\pi r$ |
| $C = 2\pi 5$ | $C = 2\pi 2$ |
| $C = 10\pi$ | $C = 4\pi$ |

Circle *A*'s circumference is $10\pi - 4\pi = 6\pi$ mm larger than Circle *B*'s circumference. The correct answer is (D). On the FTCE test occasionally the answer will contain the π symbol. Other times you will be asked to use 3.14 in place of π. In this case, you would multiply 6 times 3.14 to get 18.84 squared units. Be sure to look carefully at your answer choices. If you chose (A) for the preceding problem, you misused the π symbol in your work.

## Ellipse

An **ellipse** looks much like a squashed circle, but it is actually a cross section of a particular cone. On the FTCE, you will not have to use any formulas relating to the circumference or area of an ellipse, but you may have to identify its shape.

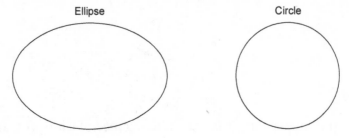

Ellipse        Circle

## Three-Dimensional Figures

There are many different three-dimensional geometric shapes: prisms, pyramids, cylinders, cones, and spheres. A prism is a solid whose opposite lateral faces are congruent. A pyramid has a polygon as its base and triangular shaped lateral faces. The lateral faces meet at a point at the top of the figure called the apex. A "pyramid" with a circular base is called a cone. A cylinder is a solid whose bases are congruent circles. Its lateral face is in the shape of a rectangle that is rolled up (think of a can of soup). A sphere is shaped like a ball.

## Prism

A solid with lateral faces and bases that are congruent polygons is called a **prism**. If the congruent polygons and lateral faces are all rectangles, it is called a **rectangular solid**.

The surface area of a prism is the sum of the areas of all the faces. The area of each face is referred to as a lateral area.

The volume of a prism equals the area of the base ($B$) times the height ($h$).

*Note:* The area of the base means that you have already multiplied two dimensions together before multiplying by the height! You are probably more familiar with looking at the volume of a rectangular solid as being equal to the product of its length, width, and height. Unfortunately, the formula is not written that way on your math reference guide.

Look at both of the following figures and compare the formulas assuming that the height is 4, the length is 6, and the width is 5:

$$V = l \times w \times h$$
$$V = (6)(5)(4)$$
$$V = 120$$

$$V = lwh$$

$$V = B \times h$$
$$V = (6 \times 5)(4)$$
$$V = 120$$

$$B = l \times w$$

On your test, you may be asked to identify various three-dimensional figures. To do this you must know some basic terminology. The flat surfaces of three-dimensional figures are called faces. The line segment formed where two faces meet is called an edge, and the points where multiple faces meet are called vertices. Look at the rectangular prism in the preceding figure. It has 6 rectangular faces, 8 edges, and 8 vertices. Prisms always have parallelograms for their lateral faces, and their bases (ends) are congruent. The bases of the prism tell you its name. For instance, if a prism has two pentagons as bases and five rectangles for its lateral faces, it is called a pentagonal prism.

## Pyramid

Pyramids always have triangles for their lateral faces. They are also named by their bases. The famous pyramids in Egypt have squares for their bases and each has four triangles for faces. They are square pyramids. If a pyramid has a triangle for its base and three triangles for its lateral faces, we call it a triangular pyramid.

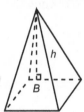

The figure formed when the vertices of a plane polygon (called the base) are joined by line segments to a point not in the same plane is called a **pyramid**.

The surface area of a pyramid equals the sum of areas of all faces.

The volume of a pyramid or cone equals $\frac{1}{3}$ times the *area of the base* ($B$) times the height ($h$).

$$V = \frac{1}{3} Bh$$

## Vertices of Pyramids and Prisms

A vertex is the point where two lines meet. You may be asked to compare different shapes based on their vertices. To calculate the number of vertices on a prism, count the number of vertices on one of the bases, then multiply by two since a prism has two bases. A rectangular prism has $4 \times 2 = 8$ vertices. To calculate the number of vertices on a pyramid, count the number of vertices on the base and add one. For instance, a rectangular pyramid has $4 + 1 = 5$ vertices.

## Cone

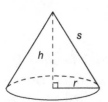

A "pyramid" with a circular base is called a **cone**. The distance from any point on the circular base to the point of the cone is called the slant height.

The surface area of a cone is given by $A = \pi r s + \pi r^2$

The volume of a cone is given by $V = \dfrac{1}{3}\pi r^2 h$

## Cylinder

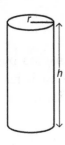

A solid with bases that are congruent circles is called a **cylinder**.

The surface area of a cylinder equals the sum of the areas of the bases and the rectangular "wrap."

$A = 2(\pi r^2) + 2(\pi r)h$

The volume of a cylinder equals the Area of the Base ($B$) times the height ($h$).

$V = Bh$

**PROBLEM**

A particular three-dimensional figure has two congruent triangular-shaped faces and three rectangular-shaped faces. What is the best name for this figure?

(A) Triangular pyramid    (B) Rectangular pyramid

(C) Triangular prism    (D) Rectangular prism

## SOLUTION

To solve this problem correctly, you must know the difference between a pyramid and a prism. A pyramid is named by the shape of its base. No matter what the shape of the base of a pyramid, its lateral faces will always be triangular. A prism is named by the shape of its base, and it has two congruent bases. With the given information, you know that the shape described is a triangular prism, answer choice (C).

The net (two-dimensional representation of the figure if its faces were laid open) of a triangular prism is shown below. Note that three of the faces are rectangular prisms (specifically squares) and the two bases are triangles.

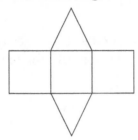

## PROBLEM

What is the best name for a three-dimensional figure with 6 vertices, 1 pentagonal base, and 5 triangular faces?

(A)  Pentagonal prism      (B)  Pentagonal pyramid

(C)  Triangular prism      (D)  Triangular pyramid

## SOLUTION

A three-dimensional figure with triangular lateral faces will be a pyramid. The shape of the base tells you the name of the pyramid. The figure described above is a pentagonal pyramid. Answer choice (B) is the correct answer.

## Spheres

A **sphere** is a three-dimensional object. Common objects like globes and balls have a spherical shape. The FTCE-GKT Math Reference Guide provides formulas for calculating the volume and surface area of a sphere. The volume is the capacity the sphere can hold. It is always a cubed measurement since volume is a three-dimensional measurement. Surface area is the area of the exterior surface of the sphere. Imagine that your sphere is an orange. The surface area would be the area of the orange's skin. This is always a two-dimensional measurement. The formulas on the math reference guide are as follows:

| **Volume** | **Surface Area** |
|---|---|
| $V = \dfrac{4}{3}\pi r^3$ | $S.A. = 4\pi r^2$ |

**PROBLEM**

Calculate the volume of a sphere with a radius of 4 cm. Use 3.14 for $\pi$ and round your answer.

    (A) 67 cm²      (B) 268 cm³      (C) 50 cm³      (D) 201 cm²

**SOLUTION**

You can eliminate choices (A) and (D), because volume is a three-dimensional measurement. Now rewrite the formula for the volume of a sphere in a simpler format:

$$V = \frac{4}{3}\pi r^3 \qquad V = \frac{4\pi r^3}{3}$$

| | |
|---|---|
| First substitute 3.14 for $\pi$ and 4 for $r$. | $\dfrac{4(3.14)(4\text{ cm})^3}{3}$ |
| Solve for your exponent. | $\dfrac{4(3.14)64\text{ cm}^3}{3}$ |
| Solve for the numerator | $\dfrac{803.84\text{ cm}^3}{3}$ |
| Divide by 3 | 267.95 cm³ |
| Round | 268 cm³ |

The correct answer is choice (B). If you chose choice (C), you forgot that $4^3 = 4 \times 4 \times 4$, not $4 \times 3$.

 **Skill 2.2. Solve problems involving ratio and proportion (e.g., scaled drawings, models, real-world scenarios).**

**Scale Drawings**

A scale drawing is a drawing of an object that is proportional in size to the actual object. Scale drawings are based on a certain conversion scale. If you know this scale, you can determine the measurements of the actual objects. For example, the scale drawing of a volleyball court shown below is drawn using the scale 1 centimeter equals 2 meters.

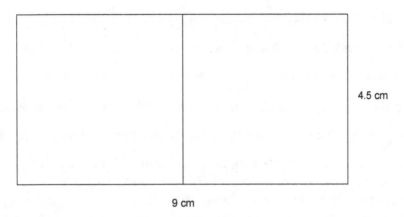

Calculate the area of this volleyball court in square meters. In the scale drawing, length is equal to 9 centimeters and width is equal to 4.5 centimeters. The scale is 1 centimeter equals 2 meters. Use this data to set up a proportion for each side of the court:

$$\frac{1 \text{ cm}}{2 \text{ m}} = \frac{9 \text{ cm}}{?} \qquad \frac{1 \text{ cm}}{2 \text{ m}} = \frac{4.5 \text{ cm}}{?}$$

So, the length of the court is 18 meters, and the width is 9 meters. To find the area, multiply length times width: $18 \times 9 = 162$. The volleyball court is 162 square meters.

Scale is often used for maps and models of real-life objects. For example, an architect wanted to draw a lighthouse that was 144.5 feet tall. She was using the scale of 1 inch = 34 feet. How many inches high would the lighthouse be in the drawing? You could set up a proportion:

$$\frac{1}{34} = \frac{x}{144.5}$$

Notice that the numerators represent the heights of the drawings in inches and the denominators represent the heights of the real buildings in feet. Solving the proportion gives $x = 4.25$. The height of the lighthouse on the drawing would be 4.25 inches.

## Ratios

A **ratio** is a comparison of two quantities. Ratios can be written in three different ways:

- with the word "to": 4 to 5

- with a colon: 4:5

- as a fraction: $\frac{4}{5}$

Ratios are used frequently in daily life, and order is very important in a ratio. For instance, a 1 to 2 ratio would mean that the item that was listed second was twice the magnitude of the item listed first. Ratios can also be used to calculate a percent. A teacher might say, "Eight of the twenty-five students are sick." This would be represented by the ratio $\frac{8}{25}$, which would equal 32%. A bakery owner could say, "We sold 56 of the 200 croissants." This could be written as $\frac{56}{200}$, which would represent 28%.

When two ratios are equal to each other, that is called a **proportion**. An example of a proportion is $\frac{12}{36} = \frac{9}{27}$. These two fractions are of equal proportion and can be simplified to see that they are equal. A fraction is in lowest terms if the only factor the numerator and the denominator have in common is 1. If both ratios simplify to the same fraction, then the ratios are equivalent and it is a proportion. Oftentimes, we use the principle of a proportion to solve for an unknown quantity.

Here's an example: There are 150 calories in an 8-ounce serving of whole milk. How many calories are in a 12-ounce serving? You can set up the following proportion to answer the question:

$$\frac{8}{150} = \frac{12}{C}$$

The first ratio has an 8 in the numerator; this represents the number of ounces given in the problem. In the denominator of the first ratio is 150. This represents the number of calories in 8 ounces of milk. This information is given in the problem. The other ratio has a 12 in the numerator because 12 represents the number of ounces of milk you are asked about in the problem. Notice how both numbers that represent the number of ounces are in the numerator. Numbers representing the same quantity must be in the same places in the ratios. The second ratio has a $C$ in the denominator. This $C$ represents the unknown number of calories we are trying to find in 12 ounces of milk. When given three of the four numbers in a proportion, you can solve for the unknown number by following a procedure. The first step is cross-multiplying. That means multiplying the numerator of one ratio by the denominator in the other ratio. Then, set those products equal to each other. The final step is to divide both sides by the number that is multiplied by the variable.

$$\frac{8}{150} = \frac{12}{C} \qquad 8 \times C = 150 \times 12 \qquad C = 225$$

Therefore, there are 225 calories in 12 ounces of whole milk.

## PROBLEM

An automobile dealer has to sell 3.5 cars for every truck to achieve the optimum profit. This year, it is estimated that 3,500 cars will be sold. How many trucks must he sell to achieve the optimum profit?

(A) 1,000    (B) 500    (C) 350    (D) 2,000

**SOLUTION**

First identify your ratio, 3.5 cars: 1 truck, or 3.5/1. We can use $t$ as our variable for trucks, and set up our equal proportion as 3,500 cars: $t$ trucks, or $\dfrac{3,500}{t}$. Now we use cross multiplication to solve:

$$\dfrac{3.5}{1} = \dfrac{3,500}{t} \quad \text{and} \quad 3.5t = (3,500)(1)$$
$$3.5t = 3,500$$
$$\dfrac{3.5t}{3.5} = \dfrac{3,500}{3.5}$$
$$t = 1000$$

The correct answer is choice (A), 1,000 trucks.

**PROBLEM**

A baker is making a new recipe for cookies. For every 6 cups of flour, he is using 1 cup of sugar. He puts 30 cups of flour and 2 cups of sugar into the batter. How many more cups of sugar does he need to add to maintain the ratio?

(A) 2          (B) 5          (C) 3          (D) 7

**SOLUTION**

First set up your ratio, 6 c flour: 1 c sugar or $\dfrac{6}{1}$. Next we make $s$ equal to the total amount of sugar in the final recipe. We can now set up our proportion and solve as follows:

$$\dfrac{6}{1} = \dfrac{30}{s} \text{ and } 6s = (30)(1)$$
$$6s = 30$$
$$\dfrac{6s}{6} = \dfrac{30}{6}$$
$$s = 5$$

For every 30 cups of flour, he needs 5 cups of sugar. Now we need to determine the total amount of sugar we need to add to get a total of 5 cups. The baker already put in 2 cups, and 5 − 2 = 3, so that answer is choice (C), 3 cups. If you chose (B), you forgot to take into consideration that the baker already put 2 cups into the bowl.

## Similar Figures

In mathematics, similar figures are two-dimensional figures that have the same shape. Usually similar figures have different sizes; however, two identical figures (which are congruent) are considered similar because they fit the definition of similar figures. Corresponding sides of similar figures have the same ratio to each other, called the scale factor. The ratio of any pair of corresponding sides of similar figure is the same. The corresponding angles of similar figures are congruent. The two triangles below are similar. Because you know that the ratio of *AC:DF* is 6:3, you can calculate the measurement of line segment *DE*.

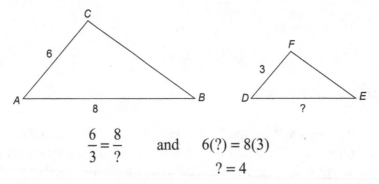

$$\frac{6}{3} = \frac{8}{?} \qquad \text{and} \qquad 6(?) = 8(3)$$
$$? = 4$$

In this example we did not simplify the 6:3 ratio in order to solve the problem, but it is important that if a ratio is your final answer on the FTCE-GKT, you remember to simplify your answer. A 6:3 ratio can be simplified by dividing both sides by their greatest common factor, 3. This gives you a ratio of 2:1. Also, it is important to be consistent when setting up your proportions. If you choose to use the measurement of the larger figure as your numerator in your ratio, you must also use the measurement from the larger figure in the numerator when you set up the proportion. In the preceding example, this means that $\frac{6}{3} = \frac{8}{4}$, but $\frac{6}{3} \neq \frac{4}{8}$.

The areas of similar figures are also proportional; however, they do not have the same ratio as the side lengths do. One right triangle has a base of 6 cm and a height of 10 cm. What would be the base and height of a similar triangle with a scale factor of 2? The base would be 12 cm and the height would be 20 cm. Let's examine the area of both triangles. The formula for finding the area of a triangle is $A = \frac{1}{2}bh$, where $b$ is the base and $h$ is the height. So the area of the original triangle is $\left(\frac{1}{2}\right)(6)(10) = 30$ cm². The area of the larger triangle is $\left(\frac{1}{2}\right)(12)(20) = 120$ cm². The area of the larger triangle is not double the area of the original triangle, as one would have expected. The area of the larger triangle is four times greater. So, what is the ratio of the areas of similar figures? The area will be the scale factor *squared*. So, if the scale factor is 3, then the area will be $3^2$ or 9 times larger.

When two figures are similar, they have 6 pairs of corresponding parts—the sides and the angles. Corresponding parts are in the same place in each similar figure.

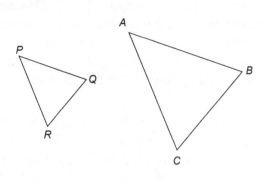

The six corresponding parts for these two similar triangles shown are:

1. *PQ* and *AB*

2. *QR* and *BC*

3. *RP* and *CA*

4. $\angle P$ and $\angle A$

5. $\angle Q$ and $\angle B$

6. $\angle R$ and $\angle C$

**PROBLEM**

Jerome has a photograph that is 6 inches by 9 inches. He wants to enlarge it by a scale factor of 2. What would be the area in square inches of Jerome's enlarged photograph?

(A) 108          (B) 216

(C) 60           (D) 120

**SOLUTION**

To solve this problem correctly, you must know that the length and width of the enlarged photograph will be twice the length and width of the original photograph. The enlarged photograph will be 12 inches by 18 inches. To find the area, multiply the length times the width. This answer is 216 square inches. The correct answer is (B).

## Congruent Figures

When two figures are **congruent**, they are the same size and shape. Corresponding parts of congruent figures are congruent. That means corresponding sides and corresponding angles are congruent. If you have two congruent regular pentagons, for example, and you know the length of one side of one of the pentagons, you can find the length of the sides of the other pentagon. Congruent figures are also considered similar. Similar figures are figures whose side lengths are proportional. The angles of similar figures are the same. If a figure is scaled up, then the new figure will be larger than the original figure. If a figure is scaled down, then the new figure will be smaller than the original figure. For example, a right triangle with sides 3, 4, and 5 cm would be similar to a right triangle with sides 18, 24, and 30 cm because 18, 24, and 30 are each six times larger than 3, 4, and 5.

## Pythagorean Theorem

The **Pythagorean Theorem** is used to find the missing side length of a right triangle. If you know two of the three sides, you can find the third using the Pythagorean Theorem. The Pythagorean Theorem is $a^2 + b^2 = c^2$, where $a$ and $b$ are the legs and $c$ is the hypotenuse of the right triangle. The legs are the two sides that make up the right angle (it does not matter which leg is $a$ and which leg is $b$.) The hypotenuse is the longest side of the right triangle and is opposite the right angle.

There are many situations in real life where you can apply the Pythagorean Theorem. Oftentimes, these problems do not explicitly state that you need to use the Pythagorean theorem. By reading the problem, you have to recognize that the information you are looking for is a side length of a right triangle. If you are given the length of a ladder and how far its base is from a building, you may be asked how high up the building the top of the ladder falls. In the diagram below, if you knew the length of the ladder and the distance of the base of the ladder from the building, you could find how high up the building the top of the ladder is. In this example, the ladder is the hypotenuse and the ground and the wall are the legs of a right triangle.

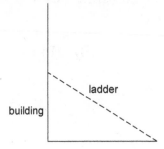

On the FTCE-GKT, you are only permitted to use a four-function calculator, which does not have a square root sign. For this reason, if you are asked to calculate a leg or hypotenuse of a right triangle, the figure will likely be a special, 3-4-5 right triangle like the ones that follow:

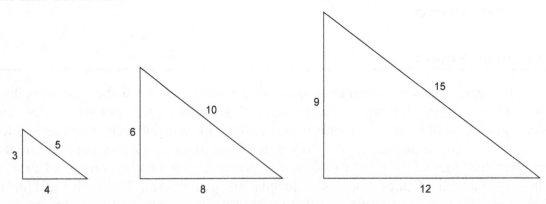

The 3-4-5 right triangle is a type of Pythagorean Triple, or a common trio of positive integers that make up the legs and hypotenuse of a right triangle. Another less common triple that occasionally shows up on this exam is the 5-12-13 right triangle. Be sure to watch for this combination. It can save you considerable time if you have these two triples memorized!

Look at the following problem:

### PROBLEM

A ten-foot ladder is leaning against a building. The ladder reaches six feet up the building. How far is the ladder from the side of the building?

### SOLUTION

Since the building and the ground form a right angle, we know that the ladder is the hypotenuse. There are two ways to solve this problem:

**The Pythagorean Theorem:**  **Scaled Proportion:**

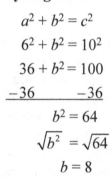

$$a^2 + b^2 = c^2$$
$$6^2 + b^2 = 10^2$$
$$36 + b^2 = 100$$
$$\underline{-36 \qquad -36}$$
$$b^2 = 64$$
$$\sqrt{b^2} = \sqrt{64}$$
$$b = 8$$

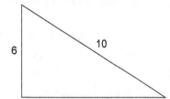

The given leg (6) and hypotenuse (10) have a common factor of 2. Divide both numbers by 2, and you get 3 for one leg and 5 for the hypotenuse. This verifies that this is a 3-4-5 right triangle that had been scaled up by a factor of 2. The missing leg would be the 4 side. $4 \times 2 = 8$, so the ladder is 8 feet from the side of the building.

### PROBLEM

A cable needs to be run from the top of a 9-foot pole to the ground, 12 feet from its base. How long will the cable be?

(A) 10 ft.      (B) 15 ft.      (C) 25 ft.      (D) 108 ft.

### SOLUTION

The 9-foot pole and the distance of 12 feet from its base make up two legs of a right triangle. 9 and 12 have a common factor of 3. $9 \div 3 = 3$ and $12 \div 3 = 4$, so this is a 3-4-5 triangle scaled up by a factor of three. Since the missing side is the 5 side, multiply 5 by a factor of 3 to get 15 ft, the length of the cable.

**Alternate Solution:** Use the Pythagorean Theorem to solve for the hypotenuse:

$$a^2 + b^2 = c^2$$
$$9^2 + 12^2 = c^2$$
$$81 + 144 = c^2$$
$$225 = c^2$$
$$\sqrt{225} = \sqrt{c^2}$$
$$15 = c$$

Using either method, the correct answer is (B), 15 ft.

## Skill 2.3. Determine an appropriate measurement unit and form (e.g., scientific notation) for real-world problems involving length, area, volume, or mass.

There are a variety of measurements that you may encounter when solving problems: length, weight, mass, perimeter, area, capacity, and volume, to name a few. It is important that you know what each measure is used for, as well as to familiarize yourself with the various units within each system. Length and perimeter are measures of distance; area is a two-dimensional measurement; and volume and capacity are three-dimensional measurements. For solids, volume can be measured in terms of cubic units. For liquids, volume can be measured in ounces, cups, pints, quarts, gallons, and liters. Weight measures the force from gravity on an object and can be measured in grams, ounces, pounds, and tons. Mass measures the amount of matter an object has.

Measuring can be done using either the metric system or customary units. It is important to be comfortable with both systems. Customary units are based on inches, feet, and yards. The standard unit of measurement in the United States is the foot, which has 12 inches in it. Three feet make up a yard, and there are 5,280 feet in a mile. Inches are broken up into fractional parts such as halves, fourths, eighths, and sixteenths. These fractions do not lend themselves to conversion to decimal numbers.

A ruler with customary units is often broken up into sixteenths. The marks on the ruler below show sixteenths.

The large line in the middle of each inch indicates a half-inch. The slightly smaller line between each inch and half-inch indicates fourths of an inch. The marks that are slightly smaller than the quarter-inch marks represent eighths of an inch. The marks that are the smallest represent sixteenths of an inch. Depending on the level of accuracy that is needed, measurements may be to the closest half-inch, quarter-inch, eighth-inch, or sixteenth-inch.

The metric system is an international system of measurement, which is simpler to work with than standard measurements because all its measurements are in base 10. Metric units of length include millimeters, centimeters, meters, and kilometers. A meter (m) is equal to 100 centimeters (cm) and 1000 mm (mm). A centimeter is equal to 10 millimeters (mm). The ruler below shows the relationship between centimeters and millimeters. Notice that the markings between centimeters show millimeters, which are $\frac{1}{10}$ of a centimeter and equal to 1 millimeter each.

Metric units of weight include grams and kilograms. The gram is the basic metric unit of mass (which for many purposes is the same as *weight*). A large paper clip weighs about 1 gram. It takes about 28 grams to make 1 ounce. Metric units of capacity include milliliters and liters. The liter is the basic metric unit of volume (or capacity). A liter is slightly larger than a quart, so it takes fewer than four liters to make a gallon.

**PROBLEM**

If five books weigh $2\frac{1}{2}$ pounds each and five notebooks weigh 4 ounces each, how many pounds do they weigh altogether?

(A) $7\frac{1}{2}$      (B) $13\frac{3}{4}$      (C) $17\frac{1}{2}$      (D) $32\frac{1}{2}$

**SOLUTION**

This problem requires many math skills including multiplying and adding fractions and converting customary units.

Calculate the weight of the books by breaking apart to multiply:

$$5 \times 2\frac{1}{2} \, lbs. = (5 \times 2) + \left(5 \times \frac{1}{2}\right) = 10 + \frac{5}{2} = 10 + 2\frac{1}{2} = 12\frac{1}{2} \, lbs.$$

Calculate the weight of the notebooks:

$$5 \times 4 \, oz. = 20 \, oz.$$

Convert the ounces to pounds:

$$\frac{20 \, oz}{1} \times \frac{1 lb}{16 oz} = \frac{20}{16} = 1\frac{4}{16} = 1\frac{1}{4} \, lbs.$$

Find a common denominator and add the weights:

$$12\frac{1}{2} + 1\frac{1}{4} = 12\frac{2}{4} + 1\frac{1}{4} = 13\frac{3}{4}$$

The correct answer is (B).

**PROBLEM**

You have a wire that is 4 ft. 8 inches long. If you bend it into a square frame, what is the area of your frame?

(A) 2 ft. 2 in.    (B) 14 in.    (C) 144 in$^2$    (D) 196 in$^2$

**SOLUTION**

First convert the mixed units into inches. Four feet is equal to 48 inches, so the wire is 48 + 8 = 56 inches long. Next, divide the wire length by four since a square has four equal sides: 56 ÷ 4 = 14 inches. Finally, use the formula $s^2$ to find the area of the frame: $14^2 = 14 \times 14 = 196$ inches squared. The correct answer is (D). ***Note:*** *If the problem asks you to convert this to square feet, remember that there are 144 square inches in one square foot. If you divide 196 by 144, you get* $1.36$ *or* $1\frac{52}{144}$ *, which simplifies to* $1\frac{13}{38}$ *square feet.*

**PROBLEM**

You are trying to tile your bathroom with tiles that are 8-inch squares. If your bathroom is 8 ft. by 12 ft., how many tiles will you need?

**SOLUTION**

To solve this problem you need to know two things: the number of tiles that fill a square foot and the number of square feet in the room.

To find the number of tiles per square foot, you first find the area of one square tile: 8 in. × 8 in. = 64 square inches. Next you find the area of one square foot in inches: 12 in. × 12 in. = 144 square inches. Finally you divided the 144 square inches by the 64 square inches in one tile: 144 ÷ 64 = 2.25. You need 2.25 tiles for each square foot of the bathroom.

To find the total number of tiles needed, multiply the length by the width of the room, then multiply your result by 2.25: 8 ft. × 12 ft. = 96 square feet. 96 × 2.25 = 216 tiles to complete your project.

Many of the problems on the General Knowledge Test will require that you convert between units. It is important that you always use your math reference guide to find equivalent units before beginning your conversions. After that, it is only a matter of correctly setting up the problem. For instance, how would you determine how many meters are in 1.4 kilometers?

**Step 1:** Put your given units in the form of a fraction with 1 in the denominator.

$$\frac{1.4 \text{ km}}{1}$$

**Step 2:** Use your math reference guide to identify your conversion.

1 kilometer = 1000 meters

**Step 3:** Multiply your given measurement by the conversion with the units you need on the top.

$$\frac{1.4 \text{ km}}{1} \times \frac{1000 \text{ m}}{1 \text{ km}}$$   (you need your answer in meters)

(put the units you started with on the bottom)

**Step 4:** Multiply

$$\frac{1.4 \ \cancel{\text{km}}}{1} \times \frac{1000 \text{ m}}{1 \ \cancel{\text{km}}} = 1400 \text{ m}$$

This method, called the factor-label method, works for both customary and metric units. When you are working with metric units, however, there is a shortcut for solving this type of problem. Since the metric system is based on powers of ten, conversions can be done by simply moving the decimal point. This method is called the metric ladder. These are the units that are used in the metric system:

| kilo- | hecto- | deka- | base (m, L, g) | deci- | centi- | milli- |
|---|---|---|---|---|---|---|

The metric ladder can be used to convert any metric unit. Let's try this method for the previous problem, 1.4 km = _____ m.

First place your finger on the unit you start with, then count the jumps to the unit you want.

| kilo- | hecto- | deka- | base (m, L, g) | deci- | centi- | milli- |
|---|---|---|---|---|---|---|

    1      2      3

Next write the number you started with, and move the decimal in the same direction and number of places you moved your finger. You will have to add zeros to have enough places.

**1.400.**

Now rewrite the number with the decimal in the new location: 1400. Since the decimal is at the end of the number, we don't have to write it. 1.4 kilometers is equal to 1400 meters.

Try it while moving from small units to larger units. 1234 mg = _____ kg. Start with your finger on milligrams, then count the jumps to kilograms:

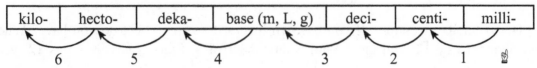

You should have counted six jumps left. Now move the decimal that many places. This time you first have to add the decimal to the end of the number and zeros to the front of the number to move the decimal:

.001234.

Now rewrite the number with the decimal in the new location: 0.001234.

1234 mg = 0.001234 kg.

In order to use this method on the FTCE-GKT, you must memorize the units in the correct order. You can use the mnemonic King Henry Died by Drinking Chocolate Milk. Generally, you will only be using kilo-, the bases (meters, liters, or grams), centi-, and milli-, but you will have to know the positions of all of the units to use this simple method of conversion.

**PROBLEM**

The distance between two posts is 8.4 meters. How many centimeters is this distance?

(A)  84          (B)  840          (C)  8,400          (D)  84,000

**SOLUTION**

Using your metric ladder, you can count two jumps right from the base unit of meters to centimeters. Move the decimal two jumps to the right, and you have 840 centimeters. The correct answer is (B).

Although you can use the factor label method to calculate any conversion, you can also use basic multiplication and division to convert units. Just remember this rule, if you are going from large to small units, multiply. If you are going from small to large, divide.

For example, if you need to convert inches (small) to feet (large), you need to divide by 12 since there are 12 inches in each foot. For example, if you have 42 inches, how many feet do you have? When you divide 42 by 12, you get 3 feet with a remainder of 6. Since your divisor is 12, you convert your remainder to a fraction, $\frac{6}{12}$, which simplifies to $\frac{1}{2}$; therefore, you have $3\frac{1}{2}$ feet.

Here's another example: If you have 16 inches, how many feet do you have? When you divide 16 by 12, you get 1 with a remainder of 4. Since your divisor is 12, your answer is $1\frac{4}{12}$, which simplifies to $1\frac{1}{3}$ feet. If you want to find out how many feet (small) you have in a given number of yards (large), multiply by 3 because every yard has 3 feet.

Let's look at this example: If you have 8 yards, how many feet do you have? Since $8 \times 3 = 24$, you have 24 feet. If you wanted to know how many inches that was, multiply 24 by 12 since 1 foot has 12 inches. $12 \times 24 = 288$. There are 288 inches in 24 feet or in 8 yards.

**PROBLEM**

How many feet are in 2.5 miles?

    (A)  2,112       (B)  4,400       (C)  5,280       (D)  13,200

**SOLUTION**

First, look up the equivalencies in your math reference guide. You will see that there are 5,280 feet in a mile. You are going from a large unit, miles, to a smaller unit, feet, so you need to multiply. Multiply 2.5 by 5,280. You have 13,200 feet in 2.5 miles. Choice (D) is correct.

## Scientific Notation and the Powers of Ten

**Scientific notation** is a way of writing really large or really small numbers in a special format. Scientific notation requires that there is **only one digit in front of the decimal point** and that the magnitude of the number is represented with a positive or negative power of ten. Notice the pattern in the powers of ten that follow:

$10^0 = 1$

$10^1 = 10$                       $10^{-1} = 0.1$

$10^2 = 100$                 $10^{-2} = 0.01$

$10^3 = 1,000$              $10^{-3} = 0.001$

$10^4 = 10,000$            $10^{-4} = 0.0001$

$10^5 = 100,000$           $10^{-5} = 0.00001$

A good trick to master using the positive powers of ten is to always first write the number 1, then add the same number of zeros as the exponent. So, $10^4$ is a 1 with four zeros behind it (10,000). You can also use your four-function calculator to solve for powers of ten ($10 \times 10 \times 10 \times 10 = 10,000$).

When you are using scientific notation, it is critical that you keep track of how many places you are moving the decimal point. For instance, if you were asked to put 1,239 in scientific notation, the decimal place would have to be moved three places left, between the 1 and the 2. But how do you use powers of ten to represent the true value of your number? Practice the following steps:

**Step 1:** Analyze the number and determine which way and how far to move the decimal.

1,239: You need to add a decimal to the end of the number and move it three places left.

**Step 2:** Move the decimal to its new location.

1.239

**Step 3:** Add $\times 10$ to the back of the number.

$1.239 \times 10$

**Step 4:** Add a positive exponent equal to the spaces you move left, or a negative exponent for the places you move right.

$1.239 \times 10^3$

Now try it with a small number like 0.0124. In order to have one whole number in front of the decimal point, the decimal must be moved two places to the right in between the 1 and the 2. When the decimal is moved, you have 1.24. Now add the proper power of ten (−2 for the two places to the right) and you have $1.24 \times 10^{-2}$.

**PROBLEM**

Put the following numbers into scientific notation:

    (A)  2,345,000    (B)  0.0045    (C)  0.132    (D)  43.8

**SOLUTION**

**Choice (A):** Move the decimal between the 2 and the 3.

Count the direction and places you move the decimal (6 left).

Add the positive exponent 6 to the power of ten: $2.345 \times 10^6$.

**Choice (B):** Move the decimal between the 4 and the 5.

Count the directions and places you move the decimal (3 right).

Add the exponent −3 to the power of ten: $4.5 \times 10^{-3}$.

**Choice (C):** Move the decimal between the 1 and the 3.

Count the direction and places you move the decimal (1 right).

Add the exponent −1 to the power of ten: $1.3 \times 10^{-1}$.

**Choice (D):** Move the decimal between the 4 and the 3.

Count the direction and places you move the decimal (1 right).

Add no exponent to the power of ten, because the 1 is understood. $4.38 \times 10$.

When a number is already in scientific notation, and we have to return it to standard form, we use the exponent to tell us where to put the decimal. If there is a negative exponent, move the decimal to the left. If the exponent is positive, move it right. When you check your work, use common sense. Multiplying a number by a positive power of ten should make it appear greater, while multiplying it by a negative power of ten should make it seem smaller. Of course, the value is not changing, just the way you express the number. You also have the option of calculating the value of the power of ten with your calculator, then multiplying your answer by the front part of the expression: $1.23 \times 10^2 = 1.23 \times (10 \times 10) = 1.23 \times 100 = 123$

## PROBLEM

Calculate the expression shown below, and express the answer in scientific notation.

$$0.006 \times 1.34$$

(A) $0.804 \times 10^{-2}$ (B) $0.804 \times 10^2$

(C) $8.04 \times 10^{-3}$ (D) $8.04 \times 10^3$

## SOLUTION

First multiply $0.006 \times 1.34$ with your calculator to get 0.00804. Now calculate how far and in what direction you have to move your decimal point (three places right). Now move the decimal and add the proper power of ten: $8.04 \times 10^{-3}$. Choice (C) is correct.

## PROBLEM

In 2003, the planet Mars was the closest it had ever been to Earth in recorded history: 34,800,000 miles away. If it were possible to freeze the planets in their orbits, how far would the round trip be from Earth to Mars and back again?

(A) $6.96 \times 10^{-7}$ (B) $34.8 \times 10^7$

(C) $6.96 \times 10^7$ (D) $3.48 \times 10^{-7}$

## SOLUTION

First multiply 34,800,000 times 2 to get 69,600,000. Now calculate how far you need to move the decimal and in which direction (7 places left). Rewrite your number with the decimal in the new position (6.96) and add the proper power of ten ($6.96 \times 10^7$). The correct answer is choice (C).

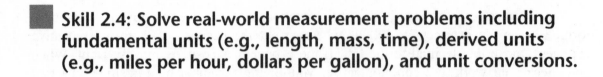

## Skill 2.4: Solve real-world measurement problems including fundamental units (e.g., length, mass, time), derived units (e.g., miles per hour, dollars per gallon), and unit conversions.

### Fundamental Units

An important step in solving problems involving measurement is figuring out the category of measurement you're working with. Generally, such problems will fall under one of these categories: length, area, angles, volume, mass, time, money, or temperature. Solving measurement problems will likely have you calling on your knowledge in several other areas of mathematics, especially algebra.

Sometimes it is helpful to estimate before performing the actual calculation to be sure your answer is reasonable. You may also estimate an answer if you do not need an exact answer. If you want to know how long it will take you to complete some errands before meeting a friend, you probably will not need an exact answer. There are times when an estimate is good enough. Estimating the result of a calculation sometimes involves rounding. If you bought a package of 8 cookies for $1.99 and wanted to know what the price per cookie is, you would divide 1.99 by 8. When you do so, you get 0.24875. That is the exact answer. However, when talking about price, we usually go to the nearest cent. You could round your answer to 25 cents. If you wanted to estimate, you also could have rounded $1.99 to $2.00. Then use mental math to divide by 8 to get 25 cents.

If you needed to estimate the area of a field that was 190 meters by 217 meters, you could round 190 meters up to 200 meters, and you could round 217 meters down to 200 meters. Therefore, the approximate or estimated area would be about $200 \times 200$, which is 40,000 meters.

The following is an example measurement problem that requires knowledge of several math topics:

> Sophie's Carpet Store charges $19.40 per square yard for the type of carpeting you'd like (padding and labor included). How much will you pay to carpet your 9 foot by 12 foot room?

One way to find the solution is to convert the room dimensions to yards (3 yards by 4 yards), then multiply to get 12 square yards. Finally, multiply 12 by the price of $19.40 per square yard, for a total price of $232.80.

What if you decided to solve the previous problem by first calculating the area of the room in square feet? 9 feet $\times$ 12 feet = 108 ft$^2$. What would you do now? There are three feet in a yard, so would you divide by 3? If so, you have just fallen into a math trap. There may be three feet in a yard, but there are 9 square feet in one square yard. You would have to divide 108 by 9 to get the correct answer of 12 yd$^2$. The cost calculation would be the same.

Remember to read word problems thoroughly to determine what information you need. For example, if you are given the length and width of a room, and you need to buy carpeting for the room, what measurement do you need to find? Perimeter? Area? Volume? You need to find the area of the room.

Here's another example: A rectangular-shaped backyard has a length of 25 feet and an area of 550 ft². If you need to know how much fence to buy to surround the yard, what measurement do you need to find? Perimeter? Area? Volume? You need to find the perimeter because the fence will surround the yard. You are given the length, which is 25 feet, but not the width. However, you are given the area, so you can find the width by dividing the area by the length. 550 ÷ 25 = 22. Therefore, the width is 22 feet. The perimeter of the backyard is found by adding both lengths and both widths. 25 + 25 + 22 + 22 = 94. The perimeter of the backyard requires 94 feet of fencing.

## Rate

A rate is a value describing one quantity in terms of another, such as miles per hour (mph) or meters per second (mps). An important formula used when working with rate is

$$\text{Distance} = \text{Rate} \times \text{Time or } d = rt.$$

(You can use the word *dirt* to remember this commonly used formula.) For example, if you are driving 40 mph for 2 hours, how many miles will you cover? When you multiply 40 by 2 and get 80 (miles), you are using the formula, $d = rt$.

### PROBLEM

You are on a road trip. The first day you drove 200 miles in 4 hours. The second day you travel at the same rate of speed for another 6 hours. If you get an average of 25 miles per gallon and gas costs $3.79 a gallon, how much did you spend on gas during the trip?

### SOLUTION

**Part 1:** Calculate how far you drove. The problem states that you drove 200 miles the first day. Next calculate your rate for the first day. If distance = rate × time, then 200 miles = rate × 4 hours or 200 = 4$r$. Divide both sides by 4 to find your rate, 50 mph. Next, calculate how many miles you traveled the second day: $d = rt$, $d = (50)(6)$, $d = 300$ miles. Add your miles for both days: 200 miles + 300 miles = 500 miles.

**Part 2:** Calculate how many gallons of gas you used. If you traveled 500 miles and get 25 miles per gallon, you can divide 500 by 25 to calculate how many gallons of gas you used. 500 ÷ 25 = 20 gallons of gas.

**Part 3:** Calculate the cost of your fuel. 20 gallons × $3.79 = $75.80 on gas.

*Note: The prior problem typifies the types of multi-step problems you will see on the FTCE-GKT.*

Some of the rate problems on this test are quite rigorous. One particular type of problem will ask you to calculate distance based on traveling at specific rates, then determine how far you traveled based on how early or late you arrive, as in the example below.

### PROBLEM

You are going to a meeting. If you drive 60 mph, you will get there two hours early. If you drive 30 mph you will get there two hours late. How far do you have to drive?

| (A) 240 miles | (B) 180 miles |
|---|---|
| (C) 120 miles | (D) 60 miles |

### SOLUTION

(A) 240 miles. The first key to solving this problem is to determine what two hours early and two hours late means. If you were due to work at 8:00 a.m. and got there at 6:00 a.m., you would be two hours early. If you got there at 10:00 a.m., you would be two hours late. The difference between 6:00 and 10:00 a.m. is four hours. Next you need to solve each distance at both rates, 30 mph and 60 mph, looking for a four hour distance in times.

If you try every solution, you are actually solving eight individual problems. The smart strategy is to choose a distance in the middle. If after you solve the problem, the time difference is too long, then try again with a shorter distance. If it is too short, try a longer distance. Look at the solution below, paying careful attention to the difference in times as you increase your distance traveled.

| Distance (miles) | = | Rate (mph) | x | Time (hours) | Difference in arrival times |
|---|---|---|---|---|---|
| 240 | | 30 | | 8 | |
| 240 | | 60 | | 4 | 8 − 4 = 4 hours |
| 180 | | 30 | | 6 | |
| 180 | | 60 | | 3 | 6 − 3 = 3 hours |
| 120 | | 30 | | 4 | |
| 120 | | 60 | | 2 | 4 − 2 = 2 hours |
| 60 | | 30 | | 2 | |
| 60 | | 60 | | 1 | 2 − 1 = 1 hour |
| | | | | | |

You may also be asked to use net rate to determine when two vehicles meet or the time it takes to fill a draining tub. We group these types of problems together because they both use net rate in their calculations. If two vehicles are heading toward each other, you add the rates and use that figure in the distance, rate, and time formula. If you have a problem where a tub is filling while simultaneously draining, subtract the two rates to find net rate. After that, calculation is simple algebra, as shown below:

### PROBLEM

Two trains leave different cities heading toward each other at different speeds. Train A, traveling 70 miles per hour (mph), leaves Westford heading toward Eastford, 260 miles away. At the same time Train B, traveling 60 mph, leaves Eastford heading toward Westford. When do the two trains meet? How far from each city do they meet?

### SOLUTION

**When they meet:**

- First add the rates of both trains, 70 + 60 = 130 mph

- Next plug your net rate into the formula (distance = rate × time) with the given distance, 260 miles = (130mph)(t), and solve. Dividing both sides by 130 gives you a time of 2 hours.

**Where they meet:**

- Use the time they meet from above and the individual rates to calculate the distance each train traveled before they meet.

- Train A: d = (70)(2) = 140 miles

- Train B: d = (60)(2) = 120 miles

### PROBLEM

You are filling a 50-gallon tub with water at a rate of 6 gallons per minute. Unfortunately, the tub has a small leak, so the water is draining out of the bottom at a rate of one gallon per minute. How long will it take to fill the tub to the top if you do not fix the leak?

### SOLUTION

First calculate the net rate: 6 gallons flowing in, less the 1 gallon leaking out equals a net fill rate of 5 gallons per minute. Next divide the total number of gallons (50) by the fill rate (5) to find out it will take 10 minutes to fill the tub.

Another rate that is useful to know is the cost per unit. For example, if you want to compare two different size containers of laundry detergent to figure out which is the better deal, you would want to know how to find the cost per ounce. If a 50-ounce container of Detergent A costs $5.99, and a 32-ounce container of Detergent B costs $4.15, which detergent costs less (per ounce)? Divide the cost by the number of ounces to find the cost per ounce. Detergent A is approximately $0.12 per ounce and Detergent B is approximately $0.13 per ounce. Detergent A is cheaper.

## PROBLEM

Which unit price shows the best buy?

(A)  15 sodas for $8.10        (B)  12 sodas for $6.96

(C)  5 sodas for $2.80         (D)  13 sodas for $7.41

## SOLUTION

To find the unit price, divide the total price by the number of sodas. The unit price for (A) is 0.54 cents. The unit price for (B) is 0.58 cents. The unit price for (C) is 0.56 cents, and the unit price for (D) is 0.57 cents. The best buy is 15 sodas for $8.10, answer choice (A).

## PROBLEM

It took Carla $1\frac{1}{2}$ minutes to run 160 meters. At that same rate, how many meters would she run in an hour?

(A)  9600        (B)  6400        (C)  240        (D)  430

## SOLUTION

To solve the problem, first convert the fraction to a decimal: $1\frac{1}{2} = 1.5$. Next write a proportion:

$$\frac{1.5}{160} = \frac{60}{x}$$

Cross-multiply to get $1.5x = (60)(160)$. This results in $1.5x = 9600$. Divide both sides by 1.5, and $x = 6400$. Carla will run 6400 meters in 1 hour (60 minutes). The correct answer is (B).

**PROBLEM**

A marathon is 26.2 miles long. How many kilometers are in a marathon if there are approximately 1.61 kilometers in 1 mile? Round your answer to the nearest tenth of a kilometer.

(A) 42.2          (B) 16.3          (C) 33.6          (D) 24.6

**SOLUTION**

To solve this problem, you can set up and solve a proportion:

$$\frac{1.61 \text{ km}}{1 \text{ mile}} = \frac{x \text{ km}}{26.2 \text{ miles}}$$

Cross-multiply $(1.61)(26.2) = (1)(x)$ to find that there are approximately 42.2 kilometers in 26.2 miles. The correct answer is (A).

**PROBLEM**

A man takes a 375-mile trip to Miami. His large car gets 18 miles per gallon, and his small car gets 32 miles per gallon. How many gallons of gas will he save if he takes the smaller car?

(A)  11.7
(B)  15.6
(C)  21.8
(D)  24

**SOLUTION**

The difference in gas mileage in the two cars is $32 - 18 = 24$ mpg. Divide 375 by 24 and you get 15.625, which rounds to 15.6 gallons of gas saved. You could also calculate the number of gallons each car used, then subtract, but this method is more time consuming. The correct answer is (B).

## Capacity Conversions—Customary Measurements

On the FTCE-GKT, customary capacity problems can be time-consuming. Problems that require gallons to be converted to cups can take valuable time that could be better spent on more rigorous problems. Look at the following example:

A classroom teacher is planning a reading night for her students. She wants to have enough punch to serve each of her 24 students a one-cup serving. How many gallons should she purchase if the punch is sold only in 1-gallon containers?

Start with the units you are given in the numerator and the number one in the denominator, then use your math reference guide to find equivalent proportions, each time putting the unit you need on the top:

$$\frac{24 \text{ cups}}{1} \times \frac{1 \text{ pint}}{2 \text{ cups}} \times \frac{1 \text{ quart}}{2 \text{ pints}} \times \frac{1 \text{ gallon}}{4 \text{ quarts}}$$

Next, cross out any units (not the numbers) that appear in both the numerator and the denominator, then multiply:

$$\frac{24 \; \cancel{\text{cups}}}{1} \times \frac{1 \; \cancel{\text{pint}}}{2 \; \cancel{\text{cups}}} \times \frac{1 \; \cancel{\text{quart}}}{2 \; \cancel{\text{pints}}} \times \frac{1 \text{ gallon}}{4 \; \cancel{\text{quarts}}} = \frac{24 \times 1 \times 1 \times 1 \text{ gallons}}{1 \times 2 \times 2 \times 4}$$

$$= \frac{24 \text{ gallons}}{16} = 1\frac{1}{2} \text{ gallons}$$

The teacher needs to buy 2 gallons of punch since the beverage is sold only in 1-gallon containers. As you can see, this required copying three proportions from the math reference guide before solving the problem. With a little memorization, there is a quicker way to solve this type of problem. The authorship of this tale is unknown, but teachers have been using some form of this for years:

---

**The Land of Gallon**

Once there was a Land of Gallon. (Draw a large G)

In this land there were 4 queens. (Draw 4 Q's inside the G)

Each queen had a lovely princess and a handsome prince. (Draw two P's in each Q)

The princes and princesses in the land each had two adorable children. (Draw 2 C's in each P)

---

The translation? In one gallon there are 4 quarts, in each quart there are 2 pints, and in each pint there are 2 cups. You can even take it a step further and put an 8 in each C since each cup is equal to 8 fluid ounces. Once you have the diagram memorized, you have a visual way to solve these problems:

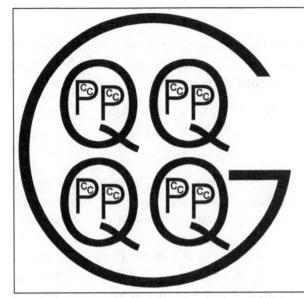

Try it! How many cups are in a half gallon? Cover up half of the image, and count the C's: 8 cups in a half gallon. How many pints in three quarts? Count the P's in three of the Q's (6). How many cups in four gallons? Count the C's in one gallon (16), then multiply by 4: $16 \times 4 = 64$ cups.

### PROBLEM

The Institute of Medicine determined that men in a temperate climate should drink about 13 cups of fluids each day. How many gallons of water is that in one week?

(A) 91.5 gallons   (B) 91 cups   (C) 16 gallons   (D) 5.7 gallons

### SOLUTION

First calculate the number of cups a man should drink a week:

$$\frac{13 \text{ cups}}{1 \text{ day}} \times 7 \text{ days} = \textbf{91 cups}$$

**Method 1:**

$$\frac{91 \text{ cups}}{1} \times \frac{1 \text{ pint}}{2 \text{ cups}} \times \frac{1 \text{ quart}}{2 \text{ pints}} \times \frac{1 \text{ gallon}}{4 \text{ quarts}} = \frac{91 \text{ gallons}}{16} = 5.7 \text{ gallons}$$

**Method 2:** Use the Land of Gallon diagram to calculate how many cups are in one gallon: 16 cups. 91 cups ÷ 16 cups = 5.7 gallons (rounded).

## Time

Problems with time are relatively straightforward, but special care has to be taken when you are calculating a period of time that starts before 12:00 and ends later. The safest strategy to use is to calculate these problems in two segments: up until 12:00, then any remaining time after. Then add the two solutions together.

PROBLEM

You have to get your children to the lacrosse field in time for a 30-minute warm-up before the 1:15 championship game in a neighboring town. You live an hour and 20 minutes from the field. What time do you need to leave the house?

    (A)  2:35        (B)  11:25        (C)  12:25        (D)  11:55

SOLUTION

First calculate what time you have to arrive at the field. Thirty minutes before 1:15 is 12:45. Next calculate your drive time in minutes: 1 hour 20 minutes = 60 minutes + 20 minutes = 80 minutes. Next, calculate how much time is between 12:00 and 12:45: 45 minutes. Subtract that from your drive time: 80 minutes − 45 minutes = 35 minutes. Finally, calculate what time it will be 35 minutes before 12:00: 11:25. Check your work: 11:25 to 12:00 is 35 minutes. 12:00 to 12:45 is 45 minutes. 35 minutes plus 45 minutes is 80 minutes. Leaving at 11:25 will get you to the field at 12:45, just in time for the 30-minute warm-up. Choice (B) is correct.

## Competency 3: Knowledge of Algebraic Thinking and the Coordinate Plane

### Skill 3.1. Determine whether two algebraic expressions are equivalent by applying properties of operations or equality.

An algebraic expression is a collection of numbers and variables or just variables that may include any of the four operations. Some examples of algebraic expressions are $3x$, $8x^2 - 3y$, $y^3$, and $\dfrac{2x}{5}$. It is important to be able to interpret algebraic expressions as well as to evaluate them. In order to do this, you need to have a basic understanding of mathematical properties and the rules that govern the addition and multiplication of negative and positive numbers.

### Adding and Subtracting Positive and Negative Numbers

If you do not feel confident dealing with negative numbers, you are not alone. Most people do not use negative numbers after they leave their formal education. When you are adding and subtracting negative and positive numbers, it is important to always remember that you are dealing with a position on the number line. A negative number moves you left on the number line, and a positive number moves you right. Take the following example: −2 + 3. If you started at −2 on the number line and jumped three whole numbers to the right, your solution would be 1. Since the four-function calculator that you will use for the FTCE-GKT will not let you use negative numbers, it is important that you estimate your answer before you solve. This will allow you to check for reasonableness.

Subtracting a negative number is the same as adding a positive number. Look at the following example: $2x − (−3) = 2x + 3$. The double negative signs are replaced by a positive sign.

## Multiplying and Dividing Negative and Positive Numbers

When you multiply positive and negative numbers, keep in mind the rule that an even number of negative numbers will result in a positive product as shown below:

| Rule | Example |
|------|---------|
| $(−a)(+b) = −ab$ | $−2(4) = −8$ |
| $(−a)(−b) = +ab$ | $−2(−4) = 8$ |
| $(−a)(+b)(+c) = −abc$ | $−2(4)(6) = −48$ |
| $(−a)(−b)(+c) = +abc$ | $−2(−4)(6) = 48$ |

Note that every time there is an *odd* number of negative numbers, the product is *negative*. Every time there is an *even* number of negative numbers, the product is *positive*.

When you divide negative and positive numbers, there are also rules to keep in mind:

| Rule | Example |
|------|---------|
| $\frac{−a}{−b} = −a ÷ −b = +(a ÷ b)$ | $\frac{−4}{−2} = −4 ÷ −2 = +2$ |
| $\frac{−a}{b} = −a ÷ b = −(a ÷ b)$ | $\frac{−4}{2} = −4 ÷ 2 = −2$ |
| $\frac{a}{−b} = a ÷ −b = −(a ÷ b)$ | $\frac{4}{−2} = 4 ÷ −2 = −2$ |

Note that if either the numerator or denominator is negative, the quotient is negative. If both are negative, the quotient is positive.

## Evaluating Algebraic Expressions

To "evaluate" an algebraic expression means to substitute in the values given for the variables to find the value of the expression. For example, the expression $x + 3y$ cannot be evaluated *until* you are given the values for both $x$ and $y$. Let's say $x = −5$ and $y = 7$. We can substitute those values into the expression:

| | |
|---|---|
| $x + 3y$ | The given algebraic expression |
| $-5 + 3(7)$ | Substitute in the values given. |
| $-5 + 21$ | Evaluate following the order of operations (multiply). |
| 16 | Evaluate following the order of operations (add). |

The value of the expression $x + 3y$ is 16 when $x = -5$ and $y = 7$.

### PROBLEM

Evaluate the expression for the given values.

$$(x + z)^2 - 3z \div x \quad x = 3 \quad \text{and} \quad z = 5$$

(A) 11 (B) 59 (C) $16\frac{1}{3}$ (D) $\frac{1}{3}$

### SOLUTION

Substitute the values for $x$ and $z$ in the algebraic expression and evaluate the expression, following the order of operations.

| | |
|---|---|
| $(x + z)^2 - 3z \div x$ | The given expression |
| $(3 + 5)^2 - 3(5) \div 3$ | Substitute in the given values. |
| $(8)^2 - 3(5) \div 3$ | Evaluate following the order of operations (parentheses). |
| $64 - 3(5) \div 3$ | Evaluate following the order of operations (exponents). |
| $64 - 15 \div 3$ | Evaluate following the order of operations (multiply). |
| $64 - 5$ | Evaluate following the order of operations (divide). |
| 59 | Evaluate following the order of operations (add). |

The correct answer is (B).

## Like Terms

Algebraic expressions can have one or more terms. Some terms can be combined, and other terms cannot. If an expression has two or more *like terms*, then they can be combined. You recognize like terms because they have the same variable to the same power ($4x^4$ and $2x^4$ are like terms). Numbers with no variables, of course, are like terms (3 and $-5$ are like terms). The following table shows some examples of like terms and unlike terms.

|  | Like Terms | Unlike Terms |
|---|---|---|
| 1. | $8 + 2 - 1$ | $4c + 3c^2$ |
| 2. | $5x + 2x - 9x$ | $2y - 5x$ |
| 3. | $2xy + 5xy$ | $x^3 - 3x^2$ |
| 4. | $-5y^2 - 3y^2$ | $3xy + 8x^2y$ |

Since like terms can be combined, the expressions in the first column of the table can be simplified.

The simplified expressions are shown below:

1.  9          2.  $-2x$          3.  $7xy$          4.  $-8y^2$

## Mathematical Properties

In order to correctly solve many of the problems on the FTCE-GKT, you need to have a basic understanding of some common mathematical properties.

The **Commutative Property** works for addition and multiplication only. The Commutative Property of Addition states that if you add two terms (they may be numbers or variables), the order does not affect the sum. That is, $4 + 3 = 3 + 4$. In this example, you can see that the answers on both sides of the equal sign are the same even though the order of the two numbers is different. This property works with variables as well. $12 + y = y + 12$. Even though we do not know the value of $y$, we can be certain that both sides of the equation are equal because the same two terms are being added on each side. The Commutative Property also works for multiplication. $9 \times 5 = 5 \times 9$ illustrates the Commutative Property of Multiplication. Both sides of the equation equal 45. If there are variables involved, such as in the example, $ab = ba$, we know both sides are equal because we are multiplying the same two numbers, just in a different order.

The **Associative Property** is a grouping property that works for both addition and multiplication. The Order of Operations tells us that the first thing we must do when simplifying expressions is to simplify operations within grouping symbols. Therefore, if given the expression $(4 + 6) + 2$, you would add 4 and 6 together before adding 2. However, let's compare the following expressions: $(4 + 6) + 2$ and $4 + (6 + 2)$. Notice that both expressions contain only addition, the same three numbers, and a set of parentheses. The difference is that the first expression groups 4 and 6 together while the second expression groups 6 and 2 together. How do the answers compare?

$(4 + 6) + 2 =$          $4 + (6 + 2) =$

$10 + 2 =$          $4 + 8 =$

$12$          $12$

Notice that both expressions yield the same answer. The Associative Property changes the numbers that are grouped together, but it does not change the answer.

To see how the Associative Property of multiplication works, we can compare the following two expressions that contain only multiplication, the same three numbers, and one set of grouping symbols. The only difference is which numbers are grouped together.

$(5 \times 8) \times 6 =$   $\qquad$   $5 \times (8 \times 6) =$

$40 \times 6 =$   $\qquad$   $5 \times 48 =$

$240$   $\qquad$   $240$

As you can see, both answers are the same even though in one expression, we multiplied 5 and 8 before multiplying by 6, and in the other expression, we multiplied 8 by 6 before multiplying by 5.

The **Distributive Property** of multiplication over addition shows that $a(b + c)$ is equal to $ab + ac$. You can prove this property is true by substituting in some numbers.

Does $4(30 + 6) = (4 \times 30) + (4 \times 6)$?

| Original Problem | $4(30 + 6)$ | $(4 \times 30) + (4 \times 6)$ |
|---|---|---|
| Step #1 | $4(36)$ | $(120) + (24)$ |
| Step #2 | $144$ | $144$ |

As you can see, the two expressions are equal. When dealing with numbers only, it does not make sense to use the Distributive Property; that is, it is not more efficient. However, when working with variables, using the Distributive Property is necessary to simplify an expression to remove parentheses. For example, $5(x + 3)$ can be rewritten as $5x + 15$. There is no other way to simplify the expression except to use the Distributive Property.

### PROBLEM

Which of the expressions below is equivalent to $35y + 60$?

(A)  $95y$   $\qquad\qquad$   (B)  $(35 + y + 60)$

(C)  $5(7y + 12)$   $\qquad\qquad$   (D)  $5 + (7y + 12)$

### SOLUTION

This problem requires being able to work with the Distributive Property. The two terms in the given expression have a GCF of 5. Therefore, you can divide both terms by 5 and take out 5 as a factor. So, $35y + 60 = 5(7y + 12)$ because $\frac{35y}{5} = 7y$ and $\frac{60}{5} = 12$. (C) is the correct answer. To check that it is correct, use the Distributive Property. Multiply 5 by both $7y$ and 12. You will get $35y + 60$; this verifies your answer.

The **Additive Identity Property** (also called the Additive Property of Zero) states that if you add zero to any number, the number retains its identity, so $53 + 0 = 53$. The **Multiplicative Identity Property** states that if you multiply any number by 1 it retains its identity, so $53 \times 1 = 53$. The **Multiplicative Property of Zero** states that if you multiply any number, positive or negative, by zero, the product is zero. $53 \times 0 = 0$ and $53 \times 200 \times 0 = 0$. It does not matter how many numbers you are multiplying together, if one of the numbers is zero, the product is zero.

### PROBLEM

The expression $2x(x - 3)$ is equal to which of the following expressions?

(A) $3x - 1$     (B) $2x^2 + 6x$     (C) $2x^2 - 6x$     (D) $2x^2 - 6$

### SOLUTION

By using the Distributive Property, $2x(x - 3) = (2x)(x) + (2x)(-3) = 2x^2 - 6x$.
The correct answer is (C).

### PROBLEM

Determine if the following algebraic expressions are true or false when $x = 0$ and $y = 1$?

(A) $2xy = 0$     (B) $2x + y = 1$     (C) $3y + x = 3$     (D) $3xy + y = 4$

### SOLUTION

This problem requires an understanding of the Identity and Zero Properties of Multiplication and Addition.

Choice (A): Anything multiplied by zero equals zero. $2(0)(1) = 0$, so this is true.

Choice (B): $2x = 2(0) = 0$. $0 + 1 = 1$, so this is true.

Choice (C): Anything multiplied by 1 keeps its identity, so $3y = 3(1) = 3$. $3 + 0 = 3$, so this is true,

Choice (D): $3xy = 3(x)(y) = 3(0)(1) = 0$. $0 + 1 = 4$, so this is false.

## Skill 3.2. Identify an algebraic expression, equation, or inequality that models a real-world situation.

Being able to translate algebraic expressions into word phrases and word phrases into algebraic expressions is a useful skill. The chart below shows some different ways to translate a variety of algebraic expressions.

| Algebraic Expressions | Word Phrases |
|---|---|
| $y + 3$ | • $y$ increased by 3<br>• $y$ plus 3<br>• 3 more than $y$<br>• $y$ and 3 |
| $7x$ | • 7 times $x$<br>• the product of $x$ and 7<br>• $x$ multiplied by 7 |
| $\dfrac{p}{3}$ | • $p$ divided by 3<br>• the quotient of $p$ and 3 |
| $m - 1$ | • $m$ decreased by 1<br>• 1 less than $m$<br>• $m$ minus 1<br>• 1 subtracted from $m$ |

Sometimes you have to translate words into algebraic expressions. For example, you could be told that Sophia is 4 years older than Gabriella and asked to write an algebraic expression for Sophia's age. Let's say Gabriella is $G$ years old; then Sophia would be $G + 4$ years old because she is 4 years older than Gabriella.

### PROBLEM

Harriet is $H$ years old. Her cousin Martha is 2 years less than three times Harriet's age. Which expression below shows the sum of Harriet's and Martha's ages?

(A)  $3H - 2$

(B)  $3H - 2 + H$

(C)  $2H - 3$

(D)  $2H - 3 + H$

### SOLUTION

To find the correct expression, you could make a "key," which clarifies what each algebraic expression means.

**MATHEMATICS**

CHAPTER
3

$H$ = Harriet's age

$3H - 2$ = Martha's age

$3H - 2 + H$ = The sum of Harriet's and Martha's ages

After you have written the key, you can use it to write the algebraic expression that means the sum of Harriet's and Martha's ages. Remember that "sum" indicates addition. Choice (B) is the correct answer. ***Note: This would further simplify to $4H - 2$.***

### PROBLEM

Your cell phone plan includes a base rate of $25.00 a month for text and calls. Any data used costs $15.00 a gigabyte, and you have budgeted to spend no more than $50.00 a month on your cell phone bill. What inequality represents how much data (d) you can use a month?

(A)  $\$50 = \$15d + \$25$     (B)  $\$15 = \$50d + \$25$

(C)  $\$50 \geq \$15d + \$25$     (D)  $\$50 \leq \$15d + \$25$

### SOLUTION

Since you want your bill to be no more than $50, you should eliminate choice (B), which has the bill as $15. Choices (A), (C), and (D) are all similar except for the signs. Eliminate choice (A) because your bill does not have to equal $50 to meet your budget. This leaves choices (C) and (D). The right side of the inequality is the amount you actually pay, so since you want it to be *less* than the left side, choice (C) is correct. It is the only choice that has your bill equal to or less than $50. ***Note:*** $\$50 \geq \$15d + \$25$ is equal to $\$15d + \$25 \leq \$50$.

### PROBLEM

To park at an airport, you pay $9.00 a day. To save money, you can buy a parking pass for $35.00 a month, then pay only $6 a day. What system of equations can represent this situation? After how many days will purchasing the pass be a better deal?

### SOLUTION

Using the formula $y = mx + b$, we can set up the equations that represent this situation. First look at the daily rate. If we use $c$ to equal the cost and $d$ to equal the number of days, we can determine that the cost is $9 per day or $c = \$9d$. Notice that since we don't pay a flat rate for a pass, we do not put anything in place of the $b$ in the equation. Next we can create a formula for purchasing

**137**

the monthly pass: $c = \$6d + \$35$. This time we put in $35 for $b$ since there is a monthly flat rate. To calculate how many days it will take to actually save money, ask yourself how much you are saving per day. You are saving $\$9 - \$6 = \$3$ per day. If you divide the $35 cost of the pass by $3 per day, you get $11\frac{2}{3}$ days. So, it's on day twelve that you actually start saving money.

## ■ Skill 3.3. Solve equations and inequalities (e.g., linear, quadratic) graphically or algebraically.

### Solving Algebraic Equations

A linear equation is an algebraic equation whose independent variable is to the first power. To solve an equation involving one operation, you must apply the inverse operation to solve it. The inverse operation means the opposite operation. The opposite of addition is subtraction and vice versa. The opposite of multiplication is division and vice versa. You must always do the same thing to both sides of an equation to keep it balanced. When you are presented with an equation, the expression on the left is equal to the expression on the right. Therefore, if you manipulate the equation in any way, you must be sure to do the same thing to both expressions. For example, if you subtract 5 from one side of an equation, you must subtract 5 from the other side, as shown below.

$$y + 5 = 12$$
$$-5 + y + 5 = 12 - 5$$
$$y = 7$$

### PROBLEM

A box of pens costs $1.89. What equation would allow you to calculate the cost ($C$) of multiple boxes ($B$) of pens?

(A)  $B = 1.89C$          (B)  $C = 1.89B$

(C)  $1.89 = B + C$        (D)  $B - 1.89 = C$

### SOLUTION

If you want, you can create a table for this problem. The relationship in the problem shows that for each box of pens, the cost is $1.89. Therefore, 2 boxes would be 2($1.89). Three boxes would be 3($1.89), etc. So, to find the total cost of $B$ boxes of pens, multiply the price for 1 box ($1.89) by $B$. The correct answer is (B), $C = 1.89B$.

When you are asked to evaluate an expression, you may be given values for any exponents in the problem. If $a + b$, and you are given $a = 2$ and $b = 3$, you would replace the variables in the equation. Once you substitute the variables, you would have $2 + 3$.

**PROBLEM**

Evaluate the expression below for $x = 2$ and $y = -3$

$$-5y + x^3$$

(A) 23        (B) -7        (C) 21        (D) -9

**SOLUTION**

| | |
|---|---|
| $-5y + x^3$ | The problem |
| $-5(-3) + (2)^3$ | Substitute in the values given. |
| $-5(-3) + 8$ | Evaluate following the order of operations (exponents). |
| $15 + 8$ | Evaluate following the order of operations (multiply). |
| $23$ | Evaluate following the order of operations (add). |

The correct answer is (A), 23.

## Solving Two-Step Equations

A two-step equation is an equation that requires performing two inverse operations to find the solution. A two-step equation has multiplication or division and addition or subtraction. You must do addition or subtraction before you do multiplication or division.

$$6y - 3 = 27$$
$$+3 \quad +3$$
$$6y = 30$$
$$\frac{6y}{6} = \frac{30}{6}$$
$$y = 5$$

$$\frac{m}{4} + 7 = 10$$
$$-7 \quad -7$$
$$\frac{m}{4} = 3$$
$$(4)\frac{m}{4} = 3(4)$$
$$m = 12$$

Some word problems lend themselves to being solved by writing and solving two-step equations.

Let's take a look at one: Jon is 5 years older than Zachary. Ben is twice Jon's age. The sum of all three of their ages is 39. Find Ben's age. You can solve this algebraically. First you should start by making a key. A key indicates what each algebraic expression represents.

$z$ = Zachary's age

$z + 5$ = Jon's age

$2(z + 5)$ = Ben's age

Write an equation based on the information given in the problem.

| | |
|---|---|
| $z + z + 5 + 2(z + 5) = 39$ | Zachary's age + Jon's age + Ben's age = 39 |
| $z + z + 5 + 2z + 10 = 39$ | Do the Distributive Property. |
| $4z + 15 = 39$ | Collect like terms. |
| $4z = 24$ | Subtract 15 from both sides. |
| $z = 6$ | Divide both sides by 4. |

Since you know that $z = 6$, use your key to determine that Zachary is 6, Jon is 11, and Ben is 22. Check and see that all three ages add to 39, which they do, so you know you are correct.

**PROBLEM**

The sum of three consecutive integers is 165. Find the largest of the three integers.

(A) 54          (B) 55          (C) 56          (D) 57

**SOLUTION**

Let's think about the difference between two consecutive whole numbers on a number line. The number to the right is always one greater than the one on the left. So if you represent the first number as $n$, the second would be $n + 1$, and the third would be $n + 1 + 1$. Now combine these in an equation and set them equal to 165:

| | |
|---|---|
| $(n) + (n + 1) + (n + 1 + 1) = 3n + 3 = 165$ | The original equation |
| $3n = 162$ | Subtract 3 from both sides. |
| $n = 54$ | Divide both sides by three. |

Since $n$ is the smallest of the three numbers, we have to solve for $(n + 1 + 1)$, the largest number. $54 + 1 + 1 = 56$. To check your work, add the three numbers: $54 + 55 + 56 = 165$, so (C), $n = 56$, is the correct answer.

**PROBLEM**

Simplify: $5x - 2(x - 3) = 6(2x + x)$

(A) $-6$          (B) $-2$          (C) $\dfrac{2}{5}$          (D) $\dfrac{15}{2}$

**SOLUTION**

| | |
|---|---|
| $5x - 2(x - 3) = 6(2x + x)$ | The original problem |
| $5x - 2(x - 3) = 6(3x)$ | Combine like terms. |
| $5x - 2x + 6 = 18x$ | Use the distributive property. |
| $3x + 6 = 18x$ | Combine like terms. |
| $3x + 6 - 3x = 18x - 3x$ | Subtract $3x$ from both sides. |
| $6 = 15x$ | Divide both sides by 15. |
| $\dfrac{6}{15} = \dfrac{15}{15}x$ | Simplify |
| $\dfrac{2}{5} = x$ | The solution |

## Solving Linear Inequalities

Inequalities are statements that show the relationship between two quantities.

There are four inequality symbols:

> Greater than

≥ Greater than or equal to

< Less than

≤ Less than or equal to

Inequalities are solved in a similar manner to solving equations. Just as in an equation, an inequality requires you to use the inverse operation of the operation that is in the problem to solve it. Also, you must do the same thing to both sides of an equation and both sides of an inequality to keep the relationship true. The main difference between solving equations and inequalities occurs when you multiply or divide an inequality by a negative number. When you do, you must *reverse* the inequality symbol to keep the inequality true. Examine the solution to the inequality below.

| | |
|---|---|
| $-8x + 2 < 26$ | Original inequality |
| $-8x < 24$ | Subtract 2 from both sides. |
| $x > -3$ | Divide both sides by $-8$ and *flip* the inequality symbol to find the solution set. |

Another difference between equations and inequalities is that for most equations, there is only one solution, while an inequality has a *range* of solutions. For example, if the solution to an inequality is $x > 5$, then any number greater than 5 is a solution. There are an infinite number of numbers that are greater than 5. In addition to whole numbers, there are also fractions and decimals.

## Graphing Linear Inequalities

Because there are often an infinite number of solutions to an inequality, they are sometimes shown on a number line.

> $>$ means "greater than" is indicated by an open circle and an arrow pointing to the right.

> $\geq$ means "greater than or equal to" is indicated by a solid circle and an arrow pointing to the right.

> $<$ means "less than" is indicated by an open circle and an arrow pointing to the left.

> $\leq$ means "less than or equal to" is indicated by a solid circle and an arrow pointing to the left.

As we said earlier, solving inequalities is just like solving an equation, except for one crucial difference: Any time you multiply or divide the equation by a negative number, you have to flip the direction of the inequality sign. Look at the following examples:

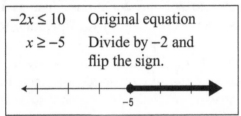

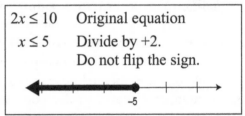

| | |
|---|---|
| $-2x \leq 10$ | Original equation |
| $x \geq -5$ | Divide by $-2$ and flip the sign. |

| | |
|---|---|
| $2x \leq 10$ | Original equation |
| $x \leq 5$ | Divide by $+2$. Do not flip the sign. |

**PROBLEM**

Which number line shows the solutions to the inequality: $-2x - 9 \leq 5$

(A) Show $x \geq 7$

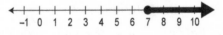

(B) Show $x \geq -7$

(C) Show $x \leq 7$

(D) Show $x \leq -7$

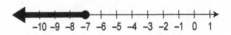

**SOLUTION**

To solve the following two-step inequality, first add 9 to both sides and then divide both sides by −2. Remember to flip the inequality symbol since you are dividing by a negative number. Your solution is $x \geq -7$, so (B) is the correct answer.

**PROBLEM**

Solve the inequality: $-2(x - 8) \leq 3x + 1$

    (A) $x \geq 3$     (B) $x \leq 3$     (C) $x \geq -3$     (D) $x \leq -3$

**SOLUTION**

| | |
|---|---|
| $-2(x - 8) \leq 3x + 1$ | The original inequality |
| $-2x + 16 \leq 3x + 1$ | Do the distributive property. |
| $\quad - 16 \qquad - 16$ | Subtract 16 from both sides. |
| $-2x \leq 3x - 15$ | |
| $- 3x - 3x$ | Subtract $3x$ from both sides. |
| $\dfrac{- 5x \leq}{- 5} \quad \dfrac{- 15}{- 5}$ | Divide both sides by −5. |
| $x \geq 3$ | Flip the inequality symbol. |

The correct answer is (A).

## Skill 3.4. Determine and solve equations or inequalities, graphically or algebraically, in real-world problems.

The FTCE-GKT will ask you to solve word problems that translate into inequalities. For instance, you may be asked to calculate the greatest amount of your income that you could spend for rent ($r$) if your payment could not be more than 70% of your income ($i$). The word **greatest** in this situation indicates that you will use a **less than or equal to sign** (≤) because your rent payment would have to be less than or equal to (.70) × (income) or $r \leq 0.70i$. If the problem asks you to calculate the least amount of money you can make to pay your monthly bills ($b$), you would use a greater than or equal to (≥) sign, and your income would have to be ≥ your total bills or $i \geq b$.

### PROBLEM

A salesman receives a base salary of $300 a month, plus 10% of his sales. How much do his average weekly sales ($s$) have to be to make enough money to cover his monthly expenses of $950?

(A) $s \leq \$650$    (B) $s \leq \$6,500$   (C) $s \geq \$1,625$   (D) $s \leq \$1,625$

### SOLUTION

First convert this to an equation with $s$ representing his sales. We have been given the total he needs to make, $950, and we know that he has to make *at least* that amount to pay his bills. We also know that his base salary is $300 plus 10% of his sales (convert the percent to a decimal: $10\% = 10/100 = 0.1$). This translates into the following equation:

$950 \leq 300 + 0.1s$    The original equation

$650 \leq 0.1s$    Subtract 300 from both sides.

$6500 \leq s$    Divide both sides by 0.1.

What does this answer mean? It means that his *sales* have to be greater than or equal to $6,500 a month to pay his bills, but the question takes this one step further. We now have to divide his monthly sales by 4, the number of weeks in a month. $6500 \div 4 = 1625$. He has to make an average of $1,625 a week in sales. The correct answer is (C). *Note: $s \geq \$1,625$ is equal to $\$1,625 \leq s$.*

### PROBLEM

A teacher wants to purchase supplies for her class. She has budgeted $25.00 to use for the purchase. If she purchased 60 pencils for $3.00 a dozen, and erasers cost half as much as pencils, how many erasers can she still purchase?

(A) 120        (B) 100        (C) 80        (D) 60

### SOLUTION

First, calculate how much she spent on pencils. There are 12 pencils in a dozen, and 60 divided by 12 is 5. The cost of 5 dozen pencils at $3.00 a dozen equals $15.00. She is starting with $25.00, so that means she has $10.00 left to spend on erasers. Now calculate the cost of a single pencil: $\$3.00 \div 12 = \$0.25$ a pencil. If a pencil costs $0.25, and erasers cost half as much, the erasers cost $0.25/2 or $0.125. Now write your equation $\$0.125e = \$10.00$. Divide both sides by $0.125, and you have $e = 80$. She can purchase 80 erasers. The correct answer is (C).

## ■ Skill 3.5. Graph and interpret a linear equation in real-world problems (e.g., use data to plot points, explain slope and *y*-intercept, determine additional solutions).

### Graphing Linear Equations

In order to graph a linear equation, you must first have a basic understanding of the coordinate plane. The coordinate plane is made up of two perpendicular axes. The *x*-axis is horizontal, and the *y*-axis is vertical. Where the two axes intersect is called the **origin**; this point has the coordinates (0, 0). The intersection of the two axes creates four separate areas called quadrants. **Quadrant I** is in the upper right hand corner. **Quadrants II, III, and IV** are located counterclockwise to Quadrant I.

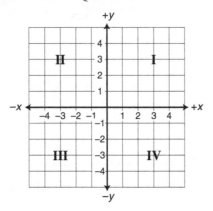

To plot a point on the coordinate plane, you must have both an ***x*-coordinate** and a ***y*-coordinate**. The *x*-coordinate tells how many spaces to move left or right, and the *y*-coordinate tells you how many spaces to move up or down. If you want to plot the point (4, 3), for example, start at the origin. Move four spaces to the right, then move three spaces up. To plot the point (−2, 5), start at the origin and move two spaces to the left, then move five spaces up. To plot (1, −8), start at the origin. Move one space to the right and then eight spaces down. To plot (0, −3), start at the origin. Do not move any spaces left or right, then move three spaces down. If you are asked to identify the coordinate of a plotted point, remember to always list the *x*-coordinate first, followed by the *y*-coordinate.

## PROBLEM

Identify the coordinates of the points in the graph.

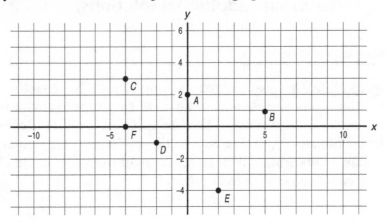

## SOLUTION

The coordinates for the points above are as follows: $A$ (0, 2), $B$ (5, 1), $C$ (–4, 3), $D$ (–2, –1), $E$ (2, –4), and $F$ (–4, 0).

## Distance Between Two Points

To find the distance between two points, use the distance formula from your math reference guide.

$$\sqrt{(x_2 - x_1)^2 + (y_2 - y_1)^2}$$

The first step to using the distance formula is to take the two points and name them Point 1 and Point 2. Let's say that Point 1 is (3, 5) and Point 2 is (4, 9). Next assign the following variables to represent the points in the equation:

| Point 1 | Point 2 |
| --- | --- |
| (3, 5) | (4, 9) |
| $(x_1, y_1)$ | $(x_2, y_2)$ |

So we assign the following values: $x_1 = 3$, $y_1 = 5$, $x_2 = 4$, and $y_2 = 9$. Now we can plug the values into the distance formula:

$$\text{Distance} = \sqrt{(x_2 - x_1)^2 + (y_2 - y_1)^2}$$

$$\text{Distance} = \sqrt{(4 - 3)^2 + (9 - 5)^2}$$

$$\text{Distance} = \sqrt{(1)^2 + (4)^2}$$

$$\text{Distance} = \sqrt{1 + 16}$$

$$\text{Distance} = \sqrt{17}, \text{ which is approximately 4.1 units.}$$

## Midpoint of a Line

To find the midpoint of a line, use the endpoints as Point 1 and Point 2, then enter them into the midpoint formula from your math reference guide. For instance, if you needed to find the midpoint of a line that had endpoints of (2, −4) and (6, 8), you could assign the following values: $x_1 = 2$, $y_1 = -4$, $x_2 = 6$, and $y_2 = 8$. *Note:* It does not matter which point you designate to represent Point 1 or Point 2, only that you do not mix them up once you have made that determination. Now enter the points into the midpoint formula:

$$\left( \frac{x_1 + x_2}{2} \right), \left( \frac{y_1 + y_2}{2} \right)$$

$$\left( \frac{2 + 6}{2} \right), \left( \frac{-4 + 8}{2} \right)$$

$$(4), (2)$$

So the midpoint of the line is located at (4, 2).

## Slope

If you know two points on a line, you can find the **slope** of the line. The slope of a line is the steepness of the line, and it can be found by dividing the vertical change between two points by the horizontal change of the two points. We can use any two points on a line to find its slope because the slope of a line is constant. The diagram below shows line *AC*, which is made up of an infinite number of points. Three of the points are labeled *A*, *B*, and *C*.

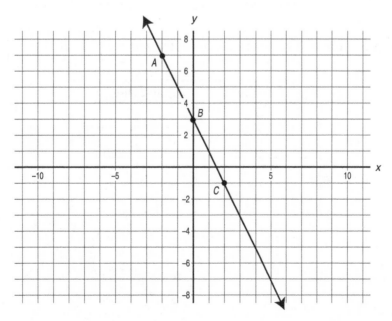

Let's use points $B$ and $C$ to find the slope of the line. The coordinates of point $B$ are $(0, 3)$, and the coordinates of point $C$ are $(2, -1)$. We can consider point $B$ as point 1 and point $C$ as point 2, so $x_1 = 0$, $y_1 = 3$, $x_2 = 2$, and $y_2 = -1$.

$$\frac{y_2 - y_1}{x_2 - x_1} = \frac{-1 - 3}{2 - 0} = \frac{-4}{2} = -2$$

Therefore, the slope passing through $(0, 3)$ and $(2, -1)$ is $-2$.

## Solving Real-World Problems Based on Data

On the FTCE-GKT, you will be asked to solve real-world problems based on data tables, line graphs, bar graphs, and word problems. These topics are also covered under Competency 4.

## Interpreting Data Tables

Tables can show relationships between two variables. Recognizing the pattern allows you to generate more values in the table. For example, look at the table below. What is the pattern between the $x$-values and the $y$-values? Notice that the $y$-values are all twice the $x$-values. Knowing that, what would be the missing $y$-value in the table?

| $x$-values | $y$-values |
|:---:|:---:|
| 7 | 14 |
| 9 | 18 |
| −3 | −6 |
| −1 | |

The missing $y$-value will be twice the $x$-value, which is $-1$. $2(-1) = -2$. The missing $y$-value is $-2$.

| $x$-values | $y$-values |
|:---:|:---:|
| 7 | 14 |
| 9 | 18 |
| −3 | −6 |
| −1 | −2 |

**PROBLEM**

Which equation shows the relationship between the *x*- and *y*-values in the table?

| *x*-values | *y*-values |
|:---:|:---:|
| 18 | 12 |
| 10 | 4 |
| 4 | −2 |

(A) $y = x - 6$     (B) $y = 2x$

(C) $x = y - 6$     (D) $x = 2y$

**SOLUTION**

To find the relationship in the table, look at the relationship between the *x*-values and *y*-values. Each *y*-value is found by taking the corresponding *x*-value and subtracting 6 from it. The correct answer is $y = x - 6$, which is answer choice (A).

## Slope and *Y*-Intercept in an Equation

The point at which a line crosses the *y*-axis is called the *y*-intercept. When matching an equation to a real-world problem with a graph, the *y*-intercept provides your first critical clue. If an equation is in slope-intercept form ($y = mx + b$), *m* gives you the slope of the line and *b* gives you the *y*-intercept. Take, for instance, the following problem: Your cell phone plan has a base cost of $40 a month, plus $15 for every 1 GB of data you use. The base cost would be the *y*-intercept. Now find the part of the problem that is variable: the slope of the line. That would be the cost of the data (*d*), which we would represent as 15*d*. The total equation would be cost = 15*d* + 40. On the FTCE-GKT you will be given word problems or graphs and asked to identify the appropriate equation. The graph of the previous problem would look like this:

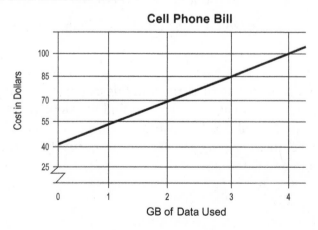

Note that the range on the $y$-axis starts at 0 and jumps to 25. Since the base cost is $40, there is no reason to include the lower numbers on the graph. The interval on the graph is 15 since we are increasing in increments of $15. When you design a graph, choose the interval that best fits your data. When choosing the range of numbers on your axis, you should always start with a number that is one interval below the lowest data point you are graphing and end with a number just over the maximum number you are using. On the FTCE-GKT you may be required to choose the best designed graph to match a word problem. Be sure to check the range, the interval, and that "jumps" in the lower end of the $y$-axis are represented properly. Also, if asked to use the graph to identify the slope of your line, you can use the rise (how far the line goes up [+] or down [−]) over the run (how far the line moves right [+] or left [−]). In this case the line is rising +15 units for every +1 unit it runs, so your slope would be $\frac{15}{1} = 15$.

### PROBLEM

Laura gets an hourly rate for helping out at her mom's office. The graph below shows Laura's earnings. What is the slope of the graph, and what does it represent?

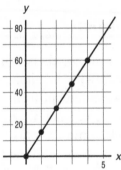

(A) The slope is $15, and it is Laura's hourly rate.

(B) The slope is 5, and it is the number of hours Laura worked.

(C) The slope is $75, and it is the total amount of money Laura earned.

(D) The slope is 0, and it is the number of hours Laura worked for 0 dollars.

### SOLUTION

The slope of a line is its rate of change. In this example, the slope would represent Laura's hourly rate. There are two ways to find the slope of the line. The first way is using the slope formula. Select two points from the line. Let's use (2, 30) and (4, 60), and label them $(x_1, y_1)$ and $(x_2, y_2)$, respectively. Substitute them into the slope formula to find the slope.

$$\frac{y_2 - y_1}{x_2 - x_1} = \frac{60 + 30}{4 - 2} = 15$$

The second method is to calculate the rise/run of the line. Counting the units up from (0, 0) to (2, 30) the rise is 30 units. Counting the units the line moves to the right between the same points, you get a run of 2 units. $\frac{30}{2} = 15$, so the slope is 15, which is Laura's hourly rate. The correct answer is (A).

**PROBLEM**

Which statement below correctly describes the air temperature on Wednesday shown in the line graph?

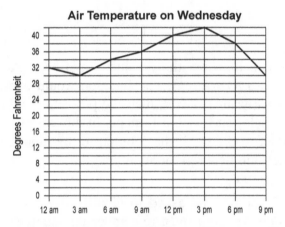

(A) The temperature rises steadily from 12 a.m. until 6 a.m., then decreases until 6 p.m., and then increases until 9 p.m.

(B) The temperature decreases after 9 a.m., increases until 12 p.m., decreases until 6 p.m., and then holds steady until 9 p.m.

(C) The temperature decreases slightly after 12 a.m., then increases until 3 p.m., and then decreases until 9 p.m.

(D) The temperature increases until 12 p.m., then decreases until 9 p.m.

**SOLUTION**

Reading a line graph requires paying close attention to the labels on the axes. This line graph shows the time on the *x*-axis and the temperature on the *y*-axis. Before reading the answer choices, take a look at the line graph and see what you notice. You can see that the temperature goes down, then up, and then down again. Now, read the answer choices to find the one that matches up with the information on the line graph. Answer choice (C) is the only correct answer.

*Note:* Can you identify how the graph above could be better designed? The range of data on the *y*-axis should go to 44 so that the top of the line is not at the very top of the graph. Also, the numbers on the *y*-axis should jump from 0 to 28 in order to make the graph more concise.

## Skill 3.6. Identify relations that satisfy the definition of a function.

All functions have three parts: an **input**, a **relationship**, and an **output**. Functions operate much like equations, but they are written a little differently. For instance, take the equation $y = x + 3$. This is a linear equation with infinite solutions. Some solutions to this equation are listed in the following table:

| x | y |
|---|---|
| 0 | 3 |
| 1 | 4 |
| 2 | 5 |

If this was written as a function, the $y$ value would be replaced with $f(x)$, and the equation would be written $f(x) = x + 3$. The function would operate in much the same way as the equation. If we wanted $x = 2$, then the problem would be $f(2) = 2 + 3 = 5$. You would get the same solution for both formats. In this case the input would be 2 (the value of $x$) and the output would be 5 (the solution to the function). But what about the relationship? The relationship between the input and the output is +3, because the output is always 3 more than the input.

On the FTCE-GKT, you will be asked to identify if a figure or a table represents a function. In order to do this, you must remember one simple rule: The value of $x$ is never repeated in a function. In a data table, that means you must check the $x$ values to be sure none are duplicates. It does not matter if numbers are repeated for the $y$ value. With a geometric figure or line graph, you can use the **vertical line test**. To do this, hold your pencil vertically and slide it across the figure or line. If it never crosses the figure in more than one place, it is a function. Look at the following examples of functions and non-functions:

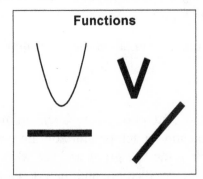

**Functions**

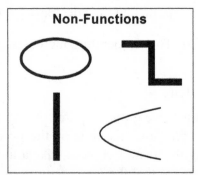

**Non-Functions**

Notice that the functions will all pass the vertical line test. The vertical line would only pass through one point in each of the figures in the function box, including the horizontal line. The images in the non-function box would not pass the test. Notice that there is a vertical line in the non-function box. Vertical lines are never functions.

If you are given a data table or a list of coordinates, review the $x$ coordinates to determine if they are functions. For instance, {(2, 2), (3, 2), and (4, 2)} would represent a function since every $x$ coordinate is different. If the points were {(2, 3), (2, 4), and (2, 5)} the figure would not be a function since the $x$ coordinate 2 repeats in the data set.

 ## Skill 3.7. Compare the slopes of two linear functions represented algebraically and graphically.

### Parallel Lines

Two lines are parallel if they lie in the same plane and do not intersect. The symbol for parallel is $\parallel$.

In the diagram below, line $XY$ is parallel to line $VW$.

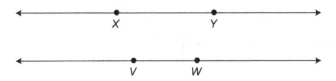

### Perpendicular Lines

Two lines or line segments are perpendicular if they intersect and form right angles. The symbol for perpendicular is $\perp$. In the diagram below, segment $AB \perp$ segment $CD$.

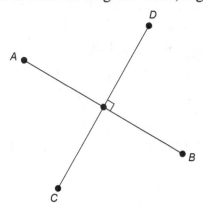

On the FTCE-GKT, you will have to identify whether a pair of lines are parallel or perpendicular based on their slope. To do this the lines must be in slope-intercept form, $y = mx + b$, with $m$ equal to the slope and $b$ equal to the $y$-intercept. Once the lines are in the proper form, compare the slopes. If they are the same, the lines are parallel. If the slopes of the lines are negative inverses of one another, they are perpendicular. To find the negative inverse of a number, you must invert it and change its sign. Here are some examples of equations that are perpendicular:

$$y = 2x + 1 \quad \text{and} \quad y = -\frac{1}{2}x + 4$$

$$y = \frac{1}{4}x - 2 \quad \text{and} \quad y = -4x + 7$$

These lines are parallel:

$$y = 2x + 1 \quad \text{and} \quad y = 2x - 3$$

$$y = \frac{1}{2}x - 4 \quad \text{and} \quad y = \frac{1}{2}x + 2$$

As you can see, the $y$-intercept has no bearing if a pair of lines is parallel or perpendicular.

## PROBLEM

Are the following lines parallel, perpendicular, or neither parallel nor perpendicular?

$$2x + y = 4 \quad \text{and} \quad 4x + 2y = 2$$

(A) Parallel　　(B) Perpendicular　　(C) Neither

## SOLUTION

Original problem:

$$2x + y = 4 \quad \text{and} \quad 4x + 2y = 2$$

Put the line in slope-intercept form by subtracting the $x$ variable and its coefficient from both sides.

$$y = -2x + 4 \quad \text{and} \quad 2y = -4x + 2$$

Divide the second equation by 2 to isolate the $y$.

$$y = -2x + 4 \quad \text{and} \quad y = -2x + 1$$

Compare the slopes

$$m = -2 \quad\quad\quad\quad m = -2$$

The lines have the same slope, so they are parallel. The correct answer is (A).

## Competency 4: Knowledge of Probability, Statistics, and Data Interpretation

■ **Skill 4.1. Analyze data presented in various forms (e.g., histograms, bar graphs, circle graphs, pictographs, line plots, tables) to solve problems.**

Information or data can be displayed in charts, tables, or a variety of graphs. The main reason that data is collected is so that it can be analyzed. Some data is better suited for being displayed in one form rather than another. For example, data that shows change over time is well suited for a line graph. Scatter plots are useful for examining trends. Venn diagrams help to see where two or more sets of data intersect. When you are given data in a chart, table, or graph, the best thing you can do is take your time reading the information. Look at some questions that you might ask yourself: What is the title? What information is on the *x*-axis and the *y*-axis? What is the scale being used? What is the time period being covered? If you are examining a pictograph, did you look at the key? It is critical to analyze all aspects of a graph before you can properly interpret its data.

### Circle Graphs

Circle graphs, also known as pie graphs or pie charts, are good for showing how the parts to a whole relate to one another. The circle graph below shows the percentages consumers spent on different areas in 2018. Notice that the portions of the pie chart are given in percents. It is possible, however, to find the actual amount of money spent on each category by calculating their values based on the average total expenditure of $29,846 that is given at the top of the graph. To find how much money was spent on housing, you could find 32% of $29,846 by completing the following computation: $0.32 \times 29846 = 9550.72$, so $9,550.72 was spent on housing.

**Consumer Expenditures in 2018**
Avg. total expenditures: $29,846

## Frequency Tables

A **frequency table** is a way to organize data to see how frequently each value occurs. A common way to organize a frequency table is to make three columns. The first column contains the data values. The second column is for tally marks, and the third column shows the number of times each data value occurs. Below is a sample of a frequency table showing how often the numbers 1–6 were tossed when a die was thrown.

| Number | Tally | Frequency |
|--------|-------|-----------|
| 1 | IIII | 4 |
| 2 | IIII | 5 |
| 3 | III | 3 |
| 4 | III | 3 |
| 5 | II | 2 |
| 6 | III | 3 |

## Stem and Leaf Plots

A stem and leaf plot is a type of frequency table that can be used to group data in an efficient manner. For instance, if students' test scores in a class were 72, 74, 77, 83, 89, and 98, you could display them as follows:

| Stem | Leaf |
|------|------|
| 7 | 2 4 7 |
| 8 | 3 9 |
| 9 | 8 |

Notice that the stem holds the tens place of each number and the leaf holds the ones value.

## Histograms

A **histogram** is a type of bar graph that is similar to a frequency table in that it shows the frequency that data occurs. It is different from a frequency table, however, because it shows the data in bar graph form (with no spaces between the bars) rather than in a table. Often histograms group data into intervals. For example, when looking at the weights of a group of individuals, the weights might be grouped in the following ways: 90–99, 100–109, 110–119, etc. When there is a lot of data, it makes more sense to group the data items in intervals rather than graph each piece of data individually.

Below is an example of a histogram that shows the breakdown of students' grades on an exam. Notice that each bar represents a range of scores rather than a specific score. Looking at the histogram, it is apparent that more students scored in the 60–80 range than in any other range.

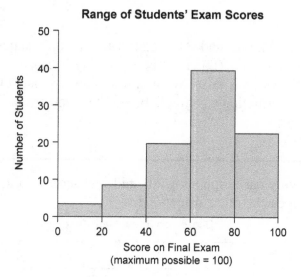

**Range of Students' Exam Scores**

**PROBLEM**

The histogram shows the number of books a group of students read last school year. Which statement about the histogram is NOT true?

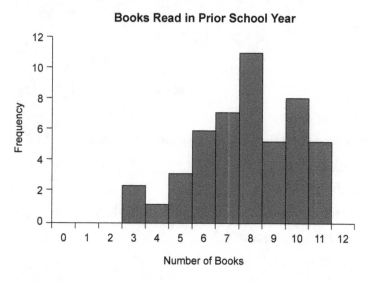

**Books Read in Prior School Year**

(A) The number of students who read 7 books is less than the number of students who read 8 books.

(B) The number of students who read 11 books is more than the sum of the number of students who read 3 books and 4 books.

(C) More students read 10 books than read 9 books.

(D) Four students read one book.

**SOLUTION**

Answer choices (A), (B), and (C) are all true. The only statement that is not true is (D). The statement for (D) could be confusing because it says, "Four students read one book," which is false. What is true, however, is, "One student read four books." When interpreting any graph, be sure that you are reading it correctly.

## Bar Graphs

Look at the following bar graph showing students' scores on a math test. There are many observations that can be made from the data.

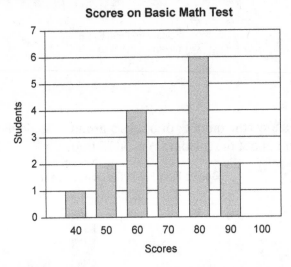

Some possible observations:

• More students scored 80 than any other score (the **mode**).

• 18 students took the test.

• The **range** on the test was 50.

• Almost half of the students scored less than 70 on the test.

• No one achieved a perfect score.

• The **median** score was 70.

**PROBLEM**

A group of seventh grade students was asked what was their favorite subject in school. Their results are depicted in the bar graph. Which statement about the results is *not* true?

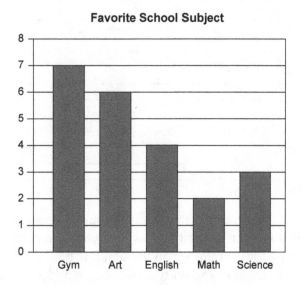

**Favorite School Subject**

(A)  Fewer students chose Math than any other subject.

(B)  Four more students chose Gym than chose Math.

(C)  Twice as many students chose Art than chose Science.

(D)  Four students chose English as their favorite subject.

**SOLUTION**

To answer this question correctly, you have to identify the statement that is not true from the answer choices. Answer choice (A) is true because only 2 students chose Math; this was the least popular subject. Answer choice (C) is true because 3 students chose Science and 6 students chose Art. Twice as many chose Art as Science. Answer choice (D) is true because the bar for English shows that 4 students chose that subject. The only answer choice that is not true is (B); 7 students chose Gym and 2 students chose Math. The difference between those two numbers is 5, not 4. Therefore, answer choice (B) is the only false statement and is thus the correct answer.

## Line Graphs

Line graphs are useful for looking at the change of some value over time. The graph below shows the high and low temperatures as they change over time:

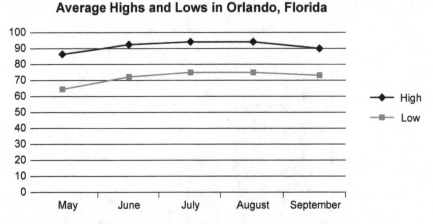

As you can see, the line graph shows that July and August were the hottest months shown in the graph. But is there a way that this data could be better represented? Look at the range of the data. The lowest number on the graph is 66 degrees, and the highest is 92 degrees. It is unnecessary to show the portion of the graph from 10 to 50 degrees because there is no activity to show there.

### PROBLEM

The line graph shows the amount of money the Pattersons have saved over the years. The x-axis shows the years, and the y-axis shows the total amount of money in dollars in the account.

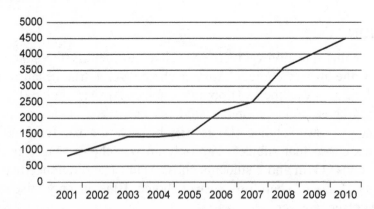

How much money did the Pattersons save from 2001 until 2010?

   (A) $4,500    (B) $4,000    (C) $3,750    (D) $3,500

**SOLUTION**

The question is asking you how much money the Pattersons saved over 9 years. It is *not* asking you how much money they have in their account in 2010. Therefore, you must find the difference between the amount of money in their account in 2010 and the amount of money in their account in 2001. $4,500 – $750 = $3,750. The correct answer is (C).

## Pictographs

A **pictograph** is a visual presentation of data using pictures or symbols instead of bars, lines, or points. The pictures in a pictograph represent a particular number. Sometimes each picture represents a quantity of one; however, other times each picture represents a larger number such as 10, 100, or 1000. Based on the size of the data, the person who is making the pictograph chooses what number each picture will represent.

Here is a sample pictograph of the different sports played by a group of elementary school students. Notice that the key indicates each soccer ball is equivalent to 10 students. Use the graph to calculate the following problem: What percentage of the students surveyed play baseball?

| baseball | ⚽ ⚽ ⚽ ⚽ ⚽ |
|---|---|
| football | ⚽ ⚽ ⚽ |
| soccer | ⚽ ⚽ ⚽ ⚽ ⚽ ⚽ |
| hockey | ⚽ ⚽ |
| basketball | ⚽ ⚽ ⚽ ⚽ |

Key: ⚽ = 10 students

First, you must be able to "read" a pictograph accurately. The number of students who play baseball is 50 (not 5). Now calculate the number who played baseball by the number surveyed: $50 ÷ 200 = 0.25$. Finally, convert this to a percent: $0.25 = 25\%$.

## Scatter Plots

Scatter plots are used to see trends in data. The points on a scatter plot do not represent a line, but can be used to make general statements about the data. The scatter plot on the next page shows an upward trend. To make a prediction using a scatter plot, draw a line in the middle of the data points, as shown on the second scatter plot.

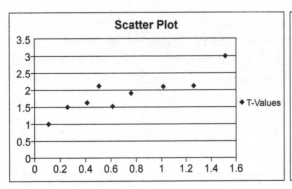

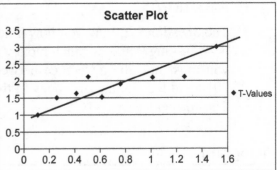

## Skill 4.2. Analyze and evaluate how the presentation of data can lead to different or inappropriate interpretations in the context of a real-world situation.

Graphs can be interpreted in many ways and misinterpretation of the data shown in a graph can result in false conclusions. Look at the graph below:

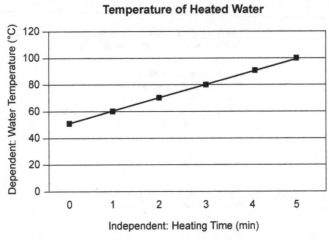

As you can see, the line graph shows a constant increase of about 10 degrees every minute. So even though the graph does not show the temperature of the water past the five-minute mark, we could extrapolate what the temperature would be based on the information that we were given. What temperature would you expect the water to be after 8 minutes? At 5 minutes, the temperature is 100 degrees; the graph shows that the water increases 10 degrees every minute, so you might expect the water to be at 130 degrees after 8 minutes. Although this temperature would follow the pattern of the graph, it would be an incorrect assumption. At sea level, water boils at 100 degrees Celsius. After that point, all added energy is used to change the state of water from a liquid to a gas. Therefore, you must pay attention to the patterns that you see in graphs, but you must also pay attention to what you know to be true in the real world. Using this real-world knowledge, you can predict that after reaching its highest temperature at 5 minutes, the temperature of the water will remain the same, 100 degrees, as time goes on. So, at 8 minutes the temperature would still be 100 degrees.

It is also important to remember that data that is presented in a graph gives the impression of being "correct." However, it is important to know that data can be presented in a variety of ways that can lead to a variety of conclusions. Depending on the scale used in the graphs, the number of years included, or the number of people included in a survey, the data can communicate different things. People who put together graphs are often trying to influence their audiences to see things a certain way that benefits the graph maker, not the consumer. Therefore, you must be cautious when reading "results," recognizing that you may not be seeing the whole picture. Do not assume that the graph you are seeing is depicting the data in an unbiased way.

**PROBLEM**

Which graph shows the greatest increase in sales?

(A)  Graph A

(B)  Graph B

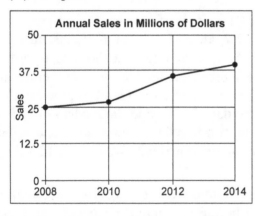

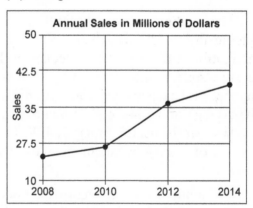

(C)  Graph C

(D)  None, they all show the same increase.

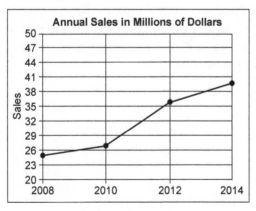

## SOLUTION

The correct choice is (D) because all the graphs show the same data: 2008 – $26 million, 2010 – $27 million, 2012 – $36 million, 2014 – $40 million. Graph A might appear larger because the interval on the *y*-axis starts at 0, not 20.

## ◼ Skill 4.3. Calculate range, mean, median, and mode of data sets.

Familiarity with the central tendencies of mean, median, mode, and standard deviation is a critical skill necessary to pass the FTCE-GKT.

The **mean** is found by adding all the data items and dividing by the number of data items you added. The mean of 4, 5, and 12 is found by adding 4 + 5 + 12, which equals 21, and then dividing by 3 since you added three terms. The mean of 4, 5, and 12 is 7. The value of the mean can be skewed by outliers, numbers that fall significantly outside the grouping of data. For example, take 2, 3, 5, 5, and 15. Most of the data falls between 2 and 5, but the addition of 15 to the group would make the mean higher than if it was not included.

The **median** is found by putting the data in order from least to greatest and then finding the middle data item. When there are an odd number of items, this is fairly straightforward. To find the median of 10, 6, 4, 8, and 12, put the data in order from least to greatest: 4, 6, 8, 10, 12; the middle number, the median, is 8. If there is an even number of data items, you must put the numbers in order from least to greatest, then find the average of the two middle numbers in the data set. To find the median of 3, 8, 4, and 11, first put the data in order: 3, 4, 8, 11. The two middle numbers are 4 and 8. Find the average of 4 and 8 by adding them together and dividing by 2. 4 + 8 = 12. 12 ÷ 2 = 6; the median is 6.

The **mode** is the data item which occurs more often than any other data item. In the data set (4, 5, 5, 7, 7, 7, 9, 9), the mode is 7 because the number 7 occurs more than any other number.

*Note:* If you have trouble remembering the differences between these terms, try using the following word association. The mean is the "mean ole' average" of the numbers. The words "median" and "middle" both start with an "m" and both have a "d" in the middle. The words "mode" and "most" both start with "mo."

**PROBLEM**

Which data set has a mean of 10?

(A)  (4, 5, 10, 13, 17)          (B)  (3, 5, 5, 8, 13)

(C)  (2, 10, 10, 10, 11)        (D)  (7, 8, 8, 12, 15)

**SOLUTION**

To find the correct set of data, the sum of all five data items must be 50 because 5 × 10 = 50 and 50 ÷ 5 = 10. Therefore, whichever set has a sum of 50 is the correct answer. The sum of the data items in answer choice (A) is 49. The sum of the data items in (B) is 34. The sum of the data items in answer choice (C) is 43. The sum of the data items in answer choice (D) is 50, so that is the correct answer.

**PROBLEM**

Which group of numbers does NOT have a mean of 30?

(A)  (20, 30, 30, 40)          (B)  (22, 24, 15, 19, 40, 60)

(C)  (10, 10, 70)               (D)  (15, 49)

**SOLUTION**

To find the mean of a set of numbers, find the sum of all of the numbers and then divide by the number of numbers there are in each set.

The mean for answer choice (A) is $(20 + 30 + 30 + 40) \div 4 = 30$

The mean for answer choice (B) is $(22 + 24 + 15 + 19 + 40 + 60) \div 6 = 30$

The mean for answer choice (C) is $(10 + 10 + 70) \div 3 = 30$

The mean for answer choice (D) is $(15 + 49) \div 2 = 32$

The only answer choice, that does not have a mean of 30 is answer choice (D), which is the correct answer.

PROBLEM

A family has five children. The four youngest are 4, 7, 9, and 11 years old. What age would be the median?

(A) 7        (B) 9        (C) 11        (D) 14

SOLUTION

If there are five children and you are given the ages of the youngest four, you can determine the median by finding the position of the middle child, or third born. The middle child is 9 years old, which is choice (B).

There are two values that give you information about how varied the data is. Knowing the **range** of data is important because it shows you how spread out the data is. To find the range, subtract the smallest data item from the largest data item. A small range lets you know that the data is grouped together closely. A large range tells you that the data is spread apart. The **standard deviation** is a statistic that shows how close the set of data is to the mean. When the data is close together around the mean, the standard deviation is small. However, when the data is spread farther apart, the standard deviation is larger.

Any standard deviation problem on the FTCE-GKT will follow a normal distribution curve, which means the data will be equally distributed on either side of the graph. Normal distribution curves follow the empirical rule: Approximately 68% of the data will fall within one standard deviation above and below the mean, 95% of the data will fall between two standard deviations above and below the mean, and 99.7% of the data will fall between three standard deviations above or below the mean. It is important to note that if a value is added equally to every number in a data set, the standard deviation does not change since it would mean an equal shift in all of the data points. It would affect measures of central tendency such as mean, median, and mode.

## Skill 4.4. Interpret the meaning of measures of central tendency (i.e., mean, median, mode) and dispersion (i.e., range, standard deviation) in the context of a real-world situation.

On the FTCE-GKT, there are many real-world word problems that require you to be proficient when calculating the meanings of measurements of central tendency. It is important that before you begin solving these problems, you have an accurate mental estimate of your answer. Be sure to check any answers for reasonableness before you select your answers on the test. When you encounter standard deviation problems, you will *not* be asked to calculate the variance or the standard deviation, but you will be asked to interpret what the standard deviation means.

## PROBLEM

A school administers a norm-referenced test to its 500 students. The average score is 50 with a standard deviation of 10 on a normal distribution curve. Approximately what number of students scored between 30 and 70?

(A) 95      (B) 150      (C) 200      (D) 475

## SOLUTION

If the standard deviation is 10, 30 is two standard deviations below the mean and 50 is two standard deviations above the mean. Since the empirical rule states that 95% of the data falls between two standard deviations above the mean and two standard deviations below the mean, multiply 500 by 0.95 to find out that 475 students scored between 30 and 70 on the test. (D) is the correct choice.

## PROBLEM

A self-employed businesswoman wants to calculate the differences in her profit margin in the first half of the year and the second. Rounded to the nearest dollar, how much more were her average sales per month during the last half of the year?

| January | $2,557 | July | $2,145 |
| --- | --- | --- | --- |
| February | $2,769 | August | $2,567 |
| March | $1,967 | September | $2,157 |
| April | $1,901 | October | $2,547 |
| May | $2,014 | November | $3,987 |
| June | $2,357 | December | $5,254 |

(A) $2,261      (B) $3,109      (C) $849      (D) $3,814

## SOLUTION

First, calculate the average sales for the first half of the year by summing the sales and dividing by 6:

$$\frac{2,557 + 2,769 + 1,967 + 1,901 + 2,014 + 2,357}{6} = 2,260.83$$

Next, calculate the average sales for the second half of the year:

$$\frac{2,145 + 2,567 + 2,157 + 2,547 + 3,987 + 5,254}{6} = 3,109.50$$

Now subtract the difference between the averages: $3,109.50 - 2,260.83 = 848.67$

Rounded to the nearest dollar, the average sales for the second half of the year are $849 higher. The correct choice is (C).

## Skill 4.5. Analyze and evaluate how the selection of statistics (e.g., mean, median, mode) can lead to different or inappropriate interpretations in the context of a real-world situation.

In the real world, the way data is presented is used to persuade an audience to think a certain way. For example, it's been reported that a greater number of parents were choosing not to immunize their children for religious reasons. In a Central Florida county, the number of religious waivers had increased from 30 to almost 150. Look at the ways we could accurately present these statistics:

Five times as many parents have gotten religious waivers for the mandatory immunizations.

120 more families have gotten religious waivers for the mandatory immunizations.

The number of religious waivers issued for immunizations have increased by 400%.

The last statement sounds like the greatest increase, but all of these statements have the same meaning. If we increase something by 400%, we are adding four times the original value to the initial value, or $30 + (30 \times 4) = 30 + 120 = 150$.

### PROBLEM

The weekly salaries of 12 employees in a company are listed below:

(500, 500, 500, 500, 500, 550, 550, 550, 600, 800, 825, 950)

Which measure of central tendency will be the highest: the mean, median, or the mode?

(A) The mode and mean will be the highest.

(B) The mean and the median will be the highest.

(C) The mean will be the highest.

(D) The median will be the highest.

### SOLUTION

Even though the mean, median, and mode are all measures of central tendency, they will be different from one another, depending on the values of the data. Solving this problem is not as difficult as you may think. Find the mode by identifying the number that is listed most often: 500. Put the numbers in order from least to greatest to find the median. There are two numbers in the middle, and they are both 550, so this is your median.

The mean, however, is harder to find, but it is not necessary to find its exact value to answer this question correctly. Notice that there are some larger values in the data. These values will pull the mean up above 500 and 550. Therefore, you know that answer choice (C) is the correct answer. (The actual mean is approximately 610.) If you state the average weekly salary is $610, that is accurate, but you are referring to the mean. If you state the typical weekly salary is $500, that is also accurate, but that is the mode. You could also say that the median weekly salary is $550. That is, you can describe the "average" using three different numbers, and all will communicate something slightly different.

### PROBLEM

A company has 90 employees. Eighty-nine employees make $50,000 a year, and one employee makes $2,000,000 a year. Which measure of central tendency would be the least representative of the data?

(A) The mean

(B) The median

(C) The mode

(D) All measures of central tendency would be equally representative.

### SOLUTION

Notice that in this problem, the mode and median are the same: $50,000. There is only one value that is much higher than all of the others, the $2,000,000 salary. We call this type of data an **outlier** since it falls well outside the grouping of most of the values in the data set. As a result, the mean will pull the "average" up higher than the other two measurements of central tendency. Therefore, the mean would be least representative of the data. Answer choice (A) is the correct answer.

## Skill 4.6. Solve and interpret real-world problems involving probability using counting procedures, tables, and tree diagrams.

**Probability** is a measure of how likely it is for an event to occur. To find the probability of an event occurring, you need to write a ratio. The numerator of the ratio is the number of times the favorable event will occur, and the denominator is the total number of events possible. For example, if you toss a penny, the probability that the penny will land tails up is $\frac{1}{2}$ because there is one tails and two possible outcomes (heads or tails). Another example is if you want to find the probability of choosing a caramel-filled chocolate out of a box of chocolates, you need to know how many chocolates are caramel-filled and how many chocolates there are in total. So, if there are 8 caramel-filled chocolates and there are 24 chocolates in the box, then the probability of choosing a caramel-filled chocolate from the box at random is $\frac{8}{24}$. It is customary to write a probability ratio in lowest terms, so the probability of choosing a caramel-filled chocolate from the box can also be written as $\frac{1}{3}$.

If you are asked to find the probability of multiple events, first find the product of the probabilities of the single events. For instance, if you need to know the probability of getting heads twice when flipping a quarter, find the probability of the first flip $\left(\frac{1}{2}\right)$, then the second event $\left(\frac{1}{2}\right)$ then multiply them together: $\frac{1}{2} \times \frac{1}{2} = \frac{1}{4}$. This is probability without replacement because you always have two sides of the quarter every time you flip it.

### PROBLEM

A bag contains 12 blue tiles, 6 red tiles, and 2 green tiles. What is the probability that you will select a green tile if you pick a tile from the bag at random?

(A) $\frac{2}{18}$      (B) $\frac{2}{20}$      (C) $\frac{1}{20}$      (D) $\frac{1}{18}$

### SOLUTION

To find the probability of selecting a green tile at random, you must know how many green tiles there are and how many tiles there are total (including the green tiles). There are 2 green tiles and a total of 20 tiles. So the probability of choosing a green tile is $\frac{2}{20}$. Answer choice (B) is correct. Note: This answer can be simplified to $\frac{1}{10}$.

## Probability Without Replacement

If you are given a more complex probability problem on the FTCE-GKT, it will most likely be a probability without replacement. Take the previous problem with the 12 blue tiles, 6 red tiles, and 2 green tiles. What is the probability of drawing two tiles at once and having them both be blue? Let's look at these as separate events. The probability of you drawing the first blue tile is $\frac{12}{20}$, which can be simplified to $\frac{3}{5}$. But when you draw the second tile, there are no longer twenty tiles in the bag. There are only nineteen tiles left in the bag and only eleven are blue. The probability of drawing the second blue tile (without replacing the first) is $\frac{11}{19}$. The probability of drawing two blue tiles at once is $\frac{3}{5} \times \frac{11}{19} = \frac{33}{95}$.

There are a multitude of problems that can be solved using probability. The important thing is to recognize what type of problem you are presented with so that you will know how to solve it correctly.

The **Fundamental Counting Principle** is a method used to calculate all of the possible combinations of a given number of events. If an event has $m$ possible outcomes and another independent event has $n$ possible outcomes, then there are $m \times n$ possible outcomes for the two events to occur together. Let's look at a specific example. If you are choosing an outfit to wear from 2 pairs of pants and 3 shirts (assuming all outfits will match), there are 6 possible outfits for you to wear because $2 \times 3 = 6$.

### PROBLEM

You have five books that you want to place on a shelf. How many ways can you arrange them?

(A)  25      (B) 50      (C) 120      (D) 125

### SOLUTION

Let's look at the first spot on the shelf. You have 5 choices to fill this spot. Now look at the second spot. You have 4 books left to choose from. When you get to the third spot, you have 3 books left to fill the spot. At the fourth spot you can choose from 2 books. And finally, there is only one book left to put in the last spot. Multiply these numbers together: $5 \times 4 \times 3 \times 2 \times 1 = 120$. There are 120 ways you can arrange 5 books on one shelf. The correct answer is (C).

## Permutations and Combinations

A **permutation** is an ordered arrangement of items that occurs when no item is used more than once and the order of arrangement makes a difference. This is the formula for permutations:

$$_nP_r = \frac{n!}{(n-r)!}$$

The notation $_nP_r$ means the number of permutations of $n$ things taken $r$ at a time. Let's look at the problem from the previous section. What if we had 5 books, but we only wanted to put 3 on the shelf? We would be taking 5 books, 3 at a time, or $_5P_3$. In this case you may find the formula more confusing than the solution. If you use the formula, you would have $\frac{5!}{(5-3)!}$. The 5! may look like some strange code, but it is just the mathematical notation for $5 \times 4 \times 3 \times 2 \times 1$. The denominator (once you have subtracted) would be 2!, which is $2 \times 1$, as shown below:

$$\frac{5!}{(5-3)!} = \frac{5 \times 4 \times 3 \times \cancel{2 \times 1}}{\cancel{2 \times 1}} = 5 \times 4 \times 3 = 60$$

Let's simplify this process and see if we can get the same solution. You have 5 books. You have 3 spots for them. You have 5 books to use in the first spot, 4 left for the second, and 3 left for the final spot, or $5 \times 4 \times 3$. In this way, permutations is like the fundamental counting principle, and you can avoid using the formula altogether.

Now, what about **combinations**? A combination is a permutation where the order makes no difference. You may think that this would make things easier, but these problems are actually a little more difficult. The notation $_nC_r$ means the number of combinations of $n$ things taken $r$ at a time, as seen in the formula below.

$$_nC_r = \frac{n!}{(n-r)!r!}$$

Once again, if you start with the fundamental counting principle, you can avoid using the formula with one small caveat: Once you have done your original calculation, you have to divide your solution by $r!$ to avoid counting duplicates. For instance, what if you have five students, A, B, C, D, and E, who are trying to fill two offices in a club? Using our take on the fundamental counting procedure, we would have 5 students to choose for the first position and four for the second position. $5 \times 4 = 20$ possible ways to fill those position, as shown below:

AB  AC  AD  AE
BA  BC  BD  BE
CA  CB  CD  CE
DA  DB  DC  DE
EA  EB  EC  ED

So what is the problem with our answer? Since order doesn't matter, AC is the same as CA. We took those five kids and put them in two positions. We can use the same method if we remember to divide our total by r! which in this case is 2! or $2 \times 1 = 2$. This will eliminate the doubles from our count as shown below:

AB  AC  AD  AE
~~BA~~  BC  BD  BE
~~CA~~  ~~CB~~  CD  CE
~~DA~~  ~~DB~~  ~~DC~~  DE
~~EA~~  ~~EB~~  ~~EC~~  ~~ED~~

Our 20 choices are now actually 10 once we removed the doubles.

## Tree Diagrams

In probability, the **sample space** is the set of all possible outcomes of an event. For example, the sample space for throwing a six-sided number cube is (1, 2, 3, 4, 5, 6). When more than one event is occurring at the same time, it is sometimes helpful to illustrate the sample space with a tree diagram. In such a way, you can see all the possible outcomes. A tree diagram shows all the possible outcomes of an event in a diagram that looks like branches of a tree. Below is a tree diagram showing all possible outcomes when tossing two coins. The last column shows in words what the tree diagram shows in branches. That is, the four ways two coins could land are (Head, Head), (Head, Tail), (Tail, Head), and (Tail, Tail).

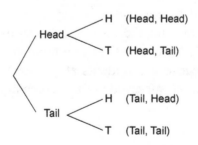

PROBLEM

Caroline tossed three coins. Use the tree diagram below to find the probability that only one of the three coins will land on heads.

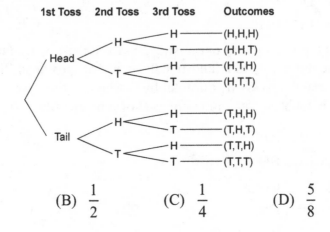

(A) $\dfrac{3}{8}$      (B) $\dfrac{1}{2}$      (C) $\dfrac{1}{4}$      (D) $\dfrac{5}{8}$

SOLUTION

The last column of the tree diagram shows the various ways three coins can land. Count the ways that show one head only (and two tails) to find that the answer is $\dfrac{3}{8}$, which is answer choice (A).

*Note:* This is different than if it asked for "at least one coin to be heads," which would be $\dfrac{7}{8}$.

## ■ Skill 4.7. Infer and analyze conclusions from sample surveys, experiments, and observational studies.

The validity of the results of sample surveys, experiments, and observational studies can be called into question if they were not conducted in an unbiased manner. For instance, say you wanted to conduct a survey of the favorite after-school activity for children. Where would you find the most valid results—by surveying one hundred students exiting an elementary school or the same number of students at a soccer game? At the school, of course, because the students at the soccer game may choose outdoor sports more often than the sample surveyed at the elementary school.

**PROBLEM**

Shaniqua wants to find the average weight of a student in her high school. Which sample would give Shaniqua the most representative results?

(A) All of the boys in 11th grade

(B) The 24 members of the boys' wrestling team

(C) The 21 students in her 9th grade science class

(D) 18 students from each of the grades 9 through 12

**SOLUTION**

Results from a sample are only as good as the sample chosen. So, in this case, you are looking for the best sample to show the average weight of a high school student. High school consists of grades 9–12 and includes both boys and girls. Therefore, choose a sample that represents all four grades and both genders. Answer choices (A), (B), and (C) all are too narrow of a sample group. Answer choice (D) includes a varied sample, which will yield the best results, so choice (D) is the correct answer.

The data gathered from an experiment can also be called into question if the variables were not properly controlled. For instance, look at the following data table:

**Mold Growth on Bread**

|  | Wet and Warm | Dry and Cold | Control |
|---|---|---|---|
| Initial Percentage Moldy | 0% | 0% | 0% |
| Final Percentage Moldy | 58% | 15% | 20% |

The data in this table really gives no information at all. Why did the wet and warm bread grow more mold—because it was moist or because it was stored in a warm environment? You can't tell because the variables were not properly controlled.

Sample surveys can also be used to make predictions about a larger population. If 56 out of 100 senior citizens surveyed preferred Product A over Product B, and there were 12,000 senior citizens living in a community, you could estimate that $12,000 \times \frac{56}{100} =$ 6,720 seniors would prefer Product A.

## PROBLEM

At West Bend High School, the student body president was tasked with the job of deciding how to spend $3,000 earned in a fundraiser. She decided to conduct a survey to determine if the student body would rather the money be spent on picnic tables or additional computers for the technology lab. Which of the following samples would give the most accurate results?

(A) She waits outside at break and surveys 1 out of every 5 students who pass her until she has surveyed 100 students.

(B) She asks everyone who sits at her table at lunch time.

(C) She waits outside at dismissal and surveys every senior who leaves campus.

(D) She selects two random homerooms from each grade level and has the teacher distribute and collect the surveys.

## SOLUTION

Choice (A) is not valid because even though she has a large sample, she may skew her results by only surveying the students who eat outside. The students in the lunchroom may have a different opinion. Choice (B) is invalid because her sample is not random or large enough. Choice (C) is not valid because her sample does not include underclassmen. Choice (D) is the best answer because the groups are selected at random, the sample size is large, and the surveys are equally distributed throughout the grade levels.

## Drill Section for Competency 1

### Drill: Integers and Real Numbers

**Addition**

1. Simplify $4 + (-7) + 2 + (-5)$.

   (A) $-6$    (B) $-4$    (C) $0$    (D) $6$    (E) $18$

2. Simplify $144 + (-317) + 213$.

   (A) $-357$    (B) $-40$    (C) $40$    (D) $257$    (E) $674$

3. What integer makes the equation $-13 + 12 + 7 + ? = 10$ a true statement?

   (A) $-22$    (B) $-10$    (C) $4$    (D) $6$    (E) $10$

4. Simplify $4 + 17 + (-29) + 13 + (-22) + (-3)$.

   (A) $-44$    (B) $-20$    (C) $23$    (D) $34$    (E) $78$

**Subtraction**

5. Simplify $319 - 428$.

   (A) $-111$    (B) $-109$    (C) $-99$    (D) $109$    (E) $747$

6. Simplify $91,203 - 37,904 + 1,073$.

   (A) $54,372$    (B) $64,701$    (C) $128,034$    (D) $129,107$    (E) $130,180$

7. Simplify $46 - 36 - 2 + 27$.

   (A) $-9$    (B) $6$    (C) $15$    (D) $35$    (E) $33$

8. Simplify $-(-4 - 7) + (-2)$.

   (A) $-22$    (B) $-13$    (C) $-9$    (D) $7$    (E) $9$

9. The peak of Mt. McKinley, the highest mountain in North America, is 6,194 meters above sea level. Badwater Basin in Death Valley, California, is 86 meters below sea level. What is the difference in elevation between the peak of Mt. McKinley and Badwater Basin?

    (A) 6,108 m    (B) 6,280 m    (C) 5,699 m    (D) 6,464 m    (E) 7,885 m

## Multiplication

10. Simplify $(-3) \times (-18) \times (-1)$.

    (A) −108    (B) −54    (C) −48    (D) 48    (E) 54

11. Simplify $|-42| \times |7|$.

    (A) −294    (B) −49    (C) −35    (D) 284    (E) 294

12. Simplify $(-6) \times 5 \times (-10) \times (-4) \times 0 \times 2$.

    (A) −2,400    (B) −240    (C) 0    (D) 280    (E) 2,700

13. Simplify $-|-6 \times 8|$.

    (A) −48    (B) −42    (C) 2    (D) 42    (E) 48

14. A city in Georgia had a record low temperature of −3°F one winter. During the same year, a city in Michigan experienced a record low that was nine times the record low set in Georgia. What was the record low in Michigan that year?

    (A) −31°F    (B) −27°F    (C) −21°F    (D) −12°F    (E) −6°F

## Division

15. Simplify $(-24) \div 8$.

    (A) −4    (B) −3    (C) −2    (D) 3    (E) 4

16. Simplify $(-180) \div (-12)$.

    (A) −30    (B) −15    (C) 1.5    (D) 15    (E) 216

17. Simplify $|-76| \div |-4|$.

(A) $-21$     (B) $-19$     (C) 13     (D) 19     (E) 21.5

18. Simplify $|216 \div (-6)|$

(A) $-36$     (B) $-12$     (C) 36     (D) 38     (E) 43

19. At the end of the year, a small firm has $2,996 in its account for bonuses. If the entire amount is equally divided among the 14 employees, how much does each one receive?

(A) $107     (B) $114     (C) $170     (D) $210     (E) $214

## Order of Operations

20. Simplify $\dfrac{4 + 8 \times 2}{5 - 1}$.

(A) 4     (B) 5     (C) 6     (D) 8     (E) 12

21. $96 \div 3 \div 4 \div 2 =$

(A) 65     (B) 64     (C) 16     (D) 8     (E) 4

22. $3 + 4 \times 2 - 6 \div 3 =$

(A) $-1$     (B) $\dfrac{5}{3}$     (C) $\dfrac{8}{3}$     (D) 9     (E) 12

23. $[(4 + 8) \times 3] \div 9 =$

(A) 4     (B) 8     (C) 12     (D) 24     (E) 36

24. $18 + 3 \times 4 \div 3 =$

(A) 3     (B) 5     (C) 10     (D) 22     (E) 28

25. $(29 - 17 + 4) \div 4 + |-2| =$

(A) $2\dfrac{2}{3}$     (B) 4     (C) $4\dfrac{2}{3}$     (D) 6     (E) 15

26. $(-3) \times 5 - 20 \div 4 =$

   (A) $-75$    (B) $-20$    (C) $-10$    (D) $-8\frac{3}{4}$    (E) $20$

27. $\dfrac{11 \times 2 + 2}{16 - 2 \times 2} =$

   (A) $\frac{11}{16}$    (B) $1$    (C) $2$    (D) $3\frac{2}{3}$    (E) $4$

28. $|-8 - 4| \div 3 \times 6 + (-4) =$

   (A) $20$    (B) $26$    (C) $32$    (D) $62$    (E) $212$

29. $32 \div 2 + 4 - 15 \div 3 =$

   (A) $0$    (B) $7$    (C) $15$    (D) $23$    (E) $63$

30. Simplify $|4 + (-3)| + |-2|$.

   (A) $-2$    (B) $-1$    (C) $1$    (D) $3$    (E) $9$

## Drill: Fractions

### Changing an Improper Fraction to a Mixed Number

**Directions:** Write each improper fraction as a mixed number in simplest form.

1. $\dfrac{50}{4}$

   (A) $10\frac{1}{4}$    (B) $11\frac{1}{2}$    (C) $12\frac{1}{4}$    (D) $12\frac{1}{2}$    (E) $25$

2. $\dfrac{17}{5}$

   (A) $3\frac{2}{5}$    (B) $3\frac{3}{5}$    (C) $3\frac{4}{5}$    (D) $4\frac{1}{5}$    (E) $4\frac{2}{5}$

3. $\dfrac{42}{3}$

   (A) $10\frac{3}{3}$    (B) $12$    (C) $13\frac{1}{3}$    (D) $14$    (E) $21\frac{1}{3}$

## Changing a Mixed Number to an Improper Fraction

**Directions:** Change each mixed number to an improper fraction in simplest form.

4. $2\dfrac{3}{5}$

    (A) $\dfrac{4}{5}$      (B) $\dfrac{6}{5}$      (C) $\dfrac{11}{5}$      (D) $\dfrac{13}{5}$      (E) $\dfrac{17}{5}$

5. $4\dfrac{3}{4}$

    (A) $\dfrac{7}{4}$      (B) $\dfrac{13}{4}$      (C) $\dfrac{16}{3}$      (D) $\dfrac{19}{4}$      (E) $\dfrac{21}{4}$

6. $6\dfrac{7}{6}$

    (A) $\dfrac{13}{6}$      (B) $\dfrac{43}{6}$      (C) $\dfrac{19}{36}$      (D) $\dfrac{42}{36}$      (E) $\dfrac{48}{36}$

## Adding Fractions with the Same Denominator

**Directions:** Add and write the answer in simplest form or as a mixed number.

7. $\dfrac{5}{12}+\dfrac{3}{12}=$

    (A) $\dfrac{5}{24}$      (B) $\dfrac{1}{3}$      (C) $\dfrac{8}{12}$      (D) $\dfrac{2}{3}$      (E) $1\dfrac{1}{3}$

8. $\dfrac{5}{8}+\dfrac{7}{8}+\dfrac{3}{8}=$

    (A) $\dfrac{15}{24}$      (B) $\dfrac{3}{4}$      (C) $\dfrac{5}{6}$      (D) $\dfrac{7}{8}$      (E) $1\dfrac{7}{8}$

9. $131\dfrac{2}{15}+28\dfrac{3}{15}=$

    (A) $159\dfrac{1}{6}$      (B) $159\dfrac{1}{5}$      (C) $159\dfrac{1}{3}$      (D) $159\dfrac{1}{2}$      (E) $159\dfrac{3}{5}$

## Subtracting Fractions with the Same Denominator

**Directions:** Subtract and write the answer in simplest form or as a mixed number.

10. $4\frac{7}{8} - 3\frac{1}{8} =$

    (A) $1\frac{1}{4}$     (B) $1\frac{3}{4}$     (C) $1\frac{12}{16}$     (D) $1\frac{7}{8}$     (E) 2

11. $132\frac{5}{12} - 37\frac{3}{12} =$

    (A) $94\frac{1}{6}$     (B) $95\frac{1}{12}$     (C) $95\frac{1}{6}$     (D) $105\frac{1}{6}$     (E) $169\frac{2}{3}$

12. $19\frac{1}{3} - 2\frac{2}{3} =$

    (A) $16\frac{2}{3}$     (B) $16\frac{5}{6}$     (C) $17\frac{1}{3}$     (D) $17\frac{2}{3}$     (E) $17\frac{5}{6}$

## Finding the LCD

**Directions:** Find the lowest common denominator of each group of fractions.

13. $\frac{2}{3}, \frac{5}{9},$ and $\frac{1}{6}$

    (A) 9     (B) 18     (C) 27     (D) 54     (E) 162

14. $\frac{7}{16}, \frac{5}{6},$ and $\frac{2}{3}$

    (A) 3     (B) 6     (C) 12     (D) 24     (E) 48

15. $\frac{2}{3}, \frac{1}{5},$ and $\frac{5}{6}$

    (A) 15     (B) 30     (C) 48     (D) 90     (E) 120

16. $\frac{4}{9}, \frac{2}{5},$ and $\frac{1}{3}$

    (A) 15     (B) 17     (C) 27     (D) 45     (E) 135

17. $\frac{3}{7}$, $\frac{5}{21}$, and $\frac{2}{3}$

   (A) 21          (B) 42          (C) 31          (D) 63          (E) 441

## Adding Fractions with Different Denominators

**Directions:** Add and write the answer in simplest form.

18. $\frac{1}{3} + \frac{5}{12} =$

   (A) $\frac{2}{5}$          (B) $\frac{1}{2}$          (C) $\frac{9}{12}$          (D) $\frac{3}{4}$          (E) $1\frac{1}{3}$

19. $12\frac{9}{16} + 17\frac{3}{4} + 8\frac{1}{8} =$

   (A) $37\frac{7}{16}$          (B) $38\frac{7}{16}$          (C) $38\frac{1}{2}$          (D) $38\frac{2}{3}$          (E) $39\frac{3}{16}$

20. $28\frac{4}{5} + 11\frac{16}{25} =$

   (A) $39\frac{2}{3}$          (B) $39\frac{4}{5}$          (C) $40\frac{9}{25}$          (D) $40\frac{2}{5}$          (E) $40\frac{11}{25}$

## Subtracting Fractions with Different Denominators

**Directions:** Subtract and write the answer in simplest form.

21. $8\frac{9}{12} - 2\frac{2}{3} =$

   (A) $6\frac{1}{12}$          (B) $6\frac{1}{6}$          (C) $6\frac{1}{3}$          (D) $6\frac{7}{12}$          (E) $6\frac{2}{3}$

22. $185\frac{11}{15} - 107\frac{2}{5} =$

   (A) $77\frac{2}{15}$          (B) $78\frac{1}{5}$          (C) $78\frac{3}{10}$          (D) $78\frac{1}{3}$          (E) $78\frac{9}{15}$

23. $34\frac{2}{3} - 16\frac{5}{6} =$

   (A)  16    (B)  $16\frac{1}{3}$    (C)  17    (D)  17    (E)  $17\frac{5}{6}$

## Multiplying Fractions

**Directions:** Multiply and reduce the answer.

24. $\frac{2}{3} \times \frac{4}{5} =$

   (A)  $\frac{6}{8}$    (B)  $\frac{3}{4}$    (C)  $\frac{8}{15}$    (D)  $\frac{10}{12}$    (E)  $\frac{6}{5}$

25. $5\frac{1}{3} \times \frac{3}{8} =$

   (A)  $\frac{4}{11}$    (B)  2    (C)  $\frac{8}{5}$    (D)  $5\frac{1}{8}$    (E)  $5\frac{17}{24}$

26. $6\frac{1}{2} \times 3 =$

   (A)  $9\frac{1}{2}$    (B)  $18\frac{1}{2}$    (C)  $19\frac{1}{2}$    (D)  20    (E)  $12\frac{1}{2}$

## Dividing Fractions

**Directions:** Divide and reduce the answer.

27. $\frac{3}{16} \div \frac{3}{4} =$

   (A)  $\frac{9}{64}$    (B)  $\frac{1}{4}$    (C)  $\frac{6}{16}$    (D)  $\frac{9}{16}$    (E)  $\frac{3}{4}$

28. $\frac{4}{9} \div \frac{2}{3} =$

   (A)  $\frac{1}{3}$    (B)  $\frac{1}{2}$    (C)  $\frac{2}{3}$    (D)  $\frac{7}{11}$    (E)  $\frac{8}{9}$

29. $5\frac{1}{4} \div \frac{7}{10} =$

    (A) $2\frac{4}{7}$     (B) $3\frac{27}{40}$     (C) $5\frac{19}{20}$     (D) $7\frac{1}{2}$     (E) $8\frac{1}{4}$

## Drill: Decimals

### Addition

**Directions:** Perform the following additions.

1.   $1.032 + 0.987 + 3.07 =$

    (A) 4.089    (B) 5.089    (C) 5.189    (D) 6.189    (E) 13.972

2.   $7.1 + 0.62 + 4.03827 + 5.183 =$

    (A) 0.2315127  (B) 16.45433  (C) 16.94127  (D) 18.561  (E) 40.4543

3.   $8 + 17.43 + 9.2 =$

    (A) 34.63    (B) 34.86    (C) 35.63    (D) 176.63    (E) 189.43

### Subtraction

**Directions:** Perform the following subtractions.

4.   $16.047 - 13.06 =$

    (A) 2.887    (B) 2.987    (C) 3.041    (D) 3.141    (E) 4.741

5.   $87.4 - 56.27 =$

    (A) 30.27    (B) 30.67    (C) 31.1    (D) 31.13    (E) 31.27

6.   $1,046.8 - 639.14 =$

    (A) 303.84    (B) 313.74    (C) 407.66    (D) 489.74    (E) 535.54

CHAPTER
3

FTCE GENERAL KNOWLEDGE TEST

## Multiplication

**Directions:** Perform the following multiplications.

7. $1.03 \times 2.6 =$

   (A) 2.18    (B) 2.678    (C) 2.78    (D) 3.38    (E) 3.63

8. $93 \times 4.2 =$

   (A) 39.06    (B) 97.2    (C) 223.2    (D) 390.6    (E) 3,906

9. $0.04 \times 0.23 =$

   (A) 0.0092    (B) 0.092    (C) 0.27    (D) 0.87    (E) 0.920

## Division

**Directions:** Perform the following divisions.

10. $123.39 \div 3 =$

    (A) 31.12    (B) 41.13    (C) 401.13    (D) 411.3    (E) 4,113

11. $1,428.6 \div 6$

    (A) 0.2381    (B) 2.381    (C) 23.81    (D) 238.1    (E) 2,381

12. $25.2 \div 0.3 =$

    (A) 0.84    (B) 8.04    (C) 8.4    (D) 84    (E) 840

## Comparing

**Directions:** Answer the following questions.

13. In which set below are the numbers arranged correctly from smallest to largest?

    (A) {0.98, 0.9, 0.993}    (B) {0.113, 0.3, 0.31}

    (C) {7.04, 7.26, 7.2}    (D) {0.006, 0.061, 0.06}

    (E) {12.84, 12.801, 12.6}

14. In which set below are the numbers arranged correctly from largest to smallest?

    (A) {1.018, 1.63, 1.368}      (B) {4.219, 4.29, 4.9}

    (C) {0.62, 0.6043, 0.643}     (D) {16.34, 16.304, 16.3}

    (E) {12.98, 12.601, 12.86}

15. Which is the **largest** number in this set—{0.87, 0.89, 0.889, 0.8, 0.987}?

    (A) 0.87      (B) 0.89      (C) 0.889      (D) 0.8      (E) 0.987

## Drill: Percent

### Finding Percents

**Directions:** Solve to find the correct percentages.

1. Find 3% of 80.

   (A) 0.24      (B) 2.4      (C) 24      (D) 240      (E) 2,400

2. Find 125% of 400.

   (A) 425      (B) 500      (C) 525      (D) 600      (E) 825

3. Find 300% of 4.

   (A) 12      (B) 120      (C) 1,200      (D) 12,000      (E) 120,000

4. Forty-eight percent of the 1,200 students at Central High are males. How many male students are there at Central High?

   (A) 57      (B) 576      (C) 580      (D) 600      (E) 648

5. Of every 1,000 people who take a certain medicine, 0.2% develop severe side effects. How many people out of every 1,000 who take the medicine develop the side effects?

   (A) 0.2      (B) 2      (C) 20      (D) 22      (E) 200

6. Of 220 applicants for a job, 75% were offered an initial interview. How many people were offered an initial interview?

   (A) 75      (B) 110      (C) 120      (D) 155      (E) 165

## Changing Percents to Fractions

**Directions:** Solve to find the correct fractions.

7.  What is 25% written as a fraction?

    (A) $\dfrac{1}{25}$    (B) $\dfrac{1}{5}$    (C) $\dfrac{1}{4}$    (D) $\dfrac{1}{3}$    (E) $\dfrac{1}{2}$

8.  What is 200% written as a fraction?

    (A) $\dfrac{1}{2}$    (B) $\dfrac{2}{1}$    (C) $\dfrac{20}{1}$    (D) $\dfrac{200}{1}$    (E) $\dfrac{2,000}{1}$

9.  What is 2% written as a fraction?

    (A) $\dfrac{1}{50}$    (B) $\dfrac{1}{25}$    (C) $\dfrac{1}{10}$    (D) $\dfrac{1}{4}$    (E) $\dfrac{1}{2}$

## Changing Fractions to Percents

**Directions:** Solve to find the following percentages.

10. What is $\dfrac{3}{5}$ written as a percent?

    (A) 30%    (B) 35%    (C) 53%    (D) 60%    (E) 65%

11. What is $\dfrac{17}{20}$ written as a percent?

    (A) 17%    (B) 70%    (C) 75%    (D) 80%    (E) 85%

12. What is $1\dfrac{1}{4}$ written as a percent?

    (A) 114%    (B) 120%    (C) 125%    (D) 127%    (E) 133%

## Changing Percents to Decimals

**Directions:** Convert the percentages to decimals.

13. What is 42% written as a decimal?

    (A) 0.42    (B) 4.2    (C) 42    (D) 420    (E) 422

14. What is 8% written as a decimal?

   (A)  0.0008     (B)  0.008     (C)  0.08     (D)  0.80     (E)  8

15. What is 34% written as a decimal?

   (A)  0.00034    (B)  0.0034    (C)  0.034    (D)  0.34     (E)  3.4

## Changing Decimals to Percents

**Directions:** Convert the following decimals to percents.

16. What is 1 written as a percent?

   (A)  1%     (B)  10%     (C)  100%     (D)  111%     (E)  150%

17. What is 0.08 written as a percent?

   (A)  0.08%     (B)  8%     (C)  8.8%     (D)  80%     (E)  800%

18. What is 0.645 written as a percent?

   (A)  64.5%     (B)  65%     (C)  69%     (D)  70%     (E)  645%

## Drill: Exponents

## Multiplication

**Directions:** Simplify.

1. $4^6 \times 4^2 =$

   (A)  $4^4$     (B)  $4^8$     (C)  $4^{12}$     (D)  $16^8$     (E)  $16^{12}$

2. $2^2 \times 2^5 \times 2^3 =$

   (A)  $2^{10}$     (B)  $4^{10}$     (C)  $8^{10}$     (D)  $2^{30}$     (E)  $8^{30}$

3. $m^8 n^3 \times m^2 n \times m^4 n^2 =$

   (A)  $3m^{16}n^6$     (B)  $m^{14}n^6$     (C)  $3m^{14}n^5$     (D)  $3m^{14}n^5$     (E)  $m^2$

## Division

**Directions:** Simplify.

4.  $6^5 \div 6^3 =$

    (A) 0        (B) 1        (C) 6        (D) 12        (E) 36

5.  $x^{10}y^8 \div x^7y^3 =$

    (A) $x^2y^5$        (B) $x^3y^4$        (C) $x^3y^5$        (D) $x^2y^4$        (E) $x^5y^3$

## Power to a Power

**Directions:** Simplify.

6.  $(3^6)^2 =$

    (A) $3^4$        (B) $3^8$        (C) $3^{12}$        (D) $9^{12}$        (E) $9^8$

7.  $(a^4b^3)^2 =$

    (A) $(ab)^9$        (B) $a^8b^6$        (C) $(ab)^{24}$        (D) $a^6b^5$        (E) $2a^4b^3$

8.  $(m^6n^5q^3)^2 =$

    (A) $2m^6n^5q^3$        (B) $m^4n^3q$        (C) $m^8n^7q^5$        (D) $m^{12}n^{10}q^6$        (E) $2m^{12}n^{10}q^6$

# Competency 1: Drills Answer Key

## Drill: Integers and Real Numbers

| | | | | |
|---|---|---|---|---|
| 1. (A) | 7. (D) | 13. (A) | 19. (E) | 25. (D) |
| 2. (C) | 8. (E) | 14. (B) | 20. (B) | 26. (B) |
| 3. (C) | 9. (B) | 15. (B) | 21. (E) | 27. (C) |
| 4. (B) | 10. (B) | 16. (D) | 22. (D) | 28. (A) |
| 5. (B) | 11. (E) | 17. (D) | 23. (A) | 29. (C) |
| 6. (A) | 12. (C) | 18. (C) | 24. (D) | 30. (D) |

## Drill: Fractions

| | | | | |
|---|---|---|---|---|
| 1. (D) | 7. (D) | 13. (B) | 19. (B) | 25. (B) |
| 2. (A) | 8. (E) | 14. (E) | 20. (E) | 26. (C) |
| 3. (D) | 9. (C) | 15. (B) | 21. (A) | 27. (B) |
| 4. (D) | 10. (B) | 16. (D) | 22. (D) | 28. (C) |
| 5. (D) | 11. (C) | 17. (A) | 23. (E) | 29. (D) |
| 6. (B) | 12. (A) | 18. (D) | 24. (C) | |

## Drill: Decimals

| | | | | |
|---|---|---|---|---|
| 1. (B) | 4. (B) | 7. (B) | 10. (B) | 13. (B) |
| 2. (C) | 5. (D) | 8. (D) | 11. (D) | 14. (D) |
| 3. (A) | 6. (C) | 9. (A) | 12. (D) | 15. (E) |

## Drill: Percent

| | | | | |
|---|---|---|---|---|
| 1. (B) | 5. (B) | 9. (A) | 13. (A) | 17. (B) |
| 2. (B) | 6. (E) | 10. (D) | 14. (C) | 18. (A) |
| 3. (A) | 7. (C) | 11. (E) | 15. (D) | |
| 4. (B) | 8. (B) | 12. (C) | 16. (C) | |

## Drill: Exponents

| | |
|---|---|
| 1. (B) | 5. (C) |
| 2. (A) | 6. (C) |
| 3. (B) | 7. (B) |
| 4. (E) | 8. (D) |

## Drill Section for Competency 2

### Drill: Measurement

1.  A brick walkway measuring 3 feet by 11 feet is to be built. The bricks measure 4 inches by 6 inches. How many bricks will it take to complete the walkway?

    (A) 132        (B) 198        (C) 330        (D) 1927        (E) 4752

2.  A wall to be papered is three times as long as it is wide. The total area to be covered is 192 ft². Wallpaper comes in rolls that are 2 feet wide by 8 feet long. How many rolls will it take to cover the wall?

    (A) 8        (B) 12        (C) 16        (D) 24        (E) 32

3.  A bottle of medicine containing 2 kg is to be poured into smaller containers that hold 8 grams each. How many of these smaller containers can be filled from the 2 kg bottle?

    (A) 0.5        (B) 1        (C) 5        (D) 50        (E) 250

### Drill: Metric Conversions

1.  How many centimeters are in 4.8 meters?

    (A) .48        (B) 48        (C) 480        (D) 4,800        (E) 48,000

2.  How many meters are in 330 millimeters?

    (A) .33        (B) 3.3        (C) 3,300        (D) 33,000        (E) 330,000

3.  How many kilometers is 475 meters?

    (A) 4750        (B) 47.5        (C) 4.75        (D) .475        (E) .0475

4.  How many millimeters in 7.3 centimeters?

    (A) .73        (B) 73        (C) 730        (D) 7,300        (E) 73,000

5. How many 50 mg pills can you make out of 1000 g of aspirin?

(A) 20    (B) 20,000    (C) 200,000    (D) 2,000,000    (E) 20,000,000

## Drill: Customary Conversions

1. How many inches in 45 feet?

(A) 3.75    (B) 540    (C) 1,620    (D) 135    (E) 450

2. How many feet in 114 inches?

(A) 9.5    (B) 1,368    (C) 38    (D) 12.5    (E) 1,140

3. How many miles in 14,520 feet?

(A) 1,210    (B) $403\frac{1}{3}$    (C) 2.75    (D) 8.25    (E) 14.52

4. How many square feet are in 27 square yards?

(A) 9    (B) 81    (C) 243    (D) 636    (E) 1620

## Drill: Unit Price

1. Find the unit price: 18 pieces of gum for 90 cents

(A) 0.04    (B) 0.05    (C) 0.06    (D) 16.20    (E) 1.62

2. Find the unit price: 8 balloons for $1.00

(A) 0.125    (B) 1.25    (C) 8.00    (D) 0.80    (E) 0.08

## Drill: Lines and Angles

### Intersecting Lines

1. Find *a*.

(A) 38°    (B) 68°    (C) 78°

(D) 90°    (E) 112°

2. Find *c*.

    (A) 32°     (B) 48°     (C) 58°

    (D) 82°     (E) 148°

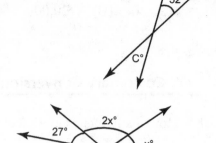

3. Determine *x*.

    (A) 21°     (B) 23°     (C) 51°

    (D) 102°    (E) 153°

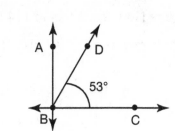

**Perpendicular Lines**

4. $\overline{BA} \perp \overline{BC}$ and $m \angle DBC = 53$. Find $m \angle ABD$.

    (A) 27°     (B) 33°     (C) 37°

    (D) 53°     (E) 90°

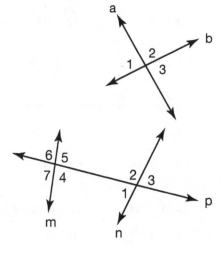

5. $m \angle 1 = 90°$. Find $m \angle 2$.

    (A) 80°     (B) 90°     (C) 100°

    (D) 135°    (E) 180°

6. If $n \perp p$, which of the following statements is true?

    (A) $\angle 1 \cong \angle 2$

    (B) $\angle 4 \cong \angle 5$

    (C) $m \angle 4 + m \angle 5 > m \angle 1 + m \angle 2$

    (D) $m \angle 3 > m \angle 2$

    (E) $m \angle 4 = 90°$

**Drill: Triangles**

**Angle Measures**

1. In △ *PQR*, ∠*Q* is a right angle. Find *m* ∠*R*.

   (A) 27°　　(B) 33°　　(C) 54°

   (D) 67°　　(E) 157°

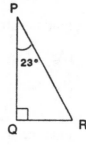

2. △ *MNO* is isosceles. If the vertex angle, ∠*N*, has a measure of 96°, find the measure of ∠*M*.

   (A) 21°　　(B) 42°　　(C) 64°

   (D) 84°　　(E) 96°

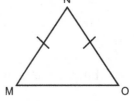

3. Find *x*.

   (A) 15°　　(B) 25°　　(C) 30°

   (D) 45°　　(E) 90°

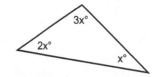

**Similar Triangles**

4. The two triangles shown are similar. Find *b*.

   (A) $2\frac{2}{3}$　　(B) 3　　(C) 4

   (D) 16　　(E) 24

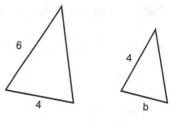

5. The two triangles shown are similar. Find *m* ∠1.

   (A) 48　　(B) 53　　(C) 74

   (D) 127　　(E) 180

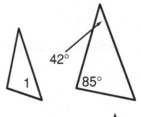

6. The two triangles shown are similar. Find *a* and *b*.

   (A) 5 and 10　　(B) 4 and 8　　(C) $4\frac{2}{3}$ and $7\frac{1}{3}$

   (D) 5 and 8　　(E) $5\frac{1}{3}$ and 8

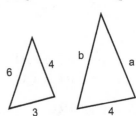

### Area

7. Find the area of △ *MNO*.

    (A) 22        (B) 49        (C) 56

    (D) 84        (E) 112

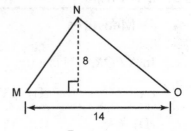

8. Find the area of △ *STU*.

    (A) 4         (B) 8         (C) 12

    (D) 6         (E) 15

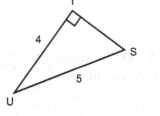

9. Find the area of △ *ABC*.

    (A) 54 cm²    (B) 81 cm²    (C) 108 cm²

    (D) 135 cm²   (E) 180 cm²

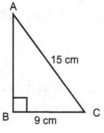

### Drill: Quadrilaterals

### Parallelograms, Rectangles, Rhombi, Squares, Trapezoids

1. Find the area of parallelogram *STUV*.

    (A) 56        (B) 90        (C) 108

    (D) 162       (E) 180

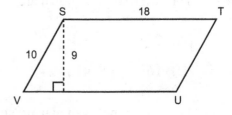

2. Find the perimeter of rectangle *PQRS*, if the area is 84 in².

    (A) 31 in     (B) 38 in     (C) 40 in

    (D) 44 in     (E) 121 in

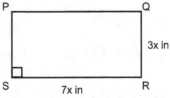

3. In rectangle *ABCD*, *AD* = 6 cm and *DC* = 8 cm. Find the length of the diagonal *AC*.

    (A) 10 cm     (B) 12 cm     (C) 20 cm

    (D) 28 cm     (E) 48 cm

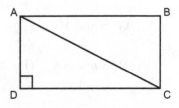

4.  You have a photograph that is 18.5 inches by 12 inches. How many square feet is the photo?

    (A)  222     (B)  144     (C)  30.5

    (D)  1.54     (E)  1.25

5.  In rhombus *DEFG*, *DE* = 7 cm. Find the perimeter of the rhombus.

    (A)  14 cm     (B)  28 cm     (C)  42 cm

    (D)  49 cm     (E)  56 cm

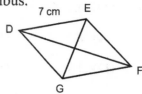

6.  A woman is planning to replace the baseboard in a 10 ft. by 12 ft. room that has a 36-inch doorway. When she bought the baseboard for the room, she knew that she would have five feet left over after completing the project. How many feet of baseboard did she buy?

    (A)  49     (B)  46     (C)  44     (D)  24     (E)  22

7.  The area of square *XYZW* is 196 cm².
    Find the perimeter of the square.

    (A)  28 cm     (B)  42 cm     (C)  56 cm

    (D)  98 cm     (E)  196 cm.

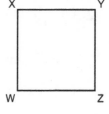

8.  A rectangle is twice as long as it is wide. It has an area of 32 cm². What is its perimeter?

    (A)  24 cm²     (B)  24 cm     (C)  12 cm²     (D)  12 cm     (E)  18 cm

9.  You have a picture that has an original size of eight inches high and ten inches wide. To fit it into a frame, you cut 1 1/2 inches from both the top and bottom and two inches off of the width. What is the new area of the picture in square inches?

    (A)  40     (B)  44     (C)  50 1/2

    (D)  52     (E)  54 1/2

10. *ABCD* is an isosceles trapezoid. Find the perimeter.

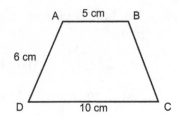

   (A) 21 cm     (B) 27 cm     (C) 30 cm

   (D) 50 cm     (E) 54 cm

11. Trapezoid *XYZW* is isosceles. If $m \angle W = 58°$ and $m \angle Z = 4x - 6°$, find $x$.

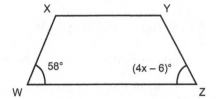

   (A) 8          (B) 12          (C) 13

   (D) 16         (E) 58

### Drill: Circles

### Circumference, Area, Concentric Circles

1.  Find the circumference of circle *A* if its radius is 3 mm.

    (A) $3\pi$ mm     (B) $6\pi$ mm     (C) $9\pi$ mm     (D) $12\pi$ mm     (E) $15\pi$ mm

2.  The circumference of circle *H* is $20\pi$ cm. Find the length of the radius.

    (A) 10 cm     (B) 20 cm     (C) $10\pi$ cm     (D) $15\pi$ cm     (E) $20\pi$ cm

3.  If the diameter of circle *X* is 9 cm and if $\pi = 3.14$, find the circumference of the circle to the nearest tenth.

    (A) 9 cm     (B) 14.1 cm     (C) 21.1 cm     (D) 24.6 cm     (E) 28.3 cm

4.  Find the area of circle *I*.

    (A) 22 mm²     (B) 121 mm²     (C) 379.94 mm²

    (D) 132 mm²     (E) $132\pi$ mm²

5. The diameter of circle $Z$ is 27 mm. Find the area of the circle.

    (A)  91.125 mm²        (B)  182.25 mm²        (C)  191.5π mm²

    (D)  182.25π mm²        (E)  729 mm²

6. The area of circle $B$ is 225π cm². Find the length of the diameter of the circle.

    (A)  15 cm        (B)  20 cm        (C)  30 cm        (D)  20π cm        (E)  25π cm

## Drill: Solids

1. Find the surface area of the rectangular prism shown.

    (A)  138 cm²        (B)  336 cm²        (C)  381 cm²

    (D)  426 cm²        (E)  540 cm²

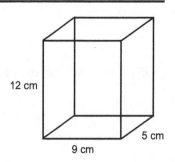

12 cm
5 cm
9 cm

2. Find the volume of the rectangular storage tank shown.

    (A)  24 m³        (B)  36 m³        (C)  38 m³

    (D)  42 m³        (E)  45 m³

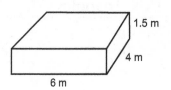

1.5 m
4 m
6 m

## Competency 2: Drills Answer Key

### Drill: Measurement

1. (B)
2. (B)
3. (E)

### Drill: Metric Conversions

1. (C)    4. (B)
2. (A)    5. (B)
3. (D)

### Drill: Customary Conversions

1. (B)    3. (C)
2. (A)    4. (C)

### Drill: Unit Price

1. (B)
2. (A)

### Drill: Lines and Angles

1. (B)    3. (C)    5. (B)
2. (A)    4. (C)    6. (A)

### Drill: Triangles

1. (D)    4. (A)    7. (C)
2. (B)    5. (B)    8. (D)
3. (C)    6. (E)    9. (A)

### Drill: Quadrilaterals

1. (D)    5. (B)    9. (A)
2. (C)    6. (B)    10. (B)
3. (A)    7. (C)    11. (D)
4. (D)    8. (B)

### Drill: Circles

1. (B)    4. (C)
2. (A)    5. (D)
3. (E)    6. (C)

### Drill: Solids

1. (D)
2. (B)

# Drill Section for Competency 3

### Drill: Coordinate Geometry

1.  Which point shown has the coordinates (−3, 2)?

    (A) A          (B) B          (C) C

    (D) D          (E) E

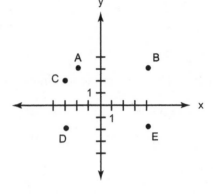

2.  What are the coordinates of the point 4 units above and 6 units to the left of point A?

    (A) (4, 3)          (B) (3, −4)          (C) (8, 3)

    (D) (4, 0)          (E) (−2, 1)

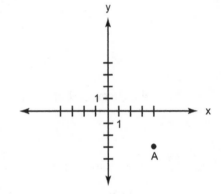

3.  Which point shown has the coordinates (2.5, −1)?

    (A) M          (B) N          (C) P

    (D) Q          (E) R

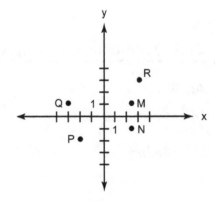

4.   The correct $x$-coordinate for point $H$ is what number?

(A)  3          (B)  4          (C)  –3

(D)  –4          (E)  –5

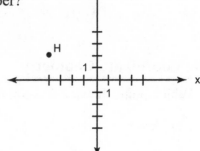

5.   The correct $y$-coordinate for point $R$ is what number?

(A)  –7          (B)  2          (C)  –2

(D)  7          (E)  8

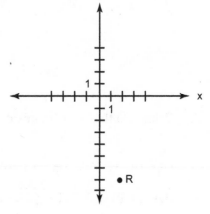

6.   Find the distance between $(4, -7)$ and $(-2, -7)$.

(A)  4          (B)  6          (C)  7          (D)  14          (E)  15

7.   What is the midpoint between $(-4, 2)$ and $(4, -6)$?

(A)  $(-2, 0)$          (B)  $(0, 2)$          (C)  $(0, -4)$          (D)  $(0, -2)$          (E)  $(0, 3)$

## Drill: Operations with Polynomials

### Addition

**Directions:** Add the following polynomials.

1.   $14m^2n^3 + 6m^2n^3 + 3m^2n^3 =$

(A)  $20m^2n^3$          (B)  $23m^6n^9$          (C)  $23m^2n^3$

(D)  $32m^6n^9$          (E)  $23m^8n^{27}$

2. $3x + 2y + 16x + 3z + 6y =$

   (A) $19x + 8y$      (B) $19x + 11yz$      (C) $19x + 8y + 3z$

   (D) $11xy + 19xz$      (E) $30xyz$

3. $(4d^2 + 7e^3 + 12f) + (3d^2 + 6e^3 + 2f) =$

   (A) $23d^2e^3f$      (B) $33d^2e^2f$      (C) $33d^4e^6f^2$

   (D) $7d^2 + 13e^3 + 14f$      (E) $23d^2 + 11e^3f$

## Subtraction

**Directions:** Subtract the following polynomials.

4. $14m^2n - 6m^2n =$

   (A) $20m^2n$      (B) $8m^2n$      (C) $8m$

   (D) $8$      (E) $8m^4n^2$

5. $7b^3 - 4c^2 - 6b^3 + 3c^2 =$

   (A) $b^3 - c^2$      (B) $-11b^2 - 3c^2$      (C) $13b^3 - c$

   (D) $7b - c$      (E) $0$

## Multiplication

**Directions:** Multiply the following polynomials.

6. $5p^2t \times 3p^2t =$

   (A) $15p^2t$      (B) $15p^4t$      (C) $15p^4t^2$

   (D) $8p^2t$      (E) $8p^4t^2$

7. $(2r + s)\,14r =$

   (A) $28rs$      (B) $28r^2 + 14sr$      (C) $16r^2 + 14rs$

   (D) $28r + 14sr$      (E) $17r^2s$

8. $(6t^2 + 2t + 1)\,3t =$

   (A) $9t^2 + 5t + 3$      (B) $18t^2 + 6t + 3$      (C) $9t^3 + 6t^2 + 3t$

   (D) $18t^3 + 6t^2 + 3t$      (E) $12t^3 + 6t^2 + 3t$

### Division

**Directions:** Divide the following polynomials.

9. $24b^4c^3 \div 6b^2c =$

    (A) $3b^2c^2$        (B) $4b^4c^3$        (C) $4b^3c^2$

    (D) $4b^2c^2$        (E) $3b^4c^3$

### Drill: Linear Equations

**Directions:** Solve for $x$.

1. $4x - 2 = 10$

    (A) $-1$     (B) $2$     (C) $3$     (D) $4$     (E) $6$

2. $7z + 1 - z = 2z - 7$

    (A) $-2$     (B) $0$     (C) $1$     (D) $2$     (E) $3$

3. $\frac{1}{3}b + 3 = \frac{1}{2}b$

    (A) $\frac{1}{2}$     (B) $2$     (C) $3\frac{3}{5}$     (D) $6$     (E) $18$

4. $0.4p + 1 = 0.7p - 2$

    (A) $0.1$     (B) $2$     (C) $5$     (D) $10$     (E) $12$

5. $4(3x + 2) - 11 = 3(3x - 2)$

    (A) $-3$     (B) $-1$     (C) $2$     (D) $3$     (E) $7$

## Drill: Inequalities

**Directions:** Find the solution set for each inequality.

1. $3m + 2 < 7$

   (A) $m \geq \dfrac{5}{3}$      (B) $m \leq 2$      (C) $m < 2$

   (D) $m > 2$      (E) $m < \dfrac{5}{3}$

2. $\dfrac{1}{2}x - 3 \leq 1$

   (A) $-4 \leq x \leq 8$      (B) $x \geq -8$      (C) $x \leq 8$

   (D) $2 \leq x \leq 8$      (E) $x \geq 8$

3. Simplify $10 < -2x < 20$

   (A) $-5 < x < 10$      (B) $10 < x < -5$      (C) $5 < x < 10$

   (D) $-10 < x < 5$      (E) $-10 < x < -5$

## Drill: Algebraic Word Problems

**Directions:** Solve the following word problems algebraically.

1. The sum of two numbers is 41. One number is one less than twice the other. Find the larger of the two numbers.

   (A) 13    (B) 14    (C) 21    (D) 27    (E) 41

2. The sum of two consecutive integers is 111. Find the value of the smaller integer.

   (A) 55    (B) 56    (C) 58    (D) 111    (E) 112

3. Zack is $n$ years old, and Josh is twice Zack's age. The sum of their ages is 33. How old is Josh?

   (A) 11    (B) 22    (C) 15    (D) 18    (E) 24

## Competency 3: Drills Answer Key

### Drill: Coordinate Geometry

| | | | |
|---|---|---|---|
| 1. (C) | | 5. (A) |
| 2. (E) | | 6. (B) |
| 3. (B) | | 7. (D) |
| 4. (D) | | |

### Drill: Operations with Polynomials

| | | |
|---|---|---|
| 1. (C) | 4. (B) | 7. (B) |
| 2. (C) | 5. (A) | 8. (D) |
| 3. (D) | 6. (C) | 9. (D) |

### Drill: Linear Equations

| | |
|---|---|
| 1. (C) | 4. (D) |
| 2. (A) | 5. (B) |
| 3. (E) | |

### Drill: Inequalities

1. (E)
2. (C)
3. (D)

### Drill: Algebraic Word Problems

1. (D)
2. (A)
3. (B)

## Drill Section for Competency 4

### Drill: Data Interpretation

**Directions:** Determine the correct response from the information provided.

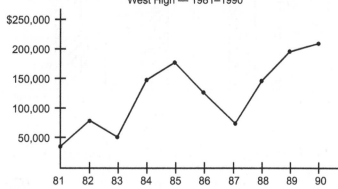

Amount of Scholarship Money Awarded to Graduating Seniors
West High — 1981–1990

1.   What was the approximate amount of scholarship money awarded in 1985?

   (A)  $150,000    (B)  $155,000    (C)  $165,000    (D)  $175,000    (E)  $190,000

2.   By how much did the scholarship money increase between 1987 and 1988?

   (A)  $25,000    (B)  $30,000    (C)  $50,000    (D)  $55,000    (E)  $75,000

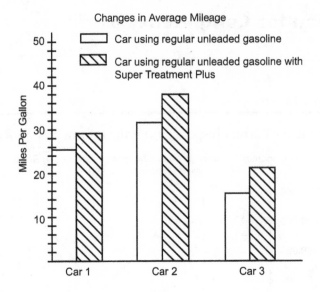

3. By how much did the mileage increase for Car 2 when the new product was used?

   (A) 5 mpg       (B) 6 mpg       (C) 7 mpg

   (D) 10 mpg      (E) 12 mpg

4. Which car's mileage increased the most in this test?

   (A) Car 1         (B) Car 2        (C) Car 3

   (D) Cars 1 and 2     (E) Cars 2 and 3

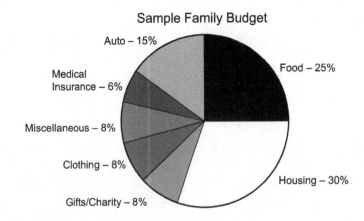

5.  Using the budget shown on the previous page, a family with an income of $4,500 a month would plan to spend what amount on housing?

    (A) $900    (B) $1125    (C) $1350    (D) $1470    (E) $1560

6.  In this sample family budget, how does the amount spent on an automobile compare to the amount spent on housing?

    (A) $\dfrac{1}{3}$    (B) $\dfrac{1}{2}$    (C) $\dfrac{2}{3}$    (D) $1\dfrac{1}{2}$    (E) 2

7.  A family with a monthly income of $3,720 spends $375 a month on clothing. By what amount do they exceed the sample budget?

    (A) $3.00    (B) $15.60    (C) $30.00    (D) $77.40    (E) $95.25

### CALORIE CHART — BREADS

| Bread | Amount | Calories |
|---|---|---|
| French Bread | 2 oz | 140 |
| Bran Bread | 1 oz | 95 |
| Whole Wheat Bread | 1 oz | 115 |
| Oatmeal Bread | 0.5 oz | 55 |
| Raisin Bread | 1 oz | 125 |

8.  One dieter eats two ounces of French bread. A second dieter eats two ounces of bran bread. The second dieter has consumed how many more calories than the first dieter?

    (A) 40    (B) 45    (C) 50    (D) 55    (E) 65

9.  One ounce of whole wheat bread has how many more calories than an ounce of oatmeal bread?

    (A) 5    (B) 15    (C) 60    (D) 75    (E) 125

### Drill: Measures of Central Tendency

## Mean

**Directions:** Find the mean of each set of numbers.

1. 18, 25, and 32

   (A) 3       (B) 25       (C) 50       (D) 75       (E) 150

2. 97, 102, 116, and 137

   (A) 40       (B) 102       (C) 109       (D) 113       (E) 116

3. 12, 15, 18, 24, and 31

   (A) 18       (B) 19.3       (C) 20       (D) 25       (E) 100

4. 7, 4, 6, 3, 11, and 14

   (A) 5       (B) 6.5       (C) 7       (D) 7.5       (E) 8

## Median

**Directions:** Find the median value of each set of numbers.

5. 3, 8, and 6

   (A) 3       (B) 6       (C) 8       (D) 17       (E) 20

6. 19, 15, 21, 27, and 12

   (A) 19       (B) 15       (C) 21       (D) 27       (E) 94

7. 29, 18, 21, and 35

   (A) 29       (B) 18       (C) 21       (D) 35       (E) 25

8. 8, 15, 7, 12, 31, 3, and 28

   (A) 7       (B) 11.6       (C) 12       (D) 14.9       (E) 104

## Mode

**Directions:** Find the mode(s) of each set of numbers.

9.  1, 3, 7, 4, 3, and 8

(A)  1          (B)  3          (C)  7          (D)  4          (E)  None

10. 12, 19, 25, and 42

(A)  12          (B)  19          (C)  25          (D)  42          (E)  None

11. 16, 14, 12, 16, 30, and 28

(A)  6          (B)  14          (C)  16          (D)  $19.\overline{3}$          (E)  None

12. 4, 3, 9, 2, 4, 5, and 2

(A)  3 and 9          (B)  5 and 9          (C)  4 and 5          (D)  2 and 4          (E)  None

## Drill: Standard Deviation

1.  The heights of adult men in the United States are shown in the table below. Out of 2,000 randomly selected men, how many would you expect to be over six feet tall?

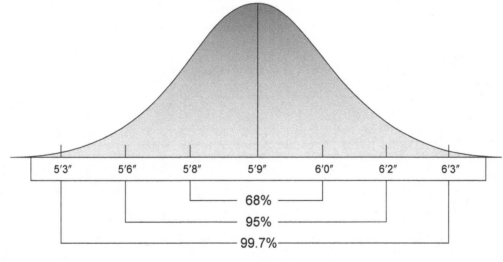

(A)  640          (B)  400          (C)  320          (D)  200          (E)  180

## Competency 4: Drills Answer Key

### Drill: Data Interpretation

| | | | | | |
|---|---|---|---|---|---|
| 1. | (D) | 4. | (E) | 7. | (D) |
| 2. | (E) | 5. | (C) | 8. | (C) |
| 3. | (B) | 6. | (B) | 9. | (A) |

### Drill: Measures of Central Tendency

| | | | | | | | |
|---|---|---|---|---|---|---|---|
| 1. | (B) | 4. | (D) | 7. | (E) | 10. | (E) |
| 2. | (D) | 5. | (B) | 8. | (C) | 11. | (C) |
| 3. | (C) | 6. | (A) | 9. | (B) | 12. | (D) |

### Drill: Standard Deviation

1. (C)

# English Language Skills

## Overview

This chapter offers comprehensive coverage of Florida's required competencies and provides 20 drills that will help build your English Language Skills. On the FTCE-GKT, you will have 40 minutes to complete the 40-question section, which covers the following key competencies:

- Knowledge of Language Structure (25%)

- Knowledge of Vocabulary Application (25%)

- Knowledge of Standard English Conventions (50%)

## Competency 1: Knowledge of Language Structure

### Skill 1.1: Evaluate correct placement of modifiers.

A misplaced modifier is one that is in the wrong place in the sentence. Misplaced modifiers come in all forms—words, phrases, and clauses. Sentences containing misplaced modifiers can be comical:

*Mom made me eat the spinach instead of my brother.*

Misplaced modifiers, like the one in the previous sentence, are usually too far away from the word or words they modify.

The sentence should read:

*Mom made me, instead of my brother, eat the spinach.*

Modifiers like *only, nearly,* and *almost* should be placed next to the word they modify and not in front of some other word, especially a verb, that they are not intended to modify. A modifier is misplaced if it appears to modify the wrong part of the sentence or if we cannot be certain what part of the sentence the writer intended it to modify. To correct a misplaced modifier, move the modifier next to the word it describes.

| | |
|---|---|
| INCORRECT: | She served hamburgers to the men on paper plates. |
| CORRECT: | She served hamburgers on paper plates to the men. |

Split infinitives also result in misplaced modifiers. Infinitives consist of the marker *to* plus the plain form of the verb. The two parts of the infinitive make up a grammatical unit that should not be split. Splitting an infinitive is placing an adverb between the *to* and the verb.

| | |
|---|---|
| INCORRECT: | The weather service expects temperatures to not rise. |
| CORRECT: | The weather service expects temperatures not to rise. |

Sometimes a split infinitive may be natural and preferable, though it may still bother some readers.

| | |
|---|---|
| EXAMPLE: | Several U.S. industries expect *to* more than *triple* their use of robots within the next decade. |

A squinting modifier is one that may refer to either a preceding or a following word, leaving the reader uncertain about what it is intended to modify. Correct a squinting modifier by moving it next to the word it is intended to modify.

| | |
|---|---|
| INCORRECT: | Snipers who fired on the soldiers often escaped capture. |
| CORRECT: | Snipers who often fired on the soldiers escaped capture. |
| | OR |
| | Snipers who fired on the soldiers escaped capture often. |

A dangling modifier is a modifier or verb in search of a subject: the modifying phrase (usually an *–ing* word group, an *-ed* or *-en* word group, or a *to + a verb* word group—participle phrase or infinitive phrase, respectively) either appears to modify the wrong word or has nothing to modify. It is left dangling at the beginning or the end of a sentence. Such sentences often look and sound correct, as in the following:

*To be a student government officer, your grades must be above average.* (However, the verbal modifier has nothing to describe. Who is *to be a student government officer*? Your grades?) Questions of this type require you to determine whether a modifier has a head-word or whether it is dangling at the beginning or the end of the sentence.

To correct a dangling modifier, reword the sentence by either 1) changing the modifying phrase to a clause with a subject, or 2) changing the subject of the sentence to the word that should be modified. Here are examples worth considering:

| | |
|---|---|
| INCORRECT: | Shortly after leaving home, the accident occurred. |
| | Who is leaving home, the accident? |
| CORRECT: | Shortly after we left home, the accident occurred. |
| | |
| INCORRECT: | To get up on time, a great effort was needed. |
| | "To get up" needs a subject. |
| CORRECT: | To get up on time, I made a great effort. |

## Skill 1.2: Apply knowledge of parallelism, including parallel expressions for parallel ideas.

This skill requires recognition of parallel expressions for parallel ideas. Parallel structure is used to express matching ideas. It refers to the grammatical balance of a series of any of the following:

**Phrases**

The squirrel ran *along the fence, up the tree,* and *into his burrow* with a mouthful of acorns.

**Adjectives**

The job market is flooded with *very talented, highly motivated,* and *well-educated* young people.

**Nouns**

You will need a *notebook, pencil,* and *dictionary* for the test.

**Clauses**

The children were told to decide *which toy they would keep* and *which toy they would give away.*

**Verbs**

The farmer *plowed, planted,* and *harvested* his corn in record time.

### Verbals

*Reading, writing,* and *calculating* are fundamental skills that all of us should possess.

### Correlative conjunctions

*Either* you will do your homework *or* you will fail.

### Repetition of structural signals

(such as articles, auxiliaries, prepositions, and conjunctions)

| | |
|---|---|
| INCORRECT: | I have quit my job, enrolled in school, and am looking for a reliable babysitter. |
| CORRECT: | I *have quit* my job, *have enrolled* in school, and *am looking* for a reliable babysitter. |

*Note:* Repetition of prepositions is considered formal and is not necessary.

You can travel *by car, by plane, or by train*; it's all up to you.

OR

You can travel *by car, plane, or train*; it's all up to you.

When a sentence contains items in a series, check for both punctuation and sentence balance. When you check for punctuation, make sure the commas are used correctly. When you check for parallelism, make sure that the conjunctions connect similar grammatical constructions, such as all adjectives or all clauses.

## Skill 1.3: Apply knowledge of a variety of effective structures.

A fragment is an incomplete construction that may or may not have a subject and a verb. Specifically, a fragment is a group of words pretending to be a sentence. Not all fragments appear as separate sentences, however. Fragments often are separated by semicolons.

| | |
|---|---|
| INCORRECT: | Traffic was stalled for ten miles on the freeway. Because repairs were being made on potholes. |
| CORRECT: | Traffic was stalled for ten miles on the freeway because repairs were being made on potholes. |
| INCORRECT: | It was a funny story; one that I had never heard before. |
| CORRECT: | It was a funny story, one that I had never heard before. |

## Comma Splices

A comma splice is the unjustifiable use of only a comma to combine what really is two separate sentences.

| | |
|---|---|
| INCORRECT: | One common error in writing is incorrect spelling, the other is the occasional use of faulty diction. |
| CORRECT: | One common error in writing is incorrect spelling; the other is the occasional use of faulty diction. |

Both run-on sentences and comma splices may be corrected in one of the following ways:

| | |
|---|---|
| RUN-ON: | Neal won the award he had the highest score. |
| COMMA SPLICE: | Neal won the award, he had the highest score. |

Separate the sentences with a period:

Neal won the award. He had the highest score.

Separate the sentences with a comma and a coordinating conjunction (*and, but, or, nor, for, yet, so*):

Neal won the award for he had the highest score.

Separate the sentences with a semicolon:

Neal won the award; he had the highest score.

Separate the sentences with a subordinating conjunction such as *although, because, since, if*:

Neal won the award because he had the highest score.

## Run-on/Fused Sentences

A run-on/fused sentence is not necessarily a long sentence or a sentence that the reader considers too long; in fact, a run-on may be two short sentences: *Dry ice does not melt it evaporates.* A run-on results when the writer fuses or runs together two separate sentences without any correct mark of punctuation separating them.

INCORRECT:    Knowing how to use a dictionary is no problem each dictionary has a section in the front of the book telling how to use it.

CORRECT:    Knowing how to use a dictionary is no problem. Each dictionary has a section in the front of the book telling how to use it.

Even if one or both of the fused sentences contains internal punctuation, the sentence is still a run-on.

INCORRECT:    Bob bought dress shoes, a suit, and a nice shirt he needed them for his sister's wedding.

CORRECT:    Bob bought dress shoes, a suit, and a nice shirt. He needed them for his sister's wedding.

## Subordination, Coordination, and Predication

Suppose, for the sake of clarity, you wanted to combine the information in these two sentences to create one statement:

*I studied a foreign language. I found English quite easy.*

How you decide to combine this information should be determined by the relationship you'd like to show between the two facts. *I studied a foreign language, and I found English quite easy* seems rather illogical. The **coordination** of the two ideas (connecting them with the coordinating conjunction *and*) is ineffective. Using **subordination** instead (connecting the sentences with a subordinating conjunction) clearly shows the degree of relative importance between the expressed ideas:

After I studied a foreign language, I found English quite easy.

When using a conjunction, be sure that the sentence parts you are joining are in agreement.

INCORRECT:    She loved him dearly but not his dog.

CORRECT:    She loved him dearly but she did not love his dog.

A common mistake that is made is to forget that each member of the pair must be followed by the same kind of construction.

INCORRECT:    They complimented them for their bravery and they thanked them for their being kind.

CORRECT:    They complimented them for their bravery and thanked them for their kindness.

*While* refers to time and should not be used as a substitute for *although*, *and*, or *but*.

> INCORRECT: While I'm usually interested in Fellini movies, I'd rather not go tonight.
>
> CORRECT: Although I'm usually interested in Fellini movies, I'd rather not go tonight.

*Where* refers to place and should not be used as a substitute for *that*.

> INCORRECT: We read in the paper where they are making great strides in DNA research.
>
> CORRECT: We read in the paper that they are making great strides in DNA research.

After words like "reason" and "explanation," use *that*, not *because*.

> INCORRECT: His explanation for his tardiness was because his alarm did not go off.
>
> CORRECT: His explanation for his tardiness was that his alarm did not go off.

## Common Syntax Errors

Syntax is defined as the arrangement of words and phrases to create well-formed sentences in a language. It is helpful for you as a test-taker to consider the most common syntax errors:

- Lack of noun/pronoun agreement

  **Incorrect Example:** Everyone should have their own log-in.

- Avoid the use of abbreviations ("&," "aka," etc.)

  **Incorrect Example:** We reviewed bank statements, reconciliations, & certificates of deposits.

- Word repetition

  **Incorrect Example:** The Miranda rights that are read to a criminal suspect in the United States, explaining the rights that are granted by the U.S. Constitution, would only seem necessary to read those rights that are granted by the country to where they are being interrogated.

- Plural vs. Possessive

  **Incorrect Example:** The boys car was a mint green Pontiac Tempest.

- Ending sentences with a preposition

  **Incorrect Example:** Never use a preposition to end a sentence with.

- Write out numbers under 10

  **Incorrect Example:** He ate 3 donuts for breakfast.

- Split infinitives

  **Incorrect Example:** The boys needed to quickly run from the store.

- Correct use of "that" versus "who"

  **Incorrect Example:** Miriam was the one that wanted the ice cream sundae.

- Correct use of "however"

  **Incorrect Example:** Conventional wisdom holds that .... However, it can also be argued that ...

- Preferred usage of "neither"/"nor"—do not use "nor" without "neither."

  **Incorrect Example:** Neither do I want to go to school but I want to go to the bank.

## Skill 1.4: Determine patterns of organization in a written passage.

Within conventional writing, text is arranged to serve the purpose of the author. The most commonly used patterns of organization are described below.

### Chronological Pattern

A chronological pattern of organization arranges information according to a progression of time, either forward or backward. When a topic is best understood in terms of different segments of time, a chronological format works well. For example, topics of a historical nature are best organized using this pattern.

When using a chronological pattern, each main section of information represents a particular period of time, and the sub-points contained within each main section refer to significant events that occurred within that time frame. A variation of this organizational pattern involves dividing a topic into "past-present-future" or "before-during-after" segments.

For example, suppose a writer's stated purpose is to describe the historical development and evolution of the city of Seattle. Assuming that the writer wanted to trace the city's first 100 years, the writer could organize the information by grouping it into four 25-year chunks. In this case, the sub-points within each main section of time represent the most significant events that occurred during that particular time frame. Notice that by breaking the 100-year span into distinct 25-year chunks, the information is more succinctly organized for the reader.

### Chronological Pattern Example

   I.   1851–1876

      A.  Significant Event #1

      B.  Significant Event #2

  II.   1876–1901

      A.  Significant Event #1

      B.  Significant Event #2

 III.   1901–1926

      A.  Significant Event #1

      B.  Significant Event #2

 IV.   1926–1951

      A.  Significant Event #1

      B.  Significant Event #2

## Sequential Pattern

A sequential pattern of organization is similar to a chronological pattern, but arranges information according to a step-by-step sequence that describes a particular process. Using a sequential pattern, each main section of information represents a main step that one would follow in the actual process. The points included within each main section represent the sub-steps one would follow. Thus, when one wishes to describe a process that follows a specific series of steps in a particular order, a sequential pattern works well.

For example, suppose a writer's stated purpose is to explain how wine is made. A sequential pattern would be effective in this case because it breaks the process down into a specific series of steps that should be followed in a precise order. Notice that a series of related smaller steps are grouped into one larger category. Thus, a process that involves many specific steps can be simplified by highlighting the most fundamental steps, which helps the reader understand the process and remember its key parts.

### Sequential Pattern Example

I.    Step One: Harvest the grapes

    A.  Harvesting procedure No. 1

    B.  Harvesting procedure No. 2

II.    Step Two: Prepare the grapes

    A.  Preparation procedure No. 1

    B.  Preparation procedure No. 2

III.    Step Three: Ferment the grapes

    A.  Fermenting procedure No. 1

    B.  Fermenting procedure No. 2

IV.    Step Four: Press the grapes

    A.  Pressing procedure No. 1

    B.  Pressing procedure No. 2

## Spatial Pattern

A spatial pattern of organization arranges information according to how things fit together in physical space (i.e., where one thing exists in relation to another). This pattern works well when a writer wishes to create a mental picture of something that has various parts distinguished by physical location. Topics involving geography, for example, are often best organized using a spatial pattern.

For example, suppose a writer wished to describe the forms of entertainment available to tourists visiting a major city. The writer could arrange the information according to "things to do" in the different districts or geographic locations of the city. Notice how this pattern of organization aids the reader. It makes sense for the writer to organize the information by physical location because the information is easy to understand and use in this format, particularly for tourists who are not familiar with the area.

### Spatial Pattern Example

I.    Downtown

    A.  Aquarium

    B.  Pike Place Market

II.    Wichita Center

    A.  Space Needle

    B.  Southern Science Center

III.    University District

    A.  University of Illinois campus

    B.  The "Park" (shops on University Avenue)

## Compare-Contrast Pattern

A compare-and-contrast pattern arranges information according to how two or more things are similar to or different from one another (or both). This is an effective pattern to use when the reader can better understand one subject when it is described in relation to another. If the reader is familiar with one topic, the writer can compare or contrast it with another topic to shed insight on it.

For example, suppose a writer's stated purpose is to help the reader make an informed decision about whether to attend a two-year college or a four-year university. One way to arrange the information is to compare and contrast the two educational options along several important dimensions, such as cost, quality of education, and variety of educational programs. In this case, the number of main sections in the outline would depend on how many dimensions or factors were considered (three in the case below). Another way to arrange the information would be to create two main sections, one that describes similarities and one that describes differences (as shown in the second example below). Notice that either format could be equally effective.

**Compare-and-Contrast Pattern Example One**

    I.   Cost of Tuition

        A.  Two-Year

        B.  Four-Year

    II.  Quality of Education

        A.  Two-year

        B.  Four-year

    III. Educational Programs

        A.  Two-year

        B.  Four-year

**Compare-and-Contrast Pattern Example Two**

    I.   Points of Comparison

        A.  Educational Programs

        B.  Cost of Tuition

    II.  Points of Contrast

        A.  Quality of Education

        B.  Type of Degree

## Advantages-Disadvantages Pattern

This pattern organizes information about a topic by dividing it up into its "good" and "bad" parts, or pros and cons. It is effective to use when a writer wishes to objectively discuss both sides of an issue without taking a stance. This allows the reader to weigh both sides of an issue. As with the compare-contrast pattern, there are a number of possible variations to an advantages-disadvantages pattern. The simplest form of this pattern is shown below.

Suppose, for example, that a writer's stated purpose is to describe the advantages and disadvantages of attending a two-year college. One way to arrange the information is to divide it into two main sections, one for the advantages and one for the disadvantages. In this scenario, the information contained within each main section will represent the specific topics of analysis (cost, accessibility, etc.).

### Advantages and Disadvantages Example

I.   Advantages

    A.  Cost

    B.  Accessibility

II.  Disadvantages

    A.  Number of educational programs

    B.  Quality of instruction

## Cause-Effect Pattern

This pattern is used to show the different causes and effects of various conditions. This pattern is particularly effective when writing a persuasive document in which the writer advocates some action to solve a problem, because it demonstrates important relationships between variables. There are two major variations to this pattern. The first is to divide the outline into two major sections—causes and effects. The second is to divide the outline according to the different causes, with the effects of each cause contained within the larger "causes" section. See the examples below.

Suppose a writer's stated purpose is to explain the causes of conflict escalation and their effects. The writer could organize the information in one of the following two ways. Again, notice that either method could work equally well.

### Cause-and-Effect Pattern Example #1

I.   Causes of Conflict Escalation

    A.  Expanding the issues

    B.  Personal attacks

  II.   Effects of these causes

      A.  Lose focus on original issue

      B.  Cycle of defensive responses

      C.  Win-Lose orientation

      D.  Negative emotions

### Cause-and-Effect Pattern Example #2

  I.   Cause: Expanding the issues

      A.  Effect: Lose focus on original issues

      B.  Effect: Cycle of defensive responses

  II.   Cause: Personal attacks

      A.  Effect: Negative emotions

      B.  Effect: Win-Lose orientation

## Problem-Solution Pattern

A problem-solution pattern divides information into two main sections, one that describes a problem and one that describes a solution. This pattern is typically used in persuasive writing, where the writer's general purpose is to convince the reader to support a given course of action. The pattern is designed to compel the reader to change an opinion or behavior by establishing that a problem exists, then providing a solution. In the problem section, the writer identifies different aspects, and provides evidence, of the problem. In the solution section, the writer identifies a potential solution and supports the effectiveness of this solution over others.

For example, suppose a writer's stated purpose is to persuade readers to adopt cycling as their primary form of transportation. First, the writer could attempt to establish that common forms of motorized transportation create compelling problems that require a solution. Then the writer could show how the proposed solution—riding a bicycle—provides a beneficial alternative to driving.

### Problem-Solution Example

  I.   Problem: Motorized Transportation

      A.  Increasing traffic congestion

      B.  Increasing pollution

      C.  Increasing "road rage" from traffic-related stress

  II.   Solution: Riding Bicycles

      A.  Bike riding reduces the number of motorized vehicles in use

      B.  Bike riding is not a source of pollution

      C.  Bike riding has physical and psychological health benefits

## Topical Pattern

This pattern is the most commonly used format, and will typically work when the other patterns do not. A topical pattern arranges information according to different subtopics within a larger topic, or the "types" of things that fall within a larger category. Using this pattern, each "type" represents a main section of information.

For example, suppose a writer wished to describe various types of wine. One way to outline this information would be to divide the type of wine by its color, as shown in the example below.

### Topical Pattern Example One

I. Red Wines

    A. European

        1. Bordeaux

        2. Burgundy

        3. Chianti

    B. Californian

        1. Cabernet Sauvignon

        2. Pinot Noir

        3. Zinfandel

II. White Wines

    A. European

        1. Bordeaux

        2. Burgundy

        3. Mosel

    B. Californian

        1. Sauvignon Blanc

        2. Chardonnay

        3. Riesling

## Competency 2: Knowledge of Vocabulary Application

### ■ Skill 2.1: Determine the meaning of unknown words, multiple-meaning words, and phrases in context.

When attempting to decipher the meaning of a new word, it is often useful to look at what comes before and after that word. The surrounding words can give you **context clues** about the meaning and structure of the new word, as well as how it is used.

### Common Types of Context Clues

**Root word and affix**—People who study birds are experts in ornithology.

**Contrast**—Unlike mammals, birds incubate their eggs outside their bodies.

**Logic**—Birds are always on the lookout for predators that might harm their young.

**Definition**—Frugivorous birds prefer eating fruit to any other kind of food.

**Example or illustration**—Some birds like to build their nests in inconspicuous spots—high up in the tops of trees, well hidden by leaves.

**Grammar**—Many birds migrate twice each year.

Beyond context clues, the following elements are helpful when determining multiple-meaning and unknown words in context:

**Root Word**—basic unit of a word

**Prefix**—word part added in front of a root word to make a new word

**Suffix**—word part added at the end of a root word to make a new word

**Synonyms**—words that mean the same or nearly the same

**Non-examples**—words that have different meanings

Finally, it is helpful to ask yourself the following questions in order to determine the meaning of unknown words:

- What is the overall intent of the text? For example, is it about science or history?

- Is the text factual or a work of fiction?

- What is the genre?

- What other words in the sentence or paragraph can provide information?

- What clues does the punctuation provide?

## Skill 2.2: Determine and select the correct use of commonly confused words, misused words, and phrases.

It is important to understand the meanings of all words—not just the ones you are asked to define. A good vocabulary will help you perform well on all sections of this test. The following information will build your skills in determining the meanings of words.

### Similar Forms and Sounds

The complex nature of language sometimes makes reading difficult. Words often become confusing when they have similar forms and sounds. Indeed the author may have a correct meaning in mind, but an incorrect word choice can alter the meaning of the sentence or even make it illogical.

NO:     Martha was always part of that *cliché*.

YES:     Martha was always part of that *clique*.

(A *cliché* is a trite or hackneyed expression; a *clique* is an exclusive group of people.)

NO:     The minister spoke of the soul's *immorality*.

YES:     The minister spoke of the soul's *immortality*.

(*Immorality* means wickedness; *immortality* means imperishable or unending life.)

NO:     Where is the nearest *stationary* store?

YES:     Where is the nearest *stationery* store?

(*Stationary* means immovable; *stationery* is paper used for writing.)

Below are groups of words that are often confused because of their similar forms and sounds.

1.  **accent**—*v.*—to stress or emphasize (You must *accent* the last syllable.)

    **ascent**—*n.*—a climb or rise (John's *ascent* of the mountain was dangerous.)

    **assent**—*n.*—consent; compliance (We need your *assent* before we can go ahead with the plans.)

2. **accept**—*v.*—to take something offered (She *accepted* the gift.)

   **except**—*prep.*—other than; but (Everyone was included in the plans *except* him.)

3. **advice**—*n.*—opinion given as to what to do or how to handle a situation (Her sister gave her *advice* on what to say at the interview.)

   **advise**—*v.*—to counsel (John's guidance counselor *advised* him on which colleges to apply to.)

4. **affect**—*v.*—to influence (Mary's suggestion did not *affect* me.)

   **effect**—1. *v.*—to cause to happen (The plan was *effected* with great success.); 2. *n.*—result (The *effect* of the medicine is excellent.)

5. **allusion**—*n.*—indirect reference (In the poem, there are many biblical *allusions.*)

   **illusion**—*n.*—false idea or conception; belief or opinion not in accord with the facts (Greg was under the *illusion* that he could win the race after missing three weeks of practice.)

6. **already**—*adv.*—previously (I had *already* read that novel.)

   **all ready**—*adv. + adj.*—prepared (The family was *all ready* to leave on vacation.)

7. **altar**—*n.*—table or stand used in religious rites (The priest stood at the *altar.*)

   **alter**—*v.*—to change (Their plans were *altered* during the strike.)

8. **capital**—1. *n.*—a city where the government meets (The senators had a meeting in Albany, the *capital* of New York.); 2. money used in business (They had enough *capital* to develop the industry.)

   **capitol**—*n.*—building in which the legislature meets (Senator Brown gave a speech at the *capitol* in Washington.)

9. **choose**—*v.*—to select (Which camera did you *choose*?)

   **chose**—(past tense, *choose*) (Susan *chose* to stay home.)

10. **cite**—*v.*—to quote (The student *cited* evidence from the text.)

    **site**—*n.*—location (They chose the *site* where the house would be built.)

11. **clothes**—*n.*—garments (Because she got caught in the rain, her *clothes* were wet.)

    **cloths**—*n.*—pieces of material (The *cloths* were used to wash the windows.)

12. **coarse**—*adj.*—rough; unrefined (Sandpaper is *coarse.*)

   **course**—1. *n.*—path of action (She did not know what *course* would solve the problem.); 2. passage (We took the long *course* to the lake.); 3. series of studies (We both enrolled in the physics *course.*); 4. part of a meal (She served a five-*course* meal.)

13. **consul**—*n.*—a person appointed by the government to live in a foreign city and represent the citizenry and business interests of his native country there (The *consul* was appointed to Naples, Italy.)

   **council**—*n.*—a group used for discussion, advisement (The *council* decided to accept his letter of resignation.)

   **counsel**—*v.*—to advise (Tom *counsels* Jerry on tax matters.)

14. **decent**—*adj.*—proper; respectable (He was very *decent* about the entire matter.)

   **descent**—1. *n.*—moving down (In Dante's *Inferno,* the *descent* into Hell was depicted graphically.); 2. ancestry (He is of Irish *descent.*)

15. **device**—1. *n.*—plan; scheme (The *device* helped her win the race.); 2. invention (We bought a *device* that opens the garage door automatically.)

   **devise**—*v.*—to contrive (He *devised* a plan so John could not win.)

16. **emigrate**—*v.*—to go away from a country (Many Japanese *emigrated* from Japan in the late 1800s.)

   **immigrate**—*v.*—to come into a country (Her relatives *immigrated* to the United States after World War I.)

17. **eminent**—*n.*—prominent (He is an *eminent* member of the community.)

   **imminent**—*adj.*—impending (The decision is *imminent.*)

   **immanent**—*adj.*—existing within (Maggie believed that religious spirit is *immanent* in human beings.)

18. **fair**—1. *adj.*—beautiful (She was *a fair* maiden.); 2. just (She tried to be *fair.*); 3. *n.*—festival (There were many games at the *fair.*)

   **fare**—*n.*—amount of money paid for transportation (The city proposed that the subway *fare* be raised.)

19. **forth**—*adv.*—onward (The soldiers moved *forth* in the blinding snow.)

   **fourth**—*n., adj.*—4th (She was the *fourth* runner-up in the beauty contest.)

20. **its**—possessive form of *it* (Our town must improve *its* roads.)

    **it's**—contraction of "it is" (*It's* time to leave the party.)

21. **later**—*adj., adv.*—at a subsequent date (We will take a vacation *later* this year.)

    **latter**—*n.*—second of the two (Susan can visit Monday or Tuesday. The *latter*, however, is preferable.)

22. **lead**—1. *n.*—(led) a metal (The handgun was made of *lead*.); 2. *v.t.*—(leed) to show the way (The camp counselor *leads* the way to the picnic grounds.)

    **led**—past tense of *lead* (The dog *led* the way.)

23. **loose**—*adj.*—free; unrestricted (The dog was let *loose* by accident.)

    **lose**—*v.*—to suffer the loss of (He was afraid he would *lose* the race.)

24. **moral**—1. *adj.*—virtuous (She is a *moral* woman with high ethical standards.); 2. *n.*—lesson taught by a story, incident, etc. (Most fables end with a *moral*.)

    **morale**—*n.*—mental condition (After the team lost the game, their *morale* was low.)

25. **of**—*prep.*—from (She is *of* French descent.)

    **off**—*adj.*—away; at a distance (The silverware fell *off* the table.)

26. **passed**—*v.*—having satisfied some requirement (He *passed* the test.)

    **past**—1. *adj.*—gone by or elapsed in time (His *past* deeds got him in trouble.); 2. *n.*—a period of time gone by (His *past* was shady.); 3. *prep.*—beyond (She ran *past* the house.)

27. **personal**—*adj.*—private (Jack was unwilling to discuss his childhood; it was too *personal*.)

    **personnel**—*n.*—staff (We lack the *personnel* to compete effectively.)

28. **principal**—*n.*—head of a school (The *principal* addressed the graduating class.)—*adj.*—most important

    **principle**—*n.*—the ultimate source, origin, or cause of something; a law, truth (The *principles* of physics were reviewed in class today.)

29. **prophecy**—*n.*—prediction of the future (His *prophecy* that he would become a doctor came true.)

    **prophesy**—*v.*—to declare or predict (He *prophesied* that we would win the lottery.)

30. **quiet**—*adj.*—still; calm (At night all is *quiet.*)

    **quite**—*adv.*—really; truly (She is *quite* a good singer.)

    **quit**—*v.*—to free oneself (Peter had little time to spare so he *quit* the chorus.)

31. **respectfully**—*adv.*—with respect, honor, esteem (He declined the offer *respectfully.*)

    **respectively**—*adv.*—in the order mentioned (Jack, Susan, and Jim, who are members of the club, were elected president, vice president, and secretary, *respectively.*)

32. **stationary**—*adj.*—immovable (The park bench is *stationary.*)

    **stationery**—*n.*—paper used for writing (The invitations were printed on yellow *stationery.*)

33. **straight**—*adj.*—not curved (The road was *straight.*)

    **strait**—1. *adj.*—restricted; narrow; confined (The patient was put in a *strait* jacket.); 2. *n.*—narrow waterway (He sailed through the *Strait* of Magellan.)

34. **than**—*conj.*—used most commonly in comparisons (Maggie is older *than* I.)

    **then**—*adv.*—soon afterward (We lived in Boston, *then* we moved to New York.)

35. **their**—possessive form of *they* (That is *their* house on Tenafly Drive.)

    **they're**—contraction of "they are" (*They're* leaving for California next week.)

    **there**—*adv.*—at that place (Who is standing *there* under the tree?)

36. **to**—*prep.*—in the direction of; toward; as (She made a turn *to* the right on Norman Street.)

    **too**—1. *adv.*—more than enough (She served *too* much for dinner.); 2. also (He is going to Maine *too.*)

    **two**—*n.*—2; one plus one (We have *two* pet rabbits.)

37. **weather**—*n.*—the general condition of the atmosphere (The *weather* is expected to be clear on Sunday.)

   **whether**—*conj.*—if it be a case or fact (We don't know *whether* the trains are late.)

38. **who's**—contraction of "who is" or "who has" (*Who's* willing to volunteer for the night shift?)

   **whose**—possessive form of *who* (*Whose* book is this?)

39. **your**—possessive form of *you* (Is this *your* seat?)

   **you're**—contraction of *you* and *are* (I know *you're* going to do well on the test.)

## Multiple Meanings

In addition to words that sound alike, you must be careful when dealing with words that have multiple meanings. For example:

   The boy was thrilled that his mother gave him a piece of chewing *gum*.

   Dentists advise people to floss their teeth to help prevent *gum* disease.

As you can see, one word can have different meanings depending on the context in which it is used.

## Connotation and Denotation

Language can become even more complicated. Not only can a single word have numerous definitions and subtle meanings, it may also take on added meanings through implication. The **connotation** is the idea suggested by its place near or association with other words or phrases. The **denotation** of a word is the direct explicit meaning.

### Connotation

Sometimes, you will be asked to tell the meaning of a word in the context of the paragraph. You may not have seen the word before, but from your understanding of the writer's intent, you should be able to figure it out. For example, read the following paragraph:

   Paris is a beautiful city, perhaps the most beautiful on earth. Long, broad avenues are lined with seventeenth- and eighteenth-century apartments, office buildings, and cafés. Flowers give the city a rich and varied look. The bridges and the river lend an air of lightness and grace to the whole urban landscape.

In this paragraph, "rich" most nearly means

(A) wealthy.

(B) polluted.

(C) colorful.

(D) dull.

If you chose "colorful" you would be right. Although "rich" literally means "wealthy" (that is its *denotation*, its literal meaning), here the writer means more than the word's literal meaning, and seems to be highlighting the variety and color that the flowers add to the avenues—that is, richness in a figurative sense. The writer is using a non-literal meaning, or *connotation* that we associate with the word "rich" to show the meaning that should be lent to it. When we think of something "rich," we usually also think of abundance, variety, color, and not merely numbers.

## Denotation

Determining the denotation of a word is different from determining a word's connotation. Read this paragraph:

Many soporifics are on the market to help people sleep. Take a glass of water and two *Sleepeze* and you get the "Z's" you need. *Sominall* supposedly helps you get the sleep you need so you can go on working. With *Morpho*, your head hits the pillow and you're asleep before the light goes out.

From this paragraph, a "soporific" is probably

(A) a drug that stimulates you to stay awake.

(B) a kind of sleeping bag.

(C) a kind of bed.

(D) a drug that helps you sleep.

What is a soporific? You can figure out what it means by looking at what is said around it. People take these "soporifics" to go to sleep, not to wake up. So it can't be (A). You can't take two beds and a glass of water to go to sleep, either. So it can't be (C). You might be able to identify what a soporific is because you recognize the brand names used as examples. So, it must be some sort of pill that you take to sleep. Because pills are usually drugs of some kind, the answer is (D).

## Figures of Speech

Figurative language helps to create imaginative and detailed writing. A figure of speech is used in the imaginative rather than the literal sense. It helps the reader to make connections between the writer's thoughts and the external world. Knowing the different types of figures of speech can help you determine the context in which a word is being used, and thereby help you determine the meaning of that word. The following are some commonly used figures of speech.

### Simile

A simile is an explicit comparison between two things. The comparison is made by using *like* or *as*.

> **Example:** Her hair was *like* straw.

> **Example:** The blanket was *as* white as snow.

### Metaphor

Like the simile, the metaphor likens two things. However, *like* or *as* are not used in the comparison.

> **Example:** "All the world's a stage." —Shakespeare

> **Example:** Grass is nature's blanket.

A common error is the mixed metaphor. This occurs when a writer uses two inconsistent metaphors in a single expression.

> **Example:** The blanket of snow clutched the earth with icy fingers.

### Hyperbole

A hyperbole is a deliberate overstatement or exaggeration used to express an idea.

> **Example:** I have told you a thousand times not to play with matches.

### Personification

Personification is the attribution of human qualities to an object, animal, or idea.

> **Example:** The wind laughed at their attempts to catch the flying papers.

## Skill 2.3: Determine diction and tone appropriate to a given audience.

### Denotation versus Connotation

Diction is word choice. The denotative meaning of a word is its *literal,* dictionary definition: what the word denotes or "means." The connotative meaning of a word is what the word connotes or "suggests"; it is a meaning apart from what the word literally means. A writer should choose a word based on the tone and context of the sentence; this ensures that a word bears the appropriate connotation while still conveying some exactness in denotation.

For example, a gift might be described as "cheap," but the directness of this word has a negative connotation—something cheap is something of little or no value. The word "inexpensive" has a more positive connotation, even though "cheap" is a synonym for "inexpensive." Questions of this type require you to make a decision regarding the appropriateness of words and phrases for the context of a sentence.

### Wordiness and Conciseness

Effective writing is concise. Wordiness, by contrast, decreases the clarity of expression by cluttering sentences with unnecessary words. Some FTCE test questions will call on your ability to detect redundancies (unnecessary repetitions), circumlocution (failure to get to the point), and padding with loose synonyms. Such questions require you to choose sentences that convey a message clearly, economically, and effectively.

Notice the difference in impact between the first and second sentences in the following pairs:

INCORRECT: The medical exam that he gave me was entirely complete.

CORRECT: The medical exam he gave me was complete.

INCORRECT: Larry asked his friend John, who was a good, old friend, if he would join him and go along with him to see the foreign film made in Japan.

CORRECT: Larry asked his good, old friend John if he would join him in seeing the Japanese film.

|           |                                                                                      |
|-----------|--------------------------------------------------------------------------------------|
| INCORRECT: | I was absolutely, totally happy with the present that my parents gave to me at 7 a.m. on the morning of my birthday. |
| CORRECT:   | I was happy with the present my parents gave me on the morning of my birthday.       |

## Tone

Aside from individual word choice, the overall tone, or attitude, of a piece of writing should be appropriate to the audience and purpose. The tone may be objective or subjective, logical or emotional, intimate or distant, serious or humorous. It can consist of many different structures and organizations of writing.

To help achieve appropriate tone is to imagine how the words sound when spoken. A journal might be like a conversation with a close friend where there is more freedom for slang and casual form of speech. A column for a newspaper may be more similar to a high school graduation speech: It can be more formal, but it can still be funny or familiar. An academic paper is similar to a formal speech at a conference: Being interesting is desirable, but there is no room for personal digressions or familiar usage of slang words. In all of the cases listed previously, there is flexibility while adapting to the audience. Writing should suit the occasion.

## Tone versus Voice

Anything you write should contain your voice: something that makes your writing sound uniquely like you. A personal conversation with a relative differs from a speech given to a group of strangers. Just as you speak to different people in different ways yet remain yourself, so should the tone of writing vary with the situation. However, the voice—the essential, individual thoughts and expression—stays your own.

Consider the following examples:

"Don't play what's there; play what's not there."

—Miles Davis (1926–1991),
American jazz musician

"The notes I handle no better than many pianists. But the pauses between the notes—ah, that is where the art resides."

—Artur Schnabel (1882–1951),
Austrian pianist

These two musicians expressed the same thought in their own unique voices.

## Competency 3: Knowledge of Standard English Conventions

### Skill 3.1: Determine and select standard verb forms.

#### Verb Forms

This section covers the principal parts of some irregular verbs, including troublesome verbs like *lie* and *lay*. The use of regular verbs like *look* and *receive* poses no real problem to most writers since the past and past participle forms end in *-ed*; it is the irregular forms that create the most confusion—for example, *seen, written,* and *begun.*

### Skill 3.2: Determine and select inappropriate shifts in verb tense.

Tense sequence indicates a logical time sequence.

**Use present tense**

in statements of universal truth:

> I learned that the sun *is* 93 million miles from Earth.

in statements about the contents of literature and other published works:

> In this book, Sandy *becomes* a nun and *writes* a book on psychology.

**Use past tense**

in statements concerning writing or publication of a book:

> He *wrote* his first book in 1949, and it *was published* in 1952.

**Use present perfect tense**

for an action that began in the past but continues into the future:

> I *have lived* here all my life.

**Use past perfect tense**

for an earlier action that is mentioned in a later action:

> Cindy ate the apple that she *had picked.*

> (First she picked it, then she ate it.)

**Use future perfect tense**

for an action that will have been completed at a specific future time:

By May, I *shall have graduated.*

**Use the present participle**

for an action that occurs at the same time as the verb:

*Speeding* down the interstate, I saw a trooper's flashing lights.

**Use the perfect participle**

for an action that occurred before the main verb:

*Having read* the directions, I started the test.

**Use the subjunctive mood**

to express a wish or state a condition contrary to fact:

*If it were not raining,* we could have a picnic.

in *that* clauses after verbs like *request, recommend, suggest, ask, require,* and *insist;* and after expressions such as *it is important* and *it is necessary:*

It is necessary that all papers *be* submitted on time.


## Skill 3.3: Determine and select agreement between subject and verb.

Agreement is the grammatical correspondence between the subject and the verb of a sentence: *I do; we do; they do; he, she, it does.*

Every English verb has five forms, two of which are the bare form (plural) and the *-s* form (singular). Simply put, singular verb forms end in *-s*; plural forms do not.

**Study these rules governing subject-verb agreement:**

A verb must agree with its subject, not with any additive phrase in the sentence such as a prepositional or verbal phrase. Ignore such phrases when deciding which verb form to use.

Your *copy* of the rules *is* on the desk.

Ms. Craig's *record* of community service and outstanding teaching *qualifies* her for a promotion.

In an inverted sentence beginning with a prepositional phrase, the verb still agrees with its subject.

At the end of the summer *come* the best *sales.*

Under the house *are* some old Mason *jars.*

**FTCE GENERAL KNOWLEDGE TEST**

Prepositional phrases beginning with compound prepositions such as *along with, together with, in addition to,* and *as well as* should be ignored, for they do not affect subject-verb agreement.

> *Gladys Knight*, as well as the Pips, *is* riding the midnight train to Georgia.

A verb must agree with its subject, not its subject complement.

> *Taxes are* a problem.
>
> A *problem is* taxes.

When a sentence begins with an expletive such as *there, here,* or *it,* the verb agrees with the subject, not the expletive.

> Surely there *are* several *alumni* who would be interested in forming a group.
>
> There *are* 50 *students* in my English class.
>
> There *is* a horrifying *study* on child abuse in *Psychology Today.*

Indefinite pronouns such as *each, either, one, everyone, everybody,* and *everything* are singular.

> *Somebody* in Detroit *loves* me.
>
> *Does either* [one] of you have a pencil?
>
> *Neither* of my brothers *has* a car.

Indefinite pronouns such as *several, few, both,* and *many* are plural.

> *Both* of my sorority sisters *have* decided to live off campus.
>
> *Few seek* the enlightenment of transcendental meditation.

Indefinite pronouns such as *all, some, most,* and *none* may be singular or plural depending on their referents.

> *Some* of the food *is* cold.
>
> *Some* of the vegetables *are* cold.
>
> I can think of some retorts, but *none* seem appropriate.
>
> *None* of the children *is* as sweet as Sally.

Fractions such as *one-half* and *one-third* may be singular or plural depending on the referent.

> *Half* of the mail *has* been delivered.
>
> *Half* of the letters *have* been read.

Subjects joined by *and* take a plural verb unless the subjects are thought to be one item or unit.

> *Jim* and *Tammy were* televangelists.
>
> *Earth, Wind, and Fire is* my favorite group.

In cases when the subjects are joined by *or, nor, either . . . or,* or *neither . . . nor,* the verb must agree with the subject closest to it.

> Either the teacher or the *students are* responsible.
>
> Neither the students nor the *teacher is* responsible.

Relative pronouns that refer to plural antecedents, such as *who, which,* or *that,* require plural verbs. However, when the relative pronoun refers to a singular subject, the pronoun takes a singular verb.

> She is one of the girls *who cheer* on Friday nights.
>
> She is the only cheerleader *who has* a broken leg.

Subjects preceded by *every, each,* and *many* are singular.

> *Every* man, woman, and child *was* given a life preserver.
>
> *Each* undergraduate *is* required to pass a proficiency exam.
>
> *Many* a tear *has* to fall before one matures.

A collective noun, such as *audience, faculty, jury,* etc., requires a singular verb when the group is regarded as a whole, and a plural verb when the members of the group are regarded as individuals.

> The *jury has* made its decision.
>
> The *faculty are* preparing their grade rosters.

Subjects preceded by *the number of* or *the percentage of* are singular, while subjects preceded by *a number of* or *a percentage of* are plural.

> *The number of* vacationers in Florida *increases* every year.
>
> *A number of* vacationers *are* young couples.

Titles of books, companies, name brands, and groups are singular or plural depending on their meaning.

> *Great Expectations is* my favorite novel.
>
> The *Rolling Stones are* performing at Hard Rock Stadium.

Certain nouns of Latin and Greek origin have unusual singular and plural forms.

| **Singular** | **Plural** |
|---|---|
| criterion | criteria |
| alumnus | alumni |
| datum | data |
| medium | media |

The *data are* available for inspection. (Note that as usage of *data* has evolved, singular verbs are used to refer to collections of information.)

The only *criterion* for membership *is* a high GPA.

Some nouns such as *deer, shrimp,* and *sheep* have the same spellings for both their singular and plural forms. In these cases, the meaning of the sentence determines whether they are singular or plural.

*Deer are* beautiful animals.

The spotted *deer is* licking the sugar cube.

Some nouns such as *scissors, jeans,* and *eyeglasses* have plural forms but no singular counterparts. These nouns almost always take plural verbs.

The *scissors are* on the table.

My new *jeans fit* me like a glove.

Words used as examples, not as grammatical parts of the sentence, require singular verbs.

*Can't is* the contraction for "cannot."

*Cats is* the plural form of "cat."

Mathematical expressions of subtraction and division require singular verbs, while expressions of addition and multiplication take either singular or plural verbs.

Ten *divided* by two *equals* five.

Five *times* two *equals* ten.

OR

Five *times* two *equal* ten.

Nouns expressing time, distance, weight, and measurement are singular when they refer to a unit and plural when they refer to separate items.

*Fifty yards is* a short distance.

*Ten years have* passed since I finished college.

Expressions of quantity are usually plural.

*Nine out of ten* dentists *recommend* that their patients floss.

Some nouns ending in *-ics*, such as *economics* and *ethics*, take singular verbs when they refer to principles or a field of study; however, when they refer to individual practices, they usually take plural verbs.

> *Ethics is* being taught in the spring.
>
> His unusual business *ethics are* what got him into trouble.

Some nouns such as *measles, news,* and *calculus* appear to be plural but are actually singular in number. These nouns require singular verbs.

> *Measles is* a very contagious disease.
>
> The *news* from Sudan is grim.
>
> *Calculus requires* great skill in algebra.

A verbal noun (infinitive or gerund) serving as a subject is treated as singular, even if the object of the verbal phrase is plural.

> *Hiding* your mistakes *does* not make them go away.
>
> *To run* five miles *is* my goal.

A noun phrase or clause acting as the subject of a sentence requires a singular verb.

> *What I need is* to be loved.
>
> *Whether there is any connection between them is* unknown.

Clauses beginning with *what* may be singular or plural depending on the meaning, that is, whether *what* means "the thing" or "the things."

> *What I want for Christmas is* a new motorcycle.
>
> *What matters are* Smith's ideas.

A plural subject followed by a singular appositive requires a plural verb; similarly, a singular subject followed by a plural appositive requires a singular verb.

> When the girls throw a party, *they* each bring a *gift*.
>
> The *board,* all ten members, *is* meeting today.

## Skill 3.4: Determine and select agreement between pronoun and antecedent.

Questions under Skill 4 test your knowledge of using an appropriate pronoun to agree with its antecedent in number (singular or plural form) and gender (masculine, feminine, or neuter). An antecedent is a noun or pronoun to which another noun or pronoun refers.

Here are the two basic rules for pronoun reference–antecedent agreement:

1. Every pronoun must have a conspicuous antecedent.

2. Every pronoun must agree with its antecedent in number, gender, and person.

When an antecedent is one of dual gender such as *student, singer, artist, person, citizen,* etc., use *his* or *her.* However, depending on the use and frequency, this may sound stilted. Some careful writers change the antecedent to a plural noun to avoid using the sexist, singular masculine pronoun *his*:

> INCORRECT: Everyone hopes that he will win the lottery.
>
> CORRECT: Most people hope that they will win the lottery.

Ordinarily, the relative pronoun *who* is used to refer to people, *which* to refer to things and places, *where* to refer to places, and *that* to refer to places or things. The distinction between *that* and *which* is a grammatical distinction (see the section on Word Choice Skills).

Many writers prefer to use *that* to refer to collective nouns.

> **Example:** A family *that* traces its lineage is usually proud of its roots.

## ■ Skill 3.5: Determine and select inappropriate pronoun shifts.

Many writers, especially students, are not sure when to use the reflexive case pronoun (which ends in *-self*) and when to use the possessive case pronoun. The rules governing the usage of the reflexive case and the possessive case are quite simple.

**Use the possessive case**

before a noun in a sentence:

> *Our* friend moved during the semester break.
>
> *My* dog has fleas, but *her* dog doesn't.

before a gerund in a sentence:

> *Her* running helps to relieve stress.
>
> *His* driving terrified her.

as a noun in a sentence:

> *Mine* was the last test graded that day.

to indicate possession:

> Karen never allows anyone else to drive *her* car.
>
> Brad thought the book was *his,* but it was someone else's.

## Use the reflexive case

as a direct object to rename the subject:

> I kicked *myself.*

as an indirect object to rename the subject:

> Henry bought *himself* a tie.

as an object of a prepositional phrase:

> Tom and Lillie baked the pie for *themselves.*

as a predicate pronoun:

> She hasn't been *herself* lately.

## Do *not* use the reflexive in place of the nominative pronoun:

| | |
|---|---|
| INCORRECT: | Both Randy and *myself* plan to go. |
| CORRECT: | Both Randy and *I* plan to go. |
| INCORRECT: | *Yourself* will take on the challenges of college. |
| CORRECT: | *You* will take on the challenges of college. |
| INCORRECT: | Either James or *yourself* will paint the mural. |
| CORRECT: | Either James or *you* will paint the mural. |

Watch out for careless use of the pronoun form:

| | |
|---|---|
| INCORRECT: | George *hisself* told me it was true. |
| CORRECT: | George *himself* told me it was true. |
| INCORRECT: | They washed the car *theirselves.* |
| CORRECT: | They washed the car *themselves.* |

Notice that reflexive pronouns are not set off by commas:

| | |
|---|---|
| INCORRECT: | Mary, *herself,* gave him the diploma. |
| CORRECT: | Mary *herself* gave him the diploma. |
| INCORRECT: | I will do it, *myself.* |
| CORRECT: | I will do it *myself.* |

## Skill 3.6: Determine and select clear pronoun references.

Pronoun-reference questions require you to determine whether the antecedent is conspicuously written in the sentence or whether it is remote, implied, ambiguous, or vague—none of which results in clear writing. Make sure that every pronoun has a conspicuous antecedent and that one pronoun substitutes only for another noun or pronoun, not for an idea or a sentence.

**Pronoun reference problems occur**

when a pronoun refers to either of two antecedents:

| | |
|---|---|
| INCORRECT: | Joanna told Tim that *she* was getting fat. |
| CORRECT: | Joanna told Tim, "*I'm* getting fat." |

when a pronoun refers to a remote antecedent:

| | |
|---|---|
| INCORRECT: | A strange car followed us closely, and *he* kept blinking his lights at us. |
| CORRECT: | A strange car followed us closely, and *its driver* kept blinking his lights at us. |

when *this, that,* and *which* refer to the general idea of the preceding clause or sentence rather than the preceding word:

| | |
|---|---|
| INCORRECT: | The students could not understand the pronoun-reference handout, *which* annoyed them very much. |
| CORRECT: | The students could not understand the pronoun-reference handout, a *fact which* annoyed them very much. |
| OR | The students were annoyed *because* they could not understand the pronoun-reference handout. |

when a pronoun refers to an unexpressed but implied noun:

| | |
|---|---|
| INCORRECT: | My husband wants me to knit a blanket, but I'm not interested in *it*. |
| CORRECT: | My husband wants me to knit a blanket, but I'm not interested in *knitting*. |

when *it* is used as something other than an expletive to postpone a subject:

INCORRECT: *It* says in today's paper that the newest shipment of cars from Detroit seems to include outright imitations of European models.

CORRECT: *Today's paper* says that the newest shipment of cars from Detroit seems to include outright imitations of European models.

INCORRECT: The football game was canceled because *it* was bad weather.

CORRECT: The football game was canceled because *the weather* was bad.

when *they* or *it* is used to refer to something or someone indefinitely, and there is no definite antecedent:

INCORRECT: At the job placement office, *they* told me to stop wearing ripped jeans to my interviews.

CORRECT: At the job placement office, *I was told* to stop wearing ripped jeans to my interviews.

when the pronoun does not agree with its antecedent in number, gender, or person:

INCORRECT: Any graduate student, if *they* are interested, may attend the lecture.

CORRECT: Any graduate student, if *he or she* is interested, may attend the lecture.

OR *All* graduate students, if *they* are interested, may attend the lecture.

INCORRECT: Many Americans are concerned that the overuse of slang and colloquialisms is corrupting *the* language.

CORRECT: Many Americans are concerned that the overuse of slang and colloquialisms is corrupting *their* language.

INCORRECT: The board of regents will not make a decision about a tuition increase until *their* March meeting.

CORRECT: The board of regents will not make a decision about a tuition increase until *its* March meeting.

when a noun or pronoun has no expressed antecedent:

> INCORRECT: In the *president's* address to the union, *he* promised no more taxes.
>
> CORRECT: In *his* address to the union, *the president* promised no more taxes.

## Skill 3.7: Determine and select pronoun case forms.

Pronoun-case questions test your knowledge of the use of nominative and objective case pronouns:

| Nominative Case | Objective Case |
|:---:|:---:|
| I | me |
| he | him |
| she | her |
| we | us |
| they | them |
| who | whom |

Among the most bedeviling questions that arise in English are when to use *I* and when to use *me*, and when to use *who* and when to use *whom*. Some writers avoid *whom* altogether, and instead of distinguishing between *I* and *me*, many writers incorrectly use *myself* (which is actually a reflexive pronoun, e.g., "I saw myself in the mirror.").

**Use the nominative case (subject pronouns)**

for the subject of a sentence:

> *We* students studied until early morning for the final.

> Alan and *I* "burned the midnight oil," too.

for pronouns in apposition to (having the same meaning as) the subject:

> Only two students, Alex and *I,* were asked to report on the meeting.

for the predicate nominative/subject complement:

> The actors nominated for the award were *she* and *I.*

for the subject of an elliptical clause:

> Molly is more experienced than *he.*

for the subject of a subordinate clause:

> Robert is the driver *who* reported the accident.

for the complement of an infinitive with no expressed subject:

> I would not want to be *he*. (Although the nominative *he* is absolutely correct, you may detect some stiltedness. That's why the objective case—*him*—may also be used after a verb.)

### Use the objective case (object pronouns)

for the direct object of a sentence:

> Mary invited *us* to her party.

for the object of a preposition:

> The books that were torn belonged to *her*.

> Just between you and *me,* I'm bored in class.

for the indirect object of a sentence:

> Walter gave a dozen red roses to *her*.

for the appositive of a direct object:

> The committee elected two delegates, Barbara and *me*.

for the object of an infinitive:

> The young boy wanted to help *us* paint the fence.

for the object of a gerund:

> Enlisting *him* was surprisingly easy.

for the object of a past participle:

> Having called the other students and *us,* the secretary went home for the day.

for a pronoun that precedes an infinitive (the subject of an infinitive):

> The supervisor told *him* to work late.

for the complement of an infinitive with an expressed subject:

> The fans thought the best player to be *him*.

for the object of an elliptical clause:

> Bill tackled Joe harder than *me*.

for the object of a verb in apposition:

> Charles invited two extra people, Carmen and *me,* to the party.

When a conjunction connects two pronouns or a pronoun and a noun, mentally remove the "and" and the other pronoun or noun to determine what the correct pronoun form should be:

> Mom gave ~~Tom and~~ myself a piece of cake.

> Mom gave ~~Tom and~~ I a piece of cake.

> Mom gave ~~Tom and~~ me a piece of cake.

The correct pronoun is now revealed:

> Mom gave *me* a piece of cake.

The only pronouns that are acceptable after *between* and other prepositions are: *me, her, him, them,* and *whom.* When deciding between *who* and *whom,* try substituting *he* for *who* and *him* for *whom*; then follow these easy transformation steps:

1. Isolate the *who* clause or the *whom* clause:

> whom we can trust

2. Invert the word order, if necessary. Place the words in the clause in the natural order of an English sentence, with the subject followed by the verb:

> we can trust whom

3. Read the final form with the *he* or *him* inserted:

> We can trust ~~whom~~ him.

When a pronoun follows a comparative conjunction like *than* or *as,* complete the elliptical construction to help you determine which pronoun is correct.

> EXAMPLE: She has more credit hours than me [do].
> She has more credit hours than I [do].

## Skill 3.8: Evaluate the correct use of adjectives and adverbs

### Correct Usage

*Adjectives* are words that modify nouns or pronouns by defining, describing, limiting, or qualifying those nouns or pronouns.

*Adverbs* are words that modify verbs, adjectives, or other adverbs and that express such ideas as time, place, manner, cause, and degree. Use adjectives as subject complements with linking verbs; use adverbs with action verbs.

| EXAMPLE: | The old man's speech was *eloquent.* | ADJECTIVE |
| | Mr. Brown speaks *eloquently.* | ADVERB |
| | Please be *careful.* | ADJECTIVE |
| | Please drive *carefully.* | ADVERB |

## Good or well

*Good* is an adjective; its use as an adverb is colloquial and nonstandard.

| INCORRECT: | He plays *good.* |
| CORRECT: | He looks *good* to be an octogenarian. |
| | The quiche tastes very *good.* |

*Well* may be either an adverb or an adjective. As an adjective, *well* means "in good health."

| CORRECT: | He plays *well.* | ADVERB |
| | My mother is not *well.* | ADJECTIVE |

## Bad or badly

*Bad* is an adjective used after sense verbs such as *look, smell, taste, feel,* or *sound,* or after linking verbs (*is, am, are, was, were*).

| INCORRECT: | I feel *badly* about the delay. |
| CORRECT: | I feel *bad* about the delay. |

*Badly* is an adverb used after all other verbs.

| INCORRECT: | It doesn't hurt very *bad.* |
| CORRECT: | It doesn't hurt very *badly.* |

## Real or really

*Real* is an adjective; its use as an adverb is colloquial and nonstandard. It means "genuine."

| INCORRECT: | He writes *real* well. |
| CORRECT: | This is *real* leather. |

*Really* is an adverb meaning "very."

|  |  |  |
|---|---|---|
| INCORRECT: | This is *really* diamond. |  |
| CORRECT: | Have a *really* nice day. |  |
| EXAMPLE: | This is *real* amethyst. | ADJECTIVE |
|  | This is *really* difficult. | ADVERB |
|  | This is a *real* crisis. | ADJECTIVE |
|  | This is *really* important. | ADVERB |

**Sort of and kind of**

*Sort of* and *kind of* are often misused in written English by writers who actually mean *rather* or *somewhat*.

|  |  |
|---|---|
| INCORRECT: | Jan was *kind of* saddened by the results of the test. |
| CORRECT: | Jan was *somewhat* saddened by the results of the test. |

## Skill 3.9: Determine and select appropriate comparative and superlative degree forms.

Competency 3's Skill 9 requires identification of appropriate comparative and superlative degree forms.

Sentences containing a faulty comparison often sound correct because their problem is not one of grammar but of logic. Read these sentences closely to make sure that like things are being compared, that the comparisons are complete, and that the comparisons are logical.

When comparing two persons or things, use the comparative, not the superlative, form of an adjective or an adverb. Use the superlative form for comparison of more than two persons or things. Use *any, other,* or *else* when comparing one thing or person with a group of which it or he or she is a part.

Most one- and two-syllable words form their comparative and superlative degrees with *-er* and *-est* suffixes, respectively. Adjectives and adverbs of more than two syllables form their comparative and superlative degrees with the addition of *more* and *most*.

| Positive | Comparative | Superlative |
| --- | --- | --- |
| good | better | best |
| old | older | oldest |
| friendly | friendlier | friendliest |
| lonely | lonelier | loneliest |
| talented | more talented | most talented |
| beautiful | more beautiful | most beautiful |

A double comparison occurs when the degree of the modifier is changed incorrectly by adding both -er and more or -est and most to the adjective or adverb.

INCORRECT: He is the *most nicest* brother.
CORRECT: He is the *nicest* brother.

INCORRECT: She is the *more meaner* of the sisters.
CORRECT: She is the *meaner* sister.

Illogical comparisons occur when there is an implied comparison between two things that are not actually being compared or that cannot be logically compared.

INCORRECT: The interest at a loan company is higher *than* a bank.
CORRECT: The interest at a loan company is higher *than* that *at* a bank.
OR The interest at a loan company is higher *than at* a bank.

Ambiguous comparisons occur when elliptical words (those omitted) create for the reader more than one interpretation of the sentence.

INCORRECT: I like Mary better than you. (than you *what*?)
CORRECT: I like Mary better than I like you.
OR I like Mary better than you do.

Incomplete comparisons occur when the basis of the comparison (the two categories being compared) is not explicitly stated.

INCORRECT: Skywriting is *more* spectacular.
CORRECT: Skywriting is *more* spectacular *than* billboard advertising.

Do not omit the words *other, any,* or *else* when comparing one thing or person with a group of which it or he or she is a part.

> INCORRECT:  Joan writes better *than any* student in her class.
>
> CORRECT:  Joan writes better *than any other* student in her class.

Do not omit the second *as* of *as . . . as* when making a point of equal or superior comparison.

> INCORRECT:  The University of West Florida is *as large* or larger than the University of North Florida.
>
> CORRECT:  The University of West Florida is *as large as* or larger than the University of Northern Florida.

Do not omit the first category of the comparison, even if the two categories are the same.

> INCORRECT:  This is one of the best, if not the best, hospital in the country.
>
> CORRECT:  This is one of the best hospitals in the country, if not the best.

The problem with the incorrect sentence is that *one of the best* requires the plural word *hospitals,* not *hospital.*

## Skill 3.10: Demonstrate command of standard spelling conventions.

Spelling questions test your ability to recognize misspelled words. This section reviews spelling tips and rules to help you spot incorrect spellings. Problems such as the distinction between *to* and *too* and *lead* and *led* are covered under the Word Choice Skills section of this review.

- Remember, *i* before *e* except after *c,* or when sounded as "a" as in *neighbor* and *weigh.*

- There are only three words in the English language that end in *-ceed*:
  exceed, proceed, succeed

- There are several words that end in *-cede*:
  accede, antecede, cede, concede, intercede, precede, recede, secede

- There is only one word in the English language that ends in *-sede*:
  supersede

Many people learn to read English phonetically—that is, by sounding out the letters of the words. However, many English words are not pronounced the way they are spelled, and those who try to spell English words phonetically often make spelling errors. It is better to memorize the correct spelling of English words rather than relying on phonetics to spell correctly.

 ## Skill 3.11: Demonstrate command of standard punctuation.

### Commas

Commas should be placed according to standard rules of punctuation for purpose, clarity, and effect. Here's a guide to the proper use of commas:

**In a series:**

When more than one adjective describes a noun, use a comma to separate and emphasize each adjective. The comma takes the place of the word *and* in the series.

> the long, dark passageway

> another confusing, sleepless night

> an elaborate, complex, brilliant plan

> the old, grey, crumpled hat

Some adjective-noun combinations are thought of as one word. In these cases, the adjective in front of the adjective-noun combination needs no comma. The simple rule is: If you were to insert the word *and* between the adjective-noun combination, it would not make sense.

> a stately oak tree

> an exceptional wine glass

> my worst report card

> a china dinner plate

The comma is also used to separate words, phrases, and whole ideas (clauses); it still takes the place of *and* when used this way.

> an apple, a pear, a fig, and a banana

> a lovely lady, an elegant dress, and many admirers

> She lowered the shade, closed the curtain, turned off the light, and went to bed.

The only question that exists about the use of commas in a series is whether one should be used before the final item. It is standard usage to do so, although many newspapers and magazines have stopped using the final, or serial, comma. Occasionally, the omission of the comma can be confusing.

| INCORRECT: | He got on his horse, tracked a rabbit, an elk and a deer and rode on to Canton. |
|---|---|
| CORRECT: | He got on his horse, tracked a rabbit, an elk, and a deer, and rode on to Canton. |

## With a long introductory phrase:

Usually if a phrase of more than five or six words or a dependent clause precedes the subject at the beginning of a sentence, a comma is used to set it off.

After last night's fiasco at the night club, she couldn't bear the thought of looking at him again.

Whenever I try to talk about my dream to go to Mars, my wife leaves the room.

Provided you have said nothing, they will never guess who you are.

It is not necessary to use a comma with a short sentence (with an introductory phrase of less than four words).

In January she will go to Switzerland.

After I rest I'll feel better.

During the day no one is home.

If an introductory phrase includes a verb form that is being used as another part of speech (a *verbal*), it must be followed by a comma.

| INCORRECT: | When eating Mary never looked up from her plate. |
|---|---|
| CORRECT: | When eating, Mary never looked up from her plate. |
| INCORRECT: | Because of her desire to follow her faith in James wavered. |
| CORRECT: | Because of her desire to follow, her faith in James wavered. |
| INCORRECT: | Having decided to leave Mary James wrote her a letter. |
| CORRECT: | Having decided to leave Mary, James wrote her a letter. |

## To separate two main ideas:

To understand how the comma should be used to separate two main ideas, you need to be able to recognize compound sentences. When a sentence contains more than two subjects and verbs (clauses), and the two clauses are joined by a conjunction (*and, but, or, nor, for, yet*), use a comma before the conjunction to show that another clause is coming.

> I thought I knew the poem by heart, but he showed me three lines I had forgotten.

> Are we really interested in helping the children, or are we more concerned with protecting our good names?

> He is supposed to leave tomorrow, but he is not ready to go.

> Jim knows you are disappointed, and he has known it for a long time.

If the two parts of the sentence are short and closely related, it is not necessary to use a comma.

> He threw the ball and the dog ran after it.

> Jane played the piano and Michael danced.

Be careful not to confuse a sentence that has a compound verb and a single subject with a compound sentence. If the subject is the same for both verbs and not included again in the second clause, there is no need for a comma.

| | |
|---|---|
| INCORRECT: | Charles sent some flowers, and wrote a long letter explaining why he had not been able to attend. |
| CORRECT: | Charles sent some flowers and wrote a long letter explaining why he had not been able to attend. |
| INCORRECT: | Last Thursday we went to the concert with Julia, and afterwards dined at an old Italian restaurant. |
| CORRECT: | Last Thursday we went to the concert with Julia and afterwards dined at an old Italian restaurant. |
| INCORRECT: | For the third time, the teacher explained that the literacy level for high school students was much lower than it had been in previous years, and, this time, wrote the statistics on the board for everyone to see. |
| CORRECT: | For the third time, the teacher explained that the literacy level for high school students was much lower than it had been in previous years and this time wrote the statistics on the board for everyone to see. |

In general, words and phrases that stop the flow of the sentence or are unnecessary for the main idea are set off by commas.

**Abbreviations after names:**

> Did you invite John Paul, Jr., and his sister?
>
> Martha Harris, Ph.D., will be the speaker tonight.

**Interjections (an exclamation without added grammatical connection):**

> Oh, I'm so glad to see you.
>
> I tried so hard, but alas, I failed.
>
> Hey, let me out of here.

**Direct address:**

> Roy, won't you open the door for the dog?
>
> I can't understand, Mother, what you are trying to say.
>
> May I ask, Mr. President, why you called us together?
>
> Hey, lady, watch out for that car!

**Tag questions:**

> You're really hungry, aren't you?
>
> Jerry looks like his father, doesn't he?

**Geographical names and addresses:**

> The concert will take place in Chicago, Illinois, on August 12.
>
> The letter was addressed to Mrs. Marion Heartwell, 1881 Pine Lane, Palo Alto, CA 95824.
>
> (Note: No comma is needed before the zip code, because it is already clearly set off from the state name.)

**Transitional words and phrases:**

> On the other hand, I hope he gets better.
>
> In addition, the phone rang constantly this afternoon.
>
> Nevertheless, I'm going to the beach on Sunday.
>
> You'll find, therefore, that no one is more loyal than I am.

**Parenthetical words and phrases:**

> You will become, I believe, a great statesman.
>
> We know, of course, that this is the only thing to do.
>
> In fact, I planted corn last summer.
>
> The Mannes affair was, to put it mildly, a surprise.

**Unusual word order:**

> The dress, new and crisp, hung in the closet.
>
> Longingly, she stared out the window.

## With nonrestrictive elements:

Parts of a sentence that modify other parts are sometimes essential to the meaning of the sentence and sometimes not. When a modifying word or group of words is not vital to the meaning of the sentence, it is *nonessential*, and is set off by commas. Since it does not restrict the meaning of the words it modifies, it is called "nonrestrictive." Modifiers that are *essential* to the meaning of the sentence are called "restrictive" and are not set off by commas.

ESSENTIAL:     The girl *who wrote the story* is my sister.

NONESSENTIAL:  My sister, *the girl who wrote the story,* has always loved to write.

ESSENTIAL:     The cup *that is on the piano* is the one I want.

NONESSENTIAL:  The cup, *which my brother gave me last year,* is on the piano.

ESSENTIAL:     The people *who arrived late* were not seated.

NONESSENTIAL:  George, *who arrived late,* was not seated.

## To set off direct quotations:

Most direct quotes or quoted materials are set off from the rest of the sentence by commas.

"Please read your part more loudly," the director insisted.

"I won't know what to do," said Michael, "if you leave me."

The teacher said sternly, "I will not dismiss this class until I have silence."

Who was it who said, "Do not ask for whom the bell tolls; it tolls for thee"?

*Note:* Commas always go inside the closing quotation mark, even if the comma is not part of the material being quoted.

Be careful not to set off indirect quotes or quotes that are used as subjects or complements, as shown here:

"To be or not to be" is the famous beginning of a soliloquy in Shakespeare's *Hamlet.* (subject)

She said she would never come back. (indirect quote)

Back then my favorite poem was "Evangeline." (complement)

## To set off contrasting elements:

Her intelligence, not her beauty, got her the job.

Your plan will take you a little farther from, rather than closer to, your destination.

It was a reasonable, though not appealing, idea.

He wanted glory, but found happiness instead.

**In dates:**

Both forms of the date are acceptable.

> She will arrive on April 6, 2016. (U.S. style is month, day, year.)
>
> He left on 5 December 1980. (European style is day month year with no commas.)
>
> In January 2015, he handed in his resignation.
>
> On October 22, 1992, Frank and Julie were married.

Usually, when a subordinate clause is at the end of a sentence, no comma is necessary preceding the clause. However, when a subordinate clause introduces a sentence, a comma should be used after the clause.

Some common subordinating conjunctions are:

| | |
|---|---|
| after | so that |
| although | though |
| as | till |
| as if | unless |
| because | until |
| before | when |
| even though | whenever |
| if | while |
| inasmuch as | |

Usually, a comma follows the conjunctive adverb. Note also that a period can be used to separate two sentences joined by a conjunctive adverb. Some common conjunctive adverbs are:

| | |
|---|---|
| accordingly | nevertheless |
| besides | next |
| consequently | nonetheless |
| finally | now |
| furthermore | on the other hand |
| however | otherwise |
| indeed | perhaps |
| in fact | still |
| moreover | therefore |

*Then* is also used as a conjunctive adverb, but it is not usually followed by a comma.

## Semicolons

Questions testing semicolon usage require you to be able to distinguish between the semicolon and the comma, and the semicolon and the colon. This review section covers the basic uses of the semicolon: to separate independent clauses not joined by a coordinating conjunction; to separate independent clauses separated by a conjunctive adverb; and to separate items in a series with internal commas. As you can see in the previous sentence, the semicolon also is helpful when lengthy clauses follow a colon. It is important to be consistent; if you use a semicolon between *any* of the items in the series, you must use semicolons to separate *all* of the items in the series.

### Use the semicolon

to separate independent clauses that are not joined by a coordinating conjunction:

> I understand how to use commas; the semicolon I have not yet mastered.

to separate two independent clauses connected by a conjunctive adverb:

> He took great care with his work; *therefore,* he was very successful.

to combine two independent clauses connected by a coordinating conjunction if either or both of the clauses contain other internal punctuation:

> Some maintain that success in college requires intelligence, industry, and perseverance; *but* others, fewer in number, assert that only personality is important.

to separate items in a series when each item has internal punctuation:

> I bought an old, dilapidated chair; an antique table, which was in beautiful condition; and a new, ugly, blue and white rug.

> Call our customer service line for assistance: Arizona, 1-800-555-6020; New Mexico, 1-800-555-5050; California, 1-800-555-3140; or Nevada, 1-800-555-3214.

### Do *not* use the semicolon

to separate a dependent and an independent clause:

> INCORRECT:  You should not make such statements; even though they are correct.

> CORRECT:  You should not make such statements even though they are correct.

to substitute for a comma:

> INCORRECT: My roommate also likes sports; particularly football, basketball, and baseball.

> CORRECT: My roommate also likes sports, particularly football, basketball, and baseball.

to set off other types of phrases or clauses from a sentence:

> INCORRECT: Being of a cynical mind; I should ask for a recount of the ballots.

> CORRECT: Being of a cynical mind, I should ask for a recount of the ballots.

> INCORRECT: The next meeting of the club has been postponed two weeks; inasmuch as both the president and vice president are out of town.

> CORRECT: The next meeting of the club has been postponed two weeks, inasmuch as both the president and vice president are out of town.

Note: The semicolon is not a terminal mark of punctuation; therefore, it should not be followed by a capital letter unless the first word in the second clause ordinarily requires capitalization.

## Colons

While it is true that a colon is used to precede a list, one must also make sure that a complete sentence precedes the colon. The colon signals the reader that a list, explanation, or restatement of the preceding will follow. It is like an arrow, indicating that something is to follow. The difference between the colon and the semicolon and between the colon and the period is that the colon is an introductory mark, not a terminal mark. Look at the following examples:

> The Constitution provides for a separation of powers among the three branches of **government.**

> **government.** The period signals a new sentence.

> **government;** The semicolon signals an interrelated sentence.

> **government,** The comma signals a coordinating conjunction followed by another independent clause.

> **government:** The colon signals a list.

Now see the colon at work, introducing a list of the three branches of American government.

> The Constitution provides for a separation of powers among the three branches of *government:* executive, legislative, and judicial.

Ensuring that a complete sentence precedes a colon means following some rules:

**Use the colon**

to introduce a list (one item may constitute a list):

> I hate this one course: English.
>
> Three plays by William Shakespeare will be presented in repertory this summer at the University of Miami: *Hamlet, Macbeth,* and *Othello.*

to introduce a list preceded by *as follows* or *the following*:

> The reasons he cited for his success are as follows: integrity, honesty, industry, and a pleasant disposition.

to separate two independent clauses, when the second clause is a restatement or explanation of the first:

> All of my high school teachers said one thing in particular: College is going to be difficult.

to introduce a word or word group that is a restatement, explanation, or summary of the first sentence:

> These two things he loved: tofu and chickpeas.

to introduce a formal appositive:

> I am positive there is one appeal that you can't overlook: money.

to separate the introductory words from a quotation that follows, if the quotation is formal, long, or contained in its own paragraph separately:

> The actor then stated: "I would rather be able to adequately play the part of Hamlet than to perform a miraculous operation, deliver a great lecture, or build a magnificent skyscraper."

The colon should only be used after statements that are grammatically complete.

Do *not* use a colon after a verb:

> INCORRECT:  My favorite holidays are: Christmas, New Year's Eve, and Halloween.
>
> CORRECT:  My favorite holidays are Christmas, New Year's Eve, and Halloween.

Do *not* use a colon after a preposition:

> INCORRECT: I enjoy different ethnic foods such as: Greek, Chinese, and Italian.

> CORRECT: I enjoy different ethnic foods such as Greek, Chinese, and Italian.

Do *not* use a colon interchangeably with the dash:

> INCORRECT: Mathematics, German, English: these gave me the greatest difficulty of all my courses.

> CORRECT: Mathematics, German, English—these gave me the greatest difficulty of all my courses.

Information preceding the colon should be a complete sentence regardless of the explanatory information following the clause.

Do *not* use the colon before the words *for example, namely, that is,* or *for instance* even though these words may be introducing a list. Because such words already signal the reader that a series of examples will follow, the use of the colon is redundant.

> INCORRECT: She had all the traits of a great leader: namely, optimism, integrity, perseverance, confidence, and decisiveness.

> CORRECT: She had all the traits of a great leader: optimism, integrity, perseverance, confidence, and decisiveness.

## Apostrophes

Apostrophe questions require you to know when an apostrophe has been used appropriately to make a noun possessive, not plural. Remember the following rules when considering how to show possession.

Add *'s* to singular nouns and indefinite pronouns:

> Tiffany's flowers
>
> a dog's bark
>
> everybody's computer
>
> at the owner's expense
>
> today's paper

Add *'s* to singular nouns ending in *s,* unless this distorts the pronunciation:

> Delores's paper
>
> the boss's pen
>
> Dr. Wayans' class
>
> for righteousness' sake

Add *an apostrophe* to plural nouns ending in *s* or *es*:

> two cents' worth
>
> ladies' night
>
> thirteen years' experience
>
> two weeks' pay

Add *'s* to plural nouns not ending in *s:*

> men's room
>
> children's toys

Add *'s* to the last word in compound words or groups:

> brother-in-law's car
>
> someone else's paper

Add *'s* to the last noun in a pair or series when indicating joint possession or ownership:

> Joe and Edna's home
>
> Julie and Kathy's party
>
> women and children's clinic
>
> Amazon.com and the U.S. Postal Service's delivery service

Add *'s* to both nouns to show ownership or possession by each person or thing:

> Joe's and Edna's trucks (indicates trucks owned separately)
>
> Julie's and Kathy's pies (indicates separately baked pies)
>
> Ted's and Jane's marriage vows (indicates separate vows to two other people, not each other)
>
> Wakulla's and Jefferson's wildlife refuges

Possessive pronouns change their forms *without* the addition of an apostrophe:

> her, his, hers
>
> your, yours
>
> their, theirs
>
> it, its

Use the possessive form of a noun preceding a gerund:

His driving annoys me.

My bowling a strike irritated him.

Do you mind our stopping by?

We appreciate your coming.

Add 's to words and initials to show that they are plural (when there would otherwise be confusion):

three A's

Mind your p's and q's.

Add s to numbers, symbols, and letters to show that they are plural:

TVs

VCRs

the 1800s

the returning POWs

## Quotation Marks and Italics

The FTCE exam will test your knowledge of the proper use of quotation marks with other marks of punctuation, with titles, and with dialogue. The exam will also test your knowledge of the correct use of italics and underlining with titles and words used as sample words (for example, *the word is is a common verb*).

The most common use of double quotation marks (") is to set off quoted words, phrases, and sentences.

"If everybody minded their own business," said the Duchess in a hoarse growl, "the world would go round a great deal faster than it does."

"Then you would say what you mean," the March Hare went on.

"I do," Alice hastily replied: "at least—at least I mean what I say—that's the same thing, you know."

—from Lewis Carroll's *Alice in Wonderland*

Single quotation marks are used to set off quoted material within a quote.

> "Shall I bring 'The Rime of the Ancient Mariner' along with us?" she asked her brother.

> Mrs. Green said, "The doctor told me, 'Go immediately to bed when you get home!'"

> "If she said that to me," Katherine insisted, "I would tell her, 'I never intend to speak to you again! Goodbye, Susan!'"

When writing dialogue, begin a new paragraph each time the speaker changes.

> "Do you know what time it is?" asked Jane.

> "Can't you see I'm busy?" snapped Mary.

> "It's easy to see that you're in a bad mood today!" replied Jane.

Use quotation marks to enclose words used as words (sometimes italics are used for this purpose).

> "Judgment" has always been a difficult word for me to spell.

> Do you know what "abstruse" means?

> "Horse and buggy" and "bread and butter" can be used either as adjectives or as nouns.

If slang is used within more formal writing, the slang words or phrases should be set off with quotation marks.

> Harrison's decision to leave the conference and to "stick his neck out" by flying to Jamaica was applauded by the rest of the conference attendees.

When words are meant to have an unusual or specific significance to the reader, for instance irony or humor, they are sometimes placed in quotation marks.

> For years, women were not allowed to buy real estate in order to "protect" them from unscrupulous dealers.

> The "conversation" resulted in one black eye and a broken nose.

To set off titles of TV shows, poems, stories, and book chapters, use quotation marks. (Book, motion picture, newspaper, and magazine titles are underlined when handwritten and italicized when printed.)

> The article "Moving South in the Southern Rain," by Jergen Smith in the *Southern News,* attracted the attention of our editor.

> The assignment is "Childhood Development," Chapter 18 of *Human Behavior.*

> My favorite essay by Montaigne is "On Silence."

"Happy Days" led the TV ratings for years, didn't it?

You will find Keats's "Ode on a Grecian Urn" in Chapter 8 in Cody's *A Selection from the Great English Poets* (Chicago: A.C. McClurg & Company, 1905).

**Errors to avoid:**

Remember that quotation marks always come in pairs. Do not make the mistake of using only one set and forgetting about the corresponding pair. If you open quotes, you also have to close them.

| | |
|---|---|
| INCORRECT: | "You'll never convince me to move to the city, said Thurman. I consider it an insane asylum." |
| CORRECT: | "You'll never convince me to move to the city," said Thurman. "I consider it an insane asylum." |
| INCORRECT: | "Idleness and pride tax with a heavier hand than kings and parliaments," Benjamin Franklin is supposed to have said. If we can get rid of the former, we may easily bear the latter." |
| CORRECT: | "Idleness and pride tax with a heavier hand than kings and parliaments," Benjamin Franklin is supposed to have said. "If we can get rid of the former, we may easily bear the latter." |

When a quote consists of several sentences, do not put the quotation marks at the beginning and end of each sentence; put them at the beginning and end of the entire quotation.

| | |
|---|---|
| INCORRECT: | "It was during his student days in Bonn that Beethoven fastened upon Schiller's poem." "The heady sense of liberation in the verses must have appealed to him." "They appealed to every German."—John Burke |
| CORRECT: | "It was during his student days in Bonn that Beethoven fastened upon Schiller's poem. The heady sense of liberation in the verses must have appealed to him. They appealed to every German."—John Burke |

Instead of setting off a long quote with quotation marks, if it is longer than five or six lines you may want to indent and single-space it. If you do indent, do not use quotation marks.

> In his *First Inaugural Address,* Abraham Lincoln appeals to the war-torn American people:

>> We are not enemies, but friends. We must not be enemies. Though passion may have strained, it must not break our bonds of affection. The mystic chords of memory, stretching from every battlefield and patriot grave to every living heart and hearthstone all over this broad land, will yet swell the chorus of the Union when again touched, as surely they will be, by the better angels of our nature.

Be careful not to use quotation marks with indirect quotations.

| | |
|---|---|
| INCORRECT: | Mary wondered "if she would get over it." |
| CORRECT: | Mary wondered if she would get over it. |
| INCORRECT: | The nurse asked "how long it had been since we had visited the doctor's office." |
| CORRECT: | The nurse asked how long it had been since we had visited the doctor's office. |

When you quote several paragraphs, it is not sufficient to place quotation marks at the beginning and end of the entire quote. Place quotation marks at the *beginning of each paragraph,* but only at the *end of the last paragraph.* Here is an abbreviated quotation for an example:

> "Here begins an odyssey through the world of classical mythology, starting with the creation of the world . . .

> "It is true that themes similar to the classical may be found in any corpus of mythology . . . Even technology is not immune to the influence of Greece and Rome . . .

> "We need hardly mention the extent to which painters and sculptors . . . have used and adapted classical mythology to illustrate the past, to reveal the human body, to express romantic or antiromantic ideals, or to symbolize any particular point of view."

Remember that in American English commas and periods are *always* placed inside the quotation marks, even if they are not actually part of the quote.

| INCORRECT: | "Life always gets colder near the summit", Nietzsche is purported to have said, "—the cold increases, responsibility grows". |
|---|---|
| CORRECT: | "Life always gets colder near the summit," Nietzsche is purported to have said, "—the cold increases, responsibility grows." |
| INCORRECT: | "Get down here right away", John cried. "You'll miss the sunset if you don't." |
| CORRECT: | "Get down here right away," John cried. "You'll miss the sunset if you don't." |
| INCORRECT: | "If my dog could talk", Mary mused, "I'll bet he would say, 'Take me for a walk right this minute'". |
| CORRECT: | "If my dog could talk," Mary mused, "I'll bet he would say, 'Take me for a walk right this minute'." |

Other marks of punctuation, such as question marks, exclamation points, colons, and semicolons, go inside the quotation marks if they are part of the quoted material. If they are not part of the quotation, however, they go outside the quotation marks. Be careful to distinguish between the guidelines for the comma and period and those for other marks of punctuation.

| INCORRECT: | "I'll always love you"! he exclaimed. |
|---|---|
| CORRECT: | "I'll always love you!" he exclaimed. |
| INCORRECT: | Did you hear her say, "He'll be there early?" |
| CORRECT: | Did you hear her say, "He'll be there early"? |
| INCORRECT: | She called down the stairs, "When are you going"? |
| CORRECT: | She called down the stairs, "When are you going?" |
| INCORRECT: | "Let me out"! he cried. "Don't you have any pity"? |
| CORRECT: | "Let me out!" he cried. "Don't you have any pity?" |

Use only one mark of punctuation at the end of a sentence ending with a quotation mark.

| | |
|---|---|
| INCORRECT: | She thought out loud, "Will I ever finish this paper in time for that class?". |
| CORRECT: | She thought out loud, "Will I ever finish this paper in time for that class?" |
| INCORRECT: | "Not the same thing a bit!", said the Hatter. "Why, you might just as well say that 'I see what I eat' is the same thing as 'I eat what I see'!". |
| CORRECT: | "Not the same thing a bit!" said the Hatter. "Why, you might just as well say that 'I see what I eat' is the same thing as 'I eat what I see'!" |

## Skill 3.12: Demonstrate command of standard capitalization.

When a word is capitalized, it calls attention to itself. This attention should be for a good reason. There are standard uses for capital letters. In general, you should capitalize (1) all proper nouns, (2) the first word of a sentence, and (3) the first word of a direct quotation.

**You should also capitalize:**

Names of ships, aircraft, spacecraft, and trains:

| | |
|---|---|
| *Apollo 13* | *Mariner IV* |
| DC-10 | SS *United States* |
| *Sputnik II* | Boeing 707 |

Names of deities:

| | |
|---|---|
| God | Jupiter |
| Allah | Holy Ghost |
| Buddha | Venus |
| Jehovah | Shiva |

Geological periods:

| | |
|---|---|
| Neolithic Age | Cenozoic Era |
| Pleistocene Epoch | Ice Age |

Names of astronomical bodies:

Mercury                    Big Dipper

Milky Way                  Halley's Comet

Ursa Major                 North Star

Personifications:

Reliable Nature brought her promised Spring.

Bring on Melancholy in his sad night.

Historical periods:

Middle Ages                World War I

Reign of Terror            Great Depression

Christian Era              Roaring Twenties

Age of Louis XIV           Renaissance

Organizations, associations, and institutions:

Girl Scouts                North Atlantic Treaty Organization

Kiwanis Club               League of Women Voters

Florida Marlins            Unitarian Church

Smithsonian Institution    Common Market

Library of Congress        Franklin Glen High School

New York Philharmonic      Harvard University

Government and judicial groups:

United States Court of Appeals    Senate

Committee on Foreign Affairs      Parliament

Key West City Commission          Peace Corps

Arkansas Supreme Court            Census Bureau

House of Representatives          Department of State

A general term that accompanies a specific name is capitalized only if it follows the specific name. If it stands alone or comes before the specific name, it is put in lowercase:

| | |
|---|---|
| Washington State | the state of Washington |
| Senator Martinez | the senator from Florida |
| Central Park | the park |
| Golden Gate Bridge | the bridge |
| President Obama | the former president of the United States |
| Pope Francis | the pope |
| Queen Elizabeth II | the queen of England |
| Tropic of Capricorn | the tropics |
| Monroe Doctrine | the doctrine of expansion |
| Mississippi River | the river |
| Easter Day | the day |
| Treaty of Versailles | the treaty |
| Merriam-Webster's Dictionary | the dictionary |
| Equatorial Current | the equator |

Use a capital to start a sentence:

Our car would not start.

When will you leave? I need to know right away.

Never!

Let me in! Please!

When a sentence appears within a sentence, start it with a capital letter:

We had only one concern: When would we eat?

My sister said, "I'll find the Monopoly game."

He answered, "We can only stay a few minutes."

The most important words of titles are capitalized. Those words not capitalized are coordinating conjunctions (*and, or, nor, but*), articles (*a, an, the*), and short prepositions (*of, on, by, for*). The first and last word of a title must always be capitalized:

| | |
|---|---|
| *A Man for All Seasons* | "Let Me In" |
| *Crime and Punishment* | "Rubaiyat of Omar Khayyam" |
| *Of Mice and Men* | "Sonata in G Minor" |
| *Rise of the West* | "Ode to Billy Joe" |
| *Strange Life of Ivan Osokin* | "Modern Family" |

Capitalize newspaper and magazine titles:

> U.S. News & World Report
> National Geographic
> The New York Times
> The Washington Post

Capitalize radio and TV station call letters:

| | |
|---|---|
| ABC News | NBC Sports |
| Cable News Network | KNX Newsradio |
| CBC Television | HBO |

Do *not* capitalize compass directions or seasons:

| | |
|---|---|
| west | north |
| east | south |
| spring | winter |
| autumn | summer |

Capitalize regions:

| | |
|---|---|
| the South | the Northeast |
| the West | Eastern Europe |
| BUT: | the south of France |
| | the east part of town |

Capitalize specific military units:

> U.S. Army
> 7th Fleet
> German Navy
> 1st Infantry Division

Capitalize political groups and philosophies:

| | |
|---|---|
| Democratic Party | Socialist Party |
| Green Party | Nazism |
| Marxist | Federalist Party |
| Republican Party | Transcendentalism |

BUT do *not* capitalize systems of government or individual adherents to a philosophy:

| | |
|---|---|
| democracy | communism |
| fascist | agnostic |

# Drills

## Drills 1-12: Vocabulary

Although the context in which a word appears can help you determine the meaning of the word, one surefire way to know a definition is to learn it. By studying the following English Language Skills lists of words and memorizing their definitions, you will be better equipped to answer English Language Skills questions that deal with word meanings.

To benefit most from this vocabulary list, study the words and their definitions, then answer all of the drill questions that appear at the end of the review. Make sure to check your answers with the answer key. This will aid you as a test-taker significantly when you focus on questions that require you to make an effective word choice and questions that require you to have a contextual understanding in order to answer the question correctly.

## Group 1

**abstract**—*adj.*—not easy to understand; theoretical

**acclaim**—*n.*—loud approval; applause

**acquiesce**—*v.*—agree or consent to an opinion

**adamant**—*adj.*—not yielding; firm

**adversary**—*n.*—an enemy; foe

**advocate**—1. *v.*—to plead in favor of; 2. *n.*—supporter; defender

**aesthetic**—*adj.*—showing good taste; artistic

**alleviate**—*v.*—to lessen or make easier

**aloof**—*adj.*—distant in interest; reserved; cool

**altercation**—*n.*—controversy; dispute

**altruistic**—*adj.*—unselfish

**amass**—*v.*—to collect together; accumulate

**ambiguous**—*adj.*—not clear; uncertain; vague

**ambivalent**—*adj.*—undecided

**ameliorate**—*v.*—to make better; to improve

**amiable**—*adj.*—friendly

**amorphous**—*adj.*—having no determinate form

**anarchist**—*n.*—one who believes that a formal government is unnecessary

**antagonism**—*n.*—hostility; opposition

**apathy**—*n.*—lack of emotion or interest

**appease**—*v.*—to make quiet; to calm

**apprehensive**—*adj.*—fearful; aware; conscious

**arbitrary**—*adj.*—based on one's preference or whim

**arrogant**—*adj.*—acting superior to others; conceited

**articulate**—1. *v.*—to speak distinctly; 2. *adj.*—eloquent; fluent; 3. *adj.*—capable of speech; 4. *v.*—to hinge; to connect; 5. *v.*—to convey; to express effectively

## Drill 1

**Directions:** Match each word in the left column with the word in the right column that is most *opposite* in meaning.

| Word | Match |
|------|-------|
| 1. ___ articulate | A. hostile |
| 2. ___ apathy | B. concrete |
| 3. ___ amiable | C. selfish |
| 4. ___ altruistic | D. reasoned |
| 5. ___ ambivalent | E. ally |
| 6. ___ abstract | F. disperse |
| 7. ___ acquiesce | G. enthusiasm |
| 8. ___ arbitrary | H. certain |
| 9. ___ amass | I. resist |
| 10. ___ adversary | J. incoherent |

**Directions:** Match each word in the left column with the word in the right column that is most *similar* in meaning.

| Word | Match |
|------|-------|
| 11. ___ adamant | A. afraid |
| 12. ___ aesthetic | B. disagreement |
| 13. ___ apprehensive | C. tasteful |
| 14. ___ antagonism | D. insistent |
| 15. ___ altercation | E. hostility |

## Group 2

**assess**—*v.*—to estimate the value of

**astute**—*adj.*—cunning; sly; crafty

**atrophy**—*v.*—to waste away through lack of nutrition

**audacious**—*adj.*—fearless; bold

**augment**—*v.*—to increase or add to; to make larger

**austere**—*adj.*—harsh; severe; strict

**authentic**—*adj.*—real; genuine; trustworthy

**authoritarian**—*adj.*—acting as a dictator; demanding obedience

**banal**—*adj.*—common; petty; ordinary

**belittle**—*v.*—to make small; to think lightly of

**benefactor**—*n.*—one who helps others; a donor

**benevolent**—*adj.*—kind; generous

**benign**—*adj.*—mild; harmless

**biased**—*adj.*—prejudiced; influenced; not neutral

**blasphemous**—*adj.*—irreligious; away from acceptable standards

**blithe**—*adj.*—happy; cheery; merry

**brevity**—*n.*—briefness; shortness

**candid**—*adj.*—honest; truthful; sincere

**capricious**—*adj.*—changeable; fickle

**caustic**—*adj.*—burning; sarcastic; harsh

**censor**—*v.*—to examine and delete objectionable material

**censure**—*v.*—to criticize or disapprove of

**charlatan**—*n.*—an imposter; fake

**coalesce**—*v.*—to combine; come together

**collaborate**—*v.*—to work together; cooperate

## Drill 2

**Directions:** Match each word in the left column with the word in the right column that is most *opposite* in meaning.

| Word | Match |
|------|-------|
| 1. ___ augment | A. permit |
| 2. ___ biased | B. religious |
| 3. ___ banal | C. praise |
| 4. ___ benevolent | D. diminish |
| 5. ___ censor | E. dishonest |
| 6. ___ authentic | F. malicious |
| 7. ___ candid | G. neutral |
| 8. ___ belittle | H. mournful |
| 9. ___ blasphemous | I. unusual |
| 10. ___ blithe | J. ersatz |

**Directions:** Match each word in the left column with the word in the right column that is most *similar* in meaning.

| Word | Match |
|------|-------|
| 11. ___ collaborate | A. harmless |
| 12. ___ benign | B. cunning |
| 13. ___ astute | C. changeable |
| 14. ___ censure | D. cooperate |
| 15. ___ capricious | E. criticize |

## Group 3

**compatible**—*adj.*—in agreement; harmonious

**complacent**—*adj.*—content; self-satisfied; smug

**compliant**—*adj.*—yielding; obedient

**comprehensive**—*adj.*—all-inclusive; complete; thorough

**compromise**—*v.*—to settle by mutual adjustment

**concede**—1. *v.*—to acknowledge; admit; 2. to surrender; to abandon one's position

**concise**—*adj.*—in few words; brief; condensed

**condescend**—*v.*—to come down from one's position or dignity

**condone**—*v.*—to overlook; to forgive

**conspicuous**—*adj.*—easy to see; noticeable

**consternation**—*n.*—amazement or terror that causes confusion

**consummation**—*n.*—the completion; finish

**contemporary**—*adj.*—living or happening at the same time; modern

**contempt**—*n.*—scorn; disrespect

**contrite**—*adj.*—regretful; sorrowful

**conventional**—*adj.*—traditional; common; routine

**cower**—*v.*—crouch down in fear or shame

**defamation**—*n.*—any harm to a name or reputation; slander

**deference**—*n.*—a yielding to the opinion of another

**deliberate**—1. *v.*—to consider carefully; weigh in the mind; 2. *adj.*—intentional

**denounce**—*v.*—to speak out against; condemn

**depict**—*v.*—to portray in words; present a visual image

**deplete**—*v.*—to reduce; to empty

**depravity**—*n.*—moral corruption; badness

**deride**—*v.*—to ridicule; laugh at with scorn

## Drill 3

**Directions:** Match each word in the left column with the word in the right column that is most *opposite* in meaning.

| | Word | | Match |
|---|---|---|---|
| 1. | ___ deplete | A. | unintentional |
| 2. | ___ contemporary | B. | disapprove |
| 3. | ___ concise | C. | invisible |
| 4. | ___ deliberate | D. | respect |
| 5. | ___ depravity | E. | fill |
| 6. | ___ condone | F. | support |
| 7. | ___ conspicuous | G. | beginning |
| 8. | ___ consummation | H. | ancient |
| 9. | ___ denounce | I. | virtue |
| 10. | ___ contempt | J. | verbose |

**Directions:** Match each word in the left column with the word in the right column that is most *similar* in meaning.

| | Word | | Match |
|---|---|---|---|
| 11. | ___ compatible | A. | portray |
| 12. | ___ depict | B. | content |
| 13. | ___ conventional | C. | harmonious |
| 14. | ___ comprehensive | D. | thorough |
| 15. | ___ complacent | E. | common |

## Group 4

**desecrate**—*v.*—to violate a holy place or sanctuary

**detached**—*adj.*—separated; not interested; standing alone

**deter**—*v.*—to prevent; to discourage; hinder

**didactic**—1. *adj.*—instructive; 2. dogmatic; preachy

**digress**—*v.*—stray from the subject; wander from topic

**diligence**—*n.*—hard work

**discerning**—*adj.*—distinguishing one thing from another

**discord**—*n.*—disagreement; lack of harmony

**discriminating**—1. *v.*—distinguishing one thing from another; 2. *v.*—demonstrating bias; 3. *adj.*—able to distinguish

**disdain**—1. *n.*—intense dislike; 2. *v.*—look down upon; scorn

**disparage**—*v.*—to belittle; undervalue

**disparity**—*n.*—difference in form, character, or degree

**dispassionate**—*adj.*—lack of feeling; impartial

**disperse**—*v.*—to scatter; separate

**disseminate**—*v.*—to circulate; scatter

**dissent**—*v.*—to disagree; differ in opinion

**dissonance**—*n.*—harsh contradiction

**diverse**—*adj.*—different; dissimilar

**document**—1. *n.*—official paper containing information; 2. *v.*—to support; substantiate; verify

**dogmatic**—*adj.*—stubborn; biased; opinionated

**dubious**—*adj.*—doubtful; uncertain; skeptical; suspicious

**eccentric**—*adj.*—odd; peculiar; strange

**efface**—*v.*—wipe out; erase

**effervescence**—1. *n.*—liveliness; spirit; enthusiasm; 2. bubbliness

**egocentric**—*adj.*—self-centered

## Drill 4

**Directions:** Match each word in the left column with the word in the right column that is most *opposite* in meaning.

| Word | Match |
|------|-------|
| 1. ___ detached | A. agree |
| 2. ___ deter | B. certain |
| 3. ___ dissent | C. lethargy |
| 4. ___ discord | D. connected |
| 5. ___ efface | E. assist |
| 6. ___ dubious | F. respect |
| 7. ___ diligence | G. compliment |
| 8. ___ disdain | H. sanctify |
| 9. ___ desecrate | I. harmony |
| 10. ___ disparage | J. restore |

**Directions:** Match each word in the left column with the word in the right column that is most *similar* in meaning.

| Word | Match |
|------|-------|
| 11. ___ effervescence | A. stubborn |
| 12. ___ dogmatic | B. distribute |
| 13. ___ disseminate | C. substantiate |
| 14. ___ document | D. liveliness |
| 15. ___ eccentric | E. odd |

## Group 5

**elaboration**—*n.*—the act of clarifying or adding details

**eloquence**—*n.*—the ability to speak well

**elusive**—*adj.*—hard to catch; difficult to understand

**emulate**—*v.*—to imitate; copy; mimic

**endorse**—*v.*—support; to approve of; recommend

**engender**—*v.*—to create; bring about

**enhance**—*v.*—to improve; complement; make more attractive

**enigma**—*n.*—mystery; secret; perplexity

**ephemeral**—*adj.*—temporary; brief; short-lived

**equivocal**—*adj.*—doubtful; uncertain

**erratic**—*adj.*—unpredictable; strange

**erroneous**—*adj.*—untrue; inaccurate; not correct

**esoteric**—*adj.*—incomprehensible; obscure

**euphony**—*n.*—pleasant sound

**execute** –1. *v.*—put to death; kill; 2. to carry out; fulfill

**exemplary**—*adj.*—serving as an example; outstanding

**exhaustive**—*adj.*—thorough; complete

**expedient**—*adj.*—helpful; practical; worthwhile

**expedite**—*v.*—speed up

**explicit**—*adj.*—specific; definite

**extol**—*v.*—praise; commend

**extraneous**—*adj.*—irrelevant; not related; not essential

**facilitate**—*v.*—make easier; simplify

**fallacious**—*adj.*—misleading

**fanatic**—*n.*—enthusiast; extremist

## Drill 5

**Directions:** Match each word in the left column with the word in the right column that is most *opposite* in meaning.

| Word | Match |
|------|-------|
| 1. ___ extraneous | A. incomplete |
| 2. ___ ephemeral | B. delay |
| 3. ___ exhaustive | C. dependable |
| 4. ___ expedite | D. comprehensible |
| 5. ___ erroneous | E. dissonance |
| 6. ___ erratic | F. eternal |
| 7. ___ explicit | G. condemn |
| 8. ___ euphony | H. relevant |
| 9. ___ elusive | I. indefinite |
| 10. ___ extol | J. accurate |

**Directions:** Match each word in the left column with the word in the right column that is most *similar* in meaning.

| Word | Match |
|------|-------|
| 11. ___ endorse | A. enable |
| 12. ___ expedient | B. recommend |
| 13. ___ facilitate | C. create |
| 14. ___ fallacious | D. worthwhile |
| 15. ___ engender | E. deceptive |

## Group 6

**fastidious**—*adj.*—fussy; hard to please

**fervent**—*n.*—passionate; intense

**fickle**—*adj.*—changeable; unpredictable

**fortuitous**—*adj.*—accidental; happening by chance; lucky

**frivolity**—*n.*—giddiness; lack of seriousness

**fundamental**—*adj.*—basic; necessary

**furtive**—*adj.*—secretive; sly

**futile**—*adj.*—worthless; unprofitable

**glutton**—*n.*—overeater

**grandiose**—*adj.*—extravagant; flamboyant

**gravity**—*n.*—seriousness

**guile**—*n.*—slyness; deceit

**gullible**—*adj.*—easily fooled

**hackneyed**—*adj.*—commonplace; trite

**hamper**—*v.*—interfere with; hinder

**haphazard**—*adj.*—disorganized; random

**hedonistic**—*adj.*—pleasure seeking

**heed**—*v.*—obey; yield to

**heresy**—*n.*—opinion contrary to popular belief

**hindrance**—*n.*—blockage; obstacle

**humility**—*n.*—lack of pride; modesty

**hypocritical**—*adj.*—two-faced; deceptive

**hypothetical**—*adj.*—assumed; uncertain

**illuminate**—*v.*—make understandable

**illusory**—*adj.*—unreal; false; deceptive

## Drill 6

**Directions:** Match each word in the left column with the word in the right column that is most *opposite* in meaning.

| | Word | | Match |
|---|---|---|---|
| 1. ___ | heresy | A. | predictable |
| 2. ___ | fickle | B. | dispassionate |
| 3. ___ | illusory | C. | simple |
| 4. ___ | frivolity | D. | extraneous |
| 5. ___ | grandiose | E. | real |
| 6. ___ | fervent | F. | beneficial |
| 7. ___ | fundamental | G. | orthodoxy |
| 8. ___ | furtive | H. | organized |
| 9. ___ | futile | I. | candid |
| 10. ___ | haphazard | J. | seriousness |

**Directions:** Match each word in the left column with the word in the right column that is most *similar* in meaning.

| | Word | | Match |
|---|---|---|---|
| 11. ___ | glutton | A. | hinder |
| 12. ___ | heed | B. | obstacle |
| 13. ___ | hamper | C. | trite |
| 14. ___ | hackneyed | D. | overeater |
| 15. ___ | hindrance | E. | obey |

## Group 7

**immune**—*adj.*—protected; unthreatened by

**immutable**—*adj.*—unchangeable; permanent

**impartial**—*adj.*—unbiased; fair

**impetuous**—1. *adj.*—rash; impulsive; 2. forcible; violent

**implication**—*n.*—suggestion; inference

**inadvertent**—*adj.*—not on purpose; unintentional

**incessant**—*adj.*—constant; continual

**incidental**—*adj.*—extraneous; unexpected

**inclined**—1. *adj.*—apt to; likely to; 2. angled

**incoherent**—*adj.*—illogical; rambling

**incompatible**—*adj.*—disagreeing; disharmonious

**incredulous**—*adj.*—unwilling to believe; skeptical

**indifferent**—*adj.*—unconcerned

**indolent**—*adj.*—lazy; inactive

**indulgent**—*adj.*—lenient; extravagant

**inevitable**—*adj.*—sure to happen; unavoidable

**infamous**—*adj.*—having a bad reputation; notorious

**infer**—*v.*—form an opinion; conclude

**initiate**—1. *v.*—begin; admit into a group; 2. *n.*—a person who is in the process of being admitted into a group

**innate**—*adj.*—natural; inborn

**innocuous**—*adj.*—harmless; innocent

**innovate**—*v.*—introduce a change; depart from the old

**insipid**—*adj.*—uninteresting; bland

**instigate**—*v.*—start; provoke

**intangible**—*adj.*—incapable of being touched; immaterial

## Drill 7

**Directions:** Match each word in the left column with the word in the right column that is most *opposite* in meaning.

| Word | Match |
|------|-------|
| 1. ___ immutable | A. intentional |
| 2. ___ impartial | B. articulate |
| 3. ___ inadvertent | C. gullible |
| 4. ___ incoherent | D. material |
| 5. ___ incompatible | E. biased |
| 6. ___ innate | F. changeable |
| 7. ___ incredulous | G. avoidable |
| 8. ___ inevitable | H. harmonious |
| 9. ___ intangible | I. learned |
| 10. ___ indolent | J. energetic |

**Directions:** Match each word in the left column with the word in the right column that is most *similar* in meaning.

| Word | Match |
|---|---|
| 11. ___ impetuous | A. lenient |
| 12. ___ incidental | B. impulsive |
| 13. ___ infer | C. provoke |
| 14. ___ instigate | D. conclude |
| 15. ___ indulgent | E. extraneous |

## Group 8

**ironic**—*adj.*—contradictory; inconsistent; sarcastic

**irrational**—*adj.*—not logical

**jeopardy**—*n.*—danger

**kindle**—*v.*—ignite; arouse

**languid**—*adj.*—weak; fatigued

**laud**—*v.*—to praise

**lax**—*adj.*—careless; irresponsible

**lethargic**—*adj.*—lazy; passive

**levity**—*n.*—silliness; lack of seriousness

**lucid**—1. *adj.*—shining; 2. easily understood

**magnanimous**—*adj.*—forgiving; unselfish

**malicious**—*adj.*—spiteful; vindictive

**marred**—*adj.*—damaged

**meander**—*v.*—wind on a course; go aimlessly

**melancholy**—*n.*—depression; gloom

**meticulous**—*adj.*—exacting; precise

**minute**—*adj.*—extremely small; tiny

**miser**—*n.*—penny pincher; stingy person

**mitigate**—*v.*—alleviate; lessen; soothe

**morose**—*adj.*—moody; despondent

**negligence**—*n.*—carelessness

**neutral**—*adj.*—impartial; unbiased

**hostalgic**—*adj.*—longing for the past; filled with bittersweet memories

**novel**—*adj.*—new

## Drill 8

**Directions:** Match each word in the left column with the word in the right column that is most *opposite* in meaning.

| Word | Match |
|------|-------|
| 1. ___ irrational | A. extinguish |
| 2. ___ kindle | B. jovial |
| 3. ___ meticulous | C. selfish |
| 4. ___ malicious | D. logical |
| 5. ___ morose | E. seriousness |
| 6. ___ magnanimous | F. ridicule |
| 7. ___ levity | G. kindly |
| 8. ___ minute | H. sloppy |
| 9. ___ laud | I. huge |
| 10. ___ novel | J. stale |

**Directions:** Match each word in the left column with the word in the right column that is most *similar* in meaning.

| Word | Match |
|------|-------|
| 11. ___ ironic | A. lessen |
| 12. ___ marred | B. damaged |
| 13. ___ mitigate | C. sarcastic |
| 14. ___ jeopardy | D. carelessness |
| 15. ___ negligence | E. danger |

## Group 9

**nullify**—*v.*—cancel; invalidate

**objective**—1. *adj.*—open-minded; impartial; 2. *n.*—goal

**obscure**—*adj.*—not easily understood; dark

**obsolete**—*adj.*—out of date; passé

**ominous**—*adj.*—threatening

**optimism**—*n.*—hope for the best; seeing the good side

**orthodox**—*adj.*—traditional; accepted

**pagan**—1. *n.*—polytheist; 2. *adj.*—polytheistic

**partisan**—1. *n.*—supporter; follower; 2. *adj.*—biased; one-sided

**perceptive**—*adj.*—full of insight; aware

**peripheral**—*adj.*—marginal; outer

**pernicious**—*adj.*—dangerous; harmful

**pessimism**—*n.*—seeing only the gloomy side; hopelessness

**phenomenon**—1. *n.*—miracle; 2. occurrence

**philanthropy**—*n.*—charity; unselfishness

**pious**—*adj.*—religious; devout; dedicated

**placate**—*v.*—pacify

**plausible**—*adj.*—probable; feasible

**pragmatic**—*adj.*—matter-of-fact; practical

**preclude**—*v.*—inhibit; make impossible

**predecessor**—*n.*—one who has occupied an office before another

**prodigal**—*adj.*—wasteful; lavish

**prodigious**—*adj.*—exceptional; tremendous

**profound**—*adj.*—deep; knowledgeable; thorough

**profusion**—*n.*—great amount; abundance

## Drill 9

**Directions:** Match each word in the left column with the word in the right column that is most *opposite* in meaning.

| Word | Match |
|------|-------|
| 1. ___ objective | A. scantiness |
| 2. ___ obsolete | B. assist |
| 3. ___ placate | C. mundane |
| 4. ___ profusion | D. biased |
| 5. ___ peripheral | E. improbable |
| 6. ___ plausible | F. minute |
| 7. ___ preclude | G. anger |
| 8. ___ prodigious | H. pessimism |
| 9. ___ profound | I. modern |
| 10. ___ optimism | J. central |

**Directions:** Match each word in the left column with the word in the right column that is most *similar* in meaning.

|  | Word |  | Match |
|---|---|---|---|
| 11. ___ | nullify | A. | invalidate |
| 12. ___ | ominous | B. | follower |
| 13. ___ | partisan | C. | lavish |
| 14. ___ | pernicious | D. | threatening |
| 15. ___ | prodigal | E. | harmful |

## Group 10

**prosaic**—*adj.*—tiresome; ordinary

**provincial**—*adj.*—regional; unsophisticated

**provocative**—1. *adj.*—tempting; 2. irritating

**prudent**—*adj.*—wise; careful; prepared

**qualified**—*adj.*—experienced; indefinite

**rectify**—*v.*—correct

**redundant**—*adj.*—repetitious; unnecessary

**refute**—*v.*—challenge; disprove

**relegate**—*v.*—banish; put to a lower position

**relevant**—*adj.*—of concern; significant

**remorse**—*n.*—guilt; sorrow

**reprehensible**—*adj.*—wicked; disgraceful

**repudiate**—*v.*—reject; cancel

**rescind**—*v.*—retract; discard

**resignation**—1. *n.*—quitting; 2. submission

**resolution**—*n.*—proposal; promise; determination

**respite**—*n.*—recess; rest period

**reticent**—*adj.*—silent; reserved; shy

**reverent**—*adj.*—respectful

**rhetorical**—*adj.*—having to do with verbal communication

**rigor**—*n.*—severity

**sagacious**—*adj.*—wise; cunning

**sanguine**—1. *adj.*—optimistic; cheerful; 2. red

**saturate**—*v.*—soak thoroughly; drench

**scanty**—*adj.*—inadequate; sparse

## Drill 10

**Directions:** Match each word in the left column with the word in the right column that is most *opposite* in meaning.

| Word | Match |
|------|-------|
| 1. ___ provincial | A. inexperienced |
| 2. ___ reticent | B. joy |
| 3. ___ prudent | C. pessimistic |
| 4. ___ qualified | D. unrelated |
| 5. ___ relegate | E. careless |
| 6. ___ remorse | F. affirm |
| 7. ___ repudiate | G. extraordinary |
| 8. ___ sanguine | H. sophisticated |
| 9. ___ relevant | I. forward |
| 10. ___ prosaic | J. promote |

**Directions:** Match each word in the left column with the word in the right column that is most *similar* in meaning.

| Word | Match |
|------|-------|
| 11. ___ provocative | A. drench |
| 12. ___ rigor | B. tempting |
| 13. ___ saturate | C. retract |
| 14. ___ rescind | D. severity |
| 15. ___ reprehensible | E. blameworthy |

## Group 11

**scrupulous**—*adj.*—honorable; exact

**scrutinize**—*v.*—examine closely; study

**servile**—*adj.*—slavish; groveling

**skeptic**—*n.*—doubter

**slander**—*v.*—defame; maliciously misrepresent

**solemnity**—*n.*—seriousness

**solicit**—*v.*—ask; seek

**stagnant**—*adj.*—motionless; stationary

**stanza**—*n.*—group of lines in a poem having a definite pattern

**static**—*adj.*—inactive; changeless

**stoic**—*adj.*—detached; unruffled; calm

**subtle**—*adj.*—understated

**superficial**—*adj.*—on the surface; narrow-minded; lacking depth

**superfluous**—*adj.*—unnecessary; extra

**surpass**—*v.*—go beyond; outdo

**sycophant**—*n.*—flatterer

**symmetry**—*n.*—correspondence of parts; harmony

**taciturn**—*adj.*—reserved; quiet; secretive

**tedious**—*adj.*—time-consuming; burdensome; uninteresting

**temper**—*v.*—soften; pacify; compose

**tentative**—*adj.*—not confirmed; indefinite

**thrifty**—*adj.*—economical; pennywise

**tranquility**—*n.*—peace; stillness; harmony

**trepidation**—*n.*—apprehension; uneasiness

**trivial**—*adj.*—unimportant; small; worthless

## Drill 11

**Directions:** Match each word in the left column with the word in the right column that is most *opposite* in meaning.

| **Word** | | **Match** | |
|---|---|---|---|
| 1. ___ scrutinize | | A. | frivolity |
| 2. ___ skeptic | | B. | enjoyable |
| 3. ___ solemnity | | C. | prodigal |
| 4. ___ static | | D. | chaos |
| 5. ___ tedious | | E. | give |
| 6. ___ tentative | | F. | skim |
| 7. ___ thrifty | | G. | turbulent |
| 8. ___ tranquility | | H. | active |
| 9. ___ solicit | | I. | believer |
| 10. ___ stagnant | | J. | confirmed |

**Directions:** Match each word in the left column with the word in the right column that is most *similar* in meaning.

| **Word** | | **Match** | |
|---|---|---|---|
| 11. ___ symmetry | | A. | understated |
| 12. ___ superfluous | | B. | unnecessary |
| 13. ___ sycophant | | C. | balance |
| 14. ___ subtle | | D. | fear |
| 15. ___ trepidation | | E. | flatterer |

## Group 12

**tumid**—*adj.*—swollen; inflated

**undermine**—*v.*—weaken; ruin

**uniform**—*adj.*—consistent; unvaried; unchanging

**universal**—*adj.*—concerning everyone; existing everywhere

**unobtrusive**—*adj.*—inconspicuous; reserved

**unprecedented**—*adj.*—unheard of; exceptional

**unpretentious**—*adj.*—simple; plain; modest

**vacillation**—*n.*—fluctuation

**valid**—*adj.*—acceptable; legal

**vehement**—*adj.*—intense; excited; enthusiastic

**venerate**—*v.*—revere

**verbose**—*adj.*—wordy; talkative

**viable**—1. *adj.*—capable of maintaining life; 2. possible; attainable

**vigorous**—*adj.*—energetic; forceful

**vilify**—*v.*—slander

**virtuoso**—*n.*—highly skilled artist

**virulent**—*adj.*—deadly; harmful; malicious

**vital**—*adj.*—important; spirited

**volatile**—*adj.*—changeable; undependable

**vulnerable**—*adj.*—open to attack; unprotected

**wane**—*v.*—grow gradually smaller

**whimsical**—*adj.*—fanciful; amusing

**wither**—*v.*—wilt; shrivel; humiliate; cut down

**zealot**—*n.*—believer; enthusiast; fan

**zenith**—*n.*—point directly overhead in the sky

## Drill 12

**Directions:** Match each word in the left column with the word in the right column that is most *opposite* in meaning.

| | Word | | Match |
|---|---|---|---|
| 1. ___ | uniform | A. | amateur |
| 2. ___ | virtuoso | B. | trivial |
| 3. ___ | vital | C. | visible |
| 4. ___ | wane | D. | placid |
| 5. ___ | unobtrusive | E. | unacceptable |
| 6. ___ | vigorous | F. | support |
| 7. ___ | volatile | G. | constancy |
| 8. ___ | vacillation | H. | lethargic |
| 9. ___ | undermine | I. | wax |
| 10. ___ | valid | J. | varied |

**Directions:** Match each word in the left column with the word in the right column that is most *similar* in meaning.

| Word | Match |
|------|-------|
| 11. ___ wither | A. intense |
| 12. ___ whimsical | B. deadly |
| 13. ___ viable | C. amusing |
| 14. ___ vehement | D. possible |
| 15. ___ virulent | E. shrivel |

## Drill 13: Word Choice

**Directions:** Choose the correct option.

1.  His <u>principal</u> reasons for resigning were his <u>principles</u> of right and wrong.

    (A) principal . . . principals

    (B) principle . . . principals

    (C) principle . . . principles

    (D) No change is necessary.

2.  The book tells about Alzheimer's disease—how it <u>affects</u> the patient and what <u>effect</u> it has on the patient's family.

    (A) effects . . . affect

    (B) affects . . . affect

    (C) effects . . . effects

    (D) No change is necessary.

3.  The <u>amount</u> of homeless children we can help depends on the <u>number</u> of available shelters.

    (A) number . . . number

    (B) amount . . . amount

    (C) number . . . amount

    (D) No change is necessary.

4.  All students are <u>suppose to</u> pass the test before <u>achieving</u> upper-division status.

   (A) suppose to . . . achieving their

   (B) suppose to . . . being achieved

   (C) supposed to . . . achieving

   (D) No change is necessary.

5.  The reason he <u>succeeded</u> is <u>because</u> he worked hard.

   (A) succeeded . . . that

   (B) seceded . . . that

   (C) succede . . . because of

   (D) No change is necessary.

## Drill 14: Sentence Structure

**Directions:** Select the sentence that clearly and effectively states the idea and has no structural errors.

1.  (A) South of Richmond, the two roads converge together to form a single highway.

   (B) South of Richmond, the two roads converge together to form an interstate highway.

   (C) South of Richmond, the two roads converge to form an interstate highway.

   (D) South of Richmond, the two roads converge to form a single interstate highway.

2.  (A) The student depended on his parents for financial support.

   (B) The student lacked the ways and means to pay for his room and board, so he depended on his parents for this kind of money and support.

   (C) The student lacked the ways and means or the wherewithal to support himself, so his parents provided him with the financial support he needed.

   (D) The student lacked the means to pay for his room and board, so he depended on his parents for financial support.

3.  (A) Vincent van Gogh and Paul Gauguin were close personal friends and companions who enjoyed each other's company and frequently worked together on their artwork.

    (B) Vincent van Gogh and Paul Gauguin were friends who frequently painted together.

    (C) Vincent van Gogh was a close personal friend of Paul Gauguin's, and the two of them often worked together on their artwork because they enjoyed each other's company.

    (D) Vincent van Gogh, a close personal friend of Paul Gauguin's, often worked with him on their artwork.

4.  (A) A college education often involves putting away childish thoughts, which are characteristic of youngsters, and concentrating on the future, which lies ahead.

    (B) A college education involves putting away childish thoughts, which are characteristic of youngsters, and concentrating on the future.

    (C) A college education involves putting away childish thoughts and concentrating on the future.

    (D) A college education involves putting away childish thoughts and concentrating on the future which lies ahead.

5.  (A) I had the occasion to visit an Oriental pagoda while I was a tourist on vacation and visiting in Kyoto, Japan.

    (B) I visited a Japanese pagoda in Kyoto.

    (C) I had occasion to visit a pagoda when I was vacationing in Kyoto, Japan.

    (D) On my vacation, I visited a Japanese pagoda in Kyoto.

6.  (A) Many gases are invisible, odorless, and they have no taste.

    (B) Many gases are invisible, odorless, and have no taste.

    (C) Many gases are invisible, odorless, and tasteless.

    (D) Many gases are invisible and odorless and tasteless.

7.  (A)  Everyone agreed that she had neither the voice or the skill to be a speaker.

    (B)  Everyone agreed that she had neither the voice nor the skill to be a speaker.

    (C)  Everyone agreed that she had either the voice nor the skill to be a speaker.

    (D)  Everyone agreed she had no voice or skill to be a speaker.

8.  (A)  The mayor will be remembered because he kept his campaign promises and because of his refusal to accept political favors.

    (B)  The mayor will be remembered because he kept his campaign promises and because he refused to accept political favors.

    (C)  The mayor will be remembered because of his refusal to accept political favors and he kept his campaign promises.

    (D)  The mayor will be remembered because he refused to accept political favors and he kept campaign promises.

9.  (A)  While taking a shower, the doorbell rang.

    (B)  While I was taking a shower, the doorbell rang.

    (C)  While taking a shower, someone rang the doorbell.

    (D)  While taking a shower the doorbell rang.

10. (A)  He swung the bat, while the runner stole second base.

    (B)  The runner stole second base while he swung the bat.

    (C)  While he was swinging the bat, the runner stole second base.

    (D)  He stole second base while swinging the bat.

### Drill 15: Punctuation

**Directions:** Choose the correct option.

1.  Nothing grows as well in Mississippi as <u>cotton. Cotton</u> being the state's principal crop.

    (A)  cotton, cotton

    (B)  cotton; cotton

    (C)  cotton cotton

    (D)  No change is necessary.

2. It was a heart-wrenching <u>movie; one</u> that I had never seen before.

   (A) movie and

   (B) movie, one

   (C) movie. One

   (D) No change is necessary.

3. Traffic was stalled for three miles on the <u>bridge. Because</u> repairs were being made.

   (A) bridge because

   (B) bridge; because

   (C) bridge, because

   (D) No change is necessary.

4. The ability to write complete sentences comes with <u>practice writing</u> run-on sentences seems to occur naturally.

   (A) practice, writing

   (B) practice. Writing

   (C) practice and

   (D) No change is necessary.

5. Even though she had taken French classes, she could not understand native French <u>speakers they</u> all spoke too fast.

   (A) speakers, they

   (B) speakers. They

   (C) speaking

   (D) No change is necessary.

6. Indianola, <u>Mississippi, where B.B. King and my father grew up</u>, has a population of less than 50,000 people.

   (A) Mississippi where, B.B. King and my father grew up,

   (B) Mississippi where B.B. King and my father grew up,

   (C) Mississippi; where B.B. King and my father grew up,

   (D) No change is necessary.

7. John Steinbeck's best known novel *The Grapes of Wrath* is the story of the <u>Joads an Oklahoma family</u> who were driven from their dust bowl farm and forced to become migrant workers in California.

    (A) Joads, an Oklahoma family

    (B) Joads, an Oklahoma family,

    (C) Joads; an Oklahoma family

    (D) No change is necessary.

8. All students who are interested in student teaching next <u>semester, must submit an application to the Teacher Education Office.</u>

    (A) semester must submit an application to the Teacher Education Office.

    (B) semester, must submit an application, to the Teacher Education Office.

    (C) semester: must submit an application to the Teacher Education Office.

    (D) No change is necessary.

9. Whenever you travel by <u>car, or plane, you</u> must wear a seatbelt.

    (A) car or plane you      (C)   car or plane, you

    (B) car, or plane you     (D)   No change is necessary.

10. Wearing a seatbelt is not just a good <u>idea, it's</u> the law.

    (A) idea; it's           (C)   idea. It's

    (B) idea it's            (D)   No change is necessary.

## Drill 16: Subject/Verb

**Directions:** Choose the correct option.

1. If you <u>had been concerned</u> about Marilyn, you <u>would have went</u> to greater lengths to ensure her safety.

    (A) had been concern . . . would have gone

    (B) was concerned . . . would have gone

    (C) had been concerned . . . would have gone

    (D) No change is necessary.

2. Susan <u>laid</u> in bed too long and missed her class.

   (A) lays                    (C) lied

   (B) lay                     (D) No change is necessary.

3. The Great Wall of China <u>is</u> fifteen hundred miles long; it <u>was built</u> in the third century BC.

   (A) was . . . was built     (C) has been . . . was built

   (B) is . . . is built       (D) No change is necessary.

4. Joe stated that the class <u>began</u> at 10:30 a.m.

   (A) begins                  (C) was beginning

   (B) had begun               (D) No change is necessary.

5. The ceiling of the Sistine Chapel <u>was</u> painted by Michelangelo; it <u>depicted</u> scenes from the Creation in the Old Testament.

   (A) was . . . depicts       (C) has been . . . depicting

   (B) is . . . depicts        (D) No change is necessary.

6. After Christmas <u>comes</u> the best sales.

   (A) has come                (C) is coming

   (B) come                    (D) No change is necessary.

7. The bakery's specialty <u>are</u> wedding cakes.

   (A) is                      (C) be

   (B) were                    (D) No change is necessary.

8. Every man, woman, and child <u>were given</u> a life preserver.

   (A) have been given         (C) was given

   (B) had gave                (D) No change is necessary.

9. Hiding your mistakes <u>don't</u> make them go away.

   (A) doesn't                 (C) have not

   (B) do not                  (D) No change is necessary.

10. The Florida State University System's Board of Governors <u>has recommended</u> a tuition increase.

    (A) have recommended

    (C) had recommended

    (B) has recommend

    (D) No change is necessary.

## Drill 17: Pronouns

**Directions:** Choose the correct option.

1. My friend and <u>myself</u> bought tickets for *Cats*.

    (A) I

    (C) us

    (B) me

    (D) No change is necessary.

2. Alcohol and tobacco are harmful to <u>whomever</u> consumes them.

    (A) whom

    (C) whoever

    (B) who

    (D) No change is necessary.

3. Everyone is wondering <u>whom</u> her successor will be.

    (A) who

    (C) who'll

    (B) whose

    (D) No change is necessary.

4. Rosa Lee's parents discovered that it was <u>her who</u> wrecked the family car.

    (A) she who

    (C) her whom

    (B) she whom

    (D) No change is necessary.

5. A student <u>who</u> wishes to protest <u>his or her</u> grades must file a formal grievance in the dean's office.

    (A) that . . . their

    (C) whom . . . their

    (B) which . . . his

    (D) No change is necessary.

6. One of the best things about working for this company is that <u>they pay</u> big bonuses.

    (A) it pays

    (C) they paid

    (B) they always pay

    (D) No change is necessary.

7.   Every car owner should be sure that <u>their</u> automobile insurance is adequate.

    (A)  your               (C)  its

    (B)  his or her      (D)  No change is necessary.

8.   My mother wants me to become a teacher, but I'm not interested in <u>it</u>.

    (A)  this              (C)  that

    (B)  teaching       (D)  No change is necessary.

9.   Since I had not paid my electric bill, <u>they</u> sent me a disconnection notice.

    (A)  the power company   (C)  it

    (B)  he                (D)  No change is necessary.

10.  Margaret seldom wrote to her sister when <u>she</u> was away at college.

    (A)  who              (C)  her sister

    (B)  her              (D)  No change is necessary.

## Drill 18: Adverbs/Comparative/Superlative

**Directions:** Choose the correct option.

1.   Although the band performed <u>badly</u>, I feel <u>real bad</u> about missing the concert.

    (A)  badly . . . real badly   (C)  badly . . . very bad

    (B)  bad . . . badly       (D)  No change is necessary.

2.   These reports are <u>relative simple</u> to prepare.

    (A)  relatively simple    (C)  relatively simply

    (B)  relative simply     (D)  No change is necessary.

3.   He did <u>very well</u> on the test although his writing skills are not <u>good</u>.

    (A)  real well . . . good    (C)  good . . . great

    (B)  very good . . . good   (D)  No change is necessary.

4.  Shake the medicine bottle <u>good</u> before you open it.

    (A)  very good            (C)    well

    (B)  real good            (D)    No change is necessary.

5.  Though she speaks <u>fluently</u>, she writes <u>poorly</u> because she doesn't observe <u>closely</u> or think <u>clear</u>.

    (A)  fluently . . . poorly . . . closely . . . clearly

    (B)  fluent . . . poor . . . close . . . clear

    (C)  fluently . . . poor . . . closely . . . clear

    (D)  No change is necessary.

**Directions:** Select the sentence that clearly and effectively states the idea and has no structural errors.

6.  (A)  Los Angeles is larger than any city in California.

    (B)  Los Angeles is larger than all the cities in California.

    (C)  Los Angeles is larger than any other city in California.

    (D)  Los Angles is larger than most cities in California.

7.  (A)  Art history is as interesting as, if not more interesting than, music appreciation.

    (B)  Art history is as interesting, if not more interesting than, music appreciation.

    (C)  Art history is as interesting as, if not more interesting, music appreciation.

    (D)  Art history is more interesting than music appreciation.

8.  (A)  The baseball team here is as good as any other university.

    (B)  The baseball team here is as good as all the other universities.

    (C)  The baseball team here is as good as any other university's.

    (D)  The baseball team is as good as any other.

9.  (A)  I like him better than you.

    (B)  I like him better than I like you.

    (C)  I like him better.

    (D)  I like him best.

10. (A) You are the most stingiest person I know.

    (B) You are the most stingier person I know.

    (C) You are the stingiest person I know.

    (D) You are more stingy.

## Drill 19: Spelling

**Directions:** Identify the misspelled word in each set.

1. (A) probly

   (B) accommodate

   (C) acquaintance

   (D) probability

2. (A) auxiliary

   (B) atheletic

   (C) beginning

   (D) useful

3. (A) environment

   (B) existence

   (C) Febuary

   (D) January

4. (A) ocassion

   (B) occurrence

   (C) omitted

   (D) committed

5. (A) perspiration

   (B) referring

   (C) priviledge

   (D) knowledge

**Directions:** Choose the correct option.

6. <u>Preceding</u> the <u>business</u> session, lunch will be served in a <u>separate</u> room.

   (A) preceeding . . . business . . . seperate

   (B) proceeding . . . bussiness . . . seperate

   (C) proceeding . . . business . . . seperite

   (D) No change is necessary.

7. Monte <u>inadvertently</u> left <u>several</u> of his <u>libary</u> books in the cafeteria.

   (A) inadverdently . . . serveral . . . libery

   (B) inadvertently . . . several . . . library

   (C) inadvertentely . . . several . . . librery

   (D) No change is necessary.

8. Sam wished he had more <u>liesure</u> time so he could <u>persue</u> his favorite hobbies.

   (A) leisure . . . pursue

   (B) Liesure . . . pursue

   (C) leisure . . . persue

   (D) No change is necessary.

9. One of my <u>favrite charecters</u> in <u>litrature</u> is Bilbo from *The Hobbit*.

   (A) favrite . . . characters . . . literature

   (B) favorite . . . characters . . . literature

   (C) favourite . . . characters . . . literature

   (D) No change is necessary.

10. Even <u>tho</u> Joe was badly hurt in the <u>accidant</u>, the company said they were not <u>lible</u> for damages.

    (A) though . . . accidant . . . libel

    (B) though . . . accident . . . liable

    (C) though . . . acident . . . liable

    (D) No change is necessary.

## Drill 20: Capitalization

**Directions:** Choose the correct option.

1. Mexico is the southernmost country in <u>North America</u>. It borders the United States on the north; it is bordered on the <u>south</u> by Belize and Guatemala.

   (A) north America . . . South

   (B) North America . . . South

   (C) North america . . . South

   (D) No change is necessary.

2. (A) Until 1989, Tom Landry was the only Coach the Dallas cowboys ever had.

   (B) Until 1989, Tom Landry was the only coach the Dallas Cowboys ever had.

   (C) Until 1989, Tom Landry was the only Coach the Dallas Cowboys ever had.

   (D) Until 1989 Tom Landry was the only coach the Dallas cowboys ever had.

3. The <u>Northern Hemisphere</u> is the half of the <u>earth</u> that lies north of the <u>Equator.</u>

   (A) Northern hemisphere . . . earth . . . equator

   (B) Northern hemisphere . . . Earth . . . Equator

   (C) Northern Hemisphere . . . earth . . . equator

   (D) No change is necessary.

4. (A) My favorite works by Ernest Hemingway are "The Snows of Kiliman-jaro," *The Sun Also Rises,* and *For Whom the Bell Tolls.*

   (B) My favorite works by Ernest Hemingway are "The Snows Of Kilimanja-ro," *The Sun Also Rises,* and *For Whom The Bell Tolls.*

   (C) My favorite works by Ernest Hemingway are "The Snows of Kilimanja-ro," *The Sun also Rises,* and *For whom the Bell Tolls.*

   (D) My favorite works by Ernest Hemingway are The Snows Of Kilimanjaro and *The Sun Also Rises* and *For Whom The Bell Tolls.*

5.  Aphrodite (<u>Venus in Roman Mythology</u>) was the <u>Greek</u> goddess of love.

(A)  Venus in Roman mythology . . . greek

(B)  venus in roman mythology . . . Greek

(C)  Venus in Roman mythology . . . Greek

(D)  No change is necessary.

## Answer Key

### Drill 1

| | | | | | | | | | |
|---|---|---|---|---|---|---|---|---|---|
| 1. | (J) | 4. | (C) | 7. | (I) | 10. | (E) | 13. | (A) |
| 2. | (G) | 5. | (H) | 8. | (D) | 11. | (D) | 14. | (E) |
| 3. | (A) | 6. | (B) | 9. | (F) | 12. | (C) | 15. | (B) |

### Drill 2

| | | | | | | | | | |
|---|---|---|---|---|---|---|---|---|---|
| 1. | (D) | 4. | (F) | 7. | (E) | 10. | (H) | 13. | (B) |
| 2. | (G) | 5. | (A) | 8. | (C) | 11. | (D) | 14. | (E) |
| 3. | (I) | 6. | (J) | 9. | (B) | 12. | (A) | 15. | (C) |

### Drill 3

| | | | | | | | | | |
|---|---|---|---|---|---|---|---|---|---|
| 1. | (E) | 4. | (A) | 7. | (C) | 10. | (D) | 13. | (E) |
| 2. | (H) | 5. | (I) | 8. | (G) | 11. | (C) | 14. | (D) |
| 3. | (J) | 6. | (B) | 9. | (F) | 12. | (A) | 15. | (B) |

### Drill 4

| | | | | | | | | | |
|---|---|---|---|---|---|---|---|---|---|
| 1. | (D) | 4. | (I) | 7. | (C) | 10. | (G) | 13. | (B) |
| 2. | (E) | 5. | (J) | 8. | (F) | 11. | (D) | 14. | (C) |
| 3. | (A) | 6. | (B) | 9. | (H) | 12. | (A) | 15. | (E) |

## Drill 5

| | | | | |
|---|---|---|---|---|
| 1. (H) | 4. (B) | 7. (I) | 10. (G) | 13. (A) |
| 2. (F) | 5. (J) | 8. (E) | 11. (B) | 14. (E) |
| 3. (A) | 6. (C) | 9. (D) | 12. (D) | 15. (C) |

## Drill 6

| | | | | |
|---|---|---|---|---|
| 1. (G) | 4. (J) | 7. (D) | 10. (H) | 13. (A) |
| 2. (A) | 5. (C) | 8. (I) | 11. (D) | 14. (C) |
| 3. (E) | 6. (B) | 9. (F) | 12. (E) | 15. (B) |

## Drill 7

| | | | | |
|---|---|---|---|---|
| 1. (F) | 4. (B) | 7. (C) | 10. (J) | 13. (D) |
| 2. (E) | 5. (H) | 8. (G) | 11. (B) | 14. (C) |
| 3. (A) | 6. (I) | 9. (D) | 12. (E) | 15. (A) |

## Drill 8

| | | | | |
|---|---|---|---|---|
| 1. (D) | 4. (G) | 7. (E) | 10. (J) | 13. (A) |
| 2. (A) | 5. (B) | 8. (I) | 11. (C) | 14. (E) |
| 3. (H) | 6. (C) | 9. (F) | 12. (B) | 15. (D) |

## Drill 9

| | | | | |
|---|---|---|---|---|
| 1. (D) | 4. (A) | 7. (B) | 10. (H) | 13. (B) |
| 2. (I) | 5. (J) | 8. (F) | 11. (A) | 14. (E) |
| 3. (G) | 6. (E) | 9. (C) | 12. (D) | 15. (C) |

## Drill 10

| | | | | |
|---|---|---|---|---|
| 1. (H) | 4. (A) | 7. (F) | 10. (G) | 13. (A) |
| 2. (I) | 5. (J) | 8. (C) | 11. (B) | 14. (C) |
| 3. (E) | 6. (B) | 9. (D) | 12. (D) | 15. (E) |

## Drill 11

| | | | | |
|---|---|---|---|---|
| 1. (F) | 4. (H) | 7. (C) | 10. (G) | 13. (E) |
| 2. (I) | 5. (B) | 8. (D) | 11. (C) | 14. (A) |
| 3. (A) | 6. (J) | 9. (E) | 12. (B) | 15. (D) |

## Drill 12

| | | | | |
|---|---|---|---|---|
| 1. (J) | 4. (I) | 7. (D) | 10. (E) | 13. (D) |
| 2. (A) | 5. (C) | 8. (G) | 11. (E) | 14. (A) |
| 3. (B) | 6. (H) | 9. (F) | 12. (C) | 15. (B) |

## Drill 13

| | | |
|---|---|---|
| 1. (D) | 3. (A) | 5. (A) |
| 2. (D) | 4. (C) | |

## Drill 14

| | | | |
|---|---|---|---|
| 1. (C) | 4. (C) | 7. (B) | 10. (A) |
| 2. (A) | 5. (B) | 8. (B) | |
| 3. (B) | 6. (C) | 9. (B) | |

## Drill 15

| | | | |
|---|---|---|---|
| 1. (A) | 4. (B) | 7. (A) | 10. (A) |
| 2. (B) | 5. (B) | 8. (A) | |
| 3. (A) | 6. (D) | 9. (C) | |

## Drill 16

| | | | |
|---|---|---|---|
| 1. (C) | 4. (A) | 7. (A) | 10. (D) |
| 2. (B) | 5. (A) | 8. (C) | |
| 3. (D) | 6. (B) | 9. (A) | |

## Drill 17

| | | | |
|---|---|---|---|
| 1. (A) | 4. (A) | 7. (B) | 10. (C) |
| 2. (C) | 5. (D) | 8. (B) | |
| 3. (A) | 6. (A) | 9. (A) | |

## Drill 18

| | | | |
|---|---|---|---|
| 1. (C) | 4. (C) | 7. (A) | 10. (C) |
| 2. (A) | 5. (A) | 8. (C) | |
| 3. (D) | 6. (C) | 9. (B) | |

## Drill 19

| | | | |
|---|---|---|---|
| 1. (A) | 4. (A) | 7. (B) | 10. (B) |
| 2. (B) | 5. (C) | 8. (A) | |
| 3. (C) | 6. (D) | 9. (B) | |

## Drill 20

| | | |
|---|---|---|
| 1. (D) | 3. (C) | 5. (C) |
| 2. (B) | 4. (A) | |

# Writing the Essay

The FTCE-GKT contains one writing exercise. You will have 50 minutes to plan and write an essay on the topic given on the assessment. This means there's a premium on using your time efficiently.

Your work will be scored by two judges. The personal views you express will not be an issue; however, the skill with which you express those views, the logic of your arguments, and the degree to which you support your position will all be important to earning a high score. Your essay will be scored both on substance and on the composition skills demonstrated.

Writing under pressure can be frustrating, but if you study this review, practice and polish your essay skills, and have a realistic sense of what to expect, you can turn problems into possibilities. We have all the tools to help you plan and write a logical, coherent, and interesting essay.

## Why Essays Exist

People write essays for many purposes other than testing. Some of our best thinkers have written essays that we continue to read from generation to generation. Essays offer the reader a logical, coherent, and imaginative written composition showing the nature or consequences of a single controlling idea when considered from the writer's unique point of view. Writers use essays to communicate their opinion or position on a topic to readers who cannot participate in an in-person conversation. Writers use essays to help readers understand or learn about something that readers should or may want to know or do. Essays always express the author's opinion, belief, position, or knowledge (backed by evidence) about the idea or object in question.

## Pre-Writing/Brainstorming

Before you begin to write, there are certain preliminary steps you need to take. A few minutes of planning will result in a more focused, well-developed, and clearer essay. You'll have 50 minutes in all, so you should spend 5 minutes on the pre-writing process.

## Skill 1: Determine the purpose for writing.

For this test you will need to recognize and produce an excellent essay. In essence, you will be taking the principles covered in this review and utilizing them to create your own original essay. With that in mind, read the standards and explanations below to prepare to build your essay response.

Read the essay prompt very carefully and ask yourself the following questions:

- What is the meaning of the topic statement?

- Is the question asking me to persuade the reader of the validity of a certain opinion?

  – What are the advantages of the topic being discussed? What are the disadvantages of the topic being discussed?

  – What are the benefits of the topic being discussed? What are the limitations to the topic being discussed?

- Do I agree or disagree with the statement? What will be my thesis (central idea)?

- What kinds of examples can I use to support my thesis? Explore personal experiences, historical evidence, current events, and related subjects.

## Skill 2: Introduce the topic.

An introduction is like a guidebook to your whole essay. It gives background information for your topic area and outlines all the ideas you are going to present. Introductions should be about 20% of the final essay and should include some or all of the following elements:

- Introduce your topic by providing background information.

- Communicate the reason/rationale for writing about this topic within education.

- Explain any complex terminology that you will be referring to within the essay.

- Establish the topic of your essay in original language, not reiterating the prompt.

- Provide a clear thesis statement for the essay.

## Skill 3: Formulate a relevant thesis or claim.

A thesis statement is the primary claim for the whole essay and should be easily located by the reader at the end of the first paragraph. In academic writing, two purposes dominate essays:

1. Persuasion through argumentation using one, some, or all of the logical patterns described here.

2. Informing and educating through analysis and using one, some, or all of the logical patterns described here.

All of an essay's organizational strategies may be used to present an argument. The author offers reasons and/or evidence so an audience will be inclined to believe the position that the author presents about the idea under discussion.

Writers use seven basic strategies to organize information and ideas in essays to help prove their point (thesis). Any of these strategies may be marshalled in arguing for an idea and persuading a reader to see the issue the writer's way. Your job is to use strategies that are appropriate to demonstrate your thesis. For example, you may wish to use comparison and contrast techniques to demonstrate that one thing or idea is better or worse than another.

## Seven Steps to Prove a Thesis

The following seven steps can be used to prove a thesis:

1. Show how a *process* or procedure does or should work, step-by-step, on a timeline.

2. *Compare or contrast* two or more things or ideas to show important differences or similarities.

3. *Identify a problem* and then explain how to solve it.

4. *Analyze* the components of the thesis, or *classify* by its types or categories, an idea or thing to show how it is put together, how it works, or how it is designed.

5. *Explain* why something happens to produce a particular result or a set of results.

6. *Describe* the particular individual characteristics, beauty, and features of a place, person(s), time, or idea.

7. *Define* what a thing is or what an idea means.

Depending upon the purpose of the essay, one pattern tends to dominate the discussion question. (For example, the writer might use *description* and *explanation* to define the varied meanings of love.)

## Skill 4: Organize ideas and details effectively.

Decide how many paragraphs you will write. In an examination of this kind, you will probably have time for no more than four or five paragraphs. In such a format, the first paragraph will be the introduction, the next two or three will develop your thesis with specific examples as the body, and the final paragraph should be a strong conclusion.

## The Introduction

The focus of your introduction should be the thesis statement. This statement allows your reader to understand the point and direction of your essay. The statement identifies the central idea of your essay and should clearly state your attitude about the subject. It will also dictate the basic content and organization of your essay. If you do not state your thesis clearly, your essay will suffer.

The thesis is the heart of the essay. Without it, readers won't know what your major message or central idea is in the essay. The thesis must be something that can be argued or needs to be proven, not just an accepted fact. For example, "Animals are used every day in cosmetic and medical testing" is a fact—it needs no proof. But if the writer says, "Using animals for cosmetic and medical testing is cruel and should be stopped," we have a point that must be supported and defended by the writer.

The thesis can be placed in any paragraph of the essay, but in a short essay, especially one written for evaluative exam purposes, the thesis is most effective when placed in the last sentence of the opening paragraph. Consider the following sample question:

> **ESSAY TOPIC:**
>
> The sentiment has been expressed that "government is best which governs least." Evaluate whether or not government is best when it governs least.

## ASSIGNMENT:

Do you agree or disagree with this statement? Choose a specific example from current events, personal experience, or your reading to support your position.

After reading the topic statement, decide if you agree or disagree. If you agree with this statement, your thesis statement could be the following:

> "Government has the right to protect individuals from interference but no right to extend its powers and activities beyond this function."

This statement clearly states the writer's opinion in a direct manner. It also serves as a blueprint for the essay. The remainder of the introduction should give two or three brief paragraphs providing evidence to support the thesis provided by you as the writer.

## Supporting Paragraphs

The next two or three paragraphs of your essay will elaborate on the supporting examples you gave in your introduction. Each paragraph should discuss only one idea. Like the introduction, each paragraph should be coherently organized, with a topic sentence and supporting details.

The topic sentence is to each paragraph what the thesis statement is to the essay as a whole. It tells the reader what you plan to discuss in that paragraph. It has a specific subject and is neither too broad nor too narrow. It also establishes the author's attitude and gives the reader a sense of the direction in which the writer is going. An effective topic sentence also helps maintain the reader's interest.

Although it may occur in the middle or at the end of the paragraph, the topic sentence usually appears at the beginning of the paragraph. Placing it there is advantageous because it helps you stay focused on the central idea for the paragraph. The remainder of each paragraph should support the topic sentence with examples and illustrations. Each sentence should progress logically from the previous one and be centrally connected to your topic sentence. Avoid extraneous material that does not serve to develop your thesis.

# Conclusion

Your conclusion should briefly restate your thesis and explain how you have shown it to be true. Since you want to end your essay on a strong note, your conclusion should be concise and effective. The following guidelines are helpful to consider:

- Do not introduce any new topics that you cannot support. If you were watching a movie that suddenly shifted plot and characters at the end, you would be disappointed or even angry. Similarly, don't let your conclusions drift away from the major focus and message of the essay.

- Make sure your conclusion sticks to the topic and represents your perspective without any confusion about what you really mean and believe. The reader will respect you for staying true to your intentions.

- The conclusion is your last chance to grab and impress the reader. You can even use humor, if appropriate, but a dramatic close will remind the reader you are serious, even passionate, about what you believe.

## Skill 5: Provide adequate, relevant supporting material.

You may employ any one of the seven steps previously listed to prove any thesis that you maintain is true. You may also call on evidence from one or all of the four following kinds of evidence to support the thesis of your essay. Identify which kind(s) of evidence you can use to prove the points of your essay. In situations like the FTCE-GK exam, most essayists use anecdotal evidence or analogy to explain, describe, or prove a thesis. However, if you know salient facts or statistics, don't hesitate to call upon them.

The following is a helpful list of avenues for providing quality supporting material:

1. **Hard data** (facts, statistics, scientific evidence, research)—documented evidence that has been verified to be true.

2. **Anecdotal evidence**—stories from the writer's own experience and knowledge that illustrate a particular point or idea.

3. **Expert opinions**—assertions or conclusions, usually citing authorities, about the matter under discussion.

4. **Analogies**—show a resemblance between one phenomenon and another.

## Skill 6: Use effective transitions.

Transitions are like road signs that provide the reader with accurate directions as they move through the essay. They help the reader follow the smooth flow of your ideas and show a connection between major and minor ideas. Transitions are used either at the beginning of a paragraph, or to show the connections among ideas within a single paragraph. Without transitions, you will jar the reader and distract him from your ideas.

Here are some typical transitional words and phrases:

| | |
|---|---|
| **Linking similar ideas** | again, for example, likewise, also, for instance, moreover, and, further, nor, another, furthermore, of course, besides, in addition, similarly, equally important, in like manner, too |
| **Linking dissimilar/ contradictory ideas** | although, however, on the other hand, and, yet, in spite of, otherwise, as if, instead, provided that, but, nevertheless, still, conversely, on the contrary |
| **Indicating cause, purpose, or result** | as for, so, as a result, for this reason, then, because, hence, therefore, consequently, since, thus |
| **Indicating time or position** | above, before, meanwhile, across, beyond, next, afterwards, eventually, presently, around, finally, second, at once, first, thereafter, at the present time, here, thereupon |
| **Indicating an example or summary** | as a result, in any event, in other words, as I have said, in brief, in short, for example, in conclusion, on the whole, for instance, in fact, to sum up |

## Skill 7: Demonstrate mature command of language.

### Common Writing Errors

The four writing errors most often made by beginning writers are: run-ons (also known as fused sentences), fragments, lack of subject-verb agreement, and incorrect use of the object. It is critical to leave two to three minutes when done typing the essay to allow yourself time to review and edit based on these common errors.

1. **Run-ons:** "She swept the floor it was dirty" is a run-on, because the pronoun "it" stands as a noun subject and starts a new sentence. A period or semicolon is needed after "floor."

2. **Fragments:** "Before Jimmy learned how to play baseball" is a fragment, even though it has a subject and verb (Jimmy learned). The word "before" fragmentizes the clause; the reader needs to know what happened before Jimmy learned how to play baseball.

3. **Problems with subject-verb agreement:** "Either Maria or Robert are going to the game" is incorrect because either Maria is going or Robert is going, but not both. The sentence should say, "Either Maria or Robert is going to the game."

4. **Incorrect object:** Probably the most common offender in this area is saying "between you and I," which sounds correct, but isn't. "Between" is a preposition that takes the objective case "me." The correct usage is "between you and me."

The FTCE-GKT test evaluators also cite lack of thought and development, misspellings, incorrect pronouns or antecedents, and lack of development as frequently occurring problems in essays. Finally, keep in mind that clear sentences always work to your advantage. Test graders will appreciate an essay they can read with ease. Typing an essay that is free of basic errors is critical in gaining a passing score.

## Five Words Weak Writers Overuse

Weak and beginning writers overuse the vague pronouns *you, we, they, this,* and *it* often without telling exactly who or what is represented by the pronoun.

1. Beginning writers often shift to second person **"you"** when the writer means "a person." This shift confuses readers and weakens the flow of the essay. Although "you" is commonly accepted in creative writing, journalism, and other arenas, in a short, formal essay, it is best to avoid "you" altogether.

2. **"We"** is another pronoun that should be avoided. If by "we" the writer means "Americans," "society," or some other group, then he or she should say so.

3. **"They"** is often misused in essay writing, because it is overused in conversation: "I went to the doctor, and they told me to take some medicine." Tell the reader who "they" are.

4. **"This"** is usually used incorrectly without a referent: "She told me she received a gift. This sounded good to me." This what? This idea? This news? This gift? Be clear—don't make your readers guess what you mean. The word "this" should be followed by a noun or referent.

5. **"It"** is a common problem among weak writers. To what does "it" refer? Your readers don't appreciate vagueness, so take the time to be clear and complete in your expression of ideas.

## Use your own Vocabulary

Is it a good idea to use big words that sound good in the dictionary or thesaurus, but that you don't really use or understand? No. So whose vocabulary should you use? Your own. You will be most comfortable with your own level of vocabulary. This "comfort zone" doesn't give you license to be informal in a formal setting or to violate the rules of standard written English, but if you try to write in a style that is not yours, your writing will be awkward and lack a true voice. You should certainly improve and build your vocabulary at every opportunity, but remember: You should not attempt to change your vocabulary level at this point. This point is applicable for your spelling skills as a writer as well. Utilize words that you know how to spell accurately. If a word does not look like it is spelled correctly, choose another word. Basic errors in vocabulary and spelling will draw negative attention to your essay and cause the evaluators to look more closely at every sentence you have communicated.

## Avoid the Passive Voice

Use the active voice to keep your prose emphatic and direct. A weak passive verb leaves the doer unknown or seemingly unimportant. However, the passive voice is essential when the action of the verb is more important than the doer, when the doer is unknown, or when the writer wishes to place the emphasis on the receiver of the action rather than on the doer.

## ▋ Skill 8: Provide a conclusion.

Your conclusion is your chance to have the last word on the subject. The conclusion allows you to have the final say on the issues you have raised in your essay, to summarize your thoughts, to demonstrate the importance of your ideas, and to propel your reader to a new view of the subject. It is also your opportunity to make a good final impression and to end on a positive note. The conclusion gives the reader something to take away that will help him or her see things differently or appreciate the topic in personally relevant ways. The conclusion can suggest broader implications that will not only interest the reader, but also enrich his or her life in some way.

Consider the following strategies for a successful conclusion:

- **Play the "So What" Game.** If you're stuck and feel like your conclusion isn't saying anything new or interesting, imagine that a friend is reading the essay over your shoulder. Whenever you make a statement from your conclusion, imagine your friend saying, "So what?" or "Why should anybody care?"

- **Return to the theme or themes in the introduction.** This strategy brings the reader full circle. For example, if you begin by describing a scenario, you can end with the same scenario as proof that your essay is helpful in creating a new understanding. You may also refer to the introductory paragraph by using key words or parallel concepts and images that you also used in the introduction.

- **Synthesize, don't summarize.** Include a brief summary of the essay's main points, but don't simply repeat things. Instead, show your reader how the points you made and your supporting material fit together. Pull it all together.

- **Propose a course of action, a solution to an issue, or questions for further study.** This can redirect your reader's thought process and help him or her apply your information and ideas to life or to see the broader implications.

- **Point to broader implications.** For example, if your essay examines the Greensboro sit-ins or another event in the Civil Rights Movement, you could point out its impact on the Civil Rights Movement as a whole. An essay about the style of writer Virginia Woolf could point to her influence on other writers or on later feminists.

In order to fully understand successful strategies for writing the conclusion, it is helpful to examine strategies to *avoid* when writing your conclusion. The following are worth noting:

- Stating the thesis for the very first time in the conclusion.

- Introducing a new idea or subtopic in your conclusion.

- Making sentimental, emotional appeals that are out of character with the rest of your essay.

- Including evidence (quotations, statistics, etc.) that should be in the body of the essay.

## Skill 9: Use a variety of sentence patterns effectively.

### Parallelism

Sentences should use the same kind of grammatical construction for all items in a series—those usually joined by a coordinating conjunction (*and, but, or,* and *nor*). "No smoking, eating, or drinking" is parallel; "No smoking, food, or drinking" is not, because *food* is not a verb form. Making elements parallel also requires knowledge of parallel correlative pairs, that is, the use of appropriate pairs together: *neither* and *nor, either* and *or, both* with *and, whether* with *or,* and *not only* with *but also.* Parallel structure is used to express matching ideas. It refers to the grammatical balance of a series of any of the following:

**Phrases.** The squirrel ran *along the fence, up the tree,* and *into his hole* with a mouthful of acorns.

**Adjectives.** The job market is flooded with *very talented, highly motivated,* and *well-educated* young people.

**Nouns.** You will need a *notebook, pencil,* and *dictionary* for the test.

**Clauses.** The children were told to decide *which toy they would keep* and *which toy they would give away.*

**Verbs.** The farmer *plowed, planted,* and *harvested* his corn in record time.

**Verbals.** *Reading, writing,* and *calculating* are fundamental skills we should all possess.

**Correlative Conjunctions.** *Either* you will do your homework *or* you will fail.

*Note:* Correlative conjunctions must be used as pairs and not mixed with other conjunctions, such as *neither* with *or* or *not only* with *also.*

**Near-parallelisms.** Sometimes a string of seemingly parallel thoughts are not actually parallel. Consider this sentence: "I *have quit* my job, *enrolled* in school, and *am looking* for a reliable babysitter." In this sentence the writer has already *quit* and *enrolled* but is still looking for a babysitter; therefore she cannot include all three in a parallel structure. A good revision of this sentence is, "I have quit my job and enrolled in school, and I am looking for a babysitter."

## Skill 10: Maintain a consistent point of view.

Depending on the audience, essays may be written from one of three points of view:

1. *First-Person Subjective/Personal* Point of View:

    "I think . . ."

    "I believe cars are more trouble than they are worth."

    "I feel . . ."

2. *Second-Person* Point of View (We . . . You; I . . . You):

"If *you* own a car, *you* will soon find out that it is more trouble than it is worth."

3. *Third-Person* Point of View (focuses on the idea, not what "I" think of it):

"*Cars* are more trouble than *they* are worth."

Be sure to maintain a consistent point of view throughout your essay. If you begin writing in the first-person ("I"), do not shift to the second- or third-person in the middle of the essay. Such inconsistency will confuse your reader and will be penalized by the graders of your essay.

## Skill 11: Apply the conventions of standard American English.

Be sure to leave yourself enough time at the end of the exam to read over your essay for errors such as misspellings, omitted words, or incorrect punctuation. Although you will not have enough time to make large-scale revisions, take the time you do have to make any small changes that will make your essay stronger. Consider the following when proofreading your work:

- Are all your sentences complete thoughts?

- Have you written any fragments or run-on sentences?

- Are you using vocabulary correctly?

- Did you leave out any punctuation?

- Did you capitalize correctly?

- Are there any misspellings, especially of difficult words?

If you have time, read your essay backwards from end to beginning. By doing so, you may catch errors that you missed reading forward only.

In order to fully understand how the conventions will be analyzed, it is helpful to look at a sample essay. Before looking at a sample essay, you must first understand the scoring criteria for the essay.

## Essay Scoring

**SCORE of 6:**  The 6 essay is notably effective.

- The main idea is clearly established and fully developed with specific details and examples.

- Organization is notably logical and coherent.

- Focus is consistently maintained.

- Vocabulary and sentence structure are varied and effective.

- Errors in sentence structure, usage and mechanics are few and insignificant.

**SCORE of 5:**  The 5 essay is mostly effective.

- The main idea is established and mostly developed with specific details and examples.

- Organization is mostly logical and coherent.

- Focus is mostly maintained.

- Vocabulary and sentence structure are mostly varied and effective.

- Errors in sentence structure, usage, and mechanics are few and mostly insignificant.

**SCORE of 4:**  The 4 essay is adequate.

- The main idea is stated and adequately developed with some specific details and examples.

- Organization is adequately logical and coherent.

- Focus is adequately maintained.

- Vocabulary and sentence structure are somewhat varied and effective.

- Errors in sentence structure, usage, and mechanics may be present, but do not interfere with communication.

**SCORE of 3:**  The 3 essay is emergent.

- The main idea is stated and may be developed with generalizations or lists.

- Organization may be ambiguous.

- Focus is somewhat maintained.

- Vocabulary and sentence structure may be repetitive and ineffective.

- A variety of errors in sentence structure, usage, and mechanics sometimes interferes with communication.

**SCORE of 2:** The 2 essay is rudimentary.

- The main idea is incomplete or ambiguous and developed with generalizations or lists.

- Organization is rudimentary and lapses in coherence.

- Focus is confusing and distracting.

- Vocabulary is simplistic and sentence structure is disjointed.

- A variety of errors in sentence structure, usage, and mechanics frequently interfere with communication.

**SCORE of 1:** The 1 essay is weak.

- The main idea is incomplete or ambiguous and development is inadequate and/or irrelevant.

- Organization is illogical and/or incoherent.

- Focus is not established.

- Vocabulary and sentence structure are garbled and confusing.

- Significant and numerous errors in sentence structure, usage, and mechanics interfere with communication.

## Sample Essay

**Directions:** You will have 50 minutes to plan, write, and proofread an ORIGINAL essay on the topic presented. READ THE TOPIC CAREFULLY TO MAKE SURE THAT YOU KNOW WHAT YOU ARE BEING ASKED TO DO.

You must write an original essay that specifically and directly responds to the topic. Pre-prepared essays or essays that are discovered to contain memorized sentences or pre-prepared passages will be invalidated. For example, if the essay raters discover passages that appear in two or more essays, the essays and the violation will be brought to the attention of the Florida Department of Education and may result in the invalidation of your scores.

Your essay should introduce the topic and then explain the topic and/or take a position on the topic and support that position. In order for your essay to be scored, it <u>must address the entire topic</u>.

At least two raters will read your essay, and each will assign it a score. Your essay will not be scored on the position you take or the opinions you express. Your essay will be evaluated holistically according to the following criteria:

| Category | Description |
|---|---|
| Focus | The extent to which the essay states and maintains a main idea or thesis. |
| Organization | The extent to which the essay uses organizational strategies to enhance meaning and clarity. |
| Support | The extent to which the essay provides reasoned, relevant, and specific support to develop the main idea or thesis. |
| Grammar, Sentence Structure, and Usage | The extent to which the essay uses accurate grammar, effective, varied sentence structure, and appropriate, precise usage. |
| Conventions | The extent to which the essay demonstrates the ability to spell common words and to use the conventions of capitalization and punctuation accurately. |

Before you start writing, take a few minutes to plan what you want to say. Also, be sure to leave yourself a few minutes to proofread and make corrections.

---

**SAMPLE TOPIC:**

In the last 20 years, the deterioration of the environment has become a growing concern among both scientists and ordinary citizens. Choose one pressing environmental problem, explain its negative impact, and discuss possible solutions.

---

## Essay Scoring

Below are three sample essays that represent possible responses to the essay topic. Compare your own response to those given on the next few pages. Allow the strengths and weaknesses of the sample essays to help you to critique your own essay and improve your writing skills.

## ◼ ESSAY I (Score: 5–6)

There are many pressing environmental problems facing both the United States and the world today. Pollution, the misuse and squandering of resources, and the cavalier attitude many people express all contribute to the problem. My position is that one of the most pressing problems this country faces is the apathetic attitude many Americans have towards recycling.

Why is recycling so imperative? There are two major reasons. First, recycling previously used materials conserves precious natural resources. Many people never stop to think that reserves of metal ores are not unlimited. There is only so much gold, silver, tin, and other metals in the ground. Once it has all been mined, there will never be any more unless we recycle what has already been used.

Second, the United States daily generates more solid waste than any other country on earth. Our disposable consumer culture consumes fast food meals in paper or Styrofoam containers, uses disposable diapers with plastic liners that do not biodegrade, receives pounds, if not tons, of unsolicited junk mail every year, and relies more and more on prepackaged rather than fresh food.

No matter how it is accomplished, increased recycling is essential. We have to stop covering our land with garbage, and the best ways to do this are to reduce our dependence on prepackaged goods and to minimize the amount of solid waste disposed of in landfills. The best way to reduce solid waste is to recycle it. Americans need to band together to recycle, to preserve our irreplaceable natural resources, reduce pollution, and preserve our precious environment.

## Analysis

This essay presents a clearly defined thesis, and the writer elaborates on this thesis in a thoughtful and sophisticated manner. Various aspects of the problem under consideration are presented and explored, along with possible solutions. The support provided for the writer's argument is convincing and logical. There are few usage or mechanical errors to interfere with the writer's ability to communicate effectively. This writer demonstrates a comprehensive understanding of the rules of standard written English.

## ESSAY II (Score: 3–4)

A pressing environmental problem today is the way we are cutting down too many trees and not planting any replacements for them. Trees are beneficial in many ways, and without them, many environmental problems would be much worse.

One of the ways trees are beneficial is that, like all plants, they take in carbon dioxide and produce oxygen. They can actually help clean the air this way. When too many trees are cut down in a small area, the air in that area is not as good and can be unhealthy to breathe.

Another way trees are beneficial is that they provide homes for many types of birds, insects, and animals. When all the trees in an area are cut down, these animals lose their homes and sometimes they can die out and become extinct that way. Like the spotted owls in Oregon, that the loggers wanted to cut down the trees they lived in. If the loggers did cut down all the old timber stands that the spotted owls lived in, the owls would have become extinct.

But the loggers say that if they can't cut the trees down then they will be out of work, and that peoples' jobs are more important than birds. The loggers can do two things—they can either get training so they can do other jobs, or they can do what they should have done all along, and start replanting trees. For every mature tree they cut down, they should have to plant at least one tree seedling.

Cutting down the trees that we need for life, and that lots of other species depend on, is a big environmental problem that has a lot of long term consequences. Trees are too important for all of us to cut them down without thinking about the future.

## Analysis

This essay has a clear thesis, which the author supports with good examples. But the writer shifts between the chosen topic, which is that indiscriminate tree-cutting is a pressing environmental problem, and a list of the ways in which trees are beneficial and a discussion about the logging profession. Also, while there are few mistakes in usage and mechanics, the writer does have some problems with sentence structure. The essay is pedestrian and does not elaborate on the topic as much as it could have. The writer fails to provide the kind of critical analysis that the topic requires.

## ESSAY III (Score: 1–2)

The most pressing environmental problem today is that lots of people and companies don't care about the environment, and they do lots of things that hurt the environment. People throw littur out car windows and don't use trash cans, even if their all over a park, soda cans and fast food wrappers are all over the place. Cigarette butts are the worst cause the filters never rot.

Newspapers and junk mail get left to blow all over the neighborhood, and beer bottles too.

Companies pollute the air and the water. Sometimes the ground around a company has lots of toxins in it.

Now companies can buy credits from other companies that let them pollute the air even more. They dump all kinds of chemicals into lakes and rivers that kills off the fish and causes acid rain and kills off more fish and some trees and small animals and insects and then no one can go swimming or fishing in the lake. People need to respect the environment because we only have one planet, and if we keep polluting it pretty soon nothing will grow and then even the people will die.

## Analysis

The writer of this essay leaves the thesis undefined. As a result, the reader is left to infer the topic from the body of the essay. It is possible to perceive the writer's intended thesis; however, the support for this thesis is superficial. The writer presents a list of common complaints about polluters, without any critical discussion of the problems and possible solutions. Many sentences are run-ons and there are several spelling errors. Although the passage conveys the author's position on the issue, several errors in usage and mechanics distract from the message and weaken the persona.

## Ensuring Essay Success

Beyond being able to write a quality essay based on the skills previously listed, it is imperative that you are familiar with the topics that are representative of the FTCE examination especially because you only have one topic. So, how do you familiarize yourself before the exam?

- Review the representative list of topics below.

- Analyze your background level of each topic.

- Practice the topics listed below while building your prior knowledge of topics.

If you find when practicing your topics that you lack the knowledge to provide quality evidence, then research the topic and make a set of notes that can be reviewed before taking the assessment. The rationale behind this final section is the idea that if you lack sufficient knowledge of the topic you will not be prepared to be successful on the day of the exam.

### FTCE Sample Topics

1. Florida evaluates teachers using the evaluation standard: highly effective, effective, needs improvement/developing, and unsatisfactory. Each educator is evaluated using this systematic approach. Write an essay describing the costs and benefits of using this assessment evaluation for teachers.

2. Reading has become a pastime and the internet has replaced this pastime. Many students spend a significant amount of time on their smartphones. Write an essay comparing and contrasting reading as a pastime.

3. Historically, schools have required community service for students. Analyze the benefits of a program of this kind.

4. Parental involvement is part of the process of schooling. Weigh the benefits and possible detriments to this element. Use specific examples to support your argument.

5. Standards-based learning is a foundational aspect of classroom instruction. Analyze how this type of learning model benefits students and teachers. Use specific evidence to support your argument.

6. Technology integration can increase student interest in the classroom. It can also provide curriculum support for teachers. Describe an outline of how this would be successfully accomplished in the 21st century classroom.

7. Substance abuse is a growing problem within society, specifically within the context of schooling. One population believes that mandatory drug testing in school is critical while another population believes that alternate forms of intervention should be provided by the school. Assert a position on this challenge and provide support to your argument.

8. Teaching in the 21st century requires attention to student interest. Research supports the benefits of student engagement within the learning environment. Analyze two practice strategies that could be implemented in the classroom which would benefit student learning.

9. According to the Centers for Disease Control and Prevention, e-cigarettes have reduced the overall smoking rate. Some believe that this innovative tool is a gift to society while others maintain that this tool is simply raising another generation of smokers who do not understand the negative effects of smoking e-cigarettes, which are not regulated by the FDA. Assert your position on this topic by providing quality evidence.

10. Many schools are requiring students to wear uniforms. Some believe that this is advantageous while others do not agree. Evaluate the advantages and disadvantages of a program of this kind while providing specific examples to support your argument.

11. The sentiment has been expressed, "Develop a passion for learning. If you do, you will never cease to grow." Evaluate what role passion plays in the process of student learning by providing quality evidence.

12. Some schools believe that online learning is a critical aspect of student preparation in the 21st century. Some believe that this is advantageous while others do not agree. Analyze the advantages and disadvantages of this type of learning.

13. Teachers are often placed in situations that are morally ambiguous but require them to take action. Evaluate the benefits and challenges of this scenario.

14. Assessment is used to measure student achievement. Evaluate two assessments used within a research-based learning environment. Provide specific examples and evidence to support research-based evaluation in the learning environment.

15. College students are required to take remedial math courses. Provide the benefits and costs to a system of this kind by using specific examples and evidence.

16. Many students feel it is critical to communicate their lives on social media. Others feel that this type of sharing is an invasion of one's privacy. Evaluate this issue and provide an argument whether or not an individual should utilize this type of technology.

17. Schools have begun offering healthier food choices within the school community. Many believe this is a worthwhile opportunity to address the growing childhood obesity epidemic while others feel this is not the role of schools. Communicate the advantages and disadvantages to a practice of this kind.

## Avoid Scoring Confusion

It is critical that you understand how your essay will be scored. Previously in this chapter, the 6-point scoring rubric was explained and examples provided. This is the rubric that each grader will use to evaluate your essay. Remember, it is not one but two individuals who will be evaluating your essay. So, to pass this portion of the FTCE-GK, you must score an 8 as a minimum score. Each grader evaluates your writing, and then the scores are combined.

Many test-takers are confused when they receive their test scores and it reads "6" thinking this is the highest score on the rubric—why would the essay not pass? Do not confuse the rubric used by the two graders with a minimum passing score of 8. The rubric is the standard for evaluating your essay; the overall score represents the *combination* of two independent evaluations of your essay.

# PRACTICE TEST 1

# FTCE General Knowledge

# Answer Sheet

## English Language Skills

1. Ⓐ Ⓑ Ⓒ Ⓓ
2. Ⓐ Ⓑ Ⓒ Ⓓ
3. Ⓐ Ⓑ Ⓒ Ⓓ
4. Ⓐ Ⓑ Ⓒ Ⓓ
5. Ⓐ Ⓑ Ⓒ Ⓓ
6. Ⓐ Ⓑ Ⓒ Ⓓ
7. Ⓐ Ⓑ Ⓒ Ⓓ
8. Ⓐ Ⓑ Ⓒ Ⓓ
9. Ⓐ Ⓑ Ⓒ Ⓓ
10. Ⓐ Ⓑ Ⓒ Ⓓ
11. Ⓐ Ⓑ Ⓒ Ⓓ
12. Ⓐ Ⓑ Ⓒ Ⓓ
13. Ⓐ Ⓑ Ⓒ Ⓓ
14. Ⓐ Ⓑ Ⓒ Ⓓ
15. Ⓐ Ⓑ Ⓒ Ⓓ
16. Ⓐ Ⓑ Ⓒ Ⓓ
17. Ⓐ Ⓑ Ⓒ Ⓓ
18. Ⓐ Ⓑ Ⓒ Ⓓ
19. Ⓐ Ⓑ Ⓒ Ⓓ
20. Ⓐ Ⓑ Ⓒ Ⓓ
21. Ⓐ Ⓑ Ⓒ Ⓓ
22. Ⓐ Ⓑ Ⓒ Ⓓ
23. Ⓐ Ⓑ Ⓒ Ⓓ
24. Ⓐ Ⓑ Ⓒ Ⓓ
25. Ⓐ Ⓑ Ⓒ Ⓓ
26. Ⓐ Ⓑ Ⓒ Ⓓ
27. Ⓐ Ⓑ Ⓒ Ⓓ
28. Ⓐ Ⓑ Ⓒ Ⓓ
29. Ⓐ Ⓑ Ⓒ Ⓓ
30. Ⓐ Ⓑ Ⓒ Ⓓ
31. Ⓐ Ⓑ Ⓒ Ⓓ
32. Ⓐ Ⓑ Ⓒ Ⓓ
33. Ⓐ Ⓑ Ⓒ Ⓓ
34. Ⓐ Ⓑ Ⓒ Ⓓ
35. Ⓐ Ⓑ Ⓒ Ⓓ
36. Ⓐ Ⓑ Ⓒ Ⓓ
37. Ⓐ Ⓑ Ⓒ Ⓓ
38. Ⓐ Ⓑ Ⓒ Ⓓ
39. Ⓐ Ⓑ Ⓒ Ⓓ
40. Ⓐ Ⓑ Ⓒ Ⓓ

## Mathematics

1. Ⓐ Ⓑ Ⓒ Ⓓ
2. Ⓐ Ⓑ Ⓒ Ⓓ
3. Ⓐ Ⓑ Ⓒ Ⓓ
4. Ⓐ Ⓑ Ⓒ Ⓓ
5. Ⓐ Ⓑ Ⓒ Ⓓ
6. Ⓐ Ⓑ Ⓒ Ⓓ
7. Ⓐ Ⓑ Ⓒ Ⓓ
8. Ⓐ Ⓑ Ⓒ Ⓓ
9. Ⓐ Ⓑ Ⓒ Ⓓ
10. Ⓐ Ⓑ Ⓒ Ⓓ
11. Ⓐ Ⓑ Ⓒ Ⓓ
12. Ⓐ Ⓑ Ⓒ Ⓓ
13. Ⓐ Ⓑ Ⓒ Ⓓ
14. Ⓐ Ⓑ Ⓒ Ⓓ
15. Ⓐ Ⓑ Ⓒ Ⓓ
16. Ⓐ Ⓑ Ⓒ Ⓓ
17. Ⓐ Ⓑ Ⓒ Ⓓ
18. Ⓐ Ⓑ Ⓒ Ⓓ
19. Ⓐ Ⓑ Ⓒ Ⓓ
20. Ⓐ Ⓑ Ⓒ Ⓓ
21. Ⓐ Ⓑ Ⓒ Ⓓ
22. Ⓐ Ⓑ Ⓒ Ⓓ
23. Ⓐ Ⓑ Ⓒ Ⓓ
24. Ⓐ Ⓑ Ⓒ Ⓓ
25. Ⓐ Ⓑ Ⓒ Ⓓ
26. Ⓐ Ⓑ Ⓒ Ⓓ
27. Ⓐ Ⓑ Ⓒ Ⓓ
28. Ⓐ Ⓑ Ⓒ Ⓓ
29. Ⓐ Ⓑ Ⓒ Ⓓ
30. Ⓐ Ⓑ Ⓒ Ⓓ
31. Ⓐ Ⓑ Ⓒ Ⓓ
32. Ⓐ Ⓑ Ⓒ Ⓓ
33. Ⓐ Ⓑ Ⓒ Ⓓ
34. Ⓐ Ⓑ Ⓒ Ⓓ
35. Ⓐ Ⓑ Ⓒ Ⓓ
36. Ⓐ Ⓑ Ⓒ Ⓓ
37. Ⓐ Ⓑ Ⓒ Ⓓ
38. Ⓐ Ⓑ Ⓒ Ⓓ
39. Ⓐ Ⓑ Ⓒ Ⓓ
40. Ⓐ Ⓑ Ⓒ Ⓓ
41. Ⓐ Ⓑ Ⓒ Ⓓ
42. Ⓐ Ⓑ Ⓒ Ⓓ
43. Ⓐ Ⓑ Ⓒ Ⓓ
44. Ⓐ Ⓑ Ⓒ Ⓓ
45. Ⓐ Ⓑ Ⓒ Ⓓ

## Reading

1. Ⓐ Ⓑ Ⓒ Ⓓ
2. Ⓐ Ⓑ Ⓒ Ⓓ
3. Ⓐ Ⓑ Ⓒ Ⓓ
4. Ⓐ Ⓑ Ⓒ Ⓓ
5. Ⓐ Ⓑ Ⓒ Ⓓ
6. Ⓐ Ⓑ Ⓒ Ⓓ
7. Ⓐ Ⓑ Ⓒ Ⓓ
8. Ⓐ Ⓑ Ⓒ Ⓓ
9. Ⓐ Ⓑ Ⓒ Ⓓ
10. Ⓐ Ⓑ Ⓒ Ⓓ
11. Ⓐ Ⓑ Ⓒ Ⓓ
12. Ⓐ Ⓑ Ⓒ Ⓓ
13. Ⓐ Ⓑ Ⓒ Ⓓ
14. Ⓐ Ⓑ Ⓒ Ⓓ
15. Ⓐ Ⓑ Ⓒ Ⓓ
16. Ⓐ Ⓑ Ⓒ Ⓓ
17. Ⓐ Ⓑ Ⓒ Ⓓ
18. Ⓐ Ⓑ Ⓒ Ⓓ
19. Ⓐ Ⓑ Ⓒ Ⓓ
20. Ⓐ Ⓑ Ⓒ Ⓓ
21. Ⓐ Ⓑ Ⓒ Ⓓ
22. Ⓐ Ⓑ Ⓒ Ⓓ
23. Ⓐ Ⓑ Ⓒ Ⓓ
24. Ⓐ Ⓑ Ⓒ Ⓓ
25. Ⓐ Ⓑ Ⓒ Ⓓ
26. Ⓐ Ⓑ Ⓒ Ⓓ
27. Ⓐ Ⓑ Ⓒ Ⓓ
28. Ⓐ Ⓑ Ⓒ Ⓓ
29. Ⓐ Ⓑ Ⓒ Ⓓ
30. Ⓐ Ⓑ Ⓒ Ⓓ
31. Ⓐ Ⓑ Ⓒ Ⓓ
32. Ⓐ Ⓑ Ⓒ Ⓓ
33. Ⓐ Ⓑ Ⓒ Ⓓ
34. Ⓐ Ⓑ Ⓒ Ⓓ
35. Ⓐ Ⓑ Ⓒ Ⓓ
36. Ⓐ Ⓑ Ⓒ Ⓓ
37. Ⓐ Ⓑ Ⓒ Ⓓ
38. Ⓐ Ⓑ Ⓒ Ⓓ
39. Ⓐ Ⓑ Ⓒ Ⓓ
40. Ⓐ Ⓑ Ⓒ Ⓓ

# Practice Test 1: Essay

50 Minutes

**Directions:** You will have 50 minutes to plan, write, and proofread an ORIGINAL essay on the topic presented. READ THE TOPIC CAREFULLY TO MAKE SURE THAT YOU KNOW WHAT YOU ARE BEING ASKED TO DO.

You must write an <u>original essay that specifically and directly responds to the topic</u>. Pre-prepared essays or essays that are discovered to contain memorized sentences or pre-prepared passages will be invalidated. For example, if the essay raters discover passages that appear in two or more essays, the essays and the violation will be brought to the attention of the Florida Department of Education and may result in the invalidation of your scores.

Your essay should introduce the topic and then explain the topic and/or take a position on the topic and support that position. In order for your essay to be scored, it <u>must address the entire topic</u>.

At least two raters will read your essay, and each will assign it a score. Your essay will not be scored on the position you take or the opinions you express. Your essay will be evaluated holistically according to the following criteria:

| Category | Description |
| --- | --- |
| Focus | The extent to which the essay states and maintains a main idea or thesis. |
| Organization | The extent to which the essay uses organizational strategies to enhance meaning and clarity. |
| Support | The extent to which the essay provides reasoned, relevant, and specific support to develop the main idea or thesis. |
| Grammar, Sentence Structure, and Usage | The extent to which the essay uses accurate grammar, effective, varied sentence structure, and appropriate, precise usage. |
| Conventions | The extent to which the essay demonstrates the ability to spell common words and to use the conventions of capitalization and punctuation accurately. |

Before you start writing, take a few minutes to plan what you want to say. Also, be sure to leave yourself a few minutes to proofread and make corrections.

| Topic |
|---|
| Many schools are requiring students to wear uniforms. Some believe that this is advantageous while others do not agree. Evaluate the advantages and disadvantages of a program of this kind and take a position on this issue. Provide evidence to support your argument. |

# Practice Test 1: English Language Skills

40 Minutes

40 Questions

DIRECTIONS: Read each question and select the best response.

1.  **DIRECTIONS:** Choose the sentence in which the modifiers are correctly placed.

    A.  While protesting the Iraq War, clashes between Chicago police and demonstrators resulted in over 170 arrests at the Democratic National Convention.

    B.  While protesting the Iraq War, police arrested over 170 demonstrators during clashes at the Democratic National Convention.

    C.  While protesting the Iraq War, over 170 demonstrators were arrested for clashing with police at the Democratic National Convention.

    D.  While protesting the Iraq War and clashing with the Chicago police, over 170 demonstrators were arrested.

2.  **DIRECTIONS:** Choose the sentence in which the modifiers are correctly placed.

    A.  On arriving at the train station, his friends greeted Jay and took him immediately to his speaking engagement in Springfield.

    B.  On arriving at the train station, Jay was greeted by his friends, who immediately took him to his speaking engagement in Springfield.

    C.  Jay was greeted by his friends who immediately took him to his speaking engagement in Springfield, on arriving at the train station.

    D.  On arriving at the train station, Jay greeted his speaking engagement in Springfield with his friends.

3.  **DIRECTIONS**: Choose the sentence in which the modifiers are correctly placed.

    The professor's consistent late arrival is offset somewhat by the remarkable quality of his lectures.

    A.  Lately, the professor's arriving consistently

    B.  The consistent late arrival of the professor

    C.  The professor's consistently late arrival

    D.  No change is necessary.

4. **DIRECTIONS:** Choose the correct word or phrase that provides parallel structure to the sentence.

> My cousin raked the lawn, washed the trucks, cleaned the upstairs bathroom, and _____ on the sofa afterwards to watch the basketball game.

A. he relaxed

B. he was able to relax

C. relaxed

D. was relaxing

5. **DIRECTIONS:** Choose the correct word or phrase that provides parallel structure to the sentence.

> When Delores realized that her father had made lima beans and rice for dinner, she _____, claimed to feel nauseous, and excused herself from the table.

A. clutched her stomach

B. was clutching her stomach

C. did clutch her stomach

D. had clutched her stomach

6. **DIRECTIONS:** Choose the correct word or phrase that provides parallel structure to the sentence.

> The teacher sought new ways of teaching, believing her students would get more from lessons _____.

A. featuring playing, acting, and creativity.

B. featuring playing, acting, and creative things.

C. featuring playing, acting, and creating.

D. featuring play, act, and creativity.

7. **DIRECTIONS:** Choose the option that corrects an error in the underlined portion(s). If no error exists, choose "No change is necessary."

> The <u>Koran</u> <u>is considered</u> by <u>muslims</u> to be the holy word.
>      A          B           C

A. koran

B. was considered

C. Muslims

D. No change is necessary

8.  **DIRECTIONS:** Choose the option that corrects an error in the underlined portion(s). If no error exists, choose "No change is necessary."

    So tenacious is their grip on life, that sponge cells will regroup and form a new sponge even <u>when they are</u> squeezed through silk.

    A.  when it is
    B.  as they will be
    C.  after they have been
    D.  No change is necessary.

9.  **DIRECTIONS:** Choose the option that corrects an error in the underlined portion(s). If no error exists, choose "No change is necessary."

    Students must pay a penalty for overdue library <u>books, however, there</u> is a grace period.

    A.  books: however, there
    B.  books however, there
    C.  books; however, there
    D.  No change is necessary.

10. **DIRECTIONS:** Choose the option that corrects an error in the underlined portion(s). If no error exists, choose "No change is necessary."

    A <u>photograph</u> of <u>mars</u> was printed in the <u>*New York Times*</u>.
         A            B                         C

    A.  Photograph
    B.  Mars
    C.  New York Times
    D.  No change is necessary.

11. **DIRECTIONS:** Choose the option that corrects an error in the underlined portion(s). If no error exists, choose "No change is necessary."

    The ideals <u>upon which</u> American society <u>is based</u> <u>are</u> primarily those of
                 A                          B   C
    Europe and not ones derived from the native Indian culture.

    A.  upon that
    B.  was based
    C.  is
    D.  No change is necessary.

12. **DIRECTIONS:** Choose the option that corrects an error in the underlined portion(s). If no error exists, choose "No change is necessary."

The art exhibit displayed works by many famous <u>artists such as</u> Dali, Picasso, and Michelangelo.

A. artists such as;

B. artists such as:

C. artists such

D. No change is necessary.

13. **DIRECTIONS:** Choose the option that corrects an error in the underlined portion(s). If no error exists, choose "No change is necessary."

Representative Wilson pointed out, however, that the legislature

<u>had not finalized</u> the state budget and salary increases <u>had depended</u> on
     A                                                                     B

decisions <u>to be made</u> in a special session.
        C

A. has not finalized

B. depend

C. to make

D. No change is necessary.

14. **DIRECTIONS:** Choose the option that corrects an error in the underlined portion(s). If no error exists, choose "No change is necessary."

Now the city librarian, doing more than checking out books, must help <u>to</u>

<u>plan</u> puppet shows and movies for children, garage sales for <u>used</u> books,
A                                                             B

and <u>arranging</u> for guest lecturers and exhibits for children.
    C

A. the plan

B. using

C. arrangements

D. No change is necessary.

15. **DIRECTIONS:** Choose the option that corrects an error in the underlined portion(s). If no error exists, choose "No change is necessary."

    In the last three years we have added more varieties of vegetables to our garden <u>than those you suggested in the beginning</u>.

    A.   than the ones who were there in

    B.   than the ones we began with

    C.   beginning with your suggestion

    D.   No change is necessary.

16. **DIRECTIONS:** Choose the option that corrects an error in the underlined portion(s). If no error exists, choose "No change is necessary."

    As you know, I am not easily fooled by flattery, and while <u>nice words please you</u>, they don't get the job done.

    A.   pleasing you with nice words

    B.   nice words are pleasing

    C.   nice words please a person

    D.   No change is necessary.

17. **DIRECTIONS:** Choose the option that corrects an error in the underlined portion(s). If no error exists, choose "No change is necessary."

    Some pieces of the puzzle, in spite of Jane's search, <u>are still missing and probably will never be found</u>.

    A.   was still missing and probably won't be found

    B.   is missing still but never found probably

    C.   probably will be missing and never found

    D.   No change is necessary.

18. **DIRECTIONS:** Choose the option that corrects an error in the underlined portion(s).

    In order <u>to completely understand</u> the psychological <u>effects</u> of the
                      **A**                          **B**

    bubonic plague, one must realize that one-fourth to one-third of the population in an <u>affected</u> area <u>died</u>.
                           **C**       **D**

    A.   to understand

    B.   effect

    C.   effected

    D.   had died

19. **DIRECTIONS:** Choose the option that corrects an error in the underlined portion(s). If no error exists, choose "No change is necessary."

Rural roads, known in the United States as farm to market roads, have always been a vital <u>link in</u> the economy of <u>more advanced</u> nations because
          A                                              B
transportation of goods to markets <u>is</u> essential.
                                    C

A. link of

B. advanced

C. was

D. No change is necessary.

20. **DIRECTIONS:** Choose the option that corrects an error in the underlined portion(s). If no error exists, choose "No change is necessary."

<u>Many a</u> graduate wishes to return to college and <u>abide in</u> the protected
A                                                        B
environment of a university, particularly if <u>someone else</u> pays the bills.
                                              C

A. Some

B. abides in

C. someone's else

D. No change is necessary.

21. **DIRECTIONS:** Choose the option that corrects an error in the underlined portion(s). If no error exists, choose "No change is necessary."

Failing a test because the student is nervous <u>is</u> understandable; <u>to fail</u>
                                              A                    B
because <u>he or she</u> did not study is quite another matter.
        C

A. was

B. failing

C. they

D. No change is necessary.

22. **DIRECTIONS:** Choose the option that corrects an error in the underlined portion(s).

    My brother and <u>me</u> dressed as quickly as we could, but we missed the
    　　　　　　　　A

    school bus, <u>which</u> made <u>us</u> late for class <u>today</u>.
    　　　　　　　B　　　　　C　　　　　　　D

    A.  I

    B.  that

    C.  them

    D.  yesterday

23. **DIRECTIONS:** Choose the most effective word or phrase within the context suggested by the sentence.

    I'm sorry to be late for the meeting, but my new secretary _____ to tell me you had scheduled it earlier.

    A.  decided

    B.  neglected

    C.  refused

    D.  thought

24. **DIRECTIONS:** Choose the most effective word or phrase within the context suggested by the sentence.

    While Julie's nature was not _____, she decided to defy her own parents for their own good.

    A.  obedient

    B.  helpful

    C.  insubordinate

    D.  vain

25. **DIRECTIONS:** Read the passage; then answer the question below.

    (1) Opera refers to a dramatic art form, originating in Europe, in which the emotional content is conveyed to the audience as much through music, both vocal and instrumental, as it is through the lyrics. (2) The drama in opera is presented using the primary elements of theater such as scenery, costumes, and acting. (3) However, the words of the opera, or libretto, are sung rather than spoken. (4) The singers are accompanied by a musical ensemble ranging from a small instrumental ensemble to a full symphonic orchestra.

    What is the best placement for the sentence below?

    "By contrast, in musical theater an actor's dramatic performance is primary, and the music plays a lesser role."

    A.  after sentence 2

    B.  before sentence 1

    C.  before sentence 4

    D.  between sentences 1 and 2

26. **DIRECTIONS:** Read the passage; then answer the question below.

    (1) The more we learn about dolphins, the more we realize that their society is more complex than people previously imagined. (2) They look after other dolphins when they are ill, care for pregnant mothers and protect the weakest in the community, as we do. (3) Some scientists have suggested that dolphins have a language but it is much more probable that they communicate with each other without needing words. (4) Could any of these mammals be more intelligent than man? (5) Certainly the most common argument in favor of man's superiority over them—that we can kill them more easily than they can kill us—is the least satisfactory. (6) On the contrary, the more we discover about these remarkable creatures, the less we appear superior when we destroy them.

    What is the best placement for the sentence below?

    "Dolphins are regarded as the friendliest creatures in the sea and stories of them helping drowning sailors have been common since Roman times."

    A.  before sentence 2

    B.  before sentence 1

    C.  after sentence 4

    D.  after sentence 6

27. **DIRECTIONS:** Choose the option that corrects an error in the underlined portion(s). If no error exists, choose "No change is necessary."

> *Gone With the Wind* <u>is the kind of a movie</u> producers would like to release because it would bring them fame.

A.   is which kind of a movie

B.   is the sort of movie

C.   is the kind of movie

D.   No change is necessary.

28. **DIRECTIONS:** Choose the option that corrects an error in the underlined portion(s). If no error exists, choose "No change is necessary."

> Eighteenth-century architecture, with its columns and balanced lines, <u>was characteristic of those of previous times in Greece and Rome.</u>

A.   was characteristic of those of before times in Greece and Rome

B.   is similar to characteristics of Greece and Rome

C.   was similar to architecture of Greece and Rome

D.   No change is necessary.

29. **DIRECTIONS:** Choose the option that corrects an error in the underlined portion(s). If no error exists, choose "No change is necessary."

> Plato, one of the famous Greek philosophers, won many wrestling prizes when he was a young man, thus <u>exemplifying the Greek ideal of balance between the necessity for physical activity and using one's mind.</u>

A.   to give an example of the Greek ideal of balancing

B.   serving as an example of the Greek ideal of balance between physical and mental activities

C.   an example of balancing Greek mental and athletic games

D.   No change is necessary.

30. **DIRECTIONS:** Choose the option that corrects an error in the underlined portion(s).

> The <u>assassination</u> of Abraham Lincoln <u>continued</u> to captivate
>       **A**                                    **B**
>
> Americans, encouraging the making of <u>television series, books, and</u>
> <u>movies</u> still being <u>released</u> each year.
>  **C**                  **D**

A. assassin

B. continues

C. television books and movies

D. to release

31. **DIRECTIONS:** Choose the option that corrects an error in the underlined portion(s). If no error exists, choose "No change is necessary."

> <u>Leonardo da Vinci was a man who</u> was a scientist, an architect, an engineer, and a sculptor.

A. Leonardo da Vinci which was a man who

B. The man Leonardo da Vinci

C. Leonardo da Vinci

D. No change is necessary.

32. **DIRECTIONS:** Choose the option that corrects an error in the underlined portion(s). If no error exists, choose "No change is necessary."

> <u>Among</u> the activities offered at the local high school <u>through</u> the
>  **A**                                            **B**
>
> community education program <u>are</u> singing in the couples' chorus, ballroom
>                                         **C**
>
> dancing, and Chinese cooking.

A. Between

B. threw

C. were

D. No change is necessary.

33. **DIRECTIONS:** Choose the option that corrects an error in the underlined portion(s). If no error exists, choose "No change is necessary."

> If you are <u>disappointed by</u> an inexpensive bicycle, then an option
> **A**
>
> you might consider is to work this summer and <u>save</u> your money for
> **B**
>
> <u>a more expensive model</u>.
> **C**

A. disappointed in

B. saved

C. an expensive model

D. No change is necessary.

34. **DIRECTIONS:** Choose the option that corrects an error in the underlined portion(s). If no error exists, choose "No change is necessary."

> Flooding abated and the river waters receded as the <u>rainfall finally
> let up</u>.

A. rainfall kept letting up

B. rain having let up

C. rainfall, when it finally let up

D. No change is necessary.

35. **DIRECTIONS:** Choose the option that corrects an error in the underlined portion(s). If no error exists, choose "No change is necessary."

> Unless China slows its population growth to zero, that country <u>would still
> have</u> a problem feeding its people.

A. would have

B. might have had still

C. will still have

D. No change is necessary.

36. **DIRECTIONS:** Choose the option that corrects an error in the underlined portion(s). If no error exists, choose "No change is necessary."

> In *The Music Man*, Robert Preston portrays a fast-talking traveling salesman who comes to a small town in Iowa <u>inadvertently falling in love with</u> the librarian.

A. inadvertently falling in love

B. and inadvertently falls in love with

C. afterwards he inadvertently falls in love with

D. No change is necessary.

37. **DIRECTIONS:** Choose the option that corrects an error in the underlined portion(s). If no error exists, choose "No change is necessary."

> Many naturalists have a reverence for the woods and wildlife, <u>which exhibits itself through their</u> writings or paintings.

A. which shows itself through his

B. and this exhibits itself through their

C. and exhibiting itself in

D. No change is necessary.

38. **DIRECTIONS:** Choose the most effective word or phrase within the context suggested by the sentence.

> Though pediatric care is _____ in the developed world, the prevalence of childhood obesity is much higher there than in the developing world due to higher rates of sugar consumption.

A. relative widely available

B. relatively wide available

C. relatively widely available

D. relatively wide availability

39. **DIRECTIONS:** Choose the most effective word or phrase within the context suggested by the sentence.

Before they went to dinner, the office staff _____ the incident to the insurance company.

A. renounced

B. relented

C. related

D. reserved

40. **DIRECTIONS:** Choose the most effective word or phrase within the context suggested by the sentence.

Mary Beth, _____ hates roaches, wears bug-stomping shoes wherever she goes.

A. whom

B. who

C. she

D. that

## Area

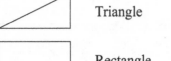

Triangle         $A = \frac{1}{2}bh$

Rectangle        $A = lw$

Trapezoid        $A = \frac{1}{2}h(b_1 + b_2)$

Parallelogram    $A = bh$

Circle           $A = \pi r^2$

| KEY | |
|---|---|
| $b$ = base | $d$ = diameter |
| $h$ = height | $r$ = radius |
| $l$ = length | $A$ = area |
| $w$ = width | $C$ = circumference |
| $S.A.$ = surface area | $V$ = volume |
| | $B$ = area of base |
| Use 3.14 or $\frac{22}{7}$ for $\pi$ | |

## Circumference

$C = \pi d$

## Surface Area

1. Surface area of a prism or pyramid equals the sum of the areas of all faces.

2. Surface area of a cylinder equals the sum of the areas of the bases and the area of its rectangular wrap.

$S.A. = 2(\pi r^2) + 2(\pi r)h$

3. Surface area of a sphere: $S.A. = 4\pi r^2$

## Volume

1. Volume of a prism or cylinder equals the <u>Area of the Base</u> ($B$) times the height ($h$).

$$V = Bh$$

2. Volume of a pyramid or cone equals $\frac{1}{3}$ times the <u>Area of the Base</u> ($B$) times the height ($h$).

$$V = \frac{1}{3}Bh$$

3. Volume of a sphere: $V = \frac{4}{3}\pi r^3$

**Pythagorean Theorem:** $a^2 + b^2 = c^2$

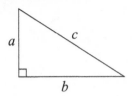

**Simple interest:** $I = prt$

$I$ = interest, $p$ = principal, $r$ = rate, $t$ = time

**Distance formula:** $d = rt$

$d$ = distance, $r$ = rate, $t$ = time

Given a line containing points $(x_1, y_1)$ and $(x_2, y_2)$.

- **Slope of line**

$$\frac{y_2 - y_1}{x_2 - x_1}$$

- **Distance between two points**

$$\sqrt{(x_2 - x_1)^2 + (y_2 - y_1)^2}$$

- **Midpoint between two points**

$$\left( \frac{x_1 + x_2}{2}, \frac{y_1 + y_2}{2} \right)$$

## Conversions

1 yard = 3 feet = 36 inches

1 mile = 1,760 yards = 5,280 feet

1 acre = 43,560 feet

1 hour = 60 minutes

1 minute = 60 seconds

1 liter = 1000 milliliters = 1000 cubic centimeters

1 meter = 100 centimeters = 1000 millimeters

1 kilometer = 1000 meters

1 gram = 1000 milligrams

1 kilogram = 1000 grams

1 cup = 8 fluid ounces

1 pint = 2 cups

1 quart = 2 pints

1 gallon = 4 quarts

1 pound = 16 ounces

1 ton = 2,000 pounds

Metric numbers with four digits are presented without a comma (e.g., 9960 kilometers). For metric numbers greater than four digits, a space is used instead of a comma (e.g., 12 500 liters).

# Practice Test 1: Mathematics

100 Minutes

45 Questions

**DIRECTIONS:** Read each question and select the best response.

1. Simplify the following expression: $6[x - 4(2x + 1)]$

   A. $4x - 16$

   B. $2x - 14$

   C. $-42x - 24$

   D. $-24x$

2. Simplify by following the order of operations: $9 - 5 \div (8 - 3) \times 3 + 6$

   A. $7\dfrac{1}{5}$

   B. $12$

   C. $22$

   D. $1$

3. Which measure of central tendency would reflect most positively on your interest in applying for a job at a company with the following salaries?

   $150,000   $75,000   $50,000   $25,000   $25,000   $25,000

   A. Mean and mode

   B. Mean and median

   C. Median only

   D. Mean only

4. Last night at the gym, the patrons worked out from 25 to 50 minutes per hour. During one hour, the gym got six visitors with an average workout time of 45 minutes. How many people could have worked out for 50 minutes, considering at least one person did?

   A. 3

   B. 4

   C. 5

   D. 6

5. Jeannie was trying to guess the name of the three-dimensional figure that Xavier was describing. Xavier's figure had:

    - 5 vertices

    - 1 rectangular base

    - 4 triangular lateral faces

    What is the name of Xavier's figure?

    A.  Rectangular prism

    B.  Rectangular pyramid

    C.  Triangular prism

    D.  Triangular pyramid

6. Carla's garden was 7 feet longer than it was wide, and it had a perimeter of 38 ft. What is the area of Carla's garden in square feet?

    A.  266

    B.  49

    C.  78

    D.  6

7. Which ordered pair is NOT a solution to the inequality: $y < \dfrac{1}{2} x - 5$?

    A.  (4, 8)

    B.  (32, 10)

    C.  (10, −1)

    D.  (6, −5)

8. Evaluate $2x^2 + 5x - 3$ when $x = -3$.

    A.  30

    B.  0

    C.  −18

    D.  −30

9. A boy has 3 blue marbles, 3 red marbles, and 3 yellow marbles. What is the probability of pulling two yellow marbles out of his pocket?

   A. $\dfrac{6}{72}$

   B. $\dfrac{1}{3}$

   C. $\dfrac{2}{3}$

   D. $\dfrac{7}{12}$

10. Current teacher salaries range from $41,000 to $65,000. If the union negotiates a flat raise of $1,000 for all teachers, which of the following statements will be true?

    A. The mean, median, and standard deviation do not change.

    B. The mean and median do not change, but the mode and standard deviation increase by $1,000.

    C. The mean, mode, and median do not change, but the standard deviation increases by $1,000.

    D. The mean, median, and mode increase by $1,000, but the standard deviation does not change.

11. If four bunches of bananas weigh $1\dfrac{3}{4}$ pounds each and 3 mangos weigh 3 ounces each, how many pounds of produce do you have altogether?

    A. $1\dfrac{11}{20}$

    B. $7\dfrac{9}{16}$

    C. 16

    D. $16\dfrac{3}{4}$

12. A student has the following test scores: 83%, 77%, 100%, and 95%. In order to get a 90% or an A in the class, what is the lowest score the student can make on the last test?

    A. 100

    B. 98

    C. 95

    D. The student cannot get an A because of the low scores.

13.  You are putting the contents of two boxes into one larger box to mail to your son at college. One box is 2 cm × 4 cm × 10 cm, and the other is 6 cm × 4 cm × 12 cm. The bigger box is 14 cm × 10 cm × 4 cm. Will the contents of the two smaller boxes fit into the larger box?

   A.  No, you need 19 more cm³ of space.

   B.  Yes, you will have 100 cm³ left over in the box.

   C.  Yes, you will have 192 cm³ left over in the box.

   D.  No, you need 16 more cm³ of space.

14.  Calculate the expression shown below and write the answer in scientific notation.

$$0.003 \times 1.25$$

   A.  $0.375 \times 10^{-2}$

   B.  $0.375 \times 10^{2}$

   C.  $3.75 \times 10^{-3}$

   D.  $3.75 \times 10^{3}$

15.  On the first day of a road trip, you drove 300 miles in 5 hours. The second day you traveled at the same rate of speed for another 7 hours. If you got an average of 27 miles per gallon and gas costs $2.59 a gallon, how much did you spend on gas during the trip?

   A.  $69.07

   B.  $56.91

   C.  $70.28

   D.  $162.34

16.  Which symbol should be in the box?

$$-\frac{7}{13} \quad \square \quad -\frac{13}{27}$$

   A.  >     B.     <       C. ≥    D.     ≤

17.  Which of the following algebraic functions is NOT true?

   A.  $2x(x + 3) = 2x^2 + 6x$

   B.  $x^4 - x^2 = x^2$

   C.  $3x^2 + 2x + (x^2 + 4) = 4x^2 + 2x + 4$

   D.  $(-2x + 3x)(3 - 3) = 0$

18. Find the slope of the line passing through the points $W$ and $Z$ in the following figure.

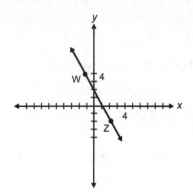

A. $-\dfrac{1}{2}$

B. $\dfrac{1}{4}$

C. $-2$

D. $2$

19. If your school has 900 students, with a teacher-to-student ratio of 1:30, how many more teachers would your principal have to hire to improve the ratio to 1:25?

A. 30

B. 6

C. 36

D. 66

20. Solve the following compound inequality:

$$-24 < -2x < -12$$

A. $12 < x < 6$

B. $-12 < x < -6$

C. $6 < x < 12$

D. $-6 < x < -12$

21. A married couple makes $24,000 each, and their total income including interest from investments is $56,000. What fraction of their income do they make from their investments?

    A. $\frac{1}{7}$

    B. $\frac{1}{5}$

    C. $\frac{1}{4}$

    D. $\frac{1}{3}$

22. A local supermarket employs 8 cashiers and stock people, 1 assistant manager, and 1 general manager with the following salaries:

    | | | | | |
    |---|---|---|---|---|
    | $18,000 | $18,000 | $18,000 | $19,000 | $21,000 |
    | $23,000 | $24,000 | $25,000 | $75,000 | $95,000 |

    To encourage people to apply to work at the store, the following sign is posted on the front door:

    > Cashiers Needed!
    >
    > Come join our team. Employees average $33,600 a year and enjoy many benefits including a discount on purchases.

    What is misleading about the sign?

    A. The amount of the employee discount is not listed.

    B. The average salary is the mean of the data, which is skewed by two large outliers.

    C. The store did not correctly calculate the mean of the data.

    D. The store should have used the median, which would have been higher than the mean.

23. If the air temperature is 65 degrees and for every meter you drill down the temperature drops by 5 degrees, what would the ground temperature be if you drilled down 20 meters?

    A. 60 degrees

    B. 45 degrees

    C. 35 degrees

    D. −35 degrees

24. You are given the equation of the following line: $y = 3x + 2$. Identify the line that is parallel to this line.

    A. $y = \dfrac{1}{3}x + 2$

    B. $y = -\dfrac{1}{3}x + 4$

    C. $y = 3x - 4$

    D. $2y = 6x + 4$

25. A realtor wants to advertise his ability to get top dollar for home sales in a particular neighborhood. What is the highest measure of central tendency for the sale price of the homes listed below?

    | 170,000 | 210,000 | 190,000 | 170,000 | 259,000 | 205,000 |

    A. The range

    B. The mean

    C. The mode

    D. The median

26. What is the probability that a six-sided die will land on a prime number?

    A. $\dfrac{1}{2}$

    B. $\dfrac{2}{3}$

    C. $\dfrac{1}{6}$

    D. $\dfrac{5}{6}$

27. Two trains leave different cities heading toward each other at different speeds. Train A, traveling at a rate of 60 miles per hour (mph), leaves Westford heading toward Eastford, 200 miles away. At the same time Train B, traveling at a rate of 40 mph, leaves Eastford heading toward Westford. How long before the trains pass each other on the tracks?

    A. 1 hour

    B. 1.5 hours

    C. 2 hours

    D. 10 hours

28. You are buying supplies for your class of 22 students. You want to buy two pencils and one pack of notebook paper for each student, but you only have time to go to one store. Using the chart below, what is the least amount you can spend on supplies?

|  | Pencils | Paper |
|---|---|---|
| Store A | 12 for $1.29 | 10-pack for $7.50 |
| Store B | 10 for $1.00 | 3-pack for $2.50 |

    A.   $25.08

    B.   $25.00

    C.   $27.66

    D.   $20.53

29. Thirty students took an exam. Five earned 40%, one earned 80%, and the rest earned 70%. Based on their scores, which of the following measures of central tendency would be the lowest?

    A.   mean

    B.   median

    C.   mode

    D.   range

30. Which answer below shows the correct simplification of $150 \div (6 + 3 \times 8) - 5$?

    A.   0

    B.   $-\dfrac{105}{36}$

    C.   $\dfrac{150}{67}$

    D.   5

31. A teacher gave a ten-question assessment to determine if her students had mastered a math standard. Based on this frequency table, what is the median score on the test?

    A. 9

    B. 7.5

    C. 7

    D. 6.5

| Mark | Tally | Frequency |
|------|-------|-----------|
| 4 | I I | 2 |
| 5 | I I | 2 |
| 6 | I I I I | 4 |
| 7 | I I I I I | 5 |
| 8 | I I I I | 4 |
| 9 | I I I I I I | 6 |
| 10 | I I I | 3 |

32. Which answer shows the following numbers in order from least to greatest?

$$-\frac{3}{4} \qquad -0.075 \qquad -1\frac{1}{2} \qquad \sqrt{4}$$

    A. $-\frac{3}{4}, -0.075, -1\frac{1}{2}, \sqrt{4}$

    B. $-\frac{3}{4}, -1\frac{1}{2}, \sqrt{4}, -0.075$

    C. $\sqrt{4}, -\frac{3}{4}, -0.075, -1\frac{1}{2}$

    D. $-1\frac{1}{2}, -\frac{3}{4}, -0.075, \sqrt{4}$

33. A middle school student conducted an experiment to determine if, with practice, mice could learn a route through a maze. The data from three of the mice are shown in the following table.

| Trial Number | Mouse 1 | Mouse 2 | Mouse 3 |
|:---:|:---:|:---:|:---:|
| 1 | 15 sec. | 16 sec. | 13 sec. |
| 2 | 16 sec. | 15 sec. | 15 sec. |
| 3 | 14 sec. | 15 sec. | 13 sec. |
| 4 | 12 sec. | 14 sec. | 12 sec. |
| 5 | 11 sec. | 12 sec. | 11 sec. |
| 6 | 12 sec. | 10 sec. | 10 sec. |
| 7 | 9 sec. | 9 sec. | 10 sec. |

Based on the data in the table, which of the following statements is false?

A. All the mice showed significant improvement from the first trial to the third trial.

B. Mouse 2 showed the greatest improvement over the course of the trials.

C. Mouse 3 showed the least improvement over the trials.

D. All three mice showed improvement from the first trial to the final trial.

34. Which graph matches with the compound inequality $1 < x < 6$?

A. Graph A

B. Graph B

C. Graph C

D. None of the graphs match

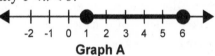
**Graph A**

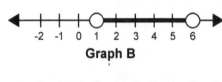
**Graph B**

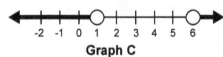
**Graph C**

35. Dante tossed three coins. Use the tree diagram below to find the probability that exactly two of the three coins will land on heads.

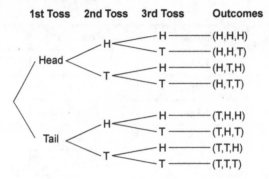

A. $\dfrac{3}{8}$

B. $\dfrac{1}{2}$

C. $\dfrac{1}{4}$

D. $\dfrac{5}{8}$

36. Some dogs and people are in a kennel. If we counted 30 heads and 104 legs in the kennel, which systems of equations could we use to determine the number of dogs ($d$) and people ($p$) that are present?

A. $d + p = 2p + 4d$

B. $2p + 4d = 30 + 104$ and $d + p = 30$

C. $d + p = 30$ and $2p + 4d = 104$

D. $d + p = 104$ and $2p + 4d = 30$

37. If a company's profit in thousands is represented by the equation $f = \dfrac{4}{3}(x - 2005) + 32$, what year will the company reach its goal of $60,000 profit?

A. 2005

B. 2026

C. 2050

D. 2065

38. How many 8-inch by 8-inch tiles are needed to cover a 12- by 16-foot room?

    A.   64

    B.   192

    C.   224

    D.   432

39. A playdough recipe calls for $\frac{1}{2}$ cup flour, $\frac{1}{3}$ cup salt, and $\frac{1}{8}$ cup water. If the teacher wants to make four batches of playdough for the class, what is the total amount of dry ingredients that will be used in the recipe?

    A.   $\frac{4}{5}$ cup

    B.   $1\frac{3}{5}$ cups

    C.   $1\frac{1}{3}$ cups

    D.   $3\frac{1}{3}$ cups

40. Which of the following is NOT a function?

    A.   A vertical line

    B.   A horizontal line

    C.   A line with a positive slope

    D.   A line with a negative slope

41. You are going to a meeting. If you drive 60 mph, you will get there two hours early. If you drive 30 mph you will get there two hours late. How far do you have to drive?

    A.   240 miles

    B.   180 miles

    C.   120 miles

    D.   60 miles

42. Investors were analyzing the profits in millions of two different companies. Based on the following tables, which statement about the companies is true?

| Company A | | | Company B | |
|---|---|---|---|---|
| Year | Profit (in millions) | | Year | Profit (in millions) |
| 1 | 2 | | 1 | 2 |
| 2 | 4 | | 3 | 4 |
| 3 | 6 | | 5 | 9 |
| 5 | 10 | | 7 | 13 |
| 10 | 20 | | 9 | 16 |

A. Company B made more profit than Company A in year 5.

B. Company A had a steady profit increase of 2 million per year.

C. Company B had a steady profit increase of 3 million per year.

D. Company A had the same yearly earnings as Company B.

43. You have five children. Two of the children are five years old, and they have a median age of nine. The range of ages is seven. Which could be the age of the second to the oldest child?

A. 14

B. 13

C. 9

D. 6

44. A magician learned a magic trick that required a red chip, a blue chip, and a green chip. If he lines up the chips in a row on the table in front of him, what is the probability that the red and blue chip will be next to each other?

A. $\frac{1}{2}$

B. $\frac{2}{3}$

C. $\frac{1}{4}$

D. $\frac{1}{3}$

45. A family is planning a trip to the Florida Keys from Orlando. If the map scale indicates that $\frac{3}{4}$ inch is equivalent to 40 miles and Key West is 280 miles from Orlando on the map, how many inches is Key West from Orlando on the map?

A. $4\frac{1}{3}$

B. $5\frac{1}{4}$

C. $6$

D. $6\frac{1}{2}$

# Practice Test 1: Reading

55 Minutes

40 Questions

**DIRECTIONS:** Read the passages and then answer the questions that follow.

## PASSAGE ONE

### Progress of Minority-Owned Businesses

Recent years have brought minority-owned businesses in the United States unprecedented opportunities. Civil rights activists have long argued that one of the principal reasons why blacks, Hispanics, and the other minority groups have difficulty establishing themselves in business is that they lack access to the sizable orders and subcontracts that are generated by large companies. Now Congress, in apparent agreement, has required by law that businesses awarded federal contracts of more than $500,000 do their best to find minority subcontractors and record their efforts to do so on forms filed with the government. Indeed, some federal and local agencies have gone so far as to set specific percentage goals for apportioning parts of public works contracts to minority enterprises.

Corporate response appears to have been substantial. According to figures collected in 1977, the total of corporate contracts with minority business rose from $77 million to $1.1 billion in 1977. The projected total of corporate contracts with minority business for the early 1980's was estimated to be over $3 billion per year with no letup anticipated in the next decade. Promising as it is for minority businesses, this increased patronage poses dangers for them, too. First, minority firms risk expanding too fast and overextending themselves financially, since most are small concerns and, unlike large businesses they often need to make substantial investments in new plants, staff, equipment, and the like in order to perform work subcontracted to them. If, sometime after, their subcontracts are for some reason reduced, such firms can face potentially crippling fixed expenses.

## PASSAGE TWO

### The World of Purchasing

Understanding the world of purchasing for minority-owned businesses is complex, but sheds light on the risks these companies face. The world of corporate purchasing can be frustrating for small entrepreneurs who get requests for elaborate formal estimates and bids. Both consume valuable time and resources and a small company's efforts must soon result in orders, or both the morale and the financial health of the business will suffer. A second risk is that white-owned companies may seek to cash in on the increasing apportionments through formation of joint ventures with minority-owned concerns, of course, in many instances there are legitimate reasons for joint ventures; clearly, white and minority enterprises can team up to acquire business that neither could on their own. Third, a minority enterprise that secures the business of one large corporate customer often runs the danger of becoming—and remaining dependent. Even in the best of circumstances, fierce competition from larger, more established companies makes it difficult for small concerns to broaden their customer bases; when such firms have nearly guaranteed orders from a single corporate benefactor, they may truly have to struggle against **complacency** arising from their current success.

1.  Identify the most accurate statement of the central idea of Passage 2.

    A.  There are significant contradictions for minority-owned businesses.

    B.  There are significant potential drawbacks for minority-owned businesses.

    C.  Experts have proposed a temporary solution to a long-standing problem between minority-owned businesses and corporations.

    D.  Experts relate a cause-and-effect relationship between minority-owned businesses and corporations.

2.  Passage 2 provides information for answering most fully which of the following questions?

    A.  What federal agencies have set percentage goals for the use of minority owned businesses in public works contracts?

    B.  To which government's agencies must businesses awarded federal contracts report their efforts to find minority subcontractors?

    C.  How widespread is the use of minority-owned concerns as fronts?

    D.  What is one set of conditions under which a small business might find itself financially overextended?

3.  According to Passage 1, civil rights activists maintain that one disadvantage under which minority-owned businesses have traditionally had to labor is that they have

    A.  been especially vulnerable to governmental regulations.

    B.  been denied bank loans at rates comparable to those afforded larger competitors.

    C.  not had sufficient opportunity to secure businesses created by large corporations.

    D.  not been able to advertise in those media that reach large numbers of potential customers.

4.  The author of Passage 2 suggests that "corporate purchasing can be frustrating for small entrepreneurs who get requests for elaborate formal estimates and bids" in order to

    A.  show both time and resources within the company are effected.

    B.  analyze the crippling fixed expenses of a minority-owned business.

    C.  record the efforts of small businesses with the government.

    D.  point to the increase in spending of small, minority-owned businesses with subcontractors.

5. The author of Passage 2 implies that the minority-owned concern that does the greater part of its business with one large corporate customer should

   A. avoid competition with the larger, more established concerns by not expanding.

   B. concentrate on securing even more business from that corporation.

   C. try to expand its customer base to avoid becoming dependent on the corporation.

   D. pass on some of the work to be done for the corporation to other minority owned concerns.

6. Which of the following is NOT a detail stated in Passage 1?

   A. Percentage goals are set by some federal and local agencies.

   B. Percentage goals set by some federal and local agencies are more specific.

   C. Percentage goals set by some federal and local agencies are less controversial.

   D. Percentage goals set by some federal and local agencies are often distributed across public works contracts.

7. Which of the following, if true, would weaken the author of Passage 1's assertion that, in the 1970s, corporate response to federal requirements was substantial?

   A. Corporate contracts with minority owned business totaled about $2 billion in 1979.

   B. Between 1970 and 1972, corporate contracts with minority owned businesses declined by 25 percent.

   C. The figures collected in 1977 under-represented the extent of corporate contracts with minority owned businesses.

   D. The $1.1 billion represented the same percentage of total corporate spending in 1977 as did $77 million in 1972.

8. The author of Passage 1 would most likely respond to the discussion of risks in Passage 2 by asserting that

   A. while abundant risks exist, opportunities are more readily available.

   B. this is not a critical argument when understanding minority-owned businesses.

   C. history is likely to repeat itself acknowledging the current context.

   D. companies must learn to overcome obstacles in order to be competitive in the marketplace.

9.  In the context of Passage 2, the word **complacency** most nearly means

    A. fervent.

    B. self-satisfaction.

    C. indifferent.

    D. zealous.

**DIRECTIONS:** Read the passage below and then answer the questions that follow.

## The Indigo Bunting's Song

In strongly territorial birds such as the indigo bunting, song is the main mechanism for securing, defining, and defending an adequate breeding area. When population density is high, only the strongest males can retain a suitable area. The weakest males do not breed or are forced to nest on poor or marginal territories. During the breeding season, the male indigo bunting sings in his territory; each song lasts two or three seconds with a very short pause between songs. Melodic and rhythmic characteristics are produced by rapid changes in sound frequency and some regularity of silent periods between sounds. These **modulated** sounds form recognizable units, called figures, each of which is reproduced again and again with remarkable consistency. Despite the large frequency range of these sounds and the rapid frequency changes that the bird makes, the number of figures is very limited. Further, although we found some unique figures in different geographical populations, more than 90 percent of all indigo bunting figures are extremely stable on a geographic basis. In our studies of isolated buntings, we found that male indigo buntings are capable of singing many more types of figures than they usually do. Thus, it would seem that they copy their figures from other buntings they hear singing.

Realizing that the ability to distinguish the songs of one species from those of another could be an important factor in the volition of the figures, we tested species recognition of a song. When we played a recording of a lazuli bunting or a painted bunting, male indigo buntings did not respond, even when a dummy of a male indigo bunting was placed near the recording device. Playing an indigo bunting song, however, usually brought an immediate response, making it clear that a male indigo bunting can readily distinguish songs of its own species from those of other species. The role of the songs' figures in interspecies recognition was then examined. We created experimental songs composed of new figures by playing a normal song backwards, which changed the detailed forms of the figures without altering frequency ranges or gross **temporal** features. Since the male indigos gave almost a full response to the backward song, we concluded that a wide range of figures and shapes can evoke positive responses. It seems likely, therefore, that a specific configuration is not essential for interspecies recognition, but it is clear that song figures must conform to a particular frequency range, must be within narrow limits of duration, and must be spaced at particular intervals. There is evidence that new figures may arise within a population through a slow process of change and selection. This variety is probably a valuable adaptation for survival: if every bird sang only a few types of figures, in dense woods or underbrush a female might have difficulty recognizing her mate's song and a male might not be able to distinguish a neighbor from a stranger. Our studies lead us to conclude that there must be a balance between song stability and conservatism, which leads to clear-cut species recognition, and song variation, which leads to individual recognition.

10. The primary purpose of this passage is to

    A.   raise new issues about the recreation of the bunting bird population.

    B.   explain an enigma occurring in the midst of bunting bird growth.

    C.   refute misconceptions about bunting bird data.

    D.   analyze a phenomenon within the ecosystem.

11. According to the passage, which of the following is true about the number and general nature of figures sung by the indigo bunting?

    A.   They are established at birth and do not change over a life-span.

    B.   They evolve slowly as the bird learns to navigate the ecosystem in which they live.

    C.   They are learned from other indigo buntings within the biological system.

    D.   They develop after the bird has been forced to marginal breeding areas moving them beyond initial patterns.

12. It can be assumed from the author that the investigation that determined the similarity among more than 90 percent of all the figures produced by birds living in different regions was undertaken to answer which of the following questions?

    A.   How many variations, if any, is there in the figure types produced by indigo buntings in different locales?

    B.   Do local populations of indigo buntings develop their own dialects of figure types?

    C.   Do figure similarities among indigo buntings decline with increasing geographic separation?

    D.   All of the above

13. Based on the passage, the existence of only a limited number of indigo bunting figures serves primarily to

    A.   ensure species survival by increasing competition among bunting birds.

    B.   increase population density by eliminating ambiguity in the figures to which the females must respond.

    C.   maintain the integrity of the species by restricting the degree of figure variation and change.

    D.   enhance species recognition by decreasing the number of figure patterns to which the bird must respond.

14. The author most likely uses the example of the dummy male indigo bunting placed near the tape recorder that played the songs of different species in order to

    A. simulate the conditions faced by bunting birds in nature.

    B. rule out visual cues as a factor in species recognition among bunting birds.

    C. supply an additional clue to species recognition for the indigo bunting.

    D. provide data on the habits of bunting species other than then indigo bunting.

15. In this context, the author uses the word **modulated** to infer the sounds are

    A. regulated.

    B. suspended.

    C. vexed.

    D. ignored.

16. Identify the most accurate statement of the central idea of the passage.

    A. The song of the indigo bunting bird is prevalent and protects the species.

    B. The female song of the indigo bunting bird defines the species.

    C. The male song of the indigo bunting bird defines the species.

    D. The song of the indigo bunting bird defines and sustains the species.

17. Which order of words describes the overall effect of the passage?

    A. song, copy, characterize, recognize

    B. volition, song, copy, recognize

    C. recognize, characterize, copy, song

    D. song, copy, recognize, volition

18. The passage supports which of the following claim about indigo bunting birds?

    A. When males are breeding they are forced to nest, relying primarily on other bunting birds.

    B. When population density is low, only the strongest males can retain an adaptable area; therefore, the weakest males do not breed or are forced to nest on less than adequate territories.

    C. When males are forced to rely on other bunting birds, they choose not to nest.

    D. When population density is high, only the strongest males can retain an adaptable area; therefore, the weakest males do not breed or are forced to nest on less than adequate territories.

19. The author of the passage points out that, "Realizing that the ability to distinguish the songs of one species from those of another could be an important factor…" in order to

    A.  demonstrate the relationship between the distinction of song and volition of the figures among bunting birds.

    B.  show the comparisons between songs and bird species.

    C.  demonstrate the correlative relationship between song and siblings among bunting birds.

    D.  show the contrasts between the number of bunting birds and songs displayed.

20. Which of the following is NOT a detail stated in the passage?

    A.  A wide range of figures shapes can evoke positive responses from bunting birds.

    B.  Bunting birds copy their figures from other buntings they hear singing.

    C.  A wide range of songs can sustain across breeding and territorial repositioning.

    D.  New figures may arise within a population through a slow process of change and selection.

21. In the context of the passage, the word **temporal** most nearly means

    A.  noble.

    B.  mundane.

    C.  daily.

    D.  lofty.

22. Which of the following is an opinion stated in the passage?

    A.  "When population density is high, only the strongest males can retain a suitable area."

    B.  "The role of the songs' figures in interspecies recognition was then examined."

    C.  "These modulated sounds form recognizable units, called figures, each of which is reproduced again and again with remarkable consistency."

    D.  "This variety is probably a valuable adaptation for survival: if every bird sang only a few types of figures, in dense woods or underbrush a female might have difficulty recognizing her mate's song and a male might not be able to distinguish a neighbor from a stranger."

23. The author mentions, "more than 90 percent of all indigo bunting figures are extremely stable on the geographic basis…" in order to

    A.  demonstrate the relationship between the number of figures and the geographical stability of the species.

    B.  show the inability of the indigo bunting bird to adapt to a new environment.

C. demonstrate the relationship between the number of figures and the adaptability of the species.

D. show the ability of the indigo bunting bird to adapt to a new environment.

24. According to the passage, why did they test for species recognition of a song?

A. In order to distinguish the figures between male and female bunting birds

B. In order to understand the relationship between male and female bunting birds

C. In order to distinguish the songs of one species from those of another

D. In order to investigate the territorial breeding grounds of bunting birds

25. According to the passage, what are the direct results of "song stability and conservatism"?

A. Individual recognition leading to song variation

B. Species recognition and song variation leading to individual recognition among bunting birds

C. Individual recognition leading to species recognition

D. Species recognition and individual recognition leading to song variation among bunting birds

26. Based on the passage, what is the best caption for this image?

A. Bunting Birds Unite

B. Extraordinary Birds

C. Bunting Song

D. Figures and Birds

**DIRECTIONS:** Read the passages below and then answer the questions that follow.

## PASSAGE ONE

### One Man's Journey

Frederick Douglass was born Frederick Augustus Washington Bailey in 1817 to a white father and a slave mother. Frederick was raised by his grandmother on a Maryland plantation until he was eight. It was then that he was sent to Baltimore by his owner to be a servant to the Auld family. Mrs. Auld recognized Frederick's intellectual acumen and defied the law of the state by teaching him to read and write.

When Mr. Auld warned that education would make the boy unfit for slavery, Frederick sought to continue his education in the streets. When his master died, Frederick was returned to the plantation to work in the fields at age 16. Later, he was hired out to work in the shipyards in Baltimore as a ship caulker. He plotted an escape but was discovered before he could get away. It took five years before he made his way to New York City and then to New Bedford, Massachusetts, eluding slave hunters by changing his name to Douglass. At an 1841 anti-slavery meeting in Massachusetts, Douglass was invited to give a talk about his experiences under slavery. His **impromptu** speech was so powerful and so eloquent that it thrust him into a career as an agent for the Massachusetts Anti-Slavery Society.

## PASSAGE TWO

### One Man's Voice

Frederick Douglass wrote his autobiography in 1845, *Narrative of the Life of Frederick Douglass, an American Slave*. The purpose was primarily to counter those who doubted his authenticity as a former slave. This work became a classic in American literature and a primary source about slavery from the point of view of a slave. His writing described his time as a slave in Maryland. It was one of five autobiographies he penned, along with dozens of noteworthy speeches, despite receiving minimal education. Douglass went on a two-year speaking tour abroad to avoid recapture by his former owner and to win new friends for the abolition movement. He returned with funds to purchase his freedom and to start his own anti-slavery newspaper. He became a consultant to Abraham Lincoln and throughout Reconstruction fought doggedly for full civil rights for freedmen; he also supported the women's rights movement. Douglass's voice created a legacy of justice and determination and his actions served as an inspiration to the civil rights movement of the 1960s and the discourse of the 21st century.

27. According to Passage 2, Douglass's autobiography was motivated by

    A.  the desire to make money for his anti-slavery movement.

    B.  the desire to start a newspaper.

    C.  his interest in authenticating his life as a slave.

    D.  his desire to educate people about slavery.

28. The central idea of Passage 1 is that Frederick Douglass

    A.  was an individual who used his power to change the laws regarding the education of slaves.

    B.  was an individual who used his experiences in order to bring awareness of injustice.

    C.  was a personal friend and confidant to a president.

    D.  was a gifted writer, speaker and teacher.

29. The author of Passage 1 details Mr. Auld's concerns in order to

    A.  provide a specific example of how the current paradigm affected Douglass's circumstances.

    B.  show the exaggeration between the world of slave and free during Douglass's lifetime.

    C.  provide a specific example of how the current paradigm predicted Douglass's circumstances.

    D.  show the exaggeration between the world of slave and African-American during Douglass's lifetime.

30. The author of Passage 1 most likely includes the example of Douglass's eloquent speech to

    A.  provide an example of how his communication limited his future opportunity.

    B.  provide an example of how his communication was a catalyst for future opportunity.

    C.  explore speech-writing as a future occupation for Douglass.

    D.  point to a reason why Lincoln relied on him as an advisor.

31. In the context of Passage, 1 **impromptu** most nearly means

    A.  unprepared.

    B.  in a quiet manner.

    C.  forceful.

    D.  elaborate.

32. What is the primary difference between Passage 1 and Passage 2?

    A. Passage 1 outlines Douglass's great literary works while Passage 2 outlines Douglass's childhood.

    B. Passage 2 depicts the rationale for Douglass's autobiography and action steps while Passage 1 provides a brief biography of Douglass.

    C. Passage 1 outlines Douglass's childhood while Passage 2 outlines Douglass's great literary works.

    D. Passage 2 provides a brief biography of Douglass while Passage 1 depicts the rationale for Douglass's autobiography and action steps.

**DIRECTIONS:** Read the passages below and then answer the questions that follow.

## PASSAGE ONE

### The Difficulty Inherent in Social Studies Texts

The **inherent** difficulty of social studies content stems mainly from the heavy technical concept load of social studies textbook passages. *Technical concepts* are one- or two-word "ideas" which have specialized meanings in social studies (for example: *government, delta, immigrants, interdependence, economy, constitution, federal, cotton belt, division of labor, and political party*). These words may have little or no meaning for students unless specific vocabulary or concept development lessons precede their first encounter with such terms. Yet basal social studies textbooks are notorious for heavy technical concept load and "thin" discussion of topics, making even the most careful independent reading low in potential benefit.

## PASSAGE TWO

### Issues with Learning Social Studies

Hard-to-pronounce names of cities, faraway countries, and foreign language names contribute to the complexity of textbook content. Many adult readers are stopped by these words, yet social studies is neither complete nor accurate without them. Add to the above problems frequent references to long periods of time or huge distances, and it becomes even more apparent why children have trouble learning from their social studies textbooks. What must a child of 9 or 10 think when the book says, "Our country was founded over 200 years ago"—or perhaps worse, "long, long ago"? What do expressions such as "far to the north," or "over a thousand miles to the east," mean to students who are not sure which direction is which and who have never traveled further than across the state or out of town?

33. The word **inherent** in Passage 1 most nearly means

    A. naturally occurring.

    B. worst.

    C. least important.

    D. foreign.

34. According to the authors of Passages 1 and 2, which of the following does NOT contribute to the ineffectiveness of social studies textbooks?

    A. Difficult terminology

    B. References to long periods of time

    C. Uninteresting topics

    D. Words that are difficult to pronounce

35. The author's primary claim in Passage 1 is that

    A. a complicated technical framework hurts social studies texts.

    B. social studies texts should be rewritten so that they are easier to understand.

    C. a complicated language pattern hurts social studies texts.

    D. the difficulties of social studies texts are necessary hurdles that must be overcome.

36. In Passage 2, the author solidifies his central claim with the use of

    A. rhetorical statements.

    B. imagery.

    C. hyperbole.

    D. symbolism.

37. The author of Passage 1 mentions "thin discussions" in order to

    A. argue the claim that social studies textbooks do not provide profitable explanations for complex terms.

    B. support the claim that social studies textbooks do not provide profitable explanations for complex terms.

    C. support the claim that social studies textbooks should not utilize complex vocabulary.

    D. argue the claim that social studies textbooks should not utilize complex vocabulary.

38. The effect of Passage 2 is

    A. to utilize, pronounce, and recognize.

    B. to consider social studies, textbooks, and discussions.

    C. to pronounce, recognize, and utilize.

    D. to mention discussions, social studies, and textbooks.

39. What is the relationship between these two sentences?

    Sentence 1: The inherent difficulty of social studies content stems mainly from the heavy technical concept load of social studies textbook passages. (paragraph 1)

    Sentence 2: Technical concepts are one- or two-word "ideas" which have specialized meaning in social studies (for example: government, delta, immigrants, interdependence, economy, constitution, federal, cotton belt, division of labor, and political party.) (paragraph 1)

    A. Sentence 2 analyzes the comment in sentence 1.

    B. Sentence 2 contradicts the main idea of sentence 1.

    C. Sentence 2 summarizes the main idea begun in sentence 1.

    D. Sentence 2 defines the main idea of sentence 1.

40. The attitude of the author of Passage 1 towards social studies texts could be best described as

    A. skeptical.

    B. inconclusive.

    C. critical.

    D. optimistic.

## Practice Test 1
## Answer Key

### ■ English Language Skills

| | | | |
|---|---|---|---|
| 1. C | 11. D | 21. B | 31. C |
| 2. B | 12. B | 22. B | 32. D |
| 3. C | 13. B | 23. B | 33. A |
| 4. C | 14. C | 24. C | 34. D |
| 5. A | 15. D | 25. D | 35. C |
| 6. C | 16. B | 26. B | 36. B |
| 7. C | 17. D | 27. C | 37. D |
| 8. C | 18. A | 28. C | 38. C |
| 9. C | 19. B | 29. B | 39. C |
| 10. B | 20. D | 30. B | 40. B |

### ■ Mathematics

| | | | |
|---|---|---|---|
| 1. C | 13. C | 24. C | 35. A |
| 2. B | 14. C | 25. B | 36. C |
| 3. D | 15. A | 26. A | 37. B |
| 4. B | 16. B | 27. C | 38. D |
| 5. B | 17. B | 28. B | 39. D |
| 6. C | 18. C | 29. A | 40. A |
| 7. A | 19. B | 30. A | 41. A |
| 8. B | 20. C | 31. B | 42. B |
| 9. A | 21. A | 32. D | 43. C |
| 10. D | 22. B | 33. A | 44. B |
| 11. B | 23. D | 34. B | 45. B |
| 12. C | | | |

(continued)

## Reading

| | | | |
|---|---|---|---|
| 1. B | 11. C | 21. B | 31. A |
| 2. D | 12. D | 22. D | 32. B |
| 3. C | 13. D | 23. A | 33. A |
| 4. A | 14. B | 24. C | 34. C |
| 5. C | 15. A | 25. B | 35. A |
| 6. C | 16. D | 26. C | 36. A |
| 7. D | 17. A | 27. C | 37. B |
| 8. A | 18. D | 28. B | 38. C |
| 9. B | 19. A | 29. A | 39. D |
| 10. D | 20. C | 30. B | 40. C |

# Practice Test 1: Correlation with FTCE Competencies

## English Language Skills

**Competency 1: Knowledge of Language Structure**

Questions: 1, 2, 3, 4, 5, 6, 25, 26, 36, 37

**Competency 2: Knowledge of Vocabulary Application**

Questions: 11, 20, 23, 24, 27, 32, 34, 38, 39, 40

**Competency 3: Knowledge of Standard English Conventions**

Questions: 7, 8, 9, 10, 12, 13, 14, 15, 16, 17, 18, 19, 21, 22, 28, 29, 30, 31, 33, 35

## Mathematics

**Competency 1: Knowledge of Number Sense, Concepts, and Operations**

Questions: 1, 2, 11, 16, 21, 30, 32, 39

**Competency 2: Knowledge of Geometry and Measurement**

Questions: 5, 6, 13, 14, 15, 19, 27, 28, 38, 41, 45

**Competency 3: Knowledge of Algebraic Thinking and the Coordinate Plain**

Questions: 7, 8, 17, 18, 20, 23, 24, 34, 36, 37, 40

**Competency 4: Knowledge of Probability, Statistics, and Data Interpretation**

Questions: 3, 4, 9, 10, 12, 22, 25, 26, 29, 31, 33, 35, 42, 43, 44

## Reading

**Competency 1: Knowledge of Key Ideas and Details Based on Text Slections**

Questions: 1, 3, 4, 5, 12, 13, 16, 20, 22, 29, 31, 32, 34, 36, 37, 38

**Competency 2: Knowledge of Craft and Structure Based on Text Selections**

Questions: 10, 11, 14, 17, 19, 23, 24, 26, 30, 33

**Competency 3: Knowledge of the Integration of Information and Ideas Based on Text Selections**

Questions: 2, 6, 7, 8, 9, 15, 18, 21, 25, 27, 28, 35, 39, 40

# Practice Test 1: Detailed Explanations of Answers

 Essay

## Sample Response Topic

At schools worldwide, students are required to wear school uniforms. This has been a debate for many years in regards to creating the most advantageous learning environment possible. As is the case with most educational issues, there are professionals on both sides of the argument. Some believe that it creates a positive element within the learning community while others believe that it is stifling for student freedom. Depending upon your vantage point, there are advantages and disadvantages to a program of this kind.

First and foremost, one of the main advantages of school uniforms is the reality that every student looks the same. Students who don't have enough means to buy expensive and fashionable clothes can surely benefit from this. Parents will also save money. Instead of buying school outfits, the money can be used to purchase school supplies. Second, and beyond the reality of saving money, the element of school uniforms can provide unity for a school community— meaning that the identity of students is found in being connected to a larger community. Therefore, if you are wearing the uniform that identifies you with a certain school, people will be able to distinguish you. Third, wearing a uniform can aid students in time management. Instead of spending an inordinate amount of time analyzing what will be worn each day, a student's time is put to use with other more fruitful activities. This is one side of the argument.

On the other hand, there are other professionals who believe school uniforms have drawbacks. For fashion aficionados, wearing a school uniform suppresses their ability to express themselves. School uniforms prevent students from wearing the clothes they want to wear. So, some students may not be comfortable with uniforms as they would not be able to choose something from their own closet. Another disadvantage worth considering is the idea that students should not have their individual freedoms controlled by an educational institution. Some professionals call into question the philosophical role schools play when they determine how each student will be dressed.

In the final analysis, wearing a school uniform has advantages and disadvantages. Advantages focus on the ideas of uniformity, time management, and finance management. Disadvantages focus on the ideas of suppression and control. School uniforms or not, learning communities should always keep students at the center of the debate— this will be a beacon of light to the conversation.

## Analysis

This essay shows a good command of the English language and depth of thought. The writer employs a traditional essay structure: The first paragraph is the introduction and the essay ends with a thesis statement. The writer gives distinct examples to support the ideas. Vocabulary is effective, transitions are good, and sentence structure is varied. This essay would merit a score of 5.

## English Language Skills

1.   **C.** In choice (C), the modifier is right next to what is being described—"demonstrators." Each of the other answer choices has a misplaced modifier.

2.   **B.** The modifier is right next to what is being described, "Jay." Also, "friends" is right next to the modifier, "who immediately took him to his speaking engagement in Springfield." Each of the other answer choices has a misplaced modifier.

3.   **C.** In this answer choice, the modifiers are placed correctly. The adverb "consistently" modifies the adjective "late." Answer choices (B) and (A) have misplaced modifiers.

4.   **C.** "Relaxed" provides parallel structure with the three other past-tense verbs in the sentence: "raked, washed, and cleaned."

5.   **A.** The blank needs to begin with a simple past tense verb. "Clutched" matches "claimed" and "excused" in the sentence providing parallel structure for the reader. Answer choices (B), (C), and (D) do not provide the parallel structure that is needed.

6.   **C.** This answer choice provides parallel structure with the ending "ing." Answer choices (A), (B) and (D) do not provide parallel structure to the sentence.

7.   **C.** Muslims must be capitalized because it is a proper noun referring to a specific group of people. Koran should be also be capitalized, so answer choice (A) is not correct. Answer choice (B) is not accurate because the sentence does not need a shift in verb tense.

8.   **C.** "After they have been" completes the proper time sequence. Choice (A), "when," and choice (B), "will be," are the wrong time sequences.

**9. C.** This is the correct answer because when joining two complete thoughts with a coordinating conjunction, you must have a semicolon at the end of the first complete thought and a comma after the coordinating conjunction. Answer choices (A) and (B) do not provide the correct punctuation needed to construct a complete sentence.

**10. B.** Any specific noun must be capitalized. So, because Mars is a specific planet, it must be capitalized. "Photograph" should not be capitalized because it is a common noun and New York Times should be capitalized and italicized because it is a specific publication.

**11. D.** Choice (A), "upon which," is a correct prepositional phrase. Choice (B), "is based," agrees with its subject, "society." In choice (C), "are" agrees with its subject, "ideals."

**12. B.** Before providing a list, the writer must include a colon, not a semicolon or comma. Therefore, answer choice (B) is the best choice.

**13. B.** Choice (B) should be "depend," not "had depended," because the use of the past perfect would indicate prior past action. There is a series of events in this sentence: first, the legislature "had not finalized" the budget, choice (A); then, Representative Wilson "pointed out" this failure. Choice (B) needs to be present tense as this situation still exists, and choice (C) is a future action.

**14. C.** In order to complete the parallelism, choice (C) should be "arrangements." "To plan" (A) is an infinitive phrase followed by noun objects: "puppet shows and movies" and "garage sales." Choice (B), "used," is a participial modifying "books."

**15. D.** The construction, "than those," clarifies the fact that more vegetables have been added. Choice (C), "your suggestion," does not contain the idea of adding more varieties of vegetables. Choices (A) and (B) end with a redundant preposition.

**16. B.** The voice must be consistent with "I," so choice (B) is the only possible correct answer. All other choices have a noun or pronoun that is not consistent with "I": choice (A), "you," and choice (C), "a person."

**17. D.** The correct answer has two concepts—pieces are missing and pieces will probably never be found. Choice (A) has an incorrect use of the verb, "was." Choice (B) has a singular verb, "is." Choice (C) indicates the pieces "probably will be missing," which is not the problem.

**18. A.** An infinitive, "to understand" should never be split by an adverbial modifier, "completely." Choice (B) "effects" is the noun form and choice (C), "affected" is the adjective form.

**19. B.** "More" is used to compare two things. Since the number of nations is not specified, "more" cannot be used in this sentence. Choice (A) is idiomatically correct; choice (C), "is," agrees in number with its subject, "transportation."

**20. D.** Choice (B) is idiomatically correct. In "someone else" (C), "else" is needed to indicate that a person other than the student would pay the bills. Choice (A) is not correct because "some" refers to two or three and the sentence is discussing a group of graduates.

**21. B.** Choice (B), "to fail," is incorrect in standard written English. The sentence contains two parallel ideas that should be expressed with the same grammatical form. Because "Failing" is a gerund, the infinitive "to fail" should be replaced with "failing" to make the construction parallel.

**22. B.** The reference in choice (B) is vague, making it sound as if the bus made the two students late; therefore, "that" is your best alternative. Answer choice (A) is a correct subject pronoun and answer choice (C) is the correct object pronoun.

**23. B.** In this sentence, the word *neglected* is the best fit because it connotes that something has been forgotten. Choices (A), (C), and (D) all fail to accurately correspond with the first part of the sentence, specifically the phrase "sorry to be late."

**24. C.** The word *insubordinate* means *disrespectful* or *disobedient*. In the context of this sentence, this is fitting because the beginning of the sentence refers to Julie as *not* doing something while the second half of the sentence implies a shift in the character.

**25. D.** The reason for this placement is because the third sentence offers specific details about drama in opera, so, this sentence bridges from the initial sentence about opera.

**26. B.** This sentence is a topic sentence. The rest of the paragraph provides specific details about dolphins and their friendly nature.

**27. C.** Choice (A) uses incorrect grammatical structure. Choice (B) is poorly worded.

**28. C.** Choice (C) is clear and concise and shows the correct comparison of architecture. Choice (A) misuses the preposition "before." Choice (B) is comparing "characteristics," not just architecture.

**29. B.** Choice (B) is clear and direct. Choice (A) is confusing, muddling the meaning of "balancing." Choice (C) has the wrong concept, "balancing games."

**30. B.** Due to the fact that the end of the sentence reads "still being released," the correct verb tense needed is present, "continues." Answer choices (A), (C), and (D) are not grammatically correct.

**31. C.** The original sentence, choice (A), contains the redundant and ungrammatical "which was a man who." Choices (B) and (D) are also unnecessarily verbose. Choice (C) makes the statement in the most direct way possible and represents correct standard usage.

**32. D.** Choice (A), "among," indicates a relationship of more than two things that do not have a one-to-one relationship with each other. The preposition in (B) is correct. "Are" (C), is a plural verb, agreeing in number with "singing, dancing, and cooking."

**33. A.** One is "disappointed by" a person or action, but "disappointed in" something that is not satisfactory. Parallel with "to work," choice (B), "save," has the word "to" omitted. Choice (C) compares the two models, one that is "inexpensive" and one that is "more expensive."

**34. D.** No change is necessary as the wording produces a complete sentence: "rainfall" is the subject and "let up" is the verb. None of the other choices produces a complete sentence.

**35. C.** This choice uses the correct tense, "will have," showing action in the future. All the other verbs listed do not show correct future verb construction.

**36. B.** The correct choice has a compound verb: "comes" and "falls in love." The salesman comes to town first, then meets and falls in love with the librarian. Choice (A), with its misplaced participial phrase, sounds as if either the town or Iowa is in love with the librarian. Choice (C) would produce a run-on sentence.

**37. D.** No change is necessary. Choice (A) misuses the pronoun "his." Choice (B) would produce a run-on sentence. Choice (C) does not indicate whose writings or paintings.

**38. C.** "Relatively" is an adverb that modifies "widely," which is an adverb that modifies the adjective "available"; therefore, the construct in answer choice (C) is the accurate grammatical construct.

**39. C.** The word *related* means "communicated," which fits the context of the sentence.

**40. B.** "Who" is used because it is the subject form and answers the verb "hates."

## Mathematics

**1.  C.**

| | |
|---|---|
| $6[x - 4(2x + 1)]$ | Original problem |
| $6[x - 8x - 4]$ | Use the distributive property to multiply $(-4)$ by $(2x)$ and $(+1)$ |
| $6[-7x - 4]$ | Combine like terms inside the brackets |
| $-42x - 24$ | Use the distributive property to multiply 6 by $(-7x)$ and $(-4)$ |

**2.  B.**

Follow the order of operations to simplify the problem.

| | |
|---|---|
| $9 - 5 \div (8 - 3) \times 3 + 6$ | Original problem |
| $9 - 5 \div (5) \times 3 + 6$ | Simplify within parentheses |
| $9 - 1 \times 3 + 6$ | Divide $(-5)$ by $(+5)$ |
| $9 - 3 + 6$ | Multiply $(-1)$ by $(+3)$ |
| $6 + 6$ | Subtract $(9 - 3)$ |
| $12$ | Solution |

**3.  D.** Since the range is not a measurement of central tendency, we solve for the mean, median, and mode for the given salaries.

**Mean:**   The average of all six salaries

($150,000 + $75,000 + $50,000 + $25,000 + $25,000 + $25,000) ÷ 6 = $58,333

**Median:**  The number that lies directly in the middle of the data sample. Order the numbers from lowest to highest. Since we are given an even amount of terms, the median is the average of the two center numbers.

~~$150,000~~  ~~$75,000~~  $50,000  $25,000  ~~$25,000~~  ~~$25,000~~

($50,000 + $25,000) ÷ 2 = $37,500

**Mode:**   The number that appears most often in the data sample.

$150,000  $75,000  $50,000  $\underline{25,000}$  $\underline{25,000}$  $\underline{25,000}$

$25,000 is the mode.

Since the mean is the highest of the measurements of central tendency, it would be the most likely to entice you to apply to work for this company.

**4. B.** First record what you already know. If the range is 25 to 50, that means 25 is the short workout and 50 is the long workout. You also know that **six** people worked out for an average of 45 minutes. You can calculate the total minutes they all worked out by working backward: $6 \times 45 = 270$ minutes, as shown below

$$25 + \underline{\quad} + \underline{\quad} + \underline{\quad} + \underline{\quad} + 50 = 270$$

Now subtract the numbers you know $(25 + 50)$ from 270. That leaves 195 minutes. The question asks how many people could have worked out for 50 minutes, so how many times can we subtract 50 from 195? Three times: $195 - (50 + 50 + 50) = 45$

Now our workout times look like this:

$$25 + \underline{45} + \underline{50} + \underline{50} + \underline{50} + 50$$

As you can see, four people could have worked out for 50 minutes.

**5. B.** A figure with 1 rectangular base and 4 triangular lateral faces will be a rectangular pyramid. The net below shows the 5 two-dimensional shapes that make up the three-dimensional shape.

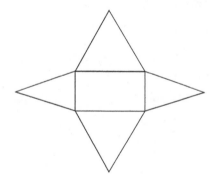

**6. C.** The perimeter of a shape is the distance around it. A rectangle has two equal lengths and two equal widths, as shown below:

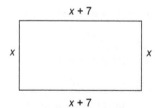

| | |
|---|---|
| $x + (x + 7) + x + (x + 7) = 38$ | Original equation |
| $4x + 14 = 38$ | Combine like terms |
| $4x + 14 - 14 = 38 - 14$ | Subtract 14 from both sides |
| $4x = 24$ | Combine like terms |

$4x \div 4 = 24 \div 4$            Divide both sides by 4

$x = 6$            The width of the rectangle

$x + 7 = 13$            The length of the rectangle

Now solve for the area of the rectangle by multiplying the length by the width: $6 \times 13 = 78$ ft².

7.   **A.** Substitute each choice into the original equation, $y < \frac{1}{2}x - 5$, to identify the choice that is not a solution.

Choice A: $(4, 8)$            $8 < \frac{1}{2}(4) - 5$

                                   $8 < 2 - 5$

                                   $8 < -3$

                                   This is false.

Choice B: $(32, 10)$         $10 < \frac{1}{2}(32) - 5$

                                   $10 < 16 - 5$

                                   $10 < 11$

                                   This is true.

Choice C: $(10, -1)$         $-1 < \frac{1}{2}(10) - 5$

                                   $-1 < 5 - 5$

                                   $-1 < 0$

                                   This is true.

Choice D: $(6, -5)$          $-5 < \frac{1}{2}(6) - 5$

                                   $-5 < 3 - 5$

                                   $-5 < -2$

                                   This is true.

8.   **B.** Substitute $-3$ for $x$, then solve:

$2x^2 + 5x - 3$            The original problem

$2(-3)^2 + 5(-3) - 3$            Substitute $-3$ for $x$

$2(9) + 5(-3) - 3$            Simplify the exponent

$18 - 15 - 3$            Multiply $2 \times 9$ and $5 \times -3$

$0$            Add and subtract from left to right to find the solution.

**9.  A.** This is an example of probability with replacement. Your chance of drawing the first yellow marble is $\dfrac{3}{9}$. Now there are only eight marbles left in the bag. Your chance of drawing the second yellow marble is $\dfrac{2}{8}$. To determine the probability of drawing two yellow marbles, multiply the probability of the individual events: $\dfrac{3}{9} \times \dfrac{2}{8} = \dfrac{6}{72}$. Sometimes on the FTCE, they simplify probability answers; sometimes they do not. If the answer is in simplest form, it would be $\dfrac{1}{12}$.

**10.  D.** When you add or subtract an equal amount to all of the terms in a data set, the standard deviation, or spread of the data, does not change. It will, however, increase or decrease the mean, median, and mode by the amount added or subtracted from each term. In this situation, every term in the data set was increased by $1,000, so the mean, median, and mode all increased by $1,000.

**11.  B.** This problem assesses multiple math skills. First, can you multiply a mixed number by a fraction? Using the distributive property, $1\dfrac{3}{4} \times 4 = (1 \times 4) + \left(\dfrac{3}{4} \times 4\right) = 4\dfrac{12}{4} = 4 + 3 = 7$ pounds of bananas. If you chose to change $1\dfrac{3}{4}$ into an improper fraction before multiplying, then $1\dfrac{3}{4} = \dfrac{7}{4}$, $and$ $\dfrac{7}{4} \times 4 = \dfrac{28}{4} = 7$ pounds. (Either method is acceptable.) Next you have to calculate the weight of the mangos in ounces, then change the total to pounds. (If you chose C, you forgot to do that!) 3 oz. $\times$ 3 = 9 oz., then change ounces to pounds by dividing by 16 since there are 16 ounces in a pound. You will get $\dfrac{9}{16}$ lbs., which is in simplest form. Add that to the 7 pounds of bananas, and the total weight of the fruit is $7\dfrac{9}{16}$ pounds.

**12.  C.** Rather than use algebra to solve this problem, it is much faster to use common sense and work backwards. Ask yourself, how many total points does the student need to get an A? We were given four scores and there is one test left, so there are five total tests. Now calculate the total points needed for a 90% or an A: $5 \times 90 = 450$ points. Next add up the other test scores: $83 + 77 + 100 + 95 = 355$ points. Finally, subtract the 355 from the needed 450 points and you will see that the student needs at least a 95 on the last test to get an A.

**13. C.** First, calculate the volumes of both small boxes and the large box.

Small box 1: 2 cm × 4 cm × 10 cm = 80 cm$^3$
Small box 2: 6 cm × 4 cm × 12 cm = 288 cm$^3$
Large box: 14 cm × 10 cm × 4 cm = 560 cm$^3$

Now subtract the volume of the two smaller boxes from that of the large box:

560 cm$^3$ − (80 cm$^3$ + 288 cm$^3$) = 560 cm$^3$ − 368 cm$^3$ = 192 cm$^3$

After you pack the larger box, you will have 192 cm$^3$ left over.

**14. C.** Multiplying 0.003 and 1.25, we get 0.00375. Since 0.003 has three numbers to the right of the decimal point and 1.25 has two numbers to the right of the decimal point, our answer has three plus two or five numbers to the right of the decimal point. To put this number into scientific notation, we must move the decimal point three places to the right and multiply our new number by 10$^{-3}$ to represent the actual value of the answer: 0.00375 = 3.75 × 10$^{-3}$.

**15. A.** This is a multistep problem using the distance formula, distance = rate × time.

Step 1. Day 1 rate:
distance = rate × time
300 miles = rate × 5 hours
rate = 300 miles/5 hours = 60 mph

Step 2. Day 2 distance:
distance = rate × time
distance = 60 mph × 7 hours
distance = 420 miles

Step 3. Calculate total miles:
Day 1 mileage + Day 2 mileage
300 miles + 420 miles = 720 miles

Step 4. Calculate gas usage (rounded to the hundredths place):
720 miles ÷ 27 mpg = 26.67 gallons

Step 5. Calculate cost of gas:
26.67 gallons × $2.59 a gallon = $69.07

**16. B.** Since these are negative numbers, it is advisable to turn the numbers into decimals rather than use the cross-product method.

$$-\frac{7}{13} = -0.54, \text{ rounded to the hundredths place}$$

$$-\frac{13}{27} = -0.48, \text{ rounded to the hundredths place}$$

When comparing the tenths place of the decimals, 0.5 appears larger than 0.4, but since we are working with negative numbers, the −0.481 would be to the right of −0.538 on the number line, so < makes the inequality true.

**17. B.** All of these expressions are true except for Choice (B). The terms $x^4$ and $x^2$ cannot be subtracted since they are unlike terms and we do not know the value of $x$. (They can, however, be divided, which yields $x^4 \div x^2 = x^2$.)

**18. C.** Note that the line passing through $W$ and $Z$ slants downward as we look at it from left to right. This means the slope should be a negative number. To find the slope of the line passing through the points $(x_1, y_1)$, and $(x_2, y_2)$, we use the formula

$$\text{slope} = \frac{y_2 - y_1}{x_2 - x_1}$$

Our points are $W = (-1, 4)$ and $Z = (2, -2)$ and so our slope is

$$\frac{(-2) - 4}{2 - (-1)} = \frac{-6}{3} = -2$$

**19. B.** This is a multistep problem:

Step 1.   Calculate the current number of teachers based on the 1:30 ratio: $1:30 = \frac{1}{30}$, so we can use this to set up a proportion as shown with $t_1$ representing the current number of teachers and using cross-products to solve for $t_1$.

$$\frac{1}{30} = \frac{t_1}{900}$$

$(1)(900) = (30)(t_1)$

$900 = 30t_1$

$30 = t_1$

Currently there are 30 teachers at the school.

Step 2. Calculate the desired number of teachers ($t_2$) using the same strategy:

The desired ratio is 1:25 or $\dfrac{1}{25}$.

$\dfrac{1}{25} = \dfrac{t_2}{900}$

$(1)(900) = (25)(t_2)$

$900 = 25t_2$

$36 = t_2$

The desired number of teachers is 36.

Step 3. Subtract the current number of teachers from the desired number of teachers to identify how many more teachers your school needs to hire: $36 - 30 = 6$ teachers.

Your school needs to hire 6 teachers to bring the student/teacher ratio to 1:25.

**20. C.** It is important to notice that the coefficient of $x$ is a negative number. This means we will be dividing through the compound inequality by a $-2$, and we will have to flip the signs:

$-24 < -2x < -12$ Write the original problem.

$\dfrac{-24}{-2} > \dfrac{-2x}{-2} > \dfrac{-12}{-2}$ Divide through by $-2$ and flip the signs.

$12 > x > 6$
$6 < x < 12$ Notice that the larger number is now on the left side of the equation. Flip the equation around so the smaller number is on the left, being careful to switch the signs back, as well. Normally on the FTCE, the inequalities are written this way, but either answer, $12 > x > 6$ or $6 < x < 12$ will be correct. You will not be given both choices.

**21. A.** Your first step is to calculate the amount of income that is from their investments: $56,000 − ($24,000 + $24,000) = $8,000. Now find the fraction of income by dividing the amount from the investment by their total income: $\dfrac{\$8000}{\$56,000}$. This simplifies to $\dfrac{1}{7}$. ***Note:*** *If you are asked to find the percent of the income, divide 8,000 by 56,000 with your calculator. You will get 0.143, which is equal to 14.3%.*

**22. B.** To solve this problem you must first calculate the average (mean) for the given salaries:

$$\dfrac{\$18,000 + \$18,000 + \$18,000 + \$19,000 + \$21,000 + \$23,000 + \$24,000 + \$25,000 + \$75,000 + \$95,000}{10} = \$33,600$$

This eliminates Choice (C) since the mean is calculated correctly.

The fact that the employee discount is not listed is not misleading, so Choice (A) can also be eliminated.

The median of the data set is $22,000, which is not higher than the mean, so Choice (D) can also be eliminated.

The correct choice is (B). By averaging in the outliers of the assistant and general managers' salaries, the store misrepresents the salary that is paid to the cashiers, who are the target audience of the sign.

**23. D.** If you were writing an equation for this problem and $t$ represented temperature and $m$ represented the number of meters below the surface, it would be $t = -5m + 65$. Notice that you are multiplying the number of meters by $-5$ since the temperature is dropping by five degrees per meter. Now you can plug in 20 for $m$: $t = -5(20) + 65 = -100 + 65 = -35$. The temperature will be 35 degrees below zero.

**24. C.** To find parallel lines, you have to identify the slope of the lines. Lines that have the same slope are parallel. When an equation is in slope intercept form, $y = mx + b$, $m$ represents the slope. The given line has a slope of $m = 3$. Choice (C) is the only line that also has a slope of 3, so it is parallel to $y = 3x + 2$.

Choice (A), $y = \dfrac{1}{3}x + 2$, has the same $y$-intercept, represented by $b$, but this only denotes where the line crosses the $y$-axis, not whether it is parallel to the original line. Choice (B), $y = -\dfrac{1}{3}x + 4$, is perpendicular to the original line because its slope is the negative inverse of 3. Choice (D), $2y = 6x + 4$, is not in slope-intercept form. If you divided the equation through by 2, you would find that it is the same line as the original equation. Since these lines touch each other at every point, they are not parallel.

**25. B.** To solve this problem, you must calculate the measurements of central tendency for the data set.

| | |
|---|---|
| Choice A: | The range is not a measure of central tendency. |
| Choice B: | To find the mean, take the average of the six numbers: (170,000 + 210,000 + 190,000 + 170,000 + 259,000 + 205,000) ÷ 6 = 1,204,000 ÷ 6 = \$200,666.67 |
| Choice C: | To find the mode, select the home price that is written most often: \$170,000 |
| Choice D: | To calculate the median, put the numbers in order from lowest to highest. Since there are an even number of prices, average the middle two prices. ~~170,000~~ ~~170,000~~ 190,000 205,000 ~~210,000~~ ~~259,000~~ (190,000 + 205,000) ÷ 2 = 395,000 ÷ 2 = \$197,500 The mean is the highest measurement of central tendency. |

**26. A.** The prime numbers between 1 and 6 are 2, 3, and 5. Therefore, the probability that a six-sided die will land on a prime number is $\dfrac{3}{6}$, which can be simplified to $\dfrac{1}{2}$.

**27. C.** The secret to solving this problem is determining the net rate, or combined rates, of the two trains. Since they are driving toward each other, you add the rates. If they had been driving the same direction and one train had been overtaking the other, you would have subtracted the rates. The net rate for the two trains is 60 mph + 40 mph = 100 mph. Now use the distance, rate, and time formula from your math reference guide, $d = r \times t$, to find the time: $200 = 100t$. Once you divide both sides of the equation by 100, you find that the two trains will pass each other in two hours.

**28. B.** Use a table to record the cost of the supplies at each store, after calculating how many items you need to purchase. If you want your students to have two pencils each, you have to purchase 44 pencils. Also, you need one pack of notebook paper per student, so that is 22 packs of paper.

Store A sells pencils by the dozen (12), so you would have to buy four packages of pencils (12 × 4 = 48) to have enough pencils. Store A sells notebook paper in 10-packs, so you would have to buy three 10-packs (3 × 10 = 30) to have enough notebook paper.

At store B, the pencils are sold in tens, so you would have to buy five units to get 44 pencils (5 × 10 = 50). Store B sells paper in 3-packs, so you would have to buy eight 3-packs (8 × 3 = 24) to have enough paper. Now complete the table:

|  | **Pencils** | **Paper** | **Total** |
|---|---|---|---|
| Store A | 4 × $1.29 = $5.16 | 3 × $7.50 = $22.50 | $5.16 + $22.50 = $27.66 |
| Store B | 5 × $1.00 = $5.00 | 8 × $2.50 = $20.00 | $5.00 + $20.00 = $25.00 |

So the least you could spend going to only one store is $25.00.

**29. A.** For this problem, you do not want to actually calculate the mean, median, and mode, but rather think about the spread of the data. If you put these numbers in order from least to greatest, you would have 40, 40, 40, 40, 40, followed by the number 70 twenty-four times, followed by 80. It is obvious that both the median and mode would have to be 70 since 70 is right in the middle of the data set and it occurs the most times. So let's think about the other numbers. Which will have the greatest impact on the mean, the five 40s or the one 80? The five 40s of course, so you know the mean will be lower than 70. The range is not a measure of central tendency, so the mean is the correct answer.

**30.  A.** Simplify by using the order of operations.

| | |
|---|---|
| $150 \div (6 + 3 \times 8) - 5$ | The problem |
| $150 \div (6 + 24) - 5$ | Simplify inside parentheses $(3 \times 8)$ |
| $150 \div (30) - 5$ | Simplify inside parentheses $(6 + 24)$ |
| $5 - 5$ | Divide 150 by 30 |
| $0$ | Subtract |

**31.  B.** The first step to solving this problem is understanding a frequency chart where each tally mark represents one score, and the frequency column gives you the sum of the tallies in each row. You do not have to write down all of the numbers in order to find the median since the numbers are already in order from least to greatest on the chart. Think about your data set. If you added up the tallies, you will see you have 26 scores on your chart. This means your median will be the average of the two most center terms. If you think about the fact that 26 divided by 2 is 13, you can deduce that the two center terms will fall in the 13th and 14th position. By counting tally marks, you will find

that the 13th term is 7 and the 14th is 8. The average of these two terms is $\dfrac{7+8}{2} = \dfrac{15}{2} = 7\dfrac{1}{2}$ or 7.5.

| Mark | Tally | Frequency | |
|---|---|---|---|
| 4 | I I | 2 | |
| 5 | I I | 2 | |
| 6 | I I I I | 4 | |
| 7 | I I I I I | 5 | Term 13 |
| 8 | I I I I | 4 | |
| 9 | I I I I I I | 6 | |
| 10 | I I I | 3 | Term 14 |

**32.  D.** To compare these numbers, change the square root to a whole number, and place them on a number line.

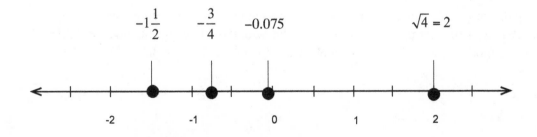

As you can see, with negative numbers, the larger the number appears (ignoring the negative sign), the smaller the actual magnitude of the number. This means $-\frac{3}{4}$ is smaller than $-0.075$, but it is larger than $-1$. The positive number is obviously larger than all of the negative numbers.

**33. A.** Choice (A) is false since Mouse 3 showed no improvement from Trial 1 to Trial 3. All the other statements are supported by the data in the table.

**34. B.** If you analyze the compound inequality $1 < x < 6$, you can break it into two separate statements: $x > 1$ **and** $x < 6$. This means the solution is the overlap of these two statements, as seen in Graph B. Graph A is incorrect because it matches $1 \le x \le 6$, read "one is less than or equal to $x$ which is less than or equal to 6." Graph C reads $x < 1$ or $x > 6$.

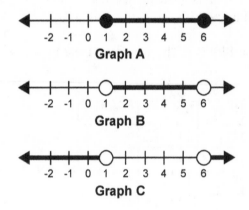

**35. A.** The third column shows which of the outcomes have two heads and as a result, only one tail. Count them to see that only three of the eight outcomes have two heads and one tail. Therefore, the probability is $\frac{3}{8}$.

**36. C.** First we can create an equation to represent the number of dogs and people in the kennel. Since there are 30 heads, the number of dogs plus the number of people can be represented by $d + p = 30$.

Each dog has 4 legs, represented by $4d$. Each person has 2 legs, represented by $2p$. There are a total of 104 legs in the barn, so we can represent this with the following equation: $2p + 4d = 104$.

The equations needed to solve this problem are $d + p = 30$ and $2p + 4d = 104$.

**37. B.** The key to this problem is to recognize that the equation represents the profit in thousands. You must use 60, not 60,000, for $f$. Looking at the equation, it is apparent that $x$ represents the year, since 2005 also is in the format of a date. Most likely that is the year the company began. Even after you have drawn these conclusions, the equation can be difficult to solve due to the fraction, $\frac{4}{3}$. By multiplying both sides of the inverse of the fraction, you can eliminate it, as shown below:

$f = \frac{4}{3}(x - 2005) + 32$        original equation

$60 = \frac{4}{3}(x - 2005) + 32$        plug in 60 for $f$

$-32 \qquad\qquad\quad -32$        subtract 32 from both sides

$28 = \frac{4}{3}(x - 2005)$

$\left(\frac{3}{4}\right)28 = \left(\frac{3}{4}\right)\left(\frac{4}{3}\right)(x - 2005)$        multiply both sides by $\frac{3}{4}$, eliminating the $\frac{4}{3}$ on the right side of the equation

$\frac{3 \times 28}{4} = (x - 2005)$

$21 = x - 2005$        multiply $\frac{3}{4} \times 28$

$+2005 \quad +2005$        add 2005 to each side

$2026 = x$        solution

The company will make a profit of 60 thousand dollars in 2026.

**38. D.** Begin by finding the number of tiles needed per square foot by finding the area of one square tile: 8 in. × 8 in. = 64 square inches. Next find the area of one square foot in inches: 12 in. × 12 in. = 144 square inches. Finally you divided the 144 square inches by the 64 square inches in one tile: 144 ÷ 64 = 2.25. You need 2.25 tiles for each square foot of the bathroom.

Now find the area of the room in square feet (12 ft. × 16 ft. = 192 ft$^2$), then multiply the area of the room by the number of tiles per square foot: 192 × 2.25 = 432. You need 432 tiles.

**39. D.** To add these fractions, we must find a common denominator for the $\frac{1}{2}$ cup flour and the $\frac{1}{3}$ cup salt. We do not need to include the water since the problem only asks for the volume of the dry ingredients. The least common multiple (LCM) of 2 and 3 is 6, so we rewrite the expression so that both fractions have 6 as a common denominator: $\frac{1}{2} = \frac{3}{6}$ and $\frac{1}{3} = \frac{2}{6}$. We can now solve the problem: $\frac{3}{6} + \frac{2}{6} = \frac{5}{6}$ cup of dry ingredients in one batch of the recipe. Since the teacher is making four batches, we now multiply $\frac{5}{6}$ by 4 to get $\frac{20}{6}$ cups of dry ingredients. Simplified, this is equal to $3\frac{1}{3}$ cups of dry ingredients.

**40. A.** For a figure to be a function, it has to pass the vertical line test. No vertical line may pass through the figure at more than one point. Choice (A), a vertical line, would be covered completely during a vertical line test, so this figure is not a function.

**41. A.** This is a rigorous, multistep problem. First of all, for this problem it is best to use the answer choices to identify the correct answer. From the word problem, we know that there needs to be a 4-hour difference between $t_1$ and $t_2$, or $t_2 - t_1 = 4$. We also can use the distance = rate × time formula, first with $r_1$ equal to 60 mph, and second with $r_2$ equal to 30 mph. We can then substitute in the given distances until we find a combination that yields a 4-hour difference in arrival times, as shown in the table.

|  | $d_1 = 60 \times t_1$ | $d_2 = 30 \times t_2 =$ | $t_2 - t_1 =$ | Result |
|---|---|---|---|---|
| 60 miles | $60 = 60 \times t_1$ <br> $t_1 = 1$ hour | $60 = 30 \times t_2$ <br> $t_2 = 2$ hours | 2 hrs – 1 hr = 1 hr | This means arriving 30 minutes early or 30 minutes late. |
| 120 miles | $120 = 60 \times t_1$ <br> $t_1 = 2$ hours | $120 = 30 \times t_2$ <br> $t_2 = 4$ hours | 4 hrs – 2 hrs = 2 hrs | This means arriving one hour early or one hour late. |
| 180 miles | $180 = 60 \times t_1$ <br> $t_1 = 3$ hours | $180 = 30 \times t_2$ <br> $t_2 = 6$ hours | 6 hrs – 3 hrs = 3 hrs | This means arriving 1.5 hours early or 1.5 hours late. |
| 240 miles | $240 = 60 \times t_1$ <br> $t_1 = 4$ hours | $240 = 30 \times t_2$ <br> $t_2 = 8$ hours | 8 hrs – 4 hrs = 4 hrs | This means that if you travel at 60 mph you will arrive 2 hours early and if you drive at 30 mph, you will arrive 2 hours late. |

Only the selection of 240 miles will result in a four-hour difference between arrival times, so this is the correct answer.

**42. B.** When you look at the relationship between the year and profit for Company A, you will always see that the profit in millions is twice the value of the year. Even though the chart does not give data for years 4, 6, 7, 8, or 9, based on the data provided, the company showed an increase of 2 million per year. (A) is incorrect because in year 5, Company A made 10 million and Company B made 9 million. (C) is incorrect because in no year did the company show an increase of 3 million from the year before. (D) is incorrect because only in year 1 did the companies have the same profit.

**43. C.** This is actually a very simple problem if you understand central tendency. Begin with what you know. If two children are 5 and the median is 9, we know over half of the puzzle:

5, 5, 9, ___, ____

Now we use what we learned about the range of the data. If you subtracted the lowest age from the highest age it would equal seven, so adding seven to the lowest age will give us the highest age:

5, 5, 9, ___, 5 + 7
5, 5, 9, ___, 12

So what ages COULD be in the second to the oldest spot? You may think that your only choices are 10 or 11, but the numbers 9 or 12 would also work since we were not given a mode for our data set. Of your choices in the problem, only 9 would satisfy the given parameters.

**44. B.** The simplest way to solve this problem is to write down the possible combinations of red, blue, and green chips and eliminate any instances where green is in the middle:

| Red First | Blue First | Green First |
|-----------|------------|-------------|
| RBG | BRG | GRB |
| ~~RGB~~ | ~~BGR~~ | GBR |

There are four combinations that do not have green in the middle, so the probability of having blue and red next to each other is $\frac{4}{6}$ or $\frac{2}{3}$. ***Note:*** *The test does not always simplify probability, so be prepared to look for either answer. You will never see both choices in the same problem.*

**45. B.** This problem can be solved with a proportion:

$$\frac{\frac{3}{4} \ inches}{40 \ miles} = \frac{x}{280 \ miles}$$

Notice that 280 is 7 times 40, so rather than use cross product, you can rename the fractions:

$$\frac{\frac{3}{4} \ inches}{40 \ miles} \times \frac{7}{7} = \frac{7x\frac{3}{4}}{280 \ miles}$$

Now multiply $7 \times \frac{3}{4}$:

$$7 \times \frac{3}{4} = \frac{21}{4} = 5\frac{1}{4}$$

Key West is $5\frac{1}{4}$ inches from Orlando on the map.

## Reading

**1.   B.** Answer choice (B) is the best choice because Passage 2 outlines "risks" for small businesses which is synonymous with "drawbacks."

**2.   D.** Passage 2 discusses many of the circumstances that surround a certain condition or challenge in the minority-owned business. Passage 2 does not provide evidence to support the other inquiries fully.

**3.   C.** Answer choice (C) is the best option because Passage 1 discusses the challenges created by large corporations and securing businesses within them as a key supporting detail. The other answer choices do not accurately provide a disadvantage discussed by the author.

**4.   A.** The author mentions the idea of subcontracts and the frustration involved in order to discuss the effect on the company by saying, "show both consume valuable time and resources and a small company's efforts." Therefore, answer (A) represents this idea communicated by the author most accurately.

**5.   C.** Answer choice (C) is the best option because the author discusses why a minority business owner would not want to be too dependent on one large corporation. The other answer choices are not accurate based on the key details of the passage.

**6.   C.** Answer choice (C) is the best answer because the selection does not discuss federal and local agencies being connected with less controversy. The other answer choices are supporting details found in Passage 1.

**7.   D.** Answer choice (D) provides the best argument that could be applied to the context of the selection and weaken the writer's position. This statistic shows the strength of the relationship between the corporate entity and federal requirements over the decade of 1970 to 1980, but does not show growth or the response being "substantial." The other answer choices would not provide further evidence to weaken the author's position.

**8.   A.** The central idea of Passage 1 is that minority-owned businesses have new opportunities. Therefore, the author would generally revert back to this central claim when faced with drawbacks or risks of minority-owned businesses.

**9.   B.** The word *complacency* is most consistent with the definition of being smug or self-satisfied. Within this context, the relationship is between the companies' success and the struggle ensuing.

**10. D.** The passage provides analytical detail mostly focused on a phenomenon. The author does not "raise new issues," "explain an enigma," or "refute misconceptions" within the passage.

**11. C.** The author discusses how and why indigo buntings learn from one another, answer choice (C). Therefore, this is the fundamental connection between the number of figures and the general nature of bunting birds.

**12. D.** Answers (A), (B), and (C) could reasonably be assumed because each key idea supported by details was mentioned in the selection.

**13. D.** The author discusses the enhancement of species recognition, so the inference found in answer choice (D) is logical.

**14. B.** This is the most logical inference because the example within the question relates most closely to "*visual cues*" and a dummy is a model of an indigo bunting bird.

**15. A.** The word *modulated* in this context is consistent with the terms *regulated* or *modified*. The other answer choices do not provide an appropriate definition of the word *modulated* that fits the context of the sentence.

**16. D.** The supporting details of the passage are most accurately summarized by the bunting bird being defined and sustained. The experimentation communicated by the author proves the importance and supports this as the passage's central claim. While (A), (B), and (C) are mentioned, they are not the primary focus.

**17. A.** The passage addresses the key words in this order: *song, copy, characterize, recognize*. While the other terms are an effect of the passage, they are not sequenced accurately. A song is created by an indigo bunting bird, copied by other bunting birds, characterized by a group of birds, and recognized by a larger population of indigo bunting birds.

**18. D.** At the beginning of the passage, the author discusses the relationship between population density and male adaptability. Then, the author follows that discussion with a conclusion based on the weakest males not breeding.

**19. A.** The author of the passage uses this quote to demonstrate that there is a causal relationship. This is supported through the quote from the author, "in the volition of the figures, we tested species recognition of a song." Then, he explains this relationship through the testing described.

**20. C.** The author of the passage mentions the key details found in (A), (B), and (D) but not (C).

**21. B.** The word *temporal* is closest in meaning to *mundane* and fits the context of the passage.

**22. D.** The word *probably* refers to the idea that the statement is opinion oriented and not absolutely fact-based. Answer choices (A), (B), and (C) focus on facts provided by the author of the passage.

**23. A.** The author provides this data in order to show that due to this high percentage, there is a clear relationship between the number of figures and geographical stability.

**24. C.** At the beginning of the second paragraph, the author discusses the idea of testing species recognition of song. Then he mentions distinguishing the song of one species from another which supports answer choice (C).

**25. B.** According to the conclusion at the end of the passage, the author mentions species recognition and song variation leading to individual recognition which are the results mentioned in (B).

**26. C.** The passage clearly speaks about the relationship between the song and the bird. Therefore, it is a logical assumption that the phrase "Bunting Song" would summarize the image based on information in the passage.

**27. C.** Douglass was interested in raising social consciousness about slavery and the primary avenue for logically accomplishing this goal was by refuting those who doubted his claim to have been a slave.

**28. B.** Choice (B) is supported by the key ideas in Passage 1. All of the other answer choices offer specific details that could be verified through the passage, but not the central claim made by the author.

**29. A.** Mr. Auld communicated his concern that Douglass would no longer fit into slavery if he became educated. The author provides this information in order to show that the paradigm or structure in which Douglass lived was built on a set of assumptions that would affect his circumstances.

**30. B.** The reason the author provides this evidence is to point to the other opportunities that Douglass was "thrust" into after his speech.

**31. A.** An *impromptu* speech is one given suddenly without preparation.

**32. B.** In Passage 1, the author discusses biographical information regarding Douglass while Passage 2 focuses on Douglass's autobiographical writing and the courageous steps chosen by Douglass throughout his lifetime.

**33. A.** The word *inherent* refers to something that is naturally occurring (A).

**34. C.** The passages specifically mention the ideas found in (A), (B), and (D), but not "uninteresting topics."

**35. A.** The author states that the difficulties of the texts are inherent (or natural) and then provides a discussion about the technical concept load found within social studies texts.

**36. A.** The author uses two rhetorical questions, or inquiries to make a point rather than providing imagery, hyperbole, or symbolism.

**37. B.** The rationale for mentioning this idea of "thin discussions" is to support the evidence that there is a lack of profitable knowledge in social studies books.

**38. C.** The ideas of pronouncing a difficult word, understanding/recognizing what it means and then the ability to utilize that word is the order of concepts provided by the author of Passage 2. The other answer choices provide words that were mentioned in the passage, but not in the appropriate order.

**39. D.** The main idea of sentence 1 is that the difficulty in social studies texts stems from the technical concept load while sentence 2 defines this central idea by telling what technical concepts are in the context of this passage to provide clarity to the reader.

**40. C.** A *critical* attitude is one that details the problematic nature of a situation or item. Therefore, as the author details the problem with the concepts found in social studies texts, he is mostly critical, not skeptical, inconclusive or optimistic.

# PRACTICE TEST 2

# FTCE General Knowledge

# Answer Sheet

## English Language Skills

| | | | |
|---|---|---|---|
| 1. Ⓐ Ⓑ Ⓒ Ⓓ | 11. Ⓐ Ⓑ Ⓒ Ⓓ | 21. Ⓐ Ⓑ Ⓒ Ⓓ | 31. Ⓐ Ⓑ Ⓒ Ⓓ |
| 2. Ⓐ Ⓑ Ⓒ Ⓓ | 12. Ⓐ Ⓑ Ⓒ Ⓓ | 22. Ⓐ Ⓑ Ⓒ Ⓓ | 32. Ⓐ Ⓑ Ⓒ Ⓓ |
| 3. Ⓐ Ⓑ Ⓒ Ⓓ | 13. Ⓐ Ⓑ Ⓒ Ⓓ | 23. Ⓐ Ⓑ Ⓒ Ⓓ | 33. Ⓐ Ⓑ Ⓒ Ⓓ |
| 4. Ⓐ Ⓑ Ⓒ Ⓓ | 14. Ⓐ Ⓑ Ⓒ Ⓓ | 24. Ⓐ Ⓑ Ⓒ Ⓓ | 34. Ⓐ Ⓑ Ⓒ Ⓓ |
| 5. Ⓐ Ⓑ Ⓒ Ⓓ | 15. Ⓐ Ⓑ Ⓒ Ⓓ | 25. Ⓐ Ⓑ Ⓒ Ⓓ | 35. Ⓐ Ⓑ Ⓒ Ⓓ |
| 6. Ⓐ Ⓑ Ⓒ Ⓓ | 16. Ⓐ Ⓑ Ⓒ Ⓓ | 26. Ⓐ Ⓑ Ⓒ Ⓓ | 36. Ⓐ Ⓑ Ⓒ Ⓓ |
| 7. Ⓐ Ⓑ Ⓒ Ⓓ | 17. Ⓐ Ⓑ Ⓒ Ⓓ | 27. Ⓐ Ⓑ Ⓒ Ⓓ | 37. Ⓐ Ⓑ Ⓒ Ⓓ |
| 8. Ⓐ Ⓑ Ⓒ Ⓓ | 18. Ⓐ Ⓑ Ⓒ Ⓓ | 28. Ⓐ Ⓑ Ⓒ Ⓓ | 38. Ⓐ Ⓑ Ⓒ Ⓓ |
| 9. Ⓐ Ⓑ Ⓒ Ⓓ | 19. Ⓐ Ⓑ Ⓒ Ⓓ | 29. Ⓐ Ⓑ Ⓒ Ⓓ | 39. Ⓐ Ⓑ Ⓒ Ⓓ |
| 10. Ⓐ Ⓑ Ⓒ Ⓓ | 20. Ⓐ Ⓑ Ⓒ Ⓓ | 30. Ⓐ Ⓑ Ⓒ Ⓓ | 40. Ⓐ Ⓑ Ⓒ Ⓓ |

## Mathematics

| | | | |
|---|---|---|---|
| 1. Ⓐ Ⓑ Ⓒ Ⓓ | 13. Ⓐ Ⓑ Ⓒ Ⓓ | 24. Ⓐ Ⓑ Ⓒ Ⓓ | 35. Ⓐ Ⓑ Ⓒ Ⓓ |
| 2. Ⓐ Ⓑ Ⓒ Ⓓ | 14. Ⓐ Ⓑ Ⓒ Ⓓ | 25. Ⓐ Ⓑ Ⓒ Ⓓ | 36. Ⓐ Ⓑ Ⓒ Ⓓ |
| 3. Ⓐ Ⓑ Ⓒ Ⓓ | 15. Ⓐ Ⓑ Ⓒ Ⓓ | 26. Ⓐ Ⓑ Ⓒ Ⓓ | 37. Ⓐ Ⓑ Ⓒ Ⓓ |
| 4. Ⓐ Ⓑ Ⓒ Ⓓ | 16. Ⓐ Ⓑ Ⓒ Ⓓ | 27. Ⓐ Ⓑ Ⓒ Ⓓ | 38. Ⓐ Ⓑ Ⓒ Ⓓ |
| 5. Ⓐ Ⓑ Ⓒ Ⓓ | 17. Ⓐ Ⓑ Ⓒ Ⓓ | 28. Ⓐ Ⓑ Ⓒ Ⓓ | 39. Ⓐ Ⓑ Ⓒ Ⓓ |
| 6. Ⓐ Ⓑ Ⓒ Ⓓ | 18. Ⓐ Ⓑ Ⓒ Ⓓ | 29. Ⓐ Ⓑ Ⓒ Ⓓ | 40. Ⓐ Ⓑ Ⓒ Ⓓ |
| 7. Ⓐ Ⓑ Ⓒ Ⓓ | 19. Ⓐ Ⓑ Ⓒ Ⓓ | 30. Ⓐ Ⓑ Ⓒ Ⓓ | 41. Ⓐ Ⓑ Ⓒ Ⓓ |
| 8. Ⓐ Ⓑ Ⓒ Ⓓ | 20. Ⓐ Ⓑ Ⓒ Ⓓ | 31. Ⓐ Ⓑ Ⓒ Ⓓ | 42. Ⓐ Ⓑ Ⓒ Ⓓ |
| 9. Ⓐ Ⓑ Ⓒ Ⓓ | 21. Ⓐ Ⓑ Ⓒ Ⓓ | 32. Ⓐ Ⓑ Ⓒ Ⓓ | 43. Ⓐ Ⓑ Ⓒ Ⓓ |
| 10. Ⓐ Ⓑ Ⓒ Ⓓ | 22. Ⓐ Ⓑ Ⓒ Ⓓ | 33. Ⓐ Ⓑ Ⓒ Ⓓ | 44. Ⓐ Ⓑ Ⓒ Ⓓ |
| 11. Ⓐ Ⓑ Ⓒ Ⓓ | 23. Ⓐ Ⓑ Ⓒ Ⓓ | 34. Ⓐ Ⓑ Ⓒ Ⓓ | 45. Ⓐ Ⓑ Ⓒ Ⓓ |
| 12. Ⓐ Ⓑ Ⓒ Ⓓ | | | |

## Reading

| | | | |
|---|---|---|---|
| 1. Ⓐ Ⓑ Ⓒ Ⓓ | 11. Ⓐ Ⓑ Ⓒ Ⓓ | 21. Ⓐ Ⓑ Ⓒ Ⓓ | 31. Ⓐ Ⓑ Ⓒ Ⓓ |
| 2. Ⓐ Ⓑ Ⓒ Ⓓ | 12. Ⓐ Ⓑ Ⓒ Ⓓ | 22. Ⓐ Ⓑ Ⓒ Ⓓ | 32. Ⓐ Ⓑ Ⓒ Ⓓ |
| 3. Ⓐ Ⓑ Ⓒ Ⓓ | 13. Ⓐ Ⓑ Ⓒ Ⓓ | 23. Ⓐ Ⓑ Ⓒ Ⓓ | 33. Ⓐ Ⓑ Ⓒ Ⓓ |
| 4. Ⓐ Ⓑ Ⓒ Ⓓ | 14. Ⓐ Ⓑ Ⓒ Ⓓ | 24. Ⓐ Ⓑ Ⓒ Ⓓ | 34. Ⓐ Ⓑ Ⓒ Ⓓ |
| 5. Ⓐ Ⓑ Ⓒ Ⓓ | 15. Ⓐ Ⓑ Ⓒ Ⓓ | 25. Ⓐ Ⓑ Ⓒ Ⓓ | 35. Ⓐ Ⓑ Ⓒ Ⓓ |
| 6. Ⓐ Ⓑ Ⓒ Ⓓ | 16. Ⓐ Ⓑ Ⓒ Ⓓ | 26. Ⓐ Ⓑ Ⓒ Ⓓ | 36. Ⓐ Ⓑ Ⓒ Ⓓ |
| 7. Ⓐ Ⓑ Ⓒ Ⓓ | 17. Ⓐ Ⓑ Ⓒ Ⓓ | 27. Ⓐ Ⓑ Ⓒ Ⓓ | 37. Ⓐ Ⓑ Ⓒ Ⓓ |
| 8. Ⓐ Ⓑ Ⓒ Ⓓ | 18. Ⓐ Ⓑ Ⓒ Ⓓ | 28. Ⓐ Ⓑ Ⓒ Ⓓ | 38. Ⓐ Ⓑ Ⓒ Ⓓ |
| 9. Ⓐ Ⓑ Ⓒ Ⓓ | 19. Ⓐ Ⓑ Ⓒ Ⓓ | 29. Ⓐ Ⓑ Ⓒ Ⓓ | 39. Ⓐ Ⓑ Ⓒ Ⓓ |
| 10. Ⓐ Ⓑ Ⓒ Ⓓ | 20. Ⓐ Ⓑ Ⓒ Ⓓ | 30. Ⓐ Ⓑ Ⓒ Ⓓ | 40. Ⓐ Ⓑ Ⓒ Ⓓ |

# Practice Test 2: Essay

50 Minutes

**Directions:** You will have 50 minutes to plan, write, and proofread an ORIGINAL essay on the topic presented. READ THE TOPIC CAREFULLY TO MAKE SURE THAT YOU KNOW WHAT YOU ARE BEING ASKED TO DO.

You must write an <u>original essay that specifically and directly responds to the topic</u>. Pre-prepared essays or essays that are discovered to contain memorized sentences or pre-prepared passages will be invalidated. For example, if the essay raters discover passages that appear in two or more essays, the essays and the violation will be brought to the attention of the Florida Department of Education and may result in the invalidation of your scores.

Your essay should introduce the topic and then explain the topic and/or take a position on the topic and support that position. In order for your essay to be scored, it <u>must address the entire topic</u>.

At least two raters will read your essay, and each will assign it a score. Your essay will not be scored on the position you take or the opinions you express. Your essay will be evaluated holistically according to the following criteria:

| Category | Description |
|---|---|
| Focus | The extent to which the essay states and maintains a main idea or thesis. |
| Organization | The extent to which the essay uses organizational strategies to enhance meaning and clarity. |
| Support | The extent to which the essay provides reasoned, relevant, and specific support to develop the main idea or thesis. |
| Grammar, Sentence Structure, and Usage | The extent to which the essay uses accurate grammar, effective, varied sentence structure, and appropriate, precise usage. |
| Conventions | The extent to which the essay demonstrates the ability to spell common words and to use the conventions of capitalization and punctuation accurately. |

Before you start writing, take a few minutes to plan what you want to say. Also, be sure to leave yourself a few minutes to proofread and make corrections.

| Topic |
| --- |
| Some schools believe that online learning is a critical aspect of student preparation in the 21st century. Some believe that this is advantageous while others do not agree. Analyze the advantages and disadvantages of this type of learning. |

# Practice Test 2: English Language Skills

40 Minutes

40 Questions

**DIRECTIONS:** Read each question and select the best response.

1. **DIRECTIONS:** Choose the sentence in which the modifiers are correctly placed.

   A. Eagerly awaiting her birthday, Mary's presents were all picked up and admired by Mary many times throughout the course of the day.

   B. Eagerly awaiting her birthday, Mary picked up and admired her presents many times throughout the day.

   C. The birthday she had been eagerly awaiting, her presents picked and admired many times.

   D. The birthday Mary had picked and was eagerly awaiting presents through the day.

2. **DIRECTIONS:** Choose the sentence in which the modifiers are correctly placed.

   A. Tired of all of the nights in hotels, Mitch was delighted when his boss finally said he didn't have to travel anymore.

   B. Mitch was delighted in all of the nights at the hotel so he didn't have to travel anymore.

   C. Tired of all of the nights in hotels, Mitch's delight was felt by Mitch when his boss finally said he didn't have to travel anymore.

   D. Mitch was staying in so many hotels that he told his boss he would not travel anymore.

3. **DIRECTIONS:** Choose the option that corrects an error in the underlined portion(s). If no error exists, choose "No change is necessary."

   > Erasmus's tomb lies inside the Basel Munster, located in Switzerland, an architectural monument which having survived medieval earthquakes, and remains one of Switzerland's most well-known buildings to this day.

   A. Erasmus's tomb lies inside the Basel Munster, located in Switzerland, an architectural monument which having survived medieval earthquakes, and

   B. Switzerland's Basel Munster, an architectural monument that survived medieval earthquakes, houses Erasmus's tomb,

   C. The tomb of Erasmus, being housed inside Switzerland's Basel Munster, is an architectural monument that survived medieval earthquakes and

   D. Erasmus's tomb lies inside Switzerland's Basel Munster, an architectural monument that survived medieval earthquakes and

4.  **DIRECTIONS:** Choose the correct word or phrase that provides parallel structure to the sentence.

    The eighteenth century Scottish philosopher Adam Smith asserted that a nation achieves the best economic results when individuals work both for their own interests and to _____.

    A.  gain more goods.

    B.  gain goods.

    C.  their own gain.

    D.  gain the most goods.

5.  **DIRECTIONS:** Choose the correct word or phrase that provides parallel structure to the sentence.

    _____ an ancient language like Latin or Greek is one way to discover the roots of Western culture; studying Judeo-Christian religious beliefs is another.

    A.  Learning

    B.  To learn

    C.  From learning

    D.  The learning

6.  **DIRECTIONS:** Choose the option that corrects an error in the underlined portion(s). If no error exists, choose "No change is necessary."

    Writing an additional sentence for each paragraph you have is easier than the writing of a brand new paragraph altogether.

    A.  one's writing of

    B.  writing

    C.  to write

    D.  when you must write

7.  **DIRECTIONS:** Choose the option that corrects an error in the underlined portion(s). If no error exists, choose "No change is necessary."

    The freshman curriculum at the community college includes <u>English</u>,
    A

    a foreign language, <u>algebra I</u> and <u>history</u>.
            B          C

    A.  english

    B.  Algebra I

    C.  History

    D.  No change is necessary

8.  **DIRECTIONS:** Choose the option that corrects an error in the underlined portion(s). If no error exists, choose "No change is necessary."

    Both professional and amateur ornithologists, <u>people who study birds</u>, recognize the Latin or scientific names of bird species.

    A.  people that study birds

    B.  people which study birds

    C.  the study of birds

    D.  No change is necessary.

9.  **DIRECTIONS:** Choose the option that corrects an error in the underlined portion(s). If no error exists, choose "No change is necessary."

    Among the states that seceded from the Union to join the Confederacy in 1860–1861 <u>were;</u> Mississippi, Florida, and Alabama.

    A.  were

    B.  were,

    C.  were:

    D.  No change is necessary

10. **DIRECTIONS:** Choose the option that corrects an error in the underlined portion(s). If no error exists, choose "No change is necessary."

The fall of the Berlin wall was an important symbol of the collapse of
              A      B

the government.
    C

A. Berlin Wall

B. could be

C. Government

D. No change is necessary

11. **DIRECTIONS:** Choose the option that corrects an error in the underlined portion(s). If no error exists, choose "No change is necessary."

The U.S. Constitution supposes what the history of all governments
             A

demonstrate, that the executive is the branch most interested in war and
    B                          C

most prone to it.

A. constitution supposes

B. demonstrates

C. more

D. No change is necessary.

12. **DIRECTIONS:** Choose the option that corrects an error in the underlined portion(s). If no error exists, choose "No change is necessary."

Senators and representatives can be reelected indefinitely: a president can
only serve two terms.

A. indefinitely but a

B. indefinitely; a

C. indefinitely, a

D. No change is necessary

13. **DIRECTIONS:** Choose the option that corrects an error in the underlined portion(s). If no error exists, choose "No change is necessary."

> <u>Nearly</u> one hundred years after the impoverished Vincent van Gogh died, his
>   **A**
>
> paintings <u>had sold</u> for more than <u>a million dollars.</u>
>   **B**            **C**

A. Near

B. have been selling

C. $1 million

D. No change is necessary.

14. **DIRECTIONS:** Choose the option that corrects an error in the underlined portion(s). If no error exists, choose "No change is necessary."

> Many athletes recruited for football by college coaches <u>expect</u> that they
>         **A**
>
> will, <u>in fact,</u> receive an education when they <u>accept</u> a scholarship.
>   **B**            **C**

A. believe

B. and should

C. except

D. No change is necessary.

15. **DIRECTIONS:** Choose the option that corrects an error in the underlined portion(s). If no error exists, choose "No change is necessary."

> Although Carmen developed an interest in classical music, <u>she did not read
> notes and had never played an instrument.</u>

A. she has never read notes and had never played an instrument

B. she does not read notes and has never played an instrument

C. it is without being able to read notes or having played an instrument

D. No change is necessary.

16. **DIRECTIONS:** Choose the option that corrects an error in the underlined portion(s). If no error exists, choose "No change is necessary."

> Political candidates must campaign on issues and ideas that strike a chord with their constituency but <u>with their goal to sway</u> undecided voters to support their candidacy.

A. within their goal to sway

B. need also to sway

C. aiming at the same time to sway

D. No change is necessary.

17. **DIRECTIONS:** Choose the option that corrects an error in the underlined portion(s). If no error exists, choose "No change is necessary."

> The major reasons students give for failing courses in college <u>is that they have demanding professors and work at</u> full- or part-time jobs.

A. are demanding professors, in addition to working at

B. are demanding professors and they work at

C. are that they have demanding professors and that they have

D. No change is necessary.

18. **DIRECTIONS:** Choose the option that corrects an error in the underlined portion(s).

> <u>Hopefully</u>, by the end of the <u>twentieth century</u>, computer scientists
>        A                                             B
>
> would invent machines with enough intelligence to work without
> breaking down <u>on</u> a regular <u>basis</u>.
>                  C              D

A. It was hoped that

B. Twentieth century

C. for

D. bases

19. **DIRECTIONS:** Choose the option that corrects an error in the underlined portion(s). If no error exists, choose "No change is necessary."

> Studies <u>showing</u> that the earth includes a <u>vast series</u> of sedimentary rocks,
>       A                                  B
>
> some with <u>embedded</u> fossils that prove the existence of ancient organisms.
>              C

  A.    show

  B.    series

  C.    embedding

  D.    No change is necessary.

20. **DIRECTIONS:** Choose the option that corrects an error in the underlined portion(s). If no error exists, choose "No change is necessary."

> When Martin Luther King, Jr., wrote his famous letter from the
>
> Birmingham jail, he advocated neither evading <u>or</u> defying the law; <u>but</u> he
>                                       A                     B
>
> accepted the idea that a penalty <u>results from</u> breaking law, even an unjust
>                                          C
>
> one.

  A.    nor

  B.    not

  C.    resulting from

  D.    No change is necessary.

21. **DIRECTIONS:** Choose the option that corrects an error in the underlined portion(s). If no error exists, choose "No change is necessary."

> <u>Having minimal exposure</u> to poetry when they attended school, most
>              A
>
> Americans <u>chose</u> to watch television or <u>to read</u> popular magazines for
>            B                             C
>
> entertainment.

  A.    Having a minimum of exposure

  B.    choose

  C.    to reading

  D.    No change is necessary.

22. **DIRECTIONS:** Choose the option that corrects an error in the underlined portion(s).

What makes <u>we</u> humans <u>different from</u> other animals <u>can be defined</u>
              A                  B                             C

at least partly by our powerful and <u>efficient</u> intelligence.
                                          D

- A. us
- B. different than
- C. is to be defined
- D. proficient

23. **DIRECTIONS:** Choose the most effective word or phrase within the context suggested by the sentence.

Can you _____ me on this issue, please?

- A. advice
- B. advise
- C. enlighten
- D. enlightening

24. **DIRECTIONS:** Choose the most effective word or phrase within the context suggested by the sentence.

Behind the sofa _____ is a collection of desiccated broccoli spears that Simon, the family cocker spaniel, carries away for Noel, who cannot stomach the vegetable.

- A. their
- B. there
- C. they're
- D. they are

25. **DIRECTIONS:** Read the passage; then answer the question below.

    (1) When a camera flash is used in a low-light environment, the subject's eyes may appear red in the finished photograph. (2) What is known as "red-eye" is the result of light from the flash reflecting off the pupils of the eyes. (3) The phenomenon of red-eye can be lessened by using the red-eye reduction feature found on many SLR cameras. (4) This feature activates a lamp which shines a small light directly into the subject's eyes. (5) When this happens, the diameter of the pupil is reduced, thus tightening the opening in the iris.

    What is the best placement for the sentence below?

    "Since a smaller pupil means a smaller host for the reflection, the chances of red-eye occurring are greatly reduced."

    A.  before sentence 1

    B.  after sentence 2

    C.  after sentence 5

    D.  before sentence 4

26. **DIRECTIONS:** Read the passage; then answer the question below.

    (1) She was so thin that you could count her vertebrae just by looking at her. (2) Apparently she was declawed by her previous owners, then abandoned or lost. (3) Since she couldn't hunt, she nearly starved. (4) Not only that, but she had an abscess on one hip. (5) The vets at the Humane Society had drained it, but it was still scabby and without fur. (6) She had a terrible cold, too. (7) She was sneezing and sniffling and her meow was just a hoarse squeak. (8) And she'd lost half her tail somewhere. (9) Instead of tapering gracefully, it had a bony knob at the end.

    What is the best placement for the sentence below?

    "When I first brought my cat home from the Humane Society she was a mangy, pitiful animal."

    A.  before sentence 1

    B.  before sentence 3

    C.  after sentence 6

    D.  after sentence 7

27. **DIRECTIONS:** Choose the option that corrects an error in the underlined portion(s). If no error exists, choose "No change is necessary."

    Having command of color, symbolism, as well as technique, Georgia O'Keeffe is considered to be a great American painter.

    A.   Having some type of command of color, symbolism, as well as technique

    B.   Having command of color, symbolism, and her technical ability

    C.   Because of her command of color, symbolism, and technique

    D.   No change is necessary.

28. **DIRECTIONS:** Choose the option that corrects an error in the underlined portion(s). If no error exists, choose "No change is necessary."

    Whether the ancient ancestors of Native Americans actually migrated or did not across a land bridge now covered by the Bering Strait remains uncertain, but that they could have has not been refuted by other theories.

    A.   Whether the ancient ancestors of Native Americans could have actually migrated or did not

    B.   That the ancient ancestors of Native Americans actually did migrate

    C.   Whether in actuality the ancient ancestors of Native Americans migrated or not

    D.   No change is necessary.

29. **DIRECTIONS:** Choose the option that corrects an error in the underlined portion(s). If no error exists, choose "No change is necessary."

    Caution in scientific experimentation can sometimes be related more to integrity than to lack of knowledge.

    A.   sometimes be inter-related to the notion of integrity than because of lack of knowledge

    B.   sometimes be related more to integrity as well as lack of knowledge

    C.   often be related to integrity as to lack of knowledge

    D.   No change is necessary.

30. **DIRECTIONS:** Choose the option that corrects an error in the underlined portion(s).

     Advances in technology over the past ten years <u>have led</u> to a steady

                                                          **A**

     increase in the global farming supply, and the <u>economy</u> of many

                                                           **B**

     communities <u>around</u> the nation are <u>benefitting</u>.

                   **C**                     **D**

     A. did lead

     B. economies

     C. across

     D. a benefit

31. **DIRECTIONS:** Choose the option that corrects an error in the underlined portion(s). If no error exists, choose "No change is necessary."

     The reason <u>a large percentage</u> of American college students <u>located</u>

                       **A**                                     **B**

     Moscow in California <u>is because they</u> were not required to learn the facts of

                                **C**

     geography.

     A. percentages

     B. locates

     C. is they

     D. No change is necessary.

32. **DIRECTIONS:** Choose the option that corrects an error in the underlined portion(s). If no error exists, choose "No change is necessary."

     When one contrasts the ideas of the Romantic William Wordsworth

     <u>with those</u> of Neoclassicist John Dryden, <u>one finds</u> that the poets

           **A**                                          **B**

     <u>differ</u> from each other as much as one might expect.

       **C**

     A. with that

     B. they find

     C. differs

     D. No change is necessary.

33. **DIRECTIONS:** Choose the option that corrects an error in the underlined portion(s). If no error exists, choose "No change is necessary."

Many political conservatives <u>contribute</u> the problems of modern American
A

society to the twin evils of the New Deal and <u>secular humanism,</u> both <u>of</u>
B

<u>which are</u> presumed to stem from Marxism.
C

A.   attribute

B.   Secular Humanism

C.   are

D.   No change is necessary.

34. **DIRECTIONS:** Choose the option that corrects an error in the underlined portion(s). If no error exists, choose "No change is necessary."

<u>Returning to the ancestral home after 12 years, the house itself seemed
much smaller to Joe</u> than it had been when he visited it as a child.

A.   Returning to Joe, the ancestral home after 12 years seemed smaller to him

B.   When Joe returned to the ancestral home after 12 years, he thought the house itself much smaller

C.   Joe returned to the ancestral home after 12 years, and then he thought the house itself much smaller

D.   No change is necessary.

35. **DIRECTIONS:** Choose the option that corrects an error in the underlined portion(s). If no error exists, choose "No change is necessary."

Historians say that the New River of North Carolina, Virginia, and West Virginia, <u>that possibly is 2,700 feet above sea level and 2,000 feet above</u> the surrounding foothills, is the oldest river in the United States.

A.   which is 2,700 feet above sea level and 2,000 feet above

B.   with a height of 2,700 feet above sea level as well as 2,000 feet above that of

C.   2,700 feet higher than sea level and ascending 2,000 feet above

D.   No change is necessary.

36. **DIRECTIONS:** Choose the option that corrects an error in the underlined portion(s). If no error exists, choose "No change is necessary."

> The age of 36 having been reached, the Ukrainian-born Polish sailor Jósef Teodor Konrad Korzeniowski changed his name to Joseph Conrad and began a new and successful career as a British novelist and short story writer.

A. Having reached the age of 36

B. When having reached the age of 36

C. When he reached the age of 36

D. No change is necessary.

37. **DIRECTIONS:** Choose the option that corrects an error in the underlined portion(s). If no error exists, choose "No change is necessary."

> During the strike, Black South African miners threw a cordon around the gold mine, and they thereby blocked it to all white workers.

A. gold mine, and they blocked everyone outside.

B. gold mine, by which all white workers were therefore blocked.

C. gold mine and therefore blocking it to all white workers.

D. No change is necessary.

38. **DIRECTIONS:** Choose the most effective word or phrase within the context suggested by the sentence.

> In the current context of professional football, strict regulations have made the design of helmets standardized; in the early days of football, _____, players often developed their own helmets to meet their specific needs.

A. nevertheless

B. in consequence

C. on the other hand

D. although

39. **DIRECTIONS:** Choose the most effective word or phrase within the context suggested by the sentence.

> After the Smiths moved, no one mourned their _____. Their noisy parties, unkempt yard, and ferocious dogs had won them no friends in the neighborhood.

A. lost

B. loss

C. losing

D. was lost

40. **DIRECTIONS:** Choose the most effective word or phrase within the context suggested by the sentence.

> Professor Duncan returned the failing exam to Lornice, _____ poor performance on the midterm confirmed her reputation as a slacker.

A. whose

B. who is

C. whomever

D. who

# Practice Test 2: Mathematics Reference Sheet

## Area

Triangle     $A = \dfrac{1}{2}bh$

Rectangle     $A = lw$

Trapezoid     $A = \dfrac{1}{2}h(b_1 + b_2)$

Parallelogram     $A = bh$

Circle     $A = \pi r^2$

| KEY | |
|---|---|
| $b$ = base | $d$ = diameter |
| $h$ = height | $r$ = radius |
| $l$ = length | $A$ = area |
| $w$ = width | $C$ = circumference |
| $S.A.$ = surface area | $V$ = volume |
| | $B$ = area of base |
| Use 3.14 or $\dfrac{22}{7}$ for $\pi$ | |

### Circumference

$C = \pi d$

## Surface Area

1. Surface area of a prism or pyramid equals the sum of the areas of all faces.

2. Surface area of a cylinder equals the sum of the areas of the bases and the area of its rectangular wrap.

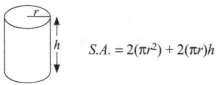

$S.A. = 2(\pi r^2) + 2(\pi r)h$

3. Surface area of a sphere: $S.A. = 4\pi r^2$

## Volume

1. Volume of a prism or cylinder equals the <u>Area of the Base</u> ($B$) times the height ($h$).

$$V = Bh$$

2. Volume of a pyramid or cone equals $\dfrac{1}{3}$ times the <u>Area of the Base</u> ($B$) times the height ($h$).

$$V = \dfrac{1}{3}Bh$$

3. Volume of a sphere: $V = \dfrac{4}{3}\pi r^3$

**Pythagorean Theorem:** $a^2 + b^2 = c^2$

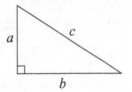

Given a line containing points $(x_1, y_1)$ and $(x_2, y_2)$.

- **Slope of line**

$$\frac{y_2 - y_1}{x_2 - x_1}$$

**Simple interest:** $I = prt$

$I$ = interest, $p$ = principal, $r$ = rate, $t$ = time

- **Distance between two points**

$$\sqrt{(x_2 - x_1)^2 + (y_2 - y_1)^2}$$

**Distance formula:** $d = rt$

$d$ = distance, $r$ = rate, $t$ = time

- **Midpoint between two points**

$$\left( \frac{x_1 + x_2}{2}, \frac{y_1 + y_2}{2} \right)$$

## Conversions

1 yard = 3 feet = 36 inches

1 mile = 1,760 yards = 5,280 feet

1 acre = 43,560 feet

1 hour = 60 minutes

1 minute = 60 seconds

1 cup = 8 fluid ounces

1 pint = 2 cups

1 quart = 2 pints

1 gallon = 4 quarts

1 pound = 16 ounces

1 ton = 2,000 pounds

1 liter = 1000 milliliters = 1000 cubic centimeters

1 meter = 100 centimeters = 1000 millimeters

1 kilometer = 1000 meters

1 gram = 1000 milligrams

1 kilogram = 1000 grams

Metric numbers with four digits are presented without a comma (e.g., 9960 kilometers). For metric numbers greater than four digits, a space is used instead of a comma (e.g., 12 500 liters).

# Practice Test 2: Mathematics

100 Minutes

45 Questions

**DIRECTIONS:** Read each question and select the best response.

1. Which of the statements below is true?

    A.   $4^3 = 3^4$

    B.   $5^0 \times 8^2 > 2^5$

    C.   $7^4 + 7^3 = 7^7$

    D.   $5^2 + 5^8 = 5^{10}$

2. The mean IQ score for 1,500 students is 100, with a standard deviation of 15. Assuming normal curve distribution, how many students have an IQ between 85 and 115? Refer to the figure shown below.

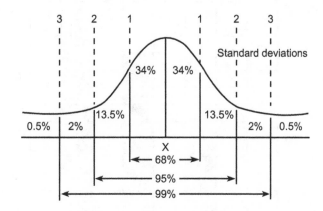

    A.   750

    B.   1,020

    C.   1,275

    D.   1,425

3. You want to make the following recipe and want to choose a big enough container.

    1 L of vanilla ice cream      50 ML chocolate sauce
    700 ML of raspberry syrup      100 ML of orange juice
    150 ML of mixer

    How many liters of ingredients will you have once you have added all of the ingredients?

    A.   1001

    B.   2

    C.   1

    D.   0.5

4.  You are playing a variation of Frisbee with some friends. The first player throws the Frisbee flying disc 3 meters forward from the starting line. The next player throws it 5 meters backwards. The third player throws the Frisbee 4 meters forward. How far is the Frisbee from the original starting line?

    A.  2 meters

    B.  3 meters

    C.  4 meters

    D.  5 meters

5.  The following graph shows the number of 8th through 10th grade students at The Eastford School. Based on the graph, how many students are sophomores?

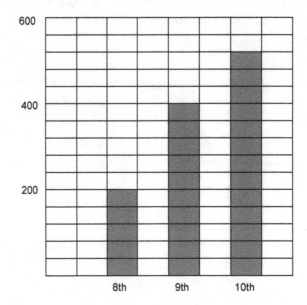

    A.  500

    B.  510

    C.  520

    D.  550

6.  A salesman makes a base salary of $250 a week, plus 3% of any sales made. Write a formula for his income if he needs to make at least $460 a week.

    A.  $250 \leq 0.03s + 460$

    B.  $250 \geq 0.03s + 460$

    C.  $460 \geq 0.03s + 250$

    D.  $460 \leq 0.03s + 250$

7.  A jewelry shop is considering adding a $95,000-a-year management position. Based on the following salaries, which measurement of central tendency would be the least affected if the store decides to add the manager's position to the current store employees?

    Current Employees: 21, 200      23,000      25,000      35,000      40,000

    A.   Median

    B.   Mean

    C.   Mode

    D.   Range

8.  Simplify the following: $|6 - 8| + 3 \div 3 \times 4^2 - 2$

    A.   12

    B.   16

    C.   8

    D.   $\dfrac{1}{8}$

9.  A farmer plants $\dfrac{3}{16}$ of 40 acres with peach trees. He plants twice as much acreage with carrots. How many acres are planted with carrots?

    A.   $\dfrac{6}{16}$

    B.   $\dfrac{3}{8}$

    C.   6

    D.   15

10. Terence wants to find the average height of a student in his high school. Which of the following would be the best choice for a sample?

    A.   The 17 students in his math class

    B.   All of the 10th-grade girls

    C.   15 students from each of the grades 9 through 12

    D.   The 30 players on the varsity and junior varsity basketball teams

11. Which of the following graphs would most favorably represent growth to potential investors?

A.
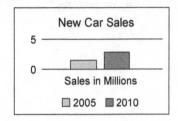

B.
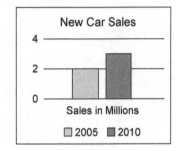

C.
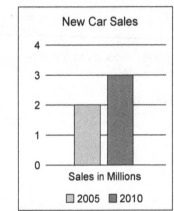

D.
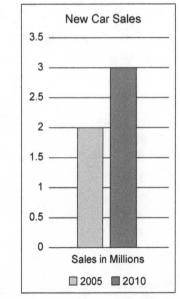

12. Which of the following does NOT have a mode of 32?

    A. {32, 32, 32, 34, 36, 37}

    B. {32, 32, 322, 322, 322}

    C. {32, 32, 32, 34, 34, 342}

    D. {30, 31, 32, 32, 33, 34}

13. A collection of data has a very large outlier. Which measure of central tendency will the outlier affect and in what way?

    A. The median will always be higher.

    B. The mode will always be higher.

    C. The range will always be higher.

    D. The mean will always be higher.

14. A woman gets two 18-inch necklaces, two 20-inch necklaces, and two 15-inch necklaces. She then purchases two more 18-inch and two more 20-inch necklaces. What is the difference in inches of the average length of her necklaces now that she has added the extra necklaces?

    A. 0.53

    B. 17.67

    C. 18.20

    D. 35.97

15. A student has the following scores on a series of exams: 59, 84, 84, 89, and 90. Which of the following scenarios would have the most positive impact on the student's average score in the class?

    A. Use the mean of the five scores to calculate the final grade.

    B. Remove the outlier before calculating the student's final average.

    C. Use the median of the scores to find the final grade.

    D. Use the mode of the data to calculate the final grade.

16. A tent is standing on four 12-foot poles. Each pole is attached 5 feet from the base with three cables. How many total feet of cables are securing the tent?

    A. 13

    B. 52

    C. 104

    D. 156

17. The scale drawing of a volleyball court is 3 centimeters by 6 centimeters. The scale is 1 centimeter equals 3 meters. What is the area of the volleyball court in square meters?

    A.  18 m²

    B.  54 m²

    C.  102 m²

    D.  162 m²

18. You are putting on a party for 24 people. You want to prepare two burgers for each guest. Hamburger buns are $0.89 for six or $1.49 for eight. What is the least amount you can spend on buns?

    A.  $3.56

    B.  $4.47

    C.  $7.12

    D.  $8.94

19. The Sunshine Shirt Company sells its shirts for $15 a shirt. Each new style of shirt costs the company $6.00 per shirt, plus a one-time silk screening fee of $150. How many shirts will the company have to sell to make a profit of $900?

    A.  60

    B.  70

    C.  117

    D.  151

20. Which of the following choices falls between 0 and 2?

    A.  $-4.037 \times 10^3$

    B.  $4.037 \times 10^3$

    C.  $-4.03 \times 10^{-2}$

    D.  $4.03 \times 10^{-2}$

21. How many 6-ounce patties could you make out of 3 pounds of hamburger?

    A.  8

    B.  10

    C.  12

    D.  16

22. There are five people, PQRST, who want to form a committee of three people. How many 3-group committees can you make if R is always on the committee?

    A. 2

    B. 4

    C. 6

    D. 12

23. The length of a picture frame is 2 inches more than twice its width. If the perimeter of the picture frame is 88 inches, what is the length of the frame in inches?

    A. 14

    B. 22

    C. 60

    D. 30

24. A triangle has angles of 20 degrees, 50 degrees, and 110 degrees. What type of triangle is it?

    A. Right scalene

    B. Acute isosceles

    C. Obtuse equilateral

    D. Scalene obtuse

25. A baseball team has won 60% of their first 70 games. They have 30 games left in the season and want to end the season with wins in 70% of their games. How many more games do they have to win to accomplish this?

    A. 28

    B. 30

    C. 36

    D. 42

26. The following table shows the hours a student studied and the scores she earned on exams. If $h$ represents the hours she studied, and $p$ represents her percentage correct, which formula represents the data in the table?

| Hours Studied | Percentage Correct |
|---|---|
| 1 | 60 |
| 2 | 70 |
| 2.5 | 75 |
| 3 | 80 |
| 4.5 | 95 |

A.  h = 10p

B.  h = 0.10p + 60

C.  p = 10h + 60

D.  p = 10h + 50

27. The following table shows the amount of time it takes to feel relief from bug bites when baking soda or ammonia is used topically. Based on the graph, which of the following statements are true?

|  | **Ant Bites** | **Tick Bites** |
|---|---|---|
| Baking Soda | 5 minutes | 10 minutes |
| Ammonia | 5 minutes | 7 minutes |

1. Baking soda is most effective for treating ant bites and tick bites.

2. Baking soda is most effective for treating all bug bites.

3. Ammonia is effective for treating all bug bites.

4. Ammonia is more effective than baking soda for treating tick bites.

A.  #1

B.  #4

C.  #3 and #4

D.  #2 and #3

28. Solve the following inequality:

$$36 \leq -2x < 54$$

A.  $x$ is greater than or equal to −18 and less than or equal to −27.

B.  $x$ is greater than or equal to −18 and less than −27.

C.  $x$ is less than or equal to −18 and greater than −27.

D.  $x$ is less than or equal to −18 and greater than or equal to −27.

29. What formula can we use to find the area of the square?

A.  $3^2$

B.  $6^2$

C.  $3 + 3$

D.  $3 \times 2 \times 2$

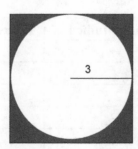

30. The following equilateral triangle is sitting on a line. Which of the following statements is true?

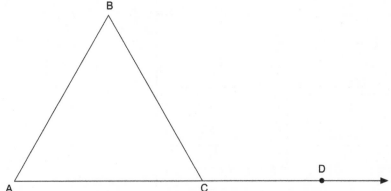

A. ∠ACB is supplementary to ∠BCD and ∠BCD is 120 degrees.

B. ∠AB and ∠CD are complementary.

C. ∠ABC and ∠D are supplementary.

D. ∠D is acute.

31. A local parking garage costs $12 a day, but if you purchase a pass that costs $25 a month, the rate drops to $8 a day. After how many days would it be more cost effective to buy the pass?

A. 8

B. 7

C. 6

D. 5

32. You have 4 pairs of pants and 3 shirts that all match, how many different ways can you choose one pair of pants and one shirt?

A. 12

B. 7

C. 4

D. 3

33. Which table correctly represents the plant growth formula $h = 2d + 4$?

A.

| d | 1 | 2 | 3 |
|---|---|---|---|
| h | 4 | 8 | 12 |

B.

| d | 1 | 2 | 3 |
|---|---|---|---|
| h | 2 | 4 | 6 |

C.

| d | 2 | 4 | 6 |
|---|---|---|---|
| h | 4 | 6 | 8 |

D.

| d | 0 | 1 | 2 |
|---|---|---|---|
| h | 4 | 6 | 8 |

34. You want to paint the walls and ceiling of a room that is 16 ft. by 14 ft. and has 8-foot ceilings. You will not paint the floor or the double doors that have an area of 6 ft. by 7 ft. Each gallon of paint covers 175 square feet. How much paint do you need to purchase to paint the walls and ceiling, but not the doors or floor?

A. 9

B. 7

C. 4

D. 3

35. Traveling from Orlando to San Francisco by air takes an average of 330 minutes. If the airplane travels at an average speed of 446 mph, how far in miles is the round trip in scientific notation?

A. $49.06 \times 10^2$

B. $4.906 \times 10^3$

C. $2.453 \times 10^3$

D. $24.53 \times 10^2$

36. If the graph represents the number of carrots or potatoes that you can buy for $180, which statement about the graph is true?

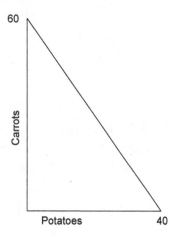

A. You can only purchase carrots without purchasing potatoes.

B. You can only purchase potatoes without purchasing carrots.

C. As you increase the amount of carrots that you buy, you also increase the amount of potatoes you can purchase.

D. As you decrease the amount of carrots that you buy, you can increase the amount of potatoes that you can purchase.

37. Laura gets an hourly rate for helping out at her dad's office. The graph below shows Laura's earnings.

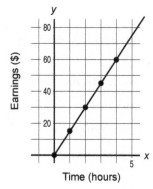

What does the slope of the graph represent?

A. The number of hours Laura worked

B. The total amount of money Laura earned

C. The number of hours Laura works for 0 dollars

D. Laura's hourly rate

38. A room is 18 feet by 21 feet. If the carpet you chose costs $6.79 per square yard, how much will it cost you to carpet the room?

    A.    $285.18

    B.    $2,566.62

    C.    $855.54

    D.    $264.81

39. On Monday it was twenty degrees below zero, on Tuesday the temperature was five degrees warmer, and on Wednesday the temperature went down seven degrees. Over the next week the temperature increased two degrees each day. What was the temperature on day nine?

    A.    −10

    B.    10

    C.    22

    D.    28

40. A family uses 1500 kilowatts of energy per month at a cost of $0.15 per kilowatt. They move to a smaller home, and now only use 900 kilowatts per month at a cost of $0.10 per kilowatt. What is the percentage of decrease in their energy costs?

    A.    40

    B.    45

    C.    55

    D.    60

41. Assuming that a student consistently received between 70 and 80 percent on test scores, how would the addition of a significantly higher outlier affect the student's mean score?

    A.    It would definitely raise the median score.

    B.    It would definitely raise the mode of the scores.

    C.    It would definitely lower the mean of the data set.

    D.    It would definitely raise the mean of the data set.

42. Which of the following data sets meets the definition of a function?

    A.

| $x$ | $y$ |
| --- | --- |
| 2 | 3 |
| 4 | 3 |
| 6 | 3 |

B.

| x | y |
|---|---|
| 2 | 2 |
| 2 | 4 |
| 2 | 6 |

C.

| x | y |
|---|---|
| 1 | 5 |
| 1 | 6 |
| 3 | 7 |

D.

| x | y |
|---|---|
| 4 | 5 |
| 3 | 6 |
| 4 | 7 |

43. During the planning stage of the fall festival, the school PTA surveyed the students at their school to determine which carnival events they preferred. The survey results are shown below.

| Event | Grades | | | | | |
|---|---|---|---|---|---|---|
| | **Kindergarten** | **1st** | **2nd** | **3rd** | **4th** | **5th** |
| Dunk Tank | 0 | 1 | 1 | 0 | 2 | 8 |
| Cake Walk | 2 | 0 | 0 | 0 | 1 | 0 |
| Pony Ride | 4 | 5 | 7 | 10 | 8 | 4 |
| Ring Toss | 0 | 0 | 1 | 0 | 1 | 0 |
| Bounce House | 5 | 6 | 8 | 9 | 10 | 18 |
| Face Painting | 1 | 1 | 0 | 1 | 0 | 0 |

Assuming that the school population is distributed equally across the grades and that the students surveyed were randomly chosen, what error did the PTA make when conducting their survey?

A. They did not provide enough options for the students to select.

B. They did not use a random selection process.

C. They did not fairly represent all grade levels in the survey.

D. They did not clearly report their results.

44. A low-level room flooded 18 in. during the storm. When pumped out, the pump removed $1\frac{1}{2}$ in. of water in 50 minutes. How many hours will it take the pump to empty the room of water?

    A.  10

    B.  60

    C.  100

    D.  600

45. The ordered pair $(7, -20)$ is a solution of which equation?

    A.  $y = -3x + 1$

    B.  $y = -x + 7$

    C.  $y = -4x + 2$

    D.  $y = -2x + 3$

# Practice Test 2: Reading

55 Minutes

40 Questions

**DIRECTIONS:** Read the passages and then answer the questions that follow.

## PASSAGE ONE

### O Captain, My Captain!

O CAPTAIN! my Captain! our fearful trip is done,

The ship has weather'd every rack, the prize we sought is won,

The port is near, the bells I hear, the people all **exulting**,

While follow eyes the steady keel, the vessel grim and daring;

But O heart! heart! heart!

O the bleeding drops of red!

Where on the deck my Captain lies,

Fallen cold and dead.


My Captain does not answer, his lips are pale and still,

My father does not feel my arm, he has no pulse nor will;

The ship is anchor'd safe and sound, its voyage closed and done,

From fearful trip the victor ship comes in with object won;

Exult, O shores! and ring, O bells!

But I, with mournful tread,

Walk the deck my Captain lies,

Fallen cold and dead.


## PASSAGE TWO

### The True Story of a Great Life

Bancroft's eulogy on Lincoln never pleased the latter's lifelong friends—those who knew him so thoroughly and well. On February 16, 1866, David Davis, who had heard it, wrote me: "You will see Mr. Bancroft's oration before this reaches you. It is able, but Mr. Lincoln is in the background. His analysis of Mr. Lincoln's character is superficial. It did not please me. How did it satisfy you?" On the 22d he again wrote: "Mr. Bancroft totally misconceived Mr. Lincoln's character in applying 'unsteadiness' and confusion to it. Mr. Lincoln grew more steady and **resolute**, and his ideas were never confused. If there were any changes in him after he got here they were for the better. I thought him always master of his subject. He was a much more self-possessed man than I thought. He thought for himself, which is a rare quality nowadays. How could Bancroft know anything about Lincoln except as he judged of him as the public do? He never saw him, and is himself as cold as an icicle. I should never have selected an old Democratic politician, and that one from Massachusetts, to deliver an eulogy on Lincoln."

Passages taken from, respectively: Walt Whitman's "O Captain! My Captain!" (1865) and *Abraham Lincoln: The True Story of a Great Life,* volume II, by William H. Herdon and Jesse W. Weik (1896).

1.  In this context, the word **exulting** in Passage 1 most nearly means

    A.  exhilarating.

    B.  frustrating.

    C.  fulfilling.

    D.  praising.


2.  How does Passage 1 differ from Passage 2?

    A.  Passage 2 is opinionated, while Passage 1 is not.

    B.  Passage 2 speaks out against funeral practices, while Passage 1 avoids the topic completely.

    C.  Passage 2 denounces a leader, while Passage 1 lauds him.

    D.  Passage 2 evaluates a eulogy, while Passage 1 is a eulogy.


3.  How would the author of Passage 1 respond to the statement made in Passage 2 that "Mr. Bancroft totally misconceived Mr. Lincoln's character in applying 'unsteadiness' and confusion to it. Mr. Lincoln grew more steady and resolute, and his ideas were never confused"?

    A.  The author would disagree that Lincoln's character is steady and resolute.

    B.  The author would agree that Lincoln's character is steady and resolute.

    C.  The author would agree that Lincoln's character is steady, but would offer examples refuting his attribute of being resolute.

    D.  The author would praise the author of Passage 2 for his critical lens in viewing a notable eulogy.


4.  In which of these ways does the content of Passage 1 differ from Passage 2?

    A.  Passage 1 uses ethos, while Passage 2 does not.

    B.  Passage 1 ignores the Civil War, while Passage 2 criticizes it.

    C.  Passage 1 addresses the current state of the nation, while Passage 2 does not.

    D.  Passage 1 is focused on instilling a bipartisan government, while Passage 2 is strongly opposed to a bipartisan government.

5.    Which of the following best describes the shift in tone between the beginning and end of Passage 1?

    A.    Triumphant to sorrowful

    B.    Charismatic to conventional

    C.    Critical to begrudging

    D.    Admiring to skeptical

6.    The central idea of Passage 2 is that

    A.    Lincoln's eulogy was anecdotally supported by his colleagues.

    B.    Lincoln's eulogy was criticized based on the mischaracterization of his qualities and ideas.

    C.    Lincoln's eulogy was not anecdotally supported by his colleagues.

    D.    Lincoln's eulogy was criticized based on the contextual understanding of the author.

7.    The critical voice in Passage 2 can best be described as

    A.    hate.

    B.    fear.

    C.    disdain.

    D.    satisfaction.

8.    In the context of Passage 2, the word **resolute** most nearly means

    A.    stalwart.

    B.    cowardly.

    C.    insincere.

    D.    respectful.

9.    Which of the following is NOT a detail stated in Passage 1?

    A.    Lincoln overcame obstacles.

    B.    Lincoln was lauded by society.

    C.    Lincoln was a valiant leader.

    D.    Lincoln was a burden for society.

### The Power Game: How Washington Works

When I came to Washington in 1962, to work at the Washington bureau of The New York Times, I thought I understood how Washington worked. I knew the usual textbook **precepts**: that the president and his cabinet were in charge of the government; that Congress declared war and passed budgets; that the secretary of State directed foreign policy; that seniority determined who wrote legislation in Congress; and that the power of southern committee chairmen—gained by seniority—was beyond the challenge of junior members; that voters elected one party or the other to govern; and the parties set how the members of Congress would vote—except for southern Democrats, who often teamed up with Republicans.

These old truisms no longer fit reality. My years as a reporter have spanned the administrations of six presidents, and over the course of that time, I have watched a stunning transformation in the way the American system of government operates. The Washington power game has been altered by many factors: new congressional assertiveness against the presidency, the revolt within congress against the seniority system, television, the merchandising of candidates, the explosion of special interest politics, the demands of political fundraising, the massive growth of staff power—and by changes in voters as well.

The political **transformations** of the past fifteen years have rewritten the old rules of the game. Presidents now have much greater difficulty marshaling governing **coalitions**. Power, instead of residing with the president, often floats away from him, and a skillful leader must learn how to ride the political waves like a surfer or be toppled. The old power oligarchy in Congress has been broken up. The new breed of senators and House members, unlike the old breed, play video politics, a different game from the old inside back room politics of Congress. Party labels mean much less now to voters and to many candidates, too. It's a new ball game, with new sets of rules, new ways of getting power leverage, new types of players, new game plans, and new tactics that affect winning and losing. It is a much looser power game now, more wide open, harder to manage and manipulate than it was more than a quarter of a century ago when I came to town.

From *The Power Game: How Washington Works* (1988), by Hedrick Smith. New York: Ballantine Books

10. According to the passage, which of the following is true about the "Washington power game"?

    A. It has a lack of staffing power.

    B. It has been altered by the demands of political fundraising.

    C. It has negated the effect of special interests.

    D. It has continuity based on congressional seniority.

11. The predominant pattern preferred by the author to make an argument is

    A. compare and contrast.

    B. summarize.

    C. cause and effect.

    D. problem and solution.

12. In the second paragraph, the writer describes the factors that have altered the power game in order to

    A. show how the political landscape shifts throughout history.

    B. provide an argument for why the political landscape is cyclical.

C. show that the political landscape does not shift throughout history.

D. provide an argument for why the political landscape is different.

13. Which words describe the overall effect of the passage?

 A. *new game, experiences, rewrite*, and *understood*

 B. *understood, rewrite, experiences*, and *new game*

 C. *new game, understood, experiences*, and *rewrite*

 D. *understood, experiences, rewrite*, and *new game*

14. The author mentions, "The political transformations of the past fifteen years have rewritten the old rules of the game" in order to do which of the following?

 A. Summarize an argument in the previous paragraph

 B. Introduce a new topic to the paragraph

 C. Link the causes in the second paragraph with the effects given in the third

 D. Introduce a contrasting point of view

15. The primary purpose of this passage is to

 A. tell a story about how political change evolves over time.

 B. persuade the reader to become involved in political transformation.

 C. analyze a situation facing the political landscape.

 D. explain different points of view regarding the political structure.

16. According to the passage, the author's attitude towards the transformation seen in the way the government operates can best be described as

 A. confusing.

 B. stunning.

 C. depressing.

 D. unfair.

17. According to the passage, what is the pivotal challenge faced by the president?

 A. Building partnerships

 B. Aligning of strategic goals

 C. Planning diplomacy

 D. Consulting infrastructure

18. In the context of the passage, the word **precepts** most nearly means

    A.  theories.

    B.  stories.

    C.  powers.

    D.  promises.


19. With which of the following description of the Washington landscape would the author of the passage mostly agree?

    A.  Easy to manipulate

    B.  Contest of wills

    C.  Shifting landscape

    D.  A power game


20. Which of the following is NOT a detail stated in the passage?

    A.  The Washington power game has been altered by many competing ideas.

    B.  Party labels mean less to voters across the continuum.

    C.  The old power oligarchy in Congress has been solidified.

    D.  The changes in Washington are focused at the operational level.


21. The word **transformations** most nearly means

    A.  successes.

    B.  changes.

    C.  regrets.

    D.  denials.


22. Identify the most accurate statement of the central idea of the passage.

    A.  Political transformations have shifted the government into a new power game.

    B.  Old truisms continue to support the shifting political landscape.

    C.  Political transformations have shifted power from journalists to the average citizen.

    D.  New politicians support the shifting government structure.

23. All of the following describe the author's attitude about Washington EXCEPT

    A. pivotal.

    B. reflective.

    C. opportunistic.

    D. optimistic.

24. The author most likely includes the example of his perspective which "…spanned the administrations of six presidents…" in order to

    A. refute claims against the author's bias.

    B. provide statistical data supporting the author's insights.

    C. refute claims against his anecdotal evidence.

    D. provide longitudinal evidence supporting the author's insights.

25. The passage provides information for answering most fully which of the following questions?

    A. What does the future hold for the political landscape?

    B. Will either party concede on power relations?

    C. How long should it take for the political landscape to shift?

    D. Why has the political landscape shifted?

26. Based on the passage, what is the best caption for this image?

    A. Washington, D.C.: Ever loving

    B. Washington, D.C.: Ever shifting

    C. Washington, D.C.: Ever corrupt

    D. Washington, D.C.: Ever constant

## PASSAGE ONE

### Education of Teachers

The waves of criticism about American education have reflected currents of social dissatisfaction for any given period of this country's history. As dynamics for change in the social order result in demands for change in the American educational system, so in turn insistence has developed for revision of teacher education (witness the more recent Holmes report (1986)). Historically, the education of American teachers has reflected evolving attitudes about public education. With slight modifications, the teacher education pattern established following the demise of the normal school during the early 1900s has persisted in most teacher preparation programs. The pattern has been one requiring certain academic and professional (educational) courses often resulting in teachers prone to teach as they had been taught.

## PASSAGE TWO

### A Target for Change

Seldom has the American school system not been the target of demands for change to meet the social priorities of the times. This theme has been traced through the following significant occurrences in education: Benjamin Franklin's advocacy in 1749 for a more useful type of education; Horace Mann's zealous proposals in the 1830s espousing the tax-supported public school; John Dewey's early twentieth century attack on traditional schools for not developing the child effectively for his or her role in society; the post-Sputnik pressure for academic rigor; the prolific criticism and accountability pressures of the 1970s; and the ensuing **disillusionment** and continued criticism of schools up to and including the twenty-first century. Each one of these historical events has marked a growth in American education.

27. The author of Passage 1 would probably agree with which of the following statements?

    A. Social dissatisfaction should drive change in American schools.

    B. Teacher education programs have changed greatly since normal schools were eliminated.

    C. Critics of American education reflect vested interests.

    D. Teachers exemplify what they know and have experienced.

28. The evolving attitudes about public education in Passage 1 are

    A. stated.

    B. unstated.

    C. biased.

    D. unwarranted.

29. One possible sequence of significant occurrences in education noted in Passage 2 is

    A.  Mann's tax-supported public schools, post-Sputnik pressures for academic rigor, and accountability of the 1970s.

    B.  Mann's tax supported public schools, Dewey's educating children for their role in society, and Franklin's advocacy.

    C.  Franklin's more useful type of education, the Holmes report, and accountability pressures of the 1970s.

    D.  Mann's tax-supported public schools, accountability pressures of the 1970s, and the post-Sputnik pressures for academic rigor.

30. Which of the following statements most obviously implies dissatisfaction with the preparation of teachers in the United States?

    A.  Demands for change in the American education system lead to insistence for revision of teacher-education programs.

    B.  The pattern of teacher education requires certain academic and professional education courses.

    C.  The education of U.S. teachers has reflected evolving attitudes about public education.

    D.  Teacher education has changed very little since the decline of the normal school.

31. After reading Passage 1, one can infer that

    A.  education is constantly changing based on different populations within a given context.

    B.  social challenges are a predictor of change within education.

    C.  social challenges are not a significant predictor of change within education.

    D.  education is multi-faceted and can be extremely complicated to change.

32. What is the relationship between these two sentences?

    > Sentence 1: The waves of criticism about American education have reflected currents of social dissatisfaction for any given period of this country's history. (paragraph 1)

    > Sentence 2: As dynamics for change in the social order result in demands for change in the American educational system, so in turn insistence has developed for revision of teacher education (witness the more recent Holmes report (1986)). (paragraph 1)

    A.  Sentence 2 analyzes the comment in sentence 1.

    B.  Sentence 2 explains the main idea of sentence 1.

    C.  Sentence 2 contradicts the main idea of sentence 1.

    D.  Sentence 2 continues the definition begun in sentence 1.

33.  In the context of Passage 2, the word **disillusionment** most nearly means

 A.  disenchantment.

 B.  naiveté.

 C.  disheartening.

 D.  enchant.

## An Enchanted River Scene

Now when I had mastered the language of this water and had come to know every **trifling** feature that bordered the great river as familiarly as I knew the letters of the alphabet, I had made a valuable acquisition. But I had lost something, too. I had lost something which could never be restored to me while I lived. All the grace, the beauty, the poetry, had gone out of the majestic river! I still kept in mind a certain wonderful sunset which I witnessed when steamboating was new to me.

A broad expanse of the river was turned to blood; in the middle distance the red hue bright-ened into gold, through which a solitary log came floating, black and conspicuous; in one place a long, slanting mark lay sparkling upon the water; in another the surface was broken by boiling, tumbling rings, that were as many-tinted as an opal; where the ruddy flush was faintest, was a smooth spot that was covered with graceful circles and radiating lines, ever so delicately traced; the shore on our left was densely wooded and the somber shadow that fell from this forest was broken in one place by a long, ruffled trail that shone like silver; and high above the forest wall a clean-stemmed dead tree waved a single leafy bough that glowed like a flame in the unob-structed splendor that was flowing from the sun. There were graceful curves, reflected images, woody heights, soft distances, and over the whole scene, far and near, the dissolving lights drifted steadily, enriching it every passing moment with new marvels of coloring.

I stood like one bewitched. I drank it in, in a speechless **rapture**. The world was new to me and I had never seen anything like this at home. But as I have said, a day came when I began to cease from noting the glories and the charms which the moon and the sun and the twilight wrought upon the river's face; another day came when I ceased altogether to note them. Then, if that sunset scene had been repeated, I should have looked upon it without rapture, and should have commented upon it inwardly after this fashion: This sun means that we are going to have wind to-morrow; that float-ing log means that the river is rising, small thanks to it; that slanting mark on the water refers to a bluff reef which is going to kill somebody's steamboat one of these nights...

From "An Enchanting River Scene" (1883), by Mark Twain

34.  In the context of the passage, the word **trifling** most nearly means

 A.  prudent.

 B.  commonplace.

 C.  trivial.

 D.  fundamental.

35.  To describe the setting of the passage, the author relies mainly on

 A.  comparison/contrast.

 B.  figurative language.

C.  cause/effect.

D.  scientific analysis.

36. The writer says, "This sun means that we are going to have wind to-morrow; that floating log means that the river is rising, small thanks to it; that slanting mark on the water refers to a bluff reef which is going to kill somebody's steamboat one of these nights...," in order to

A.  provide an example of how the writer viewed the sun.

B.  support the obstacles faced by the writer.

C.  provide an example of how the writer viewed the river.

D.  support the change in the way the writer is feeling about his subject.

37. The author describes the river with each of the following descriptions EXCEPT

A.  mercy.

B.  grace.

C.  beauty.

D.  poetry.

38. Which word best describes the writer's attitude about the setting in the second paragraph?

A.  Enthralled

B.  Repulsed

C.  Attracted

D.  Offended

39. In the third paragraph, the word **rapture** most nearly means

A.  fear.

B.  thirst.

C.  delight.

D.  innocence.

40. By the statement, "Now when I had mastered the language of this water and had come to know every **trifling** feature that bordered the great river as familiarly as I knew the letters of the alphabet, I had made a valuable acquisition," the writer is referring to

A.  the understanding of the familiar nature of the water.

B.  the understanding gained from the command of a watercraft.

C.  the understanding of the gracious waves of the water.

D.  the understanding gained from the rudimentary level of the skill.

## Practice Test 2
## Answer Key

### English Language Skills

| | | | |
|---|---|---|---|
| 1. B | 11. B | 21. B | 31. C |
| 2. A | 12. B | 22. A | 32. D |
| 3. D | 13. B | 23. B | 33. A |
| 4. C | 14. A | 24. B | 34. B |
| 5. A | 15. D | 25. C | 35. A |
| 6. B | 16. B | 26. A | 36. C |
| 7. B | 17. C | 27. C | 37. D |
| 8. D | 18. A | 28. B | 38. C |
| 9. C | 19. A | 29. D | 39. B |
| 10. A | 20. A | 30. B | 40. A |

### Mathematics

| | | | |
|---|---|---|---|
| 1. B | 13. D | 24. D | 35. B |
| 2. B | 14. A | 25. A | 36. D |
| 3. B | 15. B | 26. D | 37. D |
| 4. A | 16. D | 27. B | 38. A |
| 5. C | 17. D | 28. C | 39. A |
| 6. D | 18. C | 29. B | 40. D |
| 7. A | 19. C | 30. A | 41. D |
| 8. B | 20. D | 31. B | 42. A |
| 9. D | 21. A | 32. A | 43. C |
| 10. C | 22. C | 33. D | 44. A |
| 11. D | 23. D | 34. C | 45. A |
| 12. B | | | |

## Reading

| | | | |
|---|---|---|---|
| 1. D | 11. C | 21. B | 31. B |
| 2. D | 12. D | 22. A | 32. B |
| 3. B | 13. D | 23. D | 33. A |
| 4. C | 14. C | 24. D | 34. C |
| 5. A | 15. A | 25. D | 35. B |
| 6. B | 16. B | 26. B | 36. D |
| 7. C | 17. A | 27. D | 37. A |
| 8. A | 18. A | 28. B | 38. A |
| 9. D | 19. C | 29. A | 39. C |
| 10. B | 20. C | 30. D | 40. B |

# Practice Test 2: Correlation with FTCE Competencies

## English Language Skills

**Competency 1: Knowledge of Language Structure**

Questions: 1, 2, 3, 4, 5, 6, 25, 26, 36, 37

**Competency 2: Knowledge of Vocabulary Application**

Questions: 8, 17, 22, 23, 24, 27, 29, 38, 39, 40

**Competency 3: Knowledge of Standard English Conventions**

Questions: 7, 9, 10, 11, 12, 13, 14, 15, 16, 18, 19, 20, 21, 28, 30, 31, 32, 33, 34, 35

## Mathematics

**Competency 1: Knowledge of Number Sense, Concepts, and Operations**

Questions: 3, 4, 8, 9, 18, 20, 25, 39

**Competency 2: Knowledge of Geometry and Measurement**

Questions: 16, 17, 21, 23, 24, 29, 30, 34, 35, 38, 44

**Competency 3: Knowledge of Algebraic Thinking and the Coordinate Plain**

Questions: 1, 6, 19, 26, 28, 31, 33, 37, 40, 42, 45

**Competency 4: Knowledge of Probability, Statistics, and Data Interpretation**

Questions: 2, 5, 7, 10, 11, 12, 13, 14, 15, 22, 27, 32, 36, 41, 43

## Reading

**Competency 1: Knowledge of Key Ideas and Details Based on Text Slections**

Questions: 1, 2, 3, 4, 5, 6, 25, 26, 36, 37

**Competency 2 : Knowledge of Craft and Structure Based on Text Selections**

Questions: 8, 17, 22, 23, 24, 27, 29, 38, 39, 40

**Competency 3: Knowledge of the Integration of Information and Ideas Based on Text Selections**

Questions: 7, 9, 10, 11, 12, 13, 14, 15, 16, 18, 19, 20, 21, 28, 30, 31, 32, 33, 34, 35

# Practice Test 2: Detailed Explanations of Answers

 Essay

## Sample Response

In the current context, online learning turns out to be more and more practiced. Many traditional universities started to share their courses online for free. It represents an easy and comfortable method to achieve knowledge in almost every field, from law and accounting, to human sciences, such as psychology and sociology or history. Online learning is a great alternative to traditional universities, especially for people who can't afford the time and money to take real courses. Although many people still consider traditional schools as the best way to achieve knowledge and get a diploma, online learning proves to be a great alternative. Students have the chance to study in their own time. It represents a great way to study many fields and to boost the level of self-motivation. Online learning is so effective because students can finish their homework quickly, and there is more time left for hobbies or for finding a job.

The advantage to online learning is access to resources. This type of learning allows students to participate wherever they are. This allows them to determine and have the freedom to choose the time for study. With basically an Internet connection, a person can attend different courses. Beyond access, other advantages exist. Another set of advantages is the notion of responsibility and self-discipline of students.

The disadvantage is the way in which students are grouped. Many believe that only in the context of a small group can a person develop properly. At school, students learn how to make friends, be patient, get rid of disappointment, and especially to compete. Competition between colleagues can be very stimulating and students will only benefit from it. Online learning cannot offer human interaction. Critics of online learning, cite other disadvantages—referring to the fact that online courses cannot cope with thousands of students that try to join discussions. Finally, online learning can be difficult, if it is meant for disciplines that involve practice.

In conclusion, online learning should be seen as a complement and extension of classical forms of learning. Not even the best online course can fully replace the personal contact with a teacher, or the human relationships that develop in a group. So, while there are advantages and disadvantages to online learning; traditional classes should not be replaced with online learning.

## Analysis

This essay would receive a high score. It uses a traditional structure: the first paragraph states the topic, the second and third present development with specific examples. The fourth ends the essay and states a conclusion. The writer communicates effectively and the essay is well thought out. It is well done considering the time limit imposed on the writer by the test. This essay would merit a score of 6.

# English Language Skills

1.   **B.** Answer choices (A), (C), and (D) each have modifying phrases that do not match up to what is being modified. For example, choice (D) makes the reader believe that it is the birthday that Mary has picked, when the writer is intending for the presents to be picked.

2.   **A.** Answer choices (B), (C), and (D) have misplaced modifiers. The correct answer (A) has the modifier close to what is being modified, "Mitch."

3.   **D.** This is the correct answer because the modifiers are placed in the correct order within the sentence; "an architectural monument" follows "Basel Munster." The other answer choices have the modifiers separated from what is being modified.

4.   **C.** This choice involves parallel construction. The word *both* introduces a pair of phrases, one a prepositional phrase ("for their own interests"), the other an infinitive phrase ("to gain more goods"). Aside from being inelegant, "to gain more goods" is also not the same structure and should be changed to "their own gain" to make the two phrases perfectly parallel. Choice (C) is correct. Choices (A), (B), and (D) do not provide parallel structure to the sentence.

5.   **A.** Again, non-parallel structure is the key to this and many test items in the English Language Skills subtest. Because of the overwhelming importance of understanding balance in sentence structure, tests like this one emphasize parallel sentence structures. "To learn" clashes with "studying" in the parallel clause. Choosing "Learning" would make the clauses parallel.

6.   **B.** This sentence does not provide a parallel comparison. So, in this case, the comparison should match and state that "writing" something is easier than "the writing of something."

7.   **B.** All proper nouns must be capitalized; therefore, "English," which is a specific language, should be capitalized. Also, "Algebra I" should be capitalized because it is the name of a specific course. But answer choice (C) is not correct because "history" is not a proper noun.

8.   **D.** We can eliminate choice (C) fairly quickly as either an inappropriate or awkward appositive to "ornithology," instead of "ornithologists." (A) is not the best choice even though some may consider it acceptable. Likewise, choice (B) tends to be limited to non-restrictive clauses, unlike this one.

9.   **C.** This is the best answer because when a writer provides a list, he or she must use a colon and not a comma or semicolon before the listed items.

**10. A.** "Berlin Wall" must be capitalized because it is the name of a specific noun. The verb does not need to be changed and "government" should not be capitalized because it is not a proper noun. Therefore, the best answer choice is (A).

**11. B.** This question has several potential errors. Choice (A) calls into question the attribution of human rationality to an inanimate object, but since the Constitution actually does have logical premises, we can correctly say that the document can posit the premise stated. Choice (C) is acceptable because the superlative is referenced within the sentence; one should know that the U.S. government has three branches. Choice (B) is the verb in the clause beginning with the word "what"; it is plural, and therefore, incorrect because it does not agree with its subject, "history," a singular noun. Do not be fooled by the intervening plural word "governments."

**12. B.** This is the correct answer because the only way to separate two complete thoughts is with a semicolon or an ending punctuation mark. So, (B) provides a semicolon to separate the two complete thoughts. (A) does not provide any punctuation mark, while (C) creates a comma splice.

**13. B.** One could question the use of "nearly" (A), but it is correct. One might argue also that "million dollars" (C) should be written "$1 million," but choice (B) is clearly an incorrect use of the past perfect tense. The simple past tense ("sold"), the present progressive tense ("are selling"), or the present perfect progressive tense ("have been selling") could each be used correctly depending on the intended meaning.

**14. A.** This choice is not as obvious, but authorities agree that the use of "expect" to mean "suppose" or "believe" (the usage here) is either informal or colloquial, but not formal written English. Choice (B) is not grammatically correct. The third most likely choice, (C), brings to mind the distinction between "accept" and "except," a word pair often confused. However, "accept" is correct here.

**15. D.** Choices (B) and (C) introduce unnecessary absolute phrases beginning with "it," which makes the sentences wordy. They can be eliminated immediately. Choice (A) uses varied tenses, which make the sentence incorrect. No change is necessary.

**16. B.** Choices (A), (C), and (D) can be disqualified quickly because they are not parallel to the structure of the main clause. Choice (B) reads well and has the virtue of brevity.

**17. C.** The choices are easy to discern in this sentence. The original verb does not agree with its subject, nor is the structure parallel. Choice (A) does not logically agree with the subject ("reasons") since it names one ("demanding professors") but relegates the other reason to an afterthought. Choice (B) does not have parallel structure (phrase and clause). Choice (C) has both parallel structure and subject-verb agreement; it also names two reasons.

**18. A.** Regardless of its popular usage, "hopefully" is an adverb trying to be a clause. However, instances still exist that require a distinction between the two uses. So, in this case answer choice (A) is a better option. Answer choice (B) does not require a change in capitalization and answer choice (C) is the correct preposition. Finally, answer choice (D) is spelled correctly.

**19. A.** The two most suspicious choices are (A) and (C) because the item is a sentence fragment. No reasonable substitute for (C) would solve both the logic problem (incomplete thought) and the punctuation problem (comma splice if you omit "that"). Changing "showing" to "show" would, however, make the clause into a complete sentence with correct punctuation. Choice (B) does not provoke suspicion.

**20. A.** Again, the two most questionable choices, (A) and (B), compete for our attention. The use of "but" makes sense because it shows contrast to the previous idea. ("Don't evade or defy the law, but if caught breaking a law, accept the penalty.") The use of "or," however, is clearly not parallel to the immediately preceding use of "neither." The proper phrase is "neither . . . nor" for negative alternate choices. Choice (C) does not demand a second look.

**21. B.** This is an incorrect simple past verb tense. You have to spot the context clue "most Americans" "attended" school in the past, which suggests they no longer do so now. They must then "choose" their entertainment. Choice (A) is questionable, but the present participial phrase suggests coincidence with the time "most Americans" "attended school." It is, therefore, correct. Choice (C) is correctly an infinitive that is parallel to "to watch."

**22. A.** Choice (A) is correct, as an objective case pronoun is needed. Choice (B), (C), and (D) would make the sentence incorrect.

**23. B.** Choice (B) is correct because the word "advise" means "counsel," which fits the context of the sentence. Answer choices (A), (C), and (D) do not fit what is being asked by the writer.

**24. B.** Answer choice (B) is the correct usage for the context of this sentence. "There" is being used as referring to an item that is "behind the sofa."

**25. C.** The sentence is accurately placed after sentence 5, acting as a concluding sentence. This sentence wraps up the information being presented by the writer.

**26. A.** The best placement of this sentence, before sentence 1, is correct because the paragraph is describing the adapting of a cat to a new home. The contextual hint is "when I first," implying that this has to happen before the writer can describe the background of the cat.

**27. C.** The original suffers from inadequate causal relationship and non-parallel structure. Choice (A) is unnecessarily wordy. Choice (B) switches its structure at the end. Although it is technically parallel, it is still awkward because of the addition of the possessive pronoun "her." Choice (C) solves both problems by clearly showing cause and by being parallel (three nouns in series).

**28. B.** This sentence presents an incomplete comparison and a redundancy ("Whether"/"or did not"/"remains uncertain"). Choice (B) eliminates both problems clearly. Choices (A) and (C) are worse in both respects.

**29. D.** The sentence reads well and is perfectly balanced. Choice (A) is wordy. Choice (B) introduces an incomplete comparison ("more" but no "than"). Choice (C) awkwardly uses "as to."

**30. B.** The context of the sentence reads, "many communities" which refers to more than one. So, "economy" must also refer to more than one, "economies." The verb construct in the sentence is correct and the preposition is also accurate based on the context of the sentence.

**31. C.** The error here is known as faulty predication ("reason . . . is because"). The rule is that "because" is redundant for "reason." Choice (A) is appropriate, if a bit general, and the verb in choice (B) is correct and in the past tense.

**32. D.** All grammatical elements as shown in the sentence are correct. No change is necessary.

**33. A.** This is a colloquial, nonstandard substitution for the correct word, "attribute." Choice (B) is correctly lowercase, not capitalized. Choice (C) is a correct, if a bit stiff, phrase.

**34. B.** The original sentence has a dangling modifier (participial phrase). The house cannot return to itself, nor can "it" (pronoun for house). Choice (C) solves the original problem but is unnecessarily wordy. Choice (B) properly solves the dangling modifier problem by subordinating the return in an adverbial clause.

**35. A.** Choice (A) is the only response that makes sense. Each of the others introduces illogical comparisons or structures (non-parallel); Choices (B) and (D) are also verbose. Choice (C) is concise but not parallel.

**36. C.** This sentence suggests causal relationships between the parts of the sentence that do not belong there. Choice (B) echoes the original. Choice (C) shows clearly that the cause-effect relationship is a time relationship.

**37. D.** No change is necessary as the underlined portion is the shortest and most clear of all the choices. The syntax of (A) and (B) complicates the idea unnecessarily. (C) does not use the appropriate conjunctive adverb; "thereby" is more precise than "therefore" when referring to an event.

**38. C.** The phrase "on the other hand" fluidly connects the opposing ideas behind the two pieces of contrasting information provided in the sentence. Answer choice (D) "although" means "despite" and does not fit the context of the sentence. Answer choice (A) means "in spite of" and answer choice (B) suits a cause-and-effect relationship; neither of these options accurately fits the context of the sentence.

**39. B.** Answer choice (B) uses the noun "loss," the thing that no one mourned. Choices (A), (C), and (D) are not effective choices for the context of the sentence.

**40. A.** The correct answer choice (A) uses the possessive "whose," for Lornice's poor performance. Answer choices (B), (C), and (D) are not grammatically correct in the sentence.

## Mathematics

1.  **B.** Evaluate the expressions to find the true statement.

    Choice A:  $4^3 = 3^4$

    $4 \times 4 \times 4 = 3 \times 3 \times 3 \times 3$

    $64 \neq 81$

    Choice (A) is false.

    Choice B:  $5^0 \times 8^2 > 2^5$ (Remember, anything (except 0) to the 0 power is 1)

    $1 \times 8 \times 8 > 2 \times 2 \times 2 \times 2 \times 2.$

    $64 > 32$

    Since 64 is greater than 32, Choice (B) is true.

    Choice C:  $7^4 + 7^3 = 7^7$

    $(7 \times 7 \times 7 \times 7) + (7 \times 7 \times 7) = 7 \times 7 \times 7 \times 7 \times 7 \times 7 \times 7$

    $2{,}401 + 343 = 823{,}543$

    $2{,}744 \neq 823{,}543$

    Choice (C) is false.

    Choice D:  $5^2 + 5^8 = 5^{10}$

    $(5 \times 5) + (5 \times 5 \times 5 \times 5 \times 5 \times 5 \times 5 \times 5) = 5 \times 5 \times 5 \times 5 \times 5 \times 5 \times 5 \times 5 \times 5 \times 5$

    $25 + 390{,}625 = 9{,}765{,}625$

    $390{,}650 \neq 9{,}765{,}625$

    Choice (D) is false.

2.  **B.** The mean IQ score of 100 is given. One standard deviation above the mean is 34% of the cases, with an IQ score up to 115. One standard deviation below the mean is another 34% of the cases, with an IQ score down to 85. So, a total of 68% of the students have an IQ between 85 and 115. Therefore, $1{,}500 \times 0.68 = 1{,}020$.

3.  **B.** To solve this problem, you must convert all of the measurements to liters. Dividing by 1,000 changes milliliters to liters, which can be accomplished by moving the decimal three places left. You can then eliminate any zeros to the right of whole numbers in the decimals. Notice that when

you convert 50 ml, you have to add a zero to the left of the 5 in order to move the decimal three places.

700 mL = 0.7̶0̶0̶ L
150 mL = 0.15̶0̶ L
 50 mL = 0.05̶0̶ L
100 mL = 0.1̶0̶0̶ L

Now add these volumes to the 1 L of vanilla ice cream: $1 + 0.7 + 0.15 + 0.05 + 0.1 = 2$ liters of ingredients.

**4.   A.** To solve this problem, replace the moves with numbers using a plus sign for forward moves and a negative sign for backward moves.

The first player throws the Frisbee 3 meters forward from the starting line. (+3)

The next player throws it 5 meters backward. (−5)

The third player throws the Frisbee 4 meters forward. (+4)

How far is the Frisbee from the original starting line? $(+3 − 5 + 4 = +2)$

The Frisbee is 2 meters from the starting line.

**5.   C.** Looking at the interval on the $y$-axis, you can see that the first 200 is divided into five equal sections. By dividing 200 by 5, you will find that each horizontal line (or shaded in block) represents forty students. Now you can see that there are 400 students in the 9th grade and there are three additional boxes shaded in for the 10th grade students. If each box represents 40 students, then there are $3 \times 40$ more 10th grade students than there are 9th grade students: $400 + 120 = 520$ 10th grade students. This problem is a good reminder to be careful when reading graphs since it would be easy to make an error and assume that the graph was increasing by fifties rather than forties, which was your error if you chose (D).

**6.   D.** Begin by analyzing the equation as if you are graphing it. The base salary would be the $y$-intercept (+250) and the 3% would be the slope of the line (0.03). If we wanted to make the salesman's income equal to $460 a week, we would have $460 = 0.03s + 250$, with $s$ equaling his weekly sales. But we have to take this one step further. We want his base salary plus his commission to be greater than or equal to $460, so we write the equation as follows: $460 \leq 0.03s + 250$. Note: this can also be written $0.03s + 250 \geq 460$.

**7.   A.** This problem is asking us to see which measure of central tendency would be least affected by adding a $95,000 manager salary. Since this data set has no mode, the mode cannot be considered as a solution. Range is not a measurement of central tendency, so it is not a valid choice. We need to determine how much the median and mean will change to answer the questions.

Mean Before

$$\frac{21,200 + 23,000 + 25,000 + 35,000 + 40,000}{5} = \frac{144,200}{5} = 28,840$$

Mean After

$$\frac{21,200 + 23,000 + 25,000 + 35,000 + 40,000 + 95,000}{6} = \frac{239,200}{6} = 39,867$$

Difference: $39,867 − $28,840 = $11,027

Median Before – There is an odd number of terms, so the median is the middle term.

$25,000

Median After – There are now an even number of terms, so the median is the average of the middle two terms.

$$\frac{25,000 + 35,000}{2} = \$30,000$$

Difference: $30,000 − $25,000 = $5,000

The median is least affected.

8.  **B.** Follow the order of operations to simplify the expression.

| | |
|---|---|
| $\lvert 6 - 8 \rvert + 3 \div 3 \times 4^2 - 2$ | The problem |
| $2 + 3 \div 3 \times 4^2 - 2$ | Simplify inside the absolute value bars $\lvert 6 - 8 \rvert = \lvert -2 \rvert = 2$ |
| $2 + 3 \div 3 \times 16 - 2$ | Simplify exponents |
| $2 + 1 \times 16 - 2$ | Divide ($3 \div 3 = 1$) |
| $2 + 16 - 2$ | Multiply ($1 \times 16 = 16$) |
| $16$ | Add and subtract from left to right |

9.  **D.** First determine what fraction of the acreage is covered with carrots. If twice as many acres are planted with carrots than with peaches, we have to multiply the fraction planted with peaches $\left(\frac{3}{16}\right)$ by two: $2 \times \frac{3}{16} = \frac{6}{16} = \frac{3}{8}$. Next calculate $\frac{3}{8}$ of 40: $\frac{3}{8} \times 40 = \frac{3 \times 40}{8} = \frac{120}{8} = 15$ acres.

10. **C.** The best sample would be the one that contains the least bias. A sampling of students from each grade would be the best sample. The other choices exclude some portion of the student body.

**11. D.** Even though the graphs all depict the same data, the graph in choice (D) is proportioned so that it visually appears to show greater growth. This graph would be the best to use to favorably show growth to potential investors.

**12. B.** To identify the mode in a data set, find the term that appears most often:

Choice A: {**32, 32, 32**, 34, 36, 37}

Choice B: {32, 32, **322, 322, 322**}

Choice C: {**32, 32, 32**, 34, 34, 342}

Choice D: {30, 31, **32, 32**, 33, 34}

The mode for Choice (B) is 322, not 32, so this is the correct answer.

**13. D.** A large outlier will increase the mean, so Choice (D) is the correct answer. The range, too, will be higher, but range is not a measure of central tendency.

**14. A.** The original average is $=\dfrac{18+18+20+20+15+15}{6}=17.67$. The new average is $\dfrac{18+18+20+20+15+15+18+18+20+20}{10}=18.2$. The difference is $18.20-17.67=0.53$ inches.

**15. B.** To solve this problem, you must evaluate the effect of each scenario on the student's final grade.

Choice A: Use the mean of the five scores to calculate the final grade. To calculate the mean, add the scores and divide by the number of scores: $59 + 84 + 84 + 89 + 90 \div 5 = 406 \div 5 = 81.2$.

Choice B: Remove the outlier before calculating the student's final average. The outlier is the 59. Add the remaining scores and divide by four: $84 + 84 + 89 + 90 = 86.75$.

Choice C: Use the median of the scores to find the final grade. The median, or middle score, when the numbers are listed from lowest to highest is 84.

Choice D: Use the mode of the data to calculate the final grade. The mode of the data is 84.

Choice (B) would result in the student receiving the highest grade in the course.

**16. D.** First you must find the length of one cable. If you have memorized your Pythagorean triples, you might recognize that the tent pole, the ground, and one cable form a 5-12-13 triangle. If not, you have to use the Pythagorean Theorem, where $a$ and $b$ are the legs of the right triangle and $c$ is the hypotenuse. Don't forget that the legs meet at the right angle and the hypotenuse is the long side:

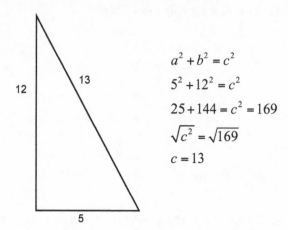

$$a^2 + b^2 = c^2$$
$$5^2 + 12^2 = c^2$$
$$25 + 144 = c^2 = 169$$
$$\sqrt{c^2} = \sqrt{169}$$
$$c = 13$$

Now you can see that the length of each cable is 13 feet long. Next you must multiply by 3 to calculate the three cables per pole and then by 4 since there are four poles holding up the tent: $13 \times 3 \times 4 = 156$. There is 156 feet of cable securing the tent.

**17. D.** First set up a proportion based on the information that is given in the problem. The scale, 1 centimeter equals 3 meters, can be written as $\dfrac{1 \text{ cm}}{3 \text{ m}}$. Set up the problem using the dimensions from the scale drawing to solve for two different proportions, the width and length of the volleyball court:

$$\frac{1 \text{ cm}}{3 \text{ m}} = \frac{3 \text{ cm}}{w \text{ m}} \quad \text{and} \quad \frac{1 \text{ cm}}{3 \text{ m}} = \frac{6 \text{ cm}}{l \text{ m}}$$

$$(1)(w) = (3)(3) \qquad (1)(l) = (3)(6)$$

$$w = 9 \text{ meters} \qquad l = 18 \text{ meters}$$

The dimensions of the court are thus 9 meters by 18 meters. Now we can calculate the area of the court (width × length): 9 m × 18 m = 162 m².

**18. C.** If you are providing two burgers for each guest, you will have to purchase 48 buns. If you purchase the buns in six-packs, you will have to buy 8 packages at $0.89 (8 × $0.89 = $7.12). If you buy them in eight-packs, you will have to buy 6 packages at $1.49 (6 × $1.49 = $8.94). If you chose choice (B), you forgot to purchase two buns per person. The least you can spend is $7.12.

**19. C.** The first step to solving this problem is determining how much the company needs to make to reach the profit goal of $900 and cover the one-time $150 cost of silk-screening. That total is $900 + $150 = $1050. If each shirt sells for $15 and costs the company $6, the profit from each shirt is $15 − $6 = $9. Now you can divide $1050 by $9 to find you need to sell 116.67 (or $116\frac{2}{3}$) shirts to reach your profit goal. Since you can't sell two-thirds of a shirt, you need to sell 117 shirts.

*Note: The test could ask you to choose a formula for this problem. If so, use p = $9s − $150. Be sure to use −$150 since this is taking away from, not adding to, your profit.*

**20. D.** We can eliminate choices (A) and (C) because they are negative, so they cannot fall between 0 and 2 on the number line. Choice (B) is much too large. Choice (D) is very close to zero, but does fall between 0 and 2 on the number line.

Or, to identify which number is between 0 and 2, take the answer choices out of scientific notation.

Choice A: $- 4.037 \times 10^3 = -4{,}037$

Choice B: $4.037 \times 10^3 = 4{,}037$

Choice C: $- 4.03 \times 10^{-2} = -0.04037$

Choice D: $4.03 \times 10^{-2} = 0.04037$

**21. A.** We first need to calculate how many ounces are in a pound. Using your math reference guide, you can see that one pound equals 16 ounces. If one pound equals 16 ounces, 3 pounds equals $3 \times 16$ ounces, or 48 ounces. Now we can divide 48 ounces into 6 ounce patties. $48 \div 6 = 8$ patties.

**22. C.** This problem is a little more complicated than it appears. In actuality, it is asking you to only fill two positions since R is a required member of the committee. The question is actually how can I take four people (PQST) in groups of two? In this case, the appropriate formula is much more difficult than the solution. This is the simple way to solve the problem. You have two open spots, so you have four choices for the first spot (we are not counting R) and three for the second spot. If we multiplied that together, there are twelve ways we could put four people in the two spots, as shown below:

| With RP | With RQ | With RS | With RT |
|---------|---------|---------|---------|
| RPQ | RQP | RSP | RTP |
| RPS | RQS | RSQ | RTQ |
| RPT | RQT | RST | RTS |

You may now think that there are twelve ways we could put four people in two committee positions, but the problem doesn't give the names of any particular positions. This means RQT is the same as RTQ and we have to eliminate the doubles:

| With RP | With RQ | With RS | With RT |
|---------|---------|---------|---------|
| RPQ | R̶Q̶P̶ | RSP | RTP |
| R̶P̶S̶ | RQS | R̶S̶Q̶ | R̶T̶Q̶ |
| R̶P̶T̶ | RQT | RST | R̶T̶S̶ |

Now you can see that there are actually <u>six</u> ways to put four people in two committee spots.

**23. D.** Begin by writing a key for the length and width of the picture frame.

$$w = \text{width}$$

$$2w + 2 = \text{length}$$

To find the perimeter of a rectangle, add all four sides together, remembering that the perimeter is made up of two widths and two lengths:

| | |
|---|---|
| $w + w + (2w + 2) + (2w + 2) = 88$ | The original equation |
| $6w + 4 = 88$ | Combine like terms |
| $6w + 4 - 4 = 88 - 4$ | Subtract 4 from both sides |
| $6w = 84$ | Combine like terms |
| $6w \div 6 = 84 \div 6$ | Divide both sides by 6 |
| $w = 14$ | Solve |

The width is 14 inches and we can substitute 14 for $w$ in $2w + 2$ to find the length. $2(14) + 2 = 30$. The length is 30 inches.

**24. D.** The given angles are all different (20 degrees, 50 degrees, and 110 degrees), so the sides are also all different lengths. This means the figure is a scalene triangle. One angle is over 90 degrees, so it is also an obtuse triangle. This triangle is a scalene obtuse triangle.

**25. A.** First you need to calculate the percentage of games that they have won. Sixty percent of seventy can be calculated by multiplying 70 by 0.60, which tells us that they have won 42 games. Next calculate how many total games are in the season. They have already played 70 and have 30 games left, so there are 100 games in the season. This means they need to win seventy percent of 100, or 70 games total. Finally, subtract the number of games they already won from the seventy wins they need: $70 - 42 = 28$. They need to win 28 of their 30 remaining games to reach their goal.

**26. D.** Looking at the pattern on the table, you can see that for every hour she studied, her score increased by 10%. So what can we infer happens when she does not study at all? According to the table, if she did not study, she would get 60% − 10%, or 50% correct. This means 50% is the base amount (or $y$-intercept) in your equation $y = mx + b$. Her increase of 10% per hours spent studying indicates that this is your slope ($m$) in the formula. The formula that represents her hours studied and percentage correct is $p = 10h + 50$.

**27. B.** In this problem, it is important to remember that a lower number on the table means that the product was more effective. You must also recognize that this data table only gives information on tick and ant bites, not on all insect bites. For this reason, you can eliminate both statements 2 and 3. Looking at statement 1, baking soda and ammonia are equally effective at treating ant bites, and baking soda is less effective at treating tick bites. For this reason, statement 1 is false. The only true statement is statement 4, which is choice (B).

**28. C.** It is important when solving inequalities that you use the following rules. First, whatever you do to one side or part of the inequality, you must do equally to the other parts. Secondly, you must flip the signs when multiplying or dividing through with a negative number, as is the case with this problem.

$36 \le -2x < 54$          The original problem

$-18 \ge x > -27$          Divide all three sections by −2 and remember to flip the signs

Now we can see $x$ must be less than or equal to −18 and greater than −27.

**29. B.** The only information given in this problem is the radius of a circle inscribed in a square. Since we know the radius is half of the diameter, we can multiply the radius of 3 by 2 to find a diameter of 6. The diameter of this circle is equal to a side of the square. Since the formula of the square is s², we can use 6² to find the area of the square.

**30. A.** To answer this question, you have to know that the angles of an equilateral triangle are all equal. If the interior angles of a triangle always equal 180 degrees, each angle in the given triangle is 180 ÷ 3 = 60 degrees. If ∠ACB is equal to 60 degrees and it is sitting on line AD, ∠BCD is equal to 180 − 60 = 120 degrees. If two angles add up to equal 180 degrees, we say that they are supplementary. For this reason, choice (A) is correct. *Note: When we write an angle name, we either only name the vertex of the angle, or we write the vertex in the middle. For instance ∠A and ∠BAC are two names for the same angle. If two angles share a vertex like ∠ACD and ∠BCD, we have to use the three-letter name to avoid confusion. You should also know that the sum of complementary angles is ninety degrees.*

**31. B.** This type of problem shows up on the test two ways. Sometimes the test asks you to calculate the number of days you have to use the pass before you begin to save money, and other times it asks you to determine the formula for both situations. We will cover both questions in this solution. Let's start with the formulas since we can use them to understand the problem. If you are paying $12 per day to park, or $12d, you would use the following formula to determine your cost: c = $12d. If you had to buy the $25 pass (your base rate) and paid $8 per day, the formula would be c = $8d + $25. The test writers expect that you will use these systems of equations to determine your solutions, but using common sense is much quicker. How much are you saving per day with the pass? $12 − $8 = $4 per day. How many days would you have to save $4 before you offset the cost of the $25 pass? $4 × 6 days would save $24, which is not enough, but $4 × 7 days would save you $28, which would cover the cost of the pass plus actually save you money. So, to make it worthwhile to buy the pass, you have to use it at least seven days.

**32. A.** To calculate the number of ways you can wear 4 pants and 3 shirts, multiply 4 by 3. There are 12 ways to wear the pants and shirts.

**33. D.** To solve this problem, you have to find the table where all of the $(d, h)$ pairs are true for the formula $h = 2d + 4$. This only happens in graph (D). If you plug in 0 for $d$, you get $h = 4$. This means that on the day you got the plant, it was already four inches tall (4 is your $y$-intercept or the $b$ in the equation $y = mx + b$). If you plug in the second value of $d$, which is 1, you will get 6. This means that after one day, the plant was six inches tall. Finally, if you plug in 2 for $d$, you will find that after two days, the plant was eight inches tall. All of the values shown in the table in choice (D) are correct. The table and formula also show that the plant is growing at a rate of two inches per day. This is your slope, $m$, in your formula $y = mx + b$.

**34. C.** Think about your room. It has a front wall and a back wall that are the same size, two identical side walls, and a ceiling. We also have to remember to exclude the area of the doors. To solve this, we are basically using a modified version of the surface area formula, $SA = 2xy + 2yz + 2xz$. It is modified because we are not painting the floor, only the ceiling. Let's use a table to organize our thinking:

| Surfaces to Paint | Dimensions | Area (ft²) |
|---|---|---|
| Front | 8 × 14 | 112 |
| Back | 8 × 14 | 112 |
| Side | 8 × 16 | 128 |
| Side | 8 × 16 | 128 |
| Ceiling | 14 × 16 | 224 |
| Total | | 704 |
| Surfaces not to paint | | |
| Area of Door | 6 × 7 | −42 |
| Total Area to Paint | | 662 |

Now we can calculate how much paint we need. If each gallon covers 175 square feet, we need 662 ÷ 175 = 3.78 gallons of paint. Since paint is sold by the gallon, we need four gallons of paint.

**35. B.** First convert the length of the trip from minutes to hours. 330 minutes ÷ 60 minutes = 5.5 hours. Next calculate the distance one way: 5.5 hours × 446 mph = 2,453 miles. Now multiply by 2 to calculate the round trip distance: 2 × 2,453 = 4,906 miles.

To convert your answer to scientific notation, move the decimal from behind the 6 to between the 4 and the 9 and multiply by $10^3$. (The exponent is the number of spaces the decimal point is moved.) The distance from Orlando to San Francisco and back again is $4.906 \times 10^3$.

**36. D.** It is important to recognize what the *y*- and *x*-intercept on the graph mean in order to choose the correct statement. Let's put the graph on a coordinate grid so that it is easier to understand:

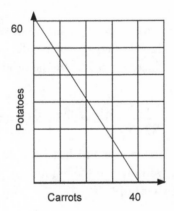

The *y*-intercept is (0, 60). This represents the 60 pounds of potatoes that could be purchased if you do not buy any carrots. The *x*-intercept is (40, 0). This represents the amount of carrots you can buy if you do not buy any potatoes. The line has a negative slope, so as you increase the amount of carrots you buy (moving from the left to the right across the line) you decrease the amount of potatoes you can purchase. This also means that purchasing less carrots, as in choice (D), will allow you to buy more potatoes.

**37. D.** The slope of a line is the hourly rate. Every hour that Laura works she earns $15.

**38. A.** This is a two-step problem. First you must calculate how many square yards of carpet are in the room. 18 feet divided by 3 feet per yard is equivalent to 6 yards, and 21 feet is equivalent to 7 yards. Then 6 yards × 7 yards is equal to 42 square yards. Now multiply 42 by $6.79, the cost per square yard: 42 × $6.79 = $285.18.

**39. A.** The key to this problem is starting with the correct number, then using a table to keep your results in order. The temperature on day one is twenty below zero, or −20. Next, you can use the increase (+) or decrease (−) line for each day to calculate the temperature as shown below:

| Day # | 1 | 2 | 3 | 4 | 5 | 6 | 7 | 8 | 9 |
|---|---|---|---|---|---|---|---|---|---|
| Increase or Decrease | | +5 | −7 | +2 | +2 | +2 | +2 | +2 | +2 |
| Temp. | −20 | −15 | −22 | −20 | −18 | −16 | −14 | −12 | −10 |

As you can see, it was ten degrees below zero on day 9. If you chose choice (D), you started with 20 above zero, or +20. If you chose (B) or (C), you made a math error. Be careful when adding and subtracting the positive and negative numbers. You should always use a number line so that you can verify that your answers make sense.

**40. D.** First we need to calculate the energy cost at the large house and at the small house. The cost at the large house is $1500 \times \$0.15 = \$225$. The cost at the small house is $900 \times \$0.10 = \$90$. To find the percentage of decrease divide the decrease in cost by the original cost at the larger house:

$$\frac{\$225 - \$90}{\$225} = \frac{\$135}{\$225} = 0.6 = 60\% \text{ decrease in cost}$$

Now check for reasonableness. You power bill has been cut by more than half, so 60% is reasonable. If you chose choice (A), you divided the amount of the new bill by the old bill rather than first calculating the decrease in your bill.

**41. D.** The addition of a significantly higher outlier would definitely raise the mean (average) of the data set. For instance, if a student has test score of 72, 76, 76, 76, and 77, the mean would be a 75.4. Adding a high outlier such as a 98 percent would raise the mean to a 79.2. This would not change the median or the mode of the data set.

**42. A.** For a data set to meet the definition of a function, no $x$ terms can be duplicated. Choice (A) is the only set that does not have duplicate data for the $x$ values.

**43. C.** For this survey sample to properly represent the population, it has to equally represent children of all grade levels. Based on the data table, over twice as many fifth graders (30) were surveyed compared to either the kindergarten (12) or first grade (13) students. This makes the data in the table an unreliable representation of the school population in the lower grades.

For this reason the correct answer is choice (C). They did not fairly represent all grade levels in the survey.

**44. A.** To solve this problem we first need to set up a proportion to determine how many minutes it will take to empty the room, then change the minutes to hours.

$\dfrac{1.5\ inches}{50\ minutes} = \dfrac{18 inches}{m}$    Set up the proportion

$1.5m = (18)(50)$    Use cross product then multiply $18 \times 50$

$\dfrac{1.5m}{1.5} = \dfrac{900}{1.5}$    Divide both sides by 1.5

$m = 600$ minutes    Solve for the minutes it takes to empty

Now since there are 60 minutes in an hour, just divide 600 min. by 60 min/hr. It will take 10 hours to empty the room.

**45. A.** Substitute $(x, y) = (7, -20)$ into each of the equations until you find one that is true.

Choice A:    $y = -3x + 1$

$-20 = -3(7) + 1$

$-20 = -21 + 1$

$-20 = -20$

This is a true statement, so choice (A) is the correct answer. The other choices do not give true statements.

Choice B:    $y = -x + 7$

$-20 = -7 + 7$

$-20 = 0$

This is a false statement.

Choice C:    $y = -4x + 2$

$-20 = -4(7) + 2$

$-20 = -28 + 2$

$-20 = -26$

This is a false statement.

Choice D:    $y = -2x + 3$

$-20 = -2(7) + 3$

$-20 = -14 + 3$

$-20 = -11$

This is a false statement.

Choice (A) is correct because $(7, -20)$ is a solution to the equation $y = -3x + 1$.

## Reading

**1.   D.** A synonym for *exulting* is *praising*; therefore, choice (D) is the best possible answer.

**2.   D.** Passage 2 assesses a eulogy while Passage 1 is an actual eulogy.

**3.   B.** The author would agree that Lincoln's character is best described as "steady and resolute" because in Passage 1 Lincoln is portrayed as a strong leader and heroic captain, thereby supporting the idea of one who is determined and admirably purposeful.

**4.   C.** Passage 1 addresses the current state of the nation, while Passage 2 does not. While Passage 1 mentions, "The ship is anchor'd safe and sound, its voyage closed and done," referring to the country's stability, Passage 2 never mentions the nation.

**5.   A.** At the start of the poem there is a triumphant tone, which can be observed in lines such as "the prize we sought is won" and "the bells I hear, the people all exulting." At the end of Passage 1, there is "mournful tread."

**6.   B.** The criticism of the eulogy communicated in Passage 2 is based on two statements: "…Mr. Lincoln's character is superficial. It did not please me…" and "Mr. Lincoln grew more steady and resolute, and his ideas were never confused." These comments support the central claim that Lincoln's eulogy was criticized based on the mischaracterization of his character and ideas.

**7.   C.** The criticism communicated through Passage 2 is focused around the area of contempt or scorn for the way his friend, Lincoln, is described in his eulogy by Bancroft. The author's attitude is not focused around hate, fear, or satisfaction.

**8.   A.** Within the context of Passage 1, the author's use of the word *resolute* is most closely related to *stalwart*, meaning *determined*.

**9.   D.** The author of Passage 1 eulogistically points to overcoming obstacles, praise from society, and being a valiant leader. However, the author does not mention a burden or barrier left behind for society. So, answer (D) is the best choice.

**10.   B.** In the second paragraph, the author points to a list of items that have shifted the "Washington power game" and the idea of political fundraising is mentioned, supporting answer choice (B).

**11.   C.** Throughout the passage, the author points to reasons and results of the shifting of the political landscape. This focuses the reader's attention on the structure of cause and effect.

**12. D.** The author provides a list of factors at the end of the paragraph in order to explain the reasons and/or rationale for change in the power game.

**13. D.** The words *understood, experiences, rewrite* and *new game* align with the order of critical points made by the author. Answer choices (A), (B), and (C) are found in the passage, but they do not represent the order which predicts the effect the details have on the reader.

**14. C.** The shift in tone is reflective of the cause-and-effect relationship between the second and third paragraph.

**15. A.** The author of the Passage is communicating in first person which means that the passage is straightforwardly telling and not persuading, explaining, or analyzing.

**16. B.** The author's tone is primarily focused around the idea of change and shifts between what was experienced in the past and what is experienced currently. Therefore, the author does not provide any details that support the idea of being confusing, depressing, or unfair.

**17. A.** The author mentions the idea of "greater difficulty marshaling governing coalitions…," referring to building partnerships. Therefore, (A) is the best option.

**18. A.** The word *precepts* aligns most closely to the definition of *theories* (A). The context is within the idea of "textbooks" which is reflective of precepts or theories.

**19. C.** While the author mentions *manipulation, wills*, and *a shift*, the primary focus is the *power game*. This theme can be seen throughout the passage.

**20. C.** The author of the passage clearly states just the opposite of answer (C) by saying that, "The old power oligarchy in Congress has been broken up." Therefore, (C) is not a detail stated in the passage.

**21. B.** The word *transformations* refers to the idea of change and does not fit the context of success, regret, or denial.

**22. A.** The author provides key details throughout the passage about the "transformations" or changes which have resulted in a new context that he terms "a new power game."

**23. D.** Throughout the passage the author refers to change, which would eliminate (A). Also, the author is reflective and discusses opportunity, eliminating choices (B) and (C).

**24. D.** The author uses this evidence to support the idea that his perspective was founded upon multiple presidencies, providing "longitudinal" support.

**25. D.** The author organizes the information in the passage through a cause-and-effect pattern. So, choice (D) is the most logical answer because the passage focuses attention on the reasons and results of the shift in the "power game."

**26. B.** The author spends the majority of time discussing the shifting political landscape or change. While the other answer choices may be true, they are never addressed within the passage.

**27. D.** Choice (B) is not supported by the passage. Choices (A) and (C) go beyond the passage. The last sentence states, "The pattern . . . resulting in teachers prone to teach as they had been taught"— thus choice (D) is the best logical option.

**28. B.** The other choices, (A), (C), and (D), are not supported by the passage. Although the passage mentions that teacher education has reflected evolving attitudes about education, the attitudes are not clearly articulated—choice (B).

**29. A.** Only choice (A) has the correct sequence; the other sequences do not follow the order as given in Passage 2.

**30. D.** Choices (A), (B), and (C) are statements about education, teacher education, and teachers. Choice (D)'s statement that teacher education has changed very little implies that this lack of change could be a source of dissatisfaction.

**31. B.** Answer choice (B) is the best option because the author of the passage hints at the social dynamics and how they affect teacher education. Answer choices (A), (C), and (D) can't be accurately assumed or inferred after reading the selection.

**32. B.** Sentence 1 communicates the main idea of the connection between social dissatisfaction and criticism of American education. Then, sentence 2 explains how this connection relates to the central idea.

**33. A.** The word in context refers most closely to being "disenchanted" not being naive, disheartened, or enchanted.

**34. C.** The word *trifling* means "trivial" and fits the context clues provided by the author stating, "as familiarly as I knew the letters of the alphabet...."

**35. B.** The writer uses a combination of the six primary elements of figurative language to communicate the setting.

**36. D.** The quote conveys the writer's shifting tone with respect to the river scene, from poetic to pragmatic. He signals this shift in a few places in the passage, contrasting his perception when "[t]he world was new to me" (in the first line of the last paragraph) with his concluding thought that he "should have looked upon it without rapture." The writer then alludes to the quote found in the question stem.

**37. A.** In the first paragraph, the author describes the river by taking stock of its beauty, poetry, and grace but does not mention mercy. So, the logical choice is (A).

**38. A.** The word *enthralled* signifies being bewitched, fascinated, or captivated by the nature being described within the paragraph.

**39. C.** The word *rapture* most clearly is defined by a feeling of enchantment or (C), delight. Answer choices (A), (B) and (D) do not fit the context of the passage.

**40. B.** The author refers to the mastery of the language of the water leading to a "valuable acquisition." Therefore, it is logical to infer that the author has gained an understanding because of his command of a watercraft.

# Notes

# Notes

# Notes

# Notes

# Notes

# Notes

# Notes

# Notes